The Forensic Psychologist's Casebook

The Forensic Psychologist's Casebook

Psychological profiling and criminal investigation

edited by

Laurence Alison

WILLAN
PUBLISHING

Published by

Willan Publishing
Culmcott House
Mill Street, Uffculme
Cullompton, Devon
EX15 3AT, UK
Tel: +44(0)1884 840337
Fax: +44(0)1884 840251
e-mail: info@willanpublishing.co.uk

Published simultaneously in the USA and Canada by

Willan Publishing
c/o ISBS, 920 NE 58th Ave, Suite 300
Portland, Oregon 97213-3644, USA
Tel: +001(0)503 287 3093
Fax: +001(0)503 280 8832
e-mail: info@isbs.com
website: www.isbs.com

ISBN 978-1-84392-101-1   Paperback
      978-1-84392-113-4   Hardback

British Library Cataloguing-in-Publication Data
A catalogue record for this book is available from the British Library

FSC
Mixed Sources
Product group from well-managed
forests and other controlled sources

Cert no. SGS-COC-2482
www.fsc.org
© 1996 Forest Stewardship Council

Project management by Deer Park Productions, Tavistock, Devon
Typeset by GCS, Leighton Buzzard, Beds
Printed and bound by TJI Digital, Padstow, Cornwall

Contents

Notes on contributors

Emily Alison

Emily has a BSc in Behavioural Science and Criminal Justice awarded by the University of Madison, Wisconsin, and an MSc in Investigative Psychology, awarded by the University of Liverpool. Her Masters degree thesis examined the relationship between crime scene behaviours and offender characteristics in homicide. She has worked as a practitioner in both the American and British correctional services and was employed as a Correctional Case Manager and outpatient therapist with Attic Correctional Services in Madison, Wisconsin, where she worked with a wide range of high-risk offenders, including the treatment of domestic violence perpetrators in a structured group work programme. She previously worked as a Treatment Manager with the National Probation Service for England and Wales (Cheshire Area) and was responsible for the Domestic Violence Prevention Programme, a 39-week community group work programme for domestic violence perpetrators. She has worked with over 200 perpetrators of domestic violence, interviewing them in great detail about their abusive and violent behaviour toward their partners. She now acts as an independent consultant, providing advice to the courts and various law enforcement agencies.

Laurence Alison

Professor Alison has worked closely alongside a number of police officers on research projects for the last ten years. He is Academic Director of the Centre for Critical Incident Research at The School of Psychology, University of Liverpool. The Centre focuses on psychological contributions to managing a variety of high-profile cases. Alongside Professor Crego (Practitioner Director) he has provided reports that have informed many debriefing sessions. He has an international track record of publishing on the subject of policing and investigation in many leading internationally recognized journals and has lectured nationally and internationally about this subject. He is on the accredited list of behavioural advisors for the National Crime and Operations Faculty and has contributed advice and training to many police forces in the UK and abroad, including the Metropolitan Police Service, Kent Police Advanced Detective Training programme, Strathclyde Police crime analysis section, the Forensic Science Institute in Krakow, and The Bundeskriminalamt in Wiesbaden.

Emma Barrett

Emma Barrett has worked for over a decade with UK law enforcement agencies and government departments, and is currently employed as a Behavioural Science Advisor with the UK government. She holds a BSc in Anthropology, a Conversion Diploma in Psychology (awarded with distinction) and an MSc in Investigative Psychology (also awarded with distinction). In addition to various work-related projects, Emma is currently carrying out research on the development of investigator expertise, in conjunction with several UK police forces, as part of a PhD at the University of Birmingham, UK. The focus of this research is the cognitive mechanisms underlying investigative situation assessment, the process by which investigators make sense of information available during complex criminal investigations. Her other research interests include interview strategies for informants and suspects, interpersonal persuasion and deception, and issues relating to the psychology of terrorism.

David Canter

Professor Canter was Professor of Psychology at the University of Surrey for ten years, where he founded the MSc course in Investigative Psychology. He continues as Professor of Psychology at the University of Liverpool. He is a Fellow of the British Psychological Society and a member of its Forensic Division and a Chartered Forensic Psychologist. He is a Fellow of the American Psychological Association and a Member of the Forensic Science Society. He has published 20 books and over 150 papers in learned professional journals, and lectured around the world on various aspects of scientific psychology. His book, *Criminal Shadows*, won the Golden Dagger Award for crime non-fiction and its US equivalent, an Anthony Award.

He has given evidence to a number of major government enquiries and to a House of Commons select committee, including unchallenged evidence to the enquiry into the Kings Cross Underground fire concerning whether the fire was accidental or malicious, and given evidence to the Appeal Courts in Belfast and in a murder trial at the Old Bailey. He has also given advice in response to requests from over 150 police investigations worldwide. He has recently been elected an Academician of the Academy of Social Sciences; this recognizes his important and seminal contributions to the social sciences.

Nina Cope

Nina Cope is currently employed as a criminologist by the Metropolitan Police Service where she is responsible for developing the profession of analysis, along with enhancing the use of criminological research in police practice. She previously worked as a lecturer and researcher at the Universities of Warwick, Cambridge and Surrey, where she contributed to the Diploma and MSc for police officers, which was delivered as part of the Strategic Command Course and conducted research on intelligence-led policing. She has a broad range of research interests in policing and crime, including analysis, intelligence-led policing, youth offending and drugs. She has also undertaken consultancy training with police forces in the UK.

Katarina Fritzon

Katarina Fritzon is a Chartered Forensic Psychologist and Course Director of the MSc in Forensic Psychology at the University of Surrey. She is an accredited behavioural investigative advisor for the National Crime and Operations Faculty, and provides regular assistance nationally and internationally to police investigations of arson. She has also provided legal consultancy on assessing interviews with psychologically vulnerable witnesses. Her research interests include developing models of criminal interactions and transactions with their victims and the environment, in particular in relation to arson and subgroups of homicide. She is also developing treatment models for fire setters and is working with NHS and privately funded hospitals in delivering interventions.

Alasdair Goodwill

Alasdair Goodwill recently completed a PhD under the direction of Prof. Alison on offender profiling and suspect prioritisation. He has conducted empirical work on geographic profiling, linking and prioritising suspects, as well as having contributed to several high profile rape and murder enquiries in the UK. He has presented much of this work at national and international conferences and has published several articles in leading journals. Currently, he is a lecturer at the Centre for Forensic and Family Psychology at the University of Birmingham.

Joanne Howard
Joanne Howard has a first degree in Politics from the University of Adelaide, South Australia, a Masters in Investigative Psychology from the University of Liverpool and she is a Rotary Foundation Academic Ambassadorial Scholar. Joanne is a Sergeant of Police with ten years of service in the South Australia Police Department. Her dissertation was titled 'Interviewing Suspects: to obtain a confession or a search for the truth?'. The majority of her service has been within the Criminal Investigation Branch investigating serious and series crimes. She is a qualified conversation management trainer and conducts interviews for recruit selection and detective training. Joanne has managed criminal investigation process projects at the corporate level and she is currently responsible for developing crime-reduction strategies for the South Australia Police. Joanne has a keen interest in 'offender debriefing' practices and is conducting further research with an aim of developing offender-based crime-reduction strategies.

Jon Ogan
Jon completed his BSc (Hons) in Psychology at Manchester Metropolitan University in 1998. The focus was on a multivariate analysis of homicide and the utility of motive in the investigation of homicide. His MSc in Criminal Justice Studies was taken at the Institute for Criminal Justice Studies, University of Portsmouth in 2000. The dissertation was on repeat victim characteristics in the sexual abuse of people with learning disabilities in Manchester. He has worked with adults with learning disabilities in Stockport and Manchester for over 12 years and is building on the MSc findings to explore victim and offender interactions and the possibility of using Smallest Space Analysis in the verification of sexual abuse allegations. This is the basis for a part-time MPhil/PhD at the Centre of Investigative Psychology, University of Liverpool. Jon also has an interest in the role of victimology in the investigation of interpersonal crimes.

David Ormerod
David Ormerod is Professor of Criminal Law at the University of Leeds, and a Barrister at the chambers of Peter Rook QC, 18 Red Lion Court,

London. His main research interests are criminal law and the law of evidence. He has written widely in these fields. One particular interest is in the area of expert evidence and in the uses of novel techniques as evidence in the criminal trial, and his publications on this include articles on psychological profiling, psychological autopsies, voice identification evidence, expert voice identification evidence and 'earprint evidence'. He is an adviser to the Law Commission and the Criminal Bar Association and is an Editor of the *Criminal Law Review* and a member of the Editorial Board of the *International Journal of Evidence and Proof.*

Louise Porter

Louise is a lecturer at the School of Psychology, University of Liverpool, and member of the Centre for Critical Incident Research. Her work focuses on leadership in small criminal groups by examining the roles of decision making, order giving and initial action in generating and perpetuating aggressive group behaviour. Her work has implications for managing criminally violent gangs, crime-reduction initiatives, educational programmes, interviewing tactics and therapeutic interventions with perpetrators and victims of such events. She has worked as the principal research assistant on two separate, externally funded projects on desistance from crime (funded by the Joseph Rowntree Foundation) and heroin rehabilitation (funded by local government agencies) and was involved in work with NACRO.

Jim Sturman QC

Jim Sturman QC is a criminal defence practitioner at the chambers of William Clegg QC, 2, Bedford Row, London WC1R 4BU. Called to the Bar in 1982 and appointed Queen's Counsel in 2002, he practises throughout England and internationally. He acted as junior counsel in *Stagg* and in the *Dallagher* appeal, and he was leading counsel in the *Dallagher* retrial. He has also appeared in several of the London City Bond 'non-disclosure' appeals having acted for Villiers at trial, on appeal and at the abuse of process hearing.

Adrian West

Adrian West qualified as a clinical psychologist in 1989. For the past 15 years he has worked in special hospitals and regional secure units in the UK. For the past ten years he has also worked as the Clinical Psychologist advisor to the National Crime and Operations Faculty. This is a specialist unit providing operational support to police forces within the UK in major crime enquiries.

Georgia Wilson

Georgia Wilson completed her Masters degree in Investigative Psychology in September 2002, for which she was awarded a distinction. Her dissertation, entitled 'Suspect prioritisation: improving decision making in the investigation of sex offences', used a diagnostic decision-making approach in its analysis of the likelihood of specified offender characteristics (distance of residence from crime, previous convictions, sentences served, age) occurring in a sample of 63 stranger sexual offences committed within Hampshire in the UK. Georgia has also contributed to police-related studies commissioned by the Home Office. She currently works as an investigator with the Independent Police Complaints Commission, which has overall responsibility for the system of complaints against the police in England and Wales. In particular, Georgia is a member of the team responsible for conducting independent investigations into the most serious categories of complaints.

Acknowledgements

I was delighted that contributors to this volume recognized the academic merits of a book on offender profiling and criminal behavioural analyses. It was clear to me that they saw the need to reach out beyond the sometimes narrow confines of journal publications to a public that is interested in our work. Despite the obvious academic benefits of journal publications and the recognition that this outlet affords, I do feel strongly that such work should not reside exclusively within a source that, to the wider community, is arcane, costly and unreachable. We have an obligation to ensure the public, practitioners and students have access to an accurate, balanced and realistic view of what really happens in a field normally surrounded by hyperbole and myth.

Many of the students and colleagues whom I have had the pleasure to work with have contributed to this volume. I should also like to note the very happy symmetry of an equal balance of male and female contributors. Most of these academics and practitioners continue to contribute directly to policy decisions in their respective professional arenas and they have all been instrumental in developing forensic psychology within their particular fields of interest. So, it has been a great privilege and honour to work with Emma Barrett, Alasdair Goodwill and Jon Ogan. In particular, Dr Louise Porter has been critical in the development of this book and, more generally, to the work of the Centre for Critical Incident Research. She has also proved an invaluable friend whom I have had the great pleasure of working alongside for the past four years.

I was fortunate enough last year to have worked with Professors Kevin Browne and Thomas-Peter and Drs Beech, Hamilton-Giachritsis, Dixon and Garrett, as well as Sue Hanson, our course administrator, during my time at the University of Birmingham. This proved a very positive experience for me and I shall miss the very friendly and collegiate atmosphere at the Centre for Forensic and Family Psychology.

At the School of Psychology, University of Liverpool, Professor Ian Donald has also been pivotal at an academic and personal level and I owe a significant debt of gratitude to him for his advice, support and friendship. In the early stages of my career, Professors Canter (Liverpool) and Furnham (University College London) provided much of the enthusiasm for investigative psychology and psychology generally and both were critical in steering me in the right direction at the right time. Professor Canter has, of course, been the leading figure in generating empirical approaches in psychological contributions to the investigation of crime. Without his initial impetus in this arena, progress would not have been so rapid nor would it have spread so far across the globe.

A number of practitioner colleagues have helped form the thinking behind this collection of readings and, indeed, my work generally. My association with the National Centre for Applied Learning Technologies and Professor Jonathan Crego in particular has been critical in recent years. As well as providing the impetus and shape to a host of issues in policing and law enforcement, he has proved a very warm friend. It has been such a pleasure to engage with Jono's boundless enthusiasm and intellectual creativity.

Stretching farther back into my association with the police service, the following have been instrumental in providing help and support: Detective Chief Superintendent Steve Watts, Detective Chief Inspector Scott Chilton, Detective Superintendent Phillip Williams, Mark Devenish Meares, Chief Superintendent Simon Merry and Detective Sergeant Ross Leonard. I am grateful for their ability to gently rubbish some of the more arcane and ignorant ideas I have held about policing as well as to contribute significantly to the ideas that have worked well. If anyone has ever held the view that the police are all cast from the same mould then they should meet this collection of officers, who represent every variation in personality and approach.

In reference to the work on offender profiling I should like to thank Lee Rainbow and Adrian West, both of whom have been open to challenge and debate views as well as to co-operate on work that seeks to professionalize the service that academics and practitioners provide. I am grateful for their insight, vision, integrity and extensive and unparalleled personal experience in this challenging area. Adrian has also provided much needed professional support and friendship.

I should also like to make special reference to the fact that my wife, Emily, has contributed significantly to this volume, though even the fact that she is named on several chapters belies the reality that she has been so instrumental to all my thinking around this book and other projects. To have such a loving and supportive wife is a rarity but to have one that is an invaluable friend, ally and professional colleague must be nothing short of a minor miracle.

Finally, I should like to thank Brian Willan for proving to be such a flexible, open and responsive publisher.

Dedications

My wife and I recently nearly lost our son. It is with great pleasure and gratitude that this book is dedicated to the individuals who saved his life at Alder Hey Children's Hospital, Liverpool. In particular, Drs Baines and Selby, the consultant paediatricians and Swapna and Eileen, the nursing staff who took 24-hour care of him in the intensive care unit, were so supportive and caring. The ICU, for me, demonstrated the clearest example of the essential qualities that all critical services should strive for: professionalism, vision, integrity, honesty and, above all, humanity. Further, the Ronald McDonald house, a charitable organization that accommodates the parents of sick children, and which has been built within a stone's throw of the hospital, provided a safe haven for us that made that harrowing week all the more bearable. All personal profits from this volume are donated with the deepest debt of gratitude to the Alder Hey Ronald McDonald House, Liverpool.

A final word: for all those who thought there may be a grain of truth or insight into recent comments in the *Spectator* about the supposedly morbid preoccupation that exemplifies a Liverpudlian attitude to grief: my experience is that Liverpudlians genuinely care when someone is suffering and I can't imagine a more comforting or reassuring place to be when the chips are down. For all international readers and those UK readers who have not paid Liverpool a visit – please make the effort to tour this wonderful city and judge for yourselves.

For Mum and Dad
For Emily and (most of all) for Heath

Preface

The casebook approach

The key issue that attracted me to editing a book on offender profiling and criminal behavioural analysis was the recognition that a number of practitioners with whom I had worked were keen to understand the science behind the advice received. I think there has been a marked difference in the last ten years in the way in which law enforcement agencies (and police officers in particular) have been keen to understand, challenge and contribute to this emerging area of forensic psychology. My early experiences with the field of profiling were almost exclusively negative, from the initial shock I experienced at the ambiguous, contradictory and seemingly entirely subjective reports that I was asked to evaluate to the very destructive self-promotion of certain 'profilers'. It is hard to underestimate the legacy that a few key cases have had on the field and it is only in very recent years that this negativity has begun to subside and be gradually replaced with greater open-mindedness as well as healthy scepticism.

Perhaps unsurprisingly, the identification of key issues has arisen from the experience of practitioners who have dealt with particularly difficult, critical cases. For this reason, I felt it was important to expand on a paper that I had written with Adrian West and Alasdair Goodwill for a special issue of *Psychology, Public Policy and Law* in which we set out the importance of examining single cases and presenting material that was informed both by scientific rigour and due consideration of the specific idiosyncratic details of the case. This 'pragmatic' approach (Fishman, 2004) has informed much of the construction of this volume and its objectives. Within the pragmatic paradigm, experienced individuals are viewed as key contributors who, in clearly explicating critical cases that they have been involved with, help contribute to an archive that serves as a starting point for deriving general principles. Fishman (1999) has promoted the idea of building a large corpus of individual case studies across fields such as therapeutic intervention, educational reform programmes (Fishman, 1999) and, in the special issue, his intention was to extend this to forensic psychology (Fishman, 2004). One potential outcome of such an approach is databases that contain rich, detailed and contextually bound resources. Archiving such information enables practitioners and academics to draw upon this corpus in the face of subsequent problems. With increasing numbers of case studies, greater confidence can be placed in extracting general trends and advocating a particular course of action without the attendant sacrifice of losing details contextually relevant to any given case. Further, experienced practitioners can use their own experience to evaluate the relevance of the archive to their own particular concerns and can decide on the extent to which their case conforms to previous cases. Additionally, researchers can use the cumulative body of evidence to extract trends in the information. This book is a first, humble effort to collect some key cases to serve as such a starting point for an archive.

The pragmatic perspective has much in common with quasi-judicial approaches to research and case-based reasoning. In the quasi-judicial method rules and interpretations emerge from comparisons and contrasts between successive cases. Similarities and differences between cases are outlined and decisions are justified by reference to these critical cases by means of coherent arguments. Unique features of critical cases provide a basis for reformulating rules and laws, while the points of similarity between the new case and previous cases preserve the extant points of law. In case-based reasoning previously successful solutions are adapted, reused and tested for success and each new revision produces a new case. This volume sets out some example cases that serve to illustrate what forensic/investigative psychologists do when preparing material for investigative purposes. During the explanation of theory and casework, I hope that the reader will appreciate the difficulties and pitfalls of working in this challenging but exciting area.

Profiling 'types' and investigating crimes

Common to all the work in this volume is the recognition that particular cases cannot easily be assigned to 'types', 'traits' or discrete, nonoverlapping entities. Instead, each case needs to be considered as possessing certain potentially unique features that must be considered within a particular context. Nowhere has this (in my view) naïve ideology of 'types' been more fervently promoted within the media and popular accounts of forensic psychology as in profiling and behavioural analysis. As my opening chapter suggests, offenders cannot be easily classified in terms of labels from which lists of background characteristics can be derived. I argue that there is little evidence in support of the utility of trait-based models of profiling. In Chapter 1 I outline the reasons why, based on an examination of the history of trait-based research, traditional profiling methods are inherently flawed. The chapter explains the dangers of too heavy a reliance on simple classifications such as 'organized' vs 'disorganized' or 'power reassurance' vs 'power assertive' rapists. Further, the chapter describes a small-scale, exploratory study of the apprehension methods involved in capturing serial killers and explains, by reference to this descriptive study, how the remit of psychological profiling can be usefully employed to develop more productive areas of research, such as assisting in detective decision-making, investigative interviewing, statement analysis and informant handling. This collection of diverse contributions from psychologists can be considered 'investigative profiling' or 'behavioural analysis' and represents an increasing corpus of studies that have been conducted by many of the individuals that have contributed to this volume, as well as an increasing number of other academics and practitioners in Europe, the United States and Canada. Alongside my intention of developing a critically evaluative stance on previous traditional contributions, the chapter hints at the complexity of major police enquiries and the pressures that they exert on senior investigating officers.

Ogan and Alison extend this idea in Chapter 2, where, by reference to the Jack the Ripper murders, they outline the range of management issues that emerge again and again in high-profile 'critical' investigations. Specifically, they highlight how many of the concerns in the 1880s that were relevant to Detective Inspectors Frederick Abberline and Edmund Reid (important investigators in the Whitechapel Murders) are still relevant in contemporary detection. With reference to archival records of this case study, alongside more contemporary comments from critical incident managers collected from a variety of focus-group studies, Ogan and Alison illustrate how critical incidents have always required not only management of the incident (in terms of detection) but also management of a large team operating within a particular culture and requiring knowledge of the perceptions of the local community, the public more generally and the voracious appetite of the media.

Barrett's very helpful chapter outlines how students may benefit from greater awareness of these issues. In Chapter 3 she sets out how students with no law enforcement background can contribute in a very direct way to policing by conducting rigorous, meaningful research that is relevant to the needs of law enforcement practitioners. She refers to two specific areas where individuals might make very significant contributions: investigative decision-making and deception, and she offers some personal observations on how students and other academic researchers might improve their understanding of the problems that matter to law enforcement professionals, and of the contribution that academic research could make in these areas. The central issue in this chapter involves the suggestion that, in order to make a strong contribution to police practice, psychologists must be prepared to devote some effort to understanding the policy and practice of law enforcement, monitor developments in policing and the criminal justice system more generally, and take advantage of opportunities to engage with law enforcement agencies.

Profiling as decision-making

In Chapter 4, Wilson and Alison illustrate some preliminary empirical work that may begin to offer a contribution to investigating stranger sex offences. They note the difficulties of such enquiries and highlight how, in such cases, there may be little or no information available about the offender and limited information about the offence itself. Further, increasingly stretched police forces have limited time and resources with which to investigate the offence. During the past half century, a number of systems have been developed to classify sex offenders: from early clinical classification systems to typologies developed specifically for criminal profiling, and most recently, to classifications based on a pragmatic approach to suspect prioritization. Wilson and Alison's chapter describes and evaluates these various classification systems and addresses how the findings of previous research can be best applied to suspect prioritization in the future.

Cope's work in Chapter 5 extends the remit of this empirical basis for contributions and notes how, increasingly, the analysis of information and intelligence has become routine in the police, influenced by a number of reform agendas, policing styles and strategic interventions that require crime problems to be identified so that resources can be allocated effectively. She notes how, in order to meet this demand, the role of the crime analyst has developed, somewhat inconsistently, across police forces and law enforcement agencies. She describes three functions of police crime analysis: to assess the nature and distribution of crime in order to efficiently allocate resources and personnel; to identify crime-suspect correlations to assist investigations; and to identify the conditions that facilitate crime and incivility so that policy-makers may make informed decisions about prevention approaches. This highlights the extent to which crime analysis supports both reactive and proactive policing.

Pitfalls

The volume then goes on to cover a range of other psychological/ behavioural contributions and reminds us of the very significant corpus of work that has been developed on police interviewing. In Chapter 6 Howard and Alison draw upon three evaluation studies that connect both with the now very large body of research on the cognitive interview and the relatively smaller body of research on interviews with suspects. The former studies involve child victim/witness interviews conducted in Norway and adult victim/witness interviews in Canada, while the latter consider interviews with suspects in Adelaide, Australia. All the studies were developed with the purpose of feeding back performance to the relevant police service involved. Further, all the studies were descriptive in nature. Broadly, their chapter illustrates how various aspects of cognitive interviewing were being adopted, though an examination of the development of the interviews over time indicates that timing of questions and progression of interviewing style must also be considered in evaluating interviews. Howard and Alison reveal how the evolution of the interview over time may reflect more of the interviewer's perspective than the interviewee's, with the third study demonstrating that interviewers' perception of the extent to which various 'truth' or 'confession' tactics were used was discrepant from the actual use, with officers overestimating the extent to which they used coercive strategies. Both studies highlight that many issues about the impact of interviews on officers, suspects and witnesses remain unanswered and that providing feedback to the police involves more than simply going through a 'checklist' of strategies. The authors conclude that, despite the plethora of studies on police interviewing, relatively little attention is given to the idea of the process being an intensely interpersonal, emotional event. This chapter concludes with the suggestion that the line between appropriate conversation, persuasion and coercion is blurred and that officers (and academics) may still be confused about the acceptability of particular interviewing styles.

The issue of 'blurred lines' of acceptable behaviour is extended in Porter's chapter on police corruption (Chapter 7). Given the sensitivity of the subject and the potential for serious repercussions of highlighting incidents of corrupt behaviour, there is often disagreement in the literature regarding what constitutes corruption, what causes it and how such behaviour can be investigated sensitively with a view to future prevention. Porter offers insight into the potential expertise of psychologists in addressing these key areas. While many elements have been linked with both the causes and prevention of corruption, there are recurring themes in the literature that reflect how the organizational culture of the police service and social pressures placed upon those involved may influence the emergence of corrupt behaviour. Her chapter assimilates the existing literature in light of organizational and social psychological dimensions, which she uses to suggest how psychologists might produce theoretical models, rooted in pragmatic evidence and informed by psychological theory, to describe the various forms of corrupt behaviour that are evident within the police and why they occur.

Guidelines

In Chapter 8 Ormerod and Sturman illustrate how the study of the inter-relationship between law and psychology is becoming increasingly common. They assert that this interest may represent an increased willingness on the part of the law to learn from psychology or, more cynically, it may represent lawyers' increased wariness about psychology, which they perceive to be trespassing into ever more sacrosanct territory, both in terms of psychology's acceptance in the courtroom and its potential to challenge hallowed precepts of the common law tradition, especially those relating to the quality of evidence, the manner of its presentation and the manner of decision-making. Ormerod and Sturman assert that psychologists would do well to bear in mind this underlying anxiety of many legal practitioners that is shared by the judiciary. In their chapter, they examine controversial uses of offender profile evidence. In doing so, they demonstrate the difficulties that prevent parties in criminal cases relying upon profiles as evidence and highlight the obstacles facing a psychologist seeking to assist the police or give evidence at trial. Their chapter is followed and developed in reference to what has now become a key case in the use and abuse of profiling work – namely *R* v *Stagg*. Alison and Canter's chapter (Chapter 9) describes the combination of strategies employed by the undercover officer (codename 'Lizzie James') in the Rachel Nickell murder enquiry. Specifically, in explaining how these rhetorical strategies were adapted by orators and developed for the specific purpose of encouraging attitude change, the authors challenged the claim (made by the clinical psychologist employed during the investigation to facilitate this pseudo-relationship) that the undercover officer did not shape the information gleaned from the suspect. They argue that, although undercover officers rely on persuasive tactics (with many probably akin to forms of interpersonal manipulation in conventional, intimate relationships), they have more sinister implications where an investigative team has the power to manipulate the suspect through the promise of a sexual relationship or the threat of the withdrawal of such 'rewards'. The singular set of material considered in this chapter, made available to the authors (who served the defence) some ten years ago, comes from a set of interactions between the female undercover officer and the suspect. As such, it presents a unique insight into the world of interpersonal manipulation, the formation and dissolution of relationships and the use of subtle rhetorical devices and manipulative stratagems. The case still represents a wealth of information about the sensitivities of working with experts, police decision-making, undercover work and the management of serious crime.

Chapter 10 extends these themes and outlines a proposed framework for articulating and assessing offender profiles and behavioural investigative advice. Alison, Goodwill and Alison go on to provide guidelines for the format of the report (caveat, competence, investigative recommendations, etc.) and set the chapter within the context of a 'profile' provided for a rape-murder case in Eastern Europe. The framework relies on a philosophy of argument developed by Stephen Toulmin in which the elements of a claim are broken down into their constituent parts. They illustrate a number of factors relevant to the provision, development and dissemination of such advice. The reports that follow in subsequent chapters represent a variety of cases and styles of working that have evolved in the past ten years, ranging from contributions to allegations of abuse to reports for the management of stalking.

The analysis of statements

Chapter 11 by Fritzon and Chapter 12 by Alison outline many of the problems alluded to in previous chapters. However, the specific focus of their work centres on a common request from investigators to experts, namely to help establish whether a particular statement is credible or not. These include the difficulty of unequivocally stating whether statements are true or false, developing clear justifications for claims made about the nature of statements and the need to examine multiple aspects of a narrative account. They present two case studies in which statements made by suspects or witnesses were proving controversial and in which the courts required some expert assessment of the way in which memory operates in such cases. In Alison's report, the case involved the defendant's controversial assertion that, subsequent to stealing and crashing a car (resulting in the death of a passenger) he retained no memory for the event. The report details the case study notes, the background literature on memory for accidents and the literature on malingering. Throughout, Alison outlines how further research in malingering and statement validation is required, and both this chapter and Fritzon's indicate how difficult it is for experts to rely on statement-validation procedures.

In Chapter 13 Canter's report on the Eddie Gilfoyle case provides a very personal insight into the working method employed to construct psychological advice. What is so interesting is how his account explains the difficulties of struggling with an area where the stakes are extremely high and there is a dearth of sufficient research. Canter explains how his involvement with the case led to re-examination of his previous conclusions in light of developing further research in the area. The notion of a particular case leading to further exploration and development of an area of research is typical of pragmatism. Part of the importance of casework is the way in which it helps inform academics of many issues in law enforcement that have barely been examined within the scientific literature.

Chapters 11 to 13 illustrate how an exclusive reliance on any of the current procedures for validating statements is too unreliable to form the basis of a prosecution or defence case. These chapters also demonstrate the need for clarity in report writing as well as the benefit of experience and knowledge of how the court is likely to respond to expert evidence. It is clear from these chapters, as well as the recommendations set out by Ormerod and Sturman in Chapter 8, that authors of such reports need to adopt a style of communication that is sympathetic with the requirements of the courts, though in practice this is always difficult, not least because psychology is an imprecise science based on probable rather than definite explanations.

The issue of presentational style and effective communication emerges in Chapter 14 and subsequent chapters. In Alison and Alison's chapter on the provision of a management programme developed for security firms, the authors indicate how their report was prepared specifically with non-psychologists in mind. The recommended responses in the report are based on principles of operant reinforcement and the authors illustrate how such concepts can be clearly expressed and can be designed to be user-friendly for clients.

The academic and the practitioner

In Chapter 15 Alison and Alison present a report prepared on behalf of a fictional police constabulary in relation to an allegation of GBH and rape within a domestic relationship. The case is based on hybridized actual cases presented to Alison and Alison in their capacity as a treatment manager for domestic violence cases and a research psychologist respectively. The case demonstrates how practitioners and academics can work effectively alongside one another in attempting to inform the courts of the research literature and in terms of the tacit knowledge of these types of scenario. This chapter brings us back to the themes set out in the early chapters, as well as in the 'Academic and Practitioner' paper by Alison *et al.* (2004), namely the benefits of practical, case-based analysis and rigorous, scientific investigation.

Chapter 16 extends these themes and presents a more personal set of reflections from two different but sympathetic perspectives, namely Alison's experience with research and West's extensive practitioner focus. This concluding chapter presents an introspective examination of the initial developments and subsequent progression of behavioural profiling and indicates that there is real reason for optimism in this most compelling of areas. As the conclusions indicate, this volume is written in the hope that familiarity with the logic of scientific enquiry and a willingness to apply the findings of investigative psychology will enhance the application of a more rational and systematic method to police investigative efforts. The purpose is to demonstrate how investigative support and advice, linked to the theoretical basis of behavioural science, can be applied effectively to the investigation of serious crime.

Having said this, the volume as a whole is clearly not designed as a definitive working method. Indeed, I would hope that many of these chapters indicate the real difficulties and pitfalls of such work. However, a central aim is to stimulate further discussion and development within an area that hitherto has failed to make publicly available what it is that forensic psychologists do when they contribute to the investigation of crime from a 'profiling' perspective.

References

Alison, L., West, A. and Goodwill, A. (2004) 'The academic and the practitioner: Pragmatists' views of offender profiling', *Psychology, Public Policy and Law*, 10 (1–2): 71–101.

Fishman, D. (1999). *The Case for Pragmatic Psychology*. New York: New York University Press.

Fishman, D. (2004) 'Background on the "Psycholegal Lexis Proposal" exploring the potential of a systematic case study database in forensic psychology', *Psychology, Public Policy and Law*, 9 (3–4): 267–74.

Part One

The Context of Criminal Investigation

Chapter 1

From trait-based profiling to psychological contributions to apprehension methods

Laurence Alison[1]

Traditional 'trait-based' profiling

Traditionally, profiling has involved the process of predicting the likely socio-demographic characteristics of an offender based on information available at the crime scene. For example, the *Crime Classification Manual*, a handbook for offender profiling issued by the FBI, explains that, 'The crime scene is presumed to reflect the murderer's behavior and personality in much the same way as furnishings reveal the homeowner's character' (Douglas *et al.*, 1992: 21). The idea of inferring one set of characteristics from one set of crime-scene actions relies on two major assumptions. Firstly, there is the issue of behavioural consistency: the variance in the crimes of serial offenders must be smaller than the variance occurring in a random comparison of different offenders. Research findings indicate that this appears to be the case for rapists (Bennell, 1998; Grubin *et al.*, 1997). Criminologists, in adopting a 'molar' approach, define behavioural consistency as the probability that an individual will repeatedly commit similar types of offences (Farrington, 1997). In contrast, psychologists have emphasized a 'molecular' analysis of criminal behaviour, where behavioural consistency is defined as the repetition of particular aspects of behaviour if the same offender engages in the same type of offence again (Canter, 1995). A number of studies have provided support for the notion of offender consistency. For example, Green *et al.* (1976) studied the consistency of burglary behaviour. Based on 14 behavioural 'markers', Green and his colleagues were able to accurately assign 14 out of 15 cases of burglary to the relevant three burglars. Similarly, Craik and Patrick (1994), Wilson *et al.* (1997), and Grubin *et al.* (1997) all concluded that behavioural consistency exists in the crime-scene behaviours of serial rapists, though only to a limited degree.

However, the second assumption, referred to as the 'homology problem' (Mokros and Alison, 2002), presents a significant hurdle for traditional profiling methods. This assumption relies on the hypothesis that the degree of similarity in the offence behaviour of any two perpetrators from a given category of crime will match the degree of similarity in their characteristics. Thus, the more similar two offenders are, the higher the resemblance in their behavioural style in the offence. The idea that the manner in which an offence is committed corresponds with a particular configuration of background characteristics differs from the more humble findings of bivariate measures of association, such as the findings of Davies *et al.* (1998) that offenders who display awareness of forensic procedures by destroying or removing semen are four times more likely to have had a previous conviction for a sexual offence than those offenders who do not take such precautions.

Traditional profiling methods make far more ambitious claims than these likelihood predictions. For example, Douglas *et al.* (1986) all refer to proposed relationships between clusters of background features from crime-scene actions in order to develop a psychological 'portrait' of the offender. When these relationships are tested, however, the results are not very promising. In the study by Davies *et al.* (1998) the integration of a range of crime-scene actions as predictors within logistic regression models failed to show a substantial improvement over the information obtained through simple base rates in the majority of instances. Similarly, in the study by House (1997), the 50 rapists in the sample appeared relatively homogeneous with respect to their criminal histories, regardless of whether they acted in a primarily aggressive, pseudo-intimate, instrumental/criminal or sadistic manner during the sexual assault. Mokros and Alison (2002) examined 100 male stranger rapes, using information on the crime-scene behaviour of 28 dichotomous variables taken directly from a police database. This represented a random sample from a total of more than 500 victim statements stored in the database. They were unable to find any clear links between sets of crime-scene behaviours and sets of background characteristics.

Traditional profiling as naïve trait psychology

Alison *et al.* (2002) state that the assumptions underlying many profiling methods are similar to assumptions inherent in naïve trait theories of personality. In the naïve trait view primary traits are seen as stable and general in that they determine a person's inclination to act consistently (stable) in a particular way across a variety of situations (general). As the notion of behavioural dispositions implies, traits are not directly observable but are inferred from behaviour (Mischel, 1999). Traditional trait-based (TTB) profiling tends to attribute behaviours to underlying, relatively context-free dispositional constructs. Thus, both TTB profiling methods and traditional trait theories are *nomothetic* in that both try to make general predictions about offenders; *deterministic* in that both make the assumption that all offenders are subject to the same set of processes that affect their behaviour in predictable ways; and finally, both are *non-situationist* in the belief that behaviour is thought to be consistent in the face of environmental influences.

Based on the evidence concerning the traditional trait approach, one would not expect a task such as offender profiling, in which global traits are derived from specific actions (or vice versa), to be possible. Moreover, the profiler's task is even more ambitious than this in that inferences are made about characteristics that are not appropriate for a psychological definition of traits (including features such as the offender's age, gender, ethnicity, marital status, degree of sexual maturity and likely reaction to police questioning (Annon, 1995; Ault and Reese, 1980; Grubin, 1995; Homant and Kennedy, 1998).

There are of course many studies of sexual offenders that support an aggregate level of research on traits. For example, Proulx *et al.* (1994) demonstrated that rapists display significantly diverse facets of personality disorder depending on their level of physical violence as demonstrated in their crime-scene behaviour. Among their findings was the observation that more violent offenders score significantly higher on the histrionic, narcissistic, antisocial and paranoid sub-scales than the less violent offenders. Langevin *et al.* (1985) report similar results for another sample of rapists.

Proulx *et al.* (1999) identified a sample of rapists according to their respective *modus operandi* into three groups: sadistic, opportunistic and anger rapists. They found substantial differences between the sadistic and the opportunistic types with respect to personality disorders. The sadistic offenders were more likely to have avoidant, schizoid and dependent tendencies, whereas the opportunistic offenders were characterized as narcissistic, paranoid and antisocial.

The study by Proulx *et al.* (1999) indicates that it may be possible to discriminate between rapists based on their crime-scene actions and that such differentiation may be reflected in personality. Such a procedure could properly be referred to as a *psychological* profile, since it refers

5

exclusively to particular psychological constructs. In contrast, the traditionalists' use of the term 'psychological profiling' relies on the generation of demographic characteristics of offenders and is, therefore, something of a misnomer.

Thus, the evidence for a nomothetic, deterministic and non-situationist model of TTB offender profiling is not compelling. Despite this and despite the admission by many profilers that their work is little more than educated guesswork, the utility of profiling seems to be generally accepted as valid. For example, Witkin (1996) reported that the FBI had 12 full-time profilers who, collectively, were involved in about 1,000 cases per year.

Interpretation of the advice

Beyond the issue of the feasibility of the process lie potential problems associated with the interpretation of the reports. To date, there has been little systematic research of such reports, and few suggestions as to how such advice might be deconstructed and evaluated. One exception is a small-scale study recently conducted on a sample of European and American offender profiles from the last decade (Alison *et al.*, 2003a). Alison *et al.* established that nearly half of the opinions expressed within these reports contained advice that could not be verified post-conviction (e.g. 'the offender has a rich fantasy life'), while over a fifth were vague or open to interpretation (e.g. 'the offender has poor social skills'). In addition, in over 80 per cent, the profiler failed to provide any justification for the advice proposed (i.e. they did not clarify what their opinion was based on).

The coding framework developed to evaluate profiles was based on Toulmin's work in the 1950s. Toulmin's work (1958), originally based on the analysis of philosophical and legal rhetoric, proposed that arguments could be broken down into various component parts to enable researchers to scrutinize the strengths and weaknesses of various aspects of any given claim. He suggested that arguments contain six interrelated components: (1) the claim, (2) the strength of the claim, (3) the grounds supporting the claim, (4) the warrant, (5) the backing, and (6) the rebuttal. Figure 1.1 illustrates how this format can be applied to the investigative domain with reference to the linking of offences. The *claim*, in this example, involves the statement that two offences are linked. In order to substantiate this claim certain components must be present. The first involves the strength, or *modality* of the claim. This may come in modal terms such as, 'probably', 'possibly', 'certainly', but in our hypothetical case this is presented as a statistical probability (i.e. 'a 99.7 per cent chance that ...'). The modality component indicates the extent to which we should rely on the claim being

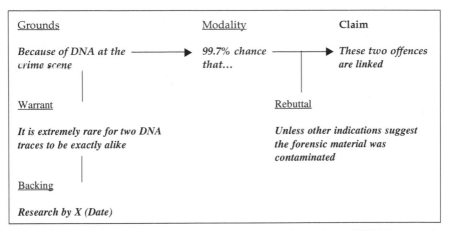

Figure 1.1 Toulmin's structure of argument using a hypothetical 'DNA' example

true, in this case the analyst is suggesting we take the claims very seriously. The *grounds* are the support for the claim. In this case, the reasoning relates to the presence of a DNA trace at the crime scene. The *warrant* authorizes the grounds because 'it is rare for two DNA traces to be exactly alike'. The *backing*, or formal support for the warrant, comes in the form of a citation to a specific example(s) of research. Finally, the *rebuttal* allows us to consider the conditions under which the claim ceases to be likely. Thus, if further evidence becomes known (for example, contamination), the claim may have to be adjusted accordingly.

There are several reasons why Toulmin's philosophy of argument is a useful method of exploring the construction of reports. Firstly, there are few clear bases upon which such advice is given. There exist few formal models of how profiling works, why it works or, indeed, if it works. Thus a framework, in which we can evaluate the justification for any given claim, allows us to identify weaknesses in those claims. It allows us to establish the certainty of the claim (modality), the conditions where the claim must be re-evaluated (rebuttal), the grounds upon which the claim is made and the warrant and backing for those grounds. In this way investigators can measure the weight and significance that can be attached to any inference or conclusion. Secondly, there is increasing pressure on investigating officers and profilers to carefully consider the potential legal ramifications of employing such advice in their inquiries (Ormerod, 1999). Profilers must approach each report with strict standards of evidentiary reliability and relevancy afforded to court procedures. Finally, by applying this framework to their own reports, profilers may gain insight into the processes that they themselves engage in when preparing material for the police.

The danger of not making the justifications of such statements clear (especially in the case of ambiguous statements) includes the potential increase in erroneous interpretation of the material. Alison *et al.* (2003b) have argued that the lack of clarity in such reports could lead to problems with the interpretation of the material in similar ways in which so-called 'Barnum effects' operate in social psychology. For example, it has long been established that people tend to accept vague and ambiguous personality descriptions as uniquely applicable to themselves without realizing that the same description could be applied to just about anyone (Forer, 1949). This has been given the name 'Forer' or 'Barnum' effect in deference to P. T. Barnum's claim that his circus included 'a little something for everyone' (Meehl, 1956). It is possible then that a contributory factor in the perception of usefulness, despite outcome measures, can be explained by the readiness to selectively fit ambiguous, unverifiable information from the profile to the offender. Therefore, after a suspect is apprehended, or if the investigating officer has a 'type' of offender in mind, it is possible that the enquiry team engage in an inferential process 'invited' by the ambiguity of the profile. As Hyman states in reference to readings from psychics, 'once the client is actively engaged in trying to make sense of the series of sometimes contradictory statements issuing from the reader, he becomes a creative problem solver trying to find coherence and meaning in the total set of statements' (Hyman, 1987: 415). To test the hypothesis that individuals engage in such processes we devised two studies in which we examined the willingness of individuals to fit the same ambiguous information to two sets of contradictory statements (profiles). In two exploratory studies with police officers and other forensic professionals as participants, Alison *et al.* (2003b) split individuals into two groups (A and B). Each group was given a questionnaire regarding a sequence of events taken from real murder cases. In part one of the exercise participants were required to read the details of this case and imagine that it was a case that they, as an investigating officer, had to deal with.

Part two of the questionnaire included an offender profile and part three incorporated the characteristics of either offender A or offender B (with group A getting offender A and group B getting offender B). In condition A the characteristics of the offender (offender A) were the genuine characteristics of the offender. In contrast, offender B was a fabricated account and was designed to be quite different from A in terms of age, preconvictions and associated knowledge (or lack thereof) of the victim. Participants were asked to rate the extent to which they felt that the profile fitted the offender. They were also asked to give a brief account of the reasons for their response.

The majority of participants in both studies rated the profile as 'generally very accurate', with no participants in either group rating the profile as either generally or very inaccurate and with no differences in the ratings of either the bogus or genuine suspect, despite the different characteristics of each. Further, in study two, in which similar results were found, investigating officers stated that the profile would assist in narrowing the range of possible suspects. In both cases, individuals appeared to have selectively attended to 'hits' in the profile with relatively less attention to misses or the fact that the profile was sufficiently ambiguous to potentially refer to quite different individuals.

Although Alison *et al.* concede that there are many limitations to this study (not least the problem of drawing conclusions from a non-significant difference and the fact that our subsequent research is beginning to establish that there are more varied responses in such studies contingent on the sophistication of the design of the study), this pen-and-paper test may underestimate the full influence of such effects in real cases. In genuine enquiries the individual providing the profile is likely to be presented to the team as an expert in his or her field, thereby increasing the credibility of the advice irrespective of content. Secondly, profilers may not always write down the information, resulting in officers relying on their memory of the advice. Finally, there may exist considerable pressure on an enquiry team to yield results, thereby resulting in a more favourable view of the advice. If a suspect does arise during the investigation, officers may wish to actively ignore the information that does not fit the suspect and, perhaps, unwittingly, exaggerate the merits of the information. They may fail to appreciate the extent to which the information could fit a wide range of individuals, a process reflecting the widely known 'confirmation bias effect' (Baron, 1988)

A bleak picture?

Much of the discussion thus far presents a rather bleak picture of profiling. However, the beliefs surrounding profiling appear to be so ingrained that many of the keenest and, indeed, brightest students have been so embroiled in the media portrayal of this field that they are often the most difficult students to encourage in developing a critical stance on such methods. In particular, many students interested in forensic and investigative psychology appear to hold the view that offender profiling is particularly useful in apprehending serial murderers. It is important to appreciate that the ways in which psychologists can contribute extends well beyond the process of profiling offenders. Indeed, the apprehension of the offender would be assisted by enhancing police decision-making and leadership skills, improving methods for interviewing witnesses and victims, developing accurate methods of recording, collating and analysing data on preconvictions of offenders, developing suspect prioritization systems based on empirical research and enhancing intelligence-led policing and the use of informants.

In order to demonstrate the many ways in which psychologists and behavioural advisors can assist in policing, this chapter now turns to an exploratory study of apprehension methods of serial killers. The study, conducted by Carrie Whyte, relates to an area of research known as 'solvability' studies.

Apprehension of serial killers: Whyte's study of solvability factors

Keppel (1989), the most vocal proponent of work in solvability studies, notes that very little has been written with regard to investigative procedures beyond those undertaken at the original crime-scene. He points to several solvability factors in homicide investigation that stretch beyond the traditional information collection process carried out at the murder/body disposal site. These include the quality of police interviews of eyewitnesses, the circumstances that led to the initial stop and arrest of the murderer, the circumstances that established probable cause to search and seize physical evidence from person/property of suspect, the quality of the investigation at the crime-scene, the quality of the scientific analysis of the physical evidence seized from the suspect and its comparison to physical evidence recovered from victims and murder scenes.

However, other than Keppel's work, most of the literature has generally been critical of the police role in apprehending offenders and has frequently concluded that the police force has little to do with solving crime. Even certain FBI officers (Ressler *et al.*, 1984) have admitted that many of the most notorious serial murderers in the US have been caught either through some fortuitous event or during some unrelated police procedure, while others have expressed the belief that serial murderers are usually discovered purely by coincidence and not by any established investigative process or through psychological assistance such as profiling (Sears, 1991).

However, Keppel (1989) is dismissive of the role of serendipity in such investigations. Although he admits that 'what usually occurs is that some patrol officer on routine duty comes across the killer' he goes on to remark that 'it then takes alert and intelligent investigators to turn this opportunity into a final resolution of the case' (p. 68). In the following study, Carrie Whyte, then a Masters student in Investigative Psychology at the University of Liverpool, sought to investigate the variety of methods of apprehension, consider types that most frequently lead to resolution of the case and establish whether particular combinations of apprehension methods are more common than others. Additionally, she wanted to establish whether the way in which an offender carries out a crime is associated with the way in which he is eventually caught.

The basic information that an investigator has to work with includes the details of the crime: the where, when, and how it occurred and identification of the victims. This information is derived through various methods, but perhaps the two prime types of evidence that may be gathered during a typical murder investigation are forensic and cor-roborative. Canter and Alison (1997) point out that the most controlled information is that gathered from the actual crime-scene. Evidence of this nature tends to be physical, such as DNA testing, ballistics and fingerprinting (Evans, 1996). Forensic evidence is highly impressive in the courtroom although, in its absence, eyewitness testimony is occasionally regarded as a factor that may sway a judge and/or jury to establish the guilt or innocence of the defendant (Loftus, 1979). However, eyewitness reports more regularly play a crucial role at the investigative stage. Police often use eyewitness reports to aid in the investigative process, whether through the identification of a suspect at a police identity parade, a 'mug shot' or publicized composite photograph or simply through the notification of the police of sightings, e.g. of a vehicle or suspicious-looking individual at or around the area where the crime took place. Additionally, police may receive information through informants or sources that are themselves often part of a potentially criminal context (Canter and Alison, 1997). Police may, for example, receive a tip-off from an accomplice of the offender due to that same individual's growing anxiety for their own safety.

In relation to investigative approaches in linking crime, a number of computerized decision support systems have been developed, such as the Violent Criminal Apprehension Programme (VICAP) (cited in Egger, 1998) and the Homicide Investigation and Tracking System (HITS) in the US (Keppel and Weis, 1993). These systems contain information not only on known offenders in the area, evidence retrieved, victimology and other factors that may help solve a particular case, they also include incidents with similar characteristics involving murder or sexual assault. In this way, such systems can be used to determine if crimes of a similar nature with a similar method of operation have been committed in a recent time period.

The sample for our study comprised a total of 101 American serial murder cases. Although it has been previously noted in the literature that serial murderers sometimes operate in pairs (Hickey (1991) found that 37 per cent of serial murders were conducted by more than one offender), we chose to focus on single perpetrators in studying apprehension methods. Although the issue of co-offending may be of some interest in relation to apprehension since it may relate to the degree to which accomplice informants contribute to bringing about apprehension, we wanted to focus, at least in this study, on single offenders in the first instance. We also focused specifically on male perpetrators. Since Hickey (1991) found that 12 per cent to 17 per cent of his sample were women, the present sample may be representative, in terms of gender, of the most general character-istics of a serial murderer population.

The age at the time of the last offence was recorded as this information was the nearest available to the offender's age at time of apprehension. The mean age for this sample of offenders was 29.6 years, with a range of 17–52 years. This conforms to previous studies that suggest that serial murderers tend to be in their late twenties to thirties. Hickey (1991), for example, found that offenders tend to be approximately 30 years of age.

Collectively, the offenders killed a total of 617 victims. Within each series between three and 23 people were murdered. The data include only those murders which the offenders were known to have conducted and for which they were convicted. The mean number of victims for each series is 8. The mean offending period was 3.75 years. However, a significant percentage were actually only killing for one year (36.4 per cent). The maximum offending period was 17 years, and 7.8 per cent of offenders managed to avoid capture for a period of ten years or more. Thus, this sample *generally* reflects the predominant characteristics of a serial murderer population in terms of a male single offender, at an average age of 30 years, with at least three victims. Data were collated from a content analysis of archival material. This took the form of published magazine articles written by investigative journalists. In all cases the journalists themselves obtained the details from the police reports and court transcripts of the cases in question.

Figure 1.2 outlines the frequency distribution for the methods by which the present sample of serial murderers were apprehended (apprehension variables). We should note that in many cases multiple apprehension methods contributed to the eventual resolution of the case. Thus eyewitness testimony may have been used in combination with, for example, a police sting or forensic evidence.

Figure 1.2 illustrates that the most frequent factor that contributed to securing the apprehension of a suspect is knowledge that an individual has been involved in previous crime (71 per cent) while the least common incident is that the offender kills himself during the commission of the crime (1 per cent). Forensic evidence was a relatively uncommon factor (12 per cent) in this study. In contrast, in 37 per cent of cases apprehension was

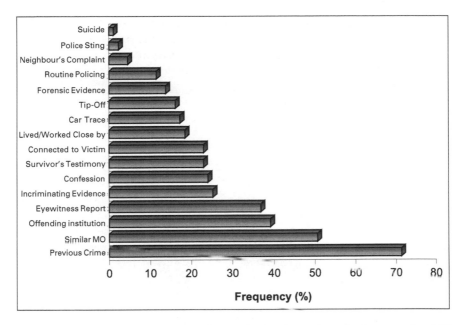

Figure 1.2 Frequency distribution for methods of apprehension in a sample of 87 serial murderers.

facilitated on the basis of eyewitness testimony. In 11.5 per cent of cases a suspect was apprehended on the basis of events unrelated to the investigation.

Apprehension roles: detective, offender, victim, informant

As stated, it was rarely the case that an offender was apprehended through a single avenue but, rather, apprehension variables tended to co-occur in varying degrees in various combinations. In order to explore, in depth, the role of differing methods of apprehension in capturing serial murderers, it is useful to consider the relationship that every apprehension variable has to every other. Based on the joint co-occurrence of apprehension variables, we found a core region surrounded by four themes. We have labelled these themes as apprehension 'roles' that relate to different emphases on the part of different 'participants' in the overall picture of serial murder apprehension. Of course, these are labels of convenience that greatly simplify the interactions of the different individuals involved in the investigation, but we would argue that they do represent thematic emphases of particular aspects of the system. We have labelled these as apprehension facilitated by *detective, offender, victim* and *informant*, where the core is represented by features essentially related to the offender's *previous history of offending*. This core represents the most frequent apprehension variable and suggests that apprehension is greatly facilitated by similarities in *modus operandi* (MO) as well as the knowledge of offenders' pre-convictions. Thus, in many cases, the offender's past, literally, catches up with him.

The sum of the frequencies for the variables incorporated within each of the four other regions is as follows: Detective = 79%, Offender = 67%, Victim = 48%, Informant = 23%.

This demonstrates that apprehension, directly through the work of the detective, represents the most frequent method of securing apprehension, while the least frequent method involves apprehension by informant. The summed frequencies also demonstrate that apprehension facilitated by the offender's own intervention/errors plays a substantial role in apprehension, while apprehension facilitated by issues associated directly with a victim help solve nearly half of all cases in the present sample. These regions are considered in more detail below, and are summarised in Figure 1.3.

Detective

This cluster of apprehension elements contains variables that involve police procedures, including the examination of forensic or eyewitness reports received by police (from an individual having witnessed the scene, a related incident or having viewed a mugshot or police composite photograph), car traces on a vehicle abandoned near the scene or one noted by an eyewitness and routine policing. This last variable is significant in that it is (a) relatively rare – thereby contradicting the belief

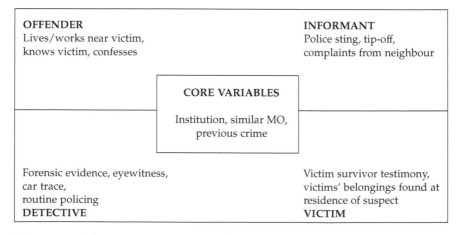

Figure 1.3 Schematic representation of co-occurrences

that this is a very frequent method and, more importantly, (b) that when it does occur in combination with other factors it is associated with overtly detective-oriented features of the case. This finding echoes Keppel's comment that it takes alert and intelligent detectives to turn the opportunity of a traffic cop arrest into a solved murder case and suggests that routine policing can be seen as another branch of detective work, rounding the actions of the police as a whole in solving crime, regardless of rank (Keppel, 1989). Thus, a central area in which psychologists may invest their research energy involves an evaluation of how this process of linking information from many disparate sources and utilizing and interpreting such patterns may be what discriminates efficient from lacklustre investigative decision-makers.[2]

Offender

This region contains variables that emphasize the offender's own part in raising his profile as a conspicuous suspect. For instance, he may have come under suspicion simply because he lives or works close by to one or more of the victims, or he has some acquaintance with the victim. Although it entails detective procedures to uncover such details, the offender fails to consider (or is not worried after having considered) the possibility that such associations increase his risk of becoming a suspect. Perhaps significantly then, also incorporated in this region is the offender's confession. This cluster, therefore, may represent actions that reflect a relatively lower degree (compared to other clusters) of concern to avoid detection and may represent actions that are suggestive of drawing attention to oneself, whether this is intentional or not.

Victim

This cluster contains only two variables, both of which are associated with evidence from a victim. Within this group the offender hoards incriminating material, such as items belonging to his victims, keeping these items as souvenirs of the murder victim in his house or on his person. The second variable involves the role of a surviving victim's testimony. Investigative and forensic psychologists have increasingly come to appreciate the influence of the role of the victim on the actions that occur during the offence, and work on suspect prioritization (see Chapter 4) has been forced to recognize victimology as a crucial component of informing decisions associated with 'profiling' offences.

Informant

Three apprehension variables relate to the receipt of information by police from a variety of potential sources or 'informants'. Police may receive complaints from neighbours that an individual is acting suspiciously or, as has occurred in some instances, there is a strange smell coming from the individual's apartment. Alternatively, police receive a tip, whether this tip is anonymous or from the accomplice's partner, friend or spouse. The final variable, the police 'sting', is set up on the receipt of suspicious information about an individual. However, this combination of elements, in this sample, was the least common means of capture.

Dominant solvability themes

The low Cronbach's values (Offender = 0.33, Detective = 0.28, Informant = 0.14, Victim = 0.11) within each cluster reveal that the regions should not be seen as discrete 'types' of apprehension method but rather as generalized themes. Therefore, one would not expect any one case to be solely represented by any one theme but rather by an emphasis of one theme with some possible influence from other regions. For example, if one were to plot the Ted Bundy case, one would find an emphasis on the detective region (routine policing, forensics, eyewitness testimony, incriminating evidence), whereas in Ed Kemper's case there is an emphasis on the offender region (victim connected, confessed). Thus, these low alpha-values suggest that it is relatively rare for a case to conform strictly to any one cluster; but rather, the majority of cases would show some bias towards a particular cluster.

The findings suggest that some methods of apprehension were more common than others. For instance, it was found that established detective procedures, such as the use of forensic science, eyewitness testimony and car traces are, collectively, very significant factors in serial murder investigation, while having access to knowledge regarding a suspect as a known offender as well as knowledge of the occurrence of recent similar crimes for the basis of linking were the most prevalent components involved in apprehension. This finding echoes Keppel's belief that traditional investigative procedures are effective in securing the apprehension of criminals (Keppel, 1989). However, it was also discovered that a number of inadvertent and, in some cases, purposeful actions by the offender can also aid the investigative process. This result tends to support the contention of a number of authors that believe serial murderers sometimes 'catch themselves' (Sears, 1991). This does not repudiate either conjecture but rather admits that both factors have a role to play in the solution of serial murder.

Frequencies for variables not previously examined within the specific context of apprehension were also low. For instance, the least frequent means of apprehension were factors relating to the receipt of information from outside sources (excluding actual eyewitnesses). Although the inclusion of more cases involving offending teams may increase the possibility of occurrence of accomplice tip-offs, frequencies remained low for notification of the police by other possible sources, such as the offender's spouse, friends or acquaintances. These results are surprising as the response of the public to the police incident room, once a serial murder investigation is publicized, is typically massive (Ressler *et al.*, 1986).

Identifying an offender on the basis of his geographical relationship to a victim has previously been the target of psychological research (Egger, 1998; Canter and Larkin, 1993). Although many of these studies have concluded that offenders typically live in close proximity to their victims (Canter and Gregory, 1994), less than one-fifth of the present sample involved the police having access to the knowledge that an offender lived or worked close by to one or more of the victims (a factor that serves to reinforce an existing suspicion on the part of the investigators). The finding of this low frequency, however, does not necessarily contradict the previous research that an offender lives near his victims. It may be that offenders do in fact live and work close to their offence sites but that detectives do not always determine this during an investigation and thus, offender apprehension is achieved through other means.

Accurate records as a foundation of detection

The core factor in apprehension in this sample appears to involve factors relating to knowledge of suspects through previous criminal records. Such a conclusion obviously has important implications for police coding procedures employed for computerized networks. Moreover, actions performed by the offender that have been described in the present research as 'conspicuous' or 'unconcealed' were also found to play a substantial role in the event of apprehension.

Perhaps the most interesting implication of the present research, however, is the recognition of recording information related to individuals' criminal histories and also the occurrence of other offences. Computerized tracking systems such as HITS and VICAP (cited in Egger, 1998; Keppel and Weis, 1993) do possess this kind of information, which facilitates comparative case analysis, and individuals with a criminal record can be instantly accessed from the system by homicide investigators. Currently, however, the success of VICAP is dependent upon the voluntary participation of local law-enforcement personnel who must complete a lengthy and detailed form in order for information to be recorded (Godwin and Canter, 1997). The present results depict that the most important information relates to previous criminal records and other similar offences. Thus, police must not underestimate the value of accurate, efficient and 'joined-up' recording systems. Indeed, the present findings serve to highlight not only the importance of putting resources toward the implementation and management of such information systems, but also pinpoint the nature of the most significant information, i.e. accurate details of an offender's previous offence history.

However, these resources need to be used wisely, and the blind collection of information without any effort to shape and evaluate the relative contribution of that information may not bear fruit. Further, the study hints at aspects of the investigative process that are far wider reaching than apprehension. The data suggest that the process of investigation is complex and multivariate and that contributions to effective media strategy, decision-making, the psychology of leadership, organizational psychology (among many others) could all enhance the professional standards of investigation.

Specific UK developments

In the United Kingdom in the last ten years we have seen improvements in certain police investigative practices. In particular, the police service has improved the process of review procedures. Further, the service has made significant commitments to the investigation and prosecution of domestic violence (for example, realization that those who are committing violent offences within the home are also often committing violence against strangers). Nevertheless, in the same period, there has been a decline in investigative experience, with the attendant potential devaluation of the role of CID as a specialism, the potentially negative consequences of which have serendipitously been more than offset by significant advances in forensic science and DNA technology. As later chapters discuss, there is a recognition in the UK of a critical shortage of experienced senior investigating officers and a need to increase investigative specialists, as well as formulate specific research agendas to enhance our knowledge of investigation and contribute to its professional development.

As this book argues, behavioural science can make a real contribution towards training and enhancing the professional standards of the police investigator role, beyond the narrow confines of traditional approaches to offender profiling.

Acknowledgements

The author would like to posthumously thank Dr. Christopher Missen for access to his substantial data set of serial killer information. This chapter is dedicated to Chris.

Notes

1 I am grateful to Adrian West for comments on (and additions to) this chapter.
2 It is important to acknowledge how difficult the detective's role is in major enquiries. Those who conscientiously choose to devote their life to intervening in society's violence repeatedly face terrible distress. Unless a dispassionate and objective attitude prevails, they are more likely to be overwhelmed. A willingness to apply a scientific attitude (which can exist alongside detective intuition) can become a critical safeguard. These are themes to which much of the book is devoted: i.e. recognition of complexity, the assistance of a scientific perspective, the ability to apply a scientific approach alongside recognition of the peculiarities of a case.

References

Alison, L., Bennett, C., Mokros, A. and Ormerod, D. (2002) 'The personality paradox in offender profiling. A theoretical review of the processes involved in deriving background characteristics from crime scene actions', *Psychology, Public Policy and Law*, 8: 115–1350.

Alison, L.J., Smith, M.D., Eastman, O. and Rainbow, L. (2003a) 'Toulmin's philosophy of argument and its relevance to offender profiling', *Psychology, Crime and Law*, 9 (2): 173–83.

Alison, L.J., Smith, M.D. and Morgan, K. (2003b) 'Interpreting the accuracy of offender profiles', *Psychology, Crime and Law*, 9 (2): 185–95.

Alison, L. and Stein, K. (2001) 'Vicious circles: Accounts of stranger sexual assault reflect abusive variants of conventional interactions', *The Journal of Forensic Psychiatry*, 12 (3): 515–38.

Annon, J.S. (1995) 'Investigative profiling: A behavioural analysis of the crime scene', *American Journal of Forensic Psychology*, 13 (4): 67–75.

Ault, R.L. and Reese, J.T. (1980) 'A psychological assessment of crime profiling', *FBI Law Enforcement Bulletin*, 49 (3): 22–25.

Baron, J. (1988) *Thinking and Deciding*. Cambridge: Cambridge University Press.

Bennell, C. (1998) *Linking Serial Sex Offences* (Unpublished MSc thesis) Liverpool, UK: University of Liverpool, Department of Psychology.

Blau, T.H. (1994) 'Psychological profiling', in T.H. Blau (ed.), *Psychological services for law enforcement* (pp. 261–274). New York: John Wiley and Sons.

Borg, I. and Lingoes, J. (1987) *Multidimensional Similarity Analysis*. New York: Springer.

Canter, D.V. (1995) 'Psychology of offender profiling', in R. Bull and D. Carson (eds), *Handbook of psychology in legal contexts* (pp. 343–355). Chichester: John Wiley and Sons.

Canter, D.V. and Alison, L J. (1997) *Criminal Detection and the Psychology of Crime*. The International Library of Criminology, Criminal Justice and Penology. Dartmouth: Ashgate.

Canter, D. and Gregory, A. (1994) 'Identifying the residential location of rapists', *Journal of the Forensic Science Society*, 34 (3): 169–75.

Canter, D. and Larkin, P. (1993) 'The environmental range of serial rapists', *Journal of Environmental Psychology*, 13: 63–9.

Copson, G. (1995) *Coals to Newcastle? Part one: A study of offender profiling* (Special interest series paper 7). London: Home Office.

Craik, M. and Patrick, A. (1994) 'Linking serial offences', *Policing*, 10: 181–87.

Davies, A., Wittebrood, K. and Jackson, J.L. (1998) *Predicting the criminal record of a stranger rapist* (Special interest series paper 12). London: Home Office, Policing and Reducing Crime Unit.

Douglas, J.E., Burgess, A.W., Burgess, A.G. and Ressler, R.K. (1992) *Crime Classification Manual: A standard system for investigating and classifying violent crime*. New York: Simon and Schuster.

Douglas, J.E., Ressler, R.K., Burgess, A.W. and Hartman, C.R. (1986) 'Criminal profiling from crime scene analysis', *Behavioural Sciences and the Law*, 4: 401–21.

Egger, S.A. (1998) *The Killers Among Us: An examination of serial murder and its investigation*. New Jersey: Prentice Hall.

Elizur, D. and Sagie, A. (1999) 'Facets of personal values: A structural analysis of life and work values', *Applied Psychology: International Review*, 48: 73–87.

Evans, C. (1996) *The Casebook of Forensic Detection: How science solved 100 of the world's most baffling crimes*. New York: Wiley and Sons Inc.

Farrington, D.P. (1997) 'Human development and criminal careers', in M. Maguire, R. Morgan and R. Reiner (eds), *The Oxford Handbook of Criminology* (2nd edn) (pp. 361–408). Oxford: Oxford University Press.

Forer, B. (1949) 'The fallacy of personal validation: A classroom demonstration of gullibility', *Journal of Abnormal and Social Psychology*, 44: 118–23.

Godwin, M. and Canter, D.V. (1997) 'Encounter and death: The spatial behaviour of US serial killers', *Policing: International Journal of Police Strategy and Management*, 20 (1): 24–38.

Green, E.J., Booth, C.E. and Biderman, M.D. (1976) 'Cluster analysis of burglary M/Os', *Journal of Police Science and Administration*, 4: 382–88.

Grubin, D. (1995) 'Offender profiling', *Journal of Forensic Psychiatry*, 6: 259–63.

Grubin, D., Kelly, P. and Ayis, S. (1997) *Linking Serious Sexual Assaults*. London: Home Office, Police Research Group.

Guttman, L.A. (1954) 'A new approach to factor analysis: The radex', in P.E. Lazarfield (ed.), *Mathematical Thinking in the Social Sciences* (pp. 258–348). Glencoe, IL: Free Press.

Guttman, L.A. (1968) 'A general non-metric technique for finding the smallest coordinate space for a configuration of points', *Psychometrika*, 33: 495–506.

Hickey, E.W. (1991) *Serial Murderers and their Victims*. Pacific Grove: Brooks/Cole.

Hodge, S. (in press) 'A multivariate model of serial sexual murder', in D.V. Canter and L.J. Alison (eds), *Profiling Rape and Murder. Offender Profiling Series Volume V*. Aldershot: Ashgate.

Homant, R.J. and Kennedy, D.B. (1998) 'Psychological aspects of crime-scene profiling: Validity research', *Criminal Justice and Behavior*, 25: 319–43.

House, J.C. (1997) 'Towards a practical application of offender profiling: The RNC's criminal suspect prioritization system' in J.L. Jackson and D.A. Bekerian (eds), *Offender Profiling: Theory, research and practice* (pp. 177–190). Chichester: John Wiley and Sons.

Hyman, R. (1987) *The Elusive Quarry: A Scientific Appraisal of Psychological Research.* New York: Prometheus Books.

Jaccard, P. (1908) 'Nouvelles recherches sur la distribution florale', *Bulletin de la Societé Vaudoise des Sciences Naturelles*, 44: 223–70.

Johnson, J.T., Cain, L.M., Falke, T.L., Hayman, J. and Perillo, E. (1985) 'The "Barnum Effect" revisited: Cognitive and motivational factors in the acceptance of personality descriptions', *Journal of Personality and Social Psychology*, 49 (5): 1378–391.

Keppel, R.D. (1989) *Serial Murder: Future implications for police investigations.* Cincinnati: Anderson Publishing Co.

Keppel, R.D. and Weis, J.G. (1993) *Improving the Investigation of Violent Crime: The homicide investigation and tracking system.* Washington, DC: US Department of Justice.

Keppel, R.D. and Weis, J.G. (1994) 'Time and distance as solvability factors in murder cases', *Journal of Forensic Sciences*, 39 (2): 386–401.

Kocsis, R.N., Irwin, H.J., Hayes, A.F. and Nunn, R. (2000) 'Expertise in psychological profiling: A comparative assessment', *Journal of Interpersonal Violence*, 15 (3): 311–31.

Langevin, R., Paitich, D. and Russon, A.E. (1985) 'Are rapists sexually anomalous, aggressive, or both?', in R. Langevin (ed.), *Erotic Preference, Gender Identity and Aggression in Men: New research studies* (pp. 17–38). Hillsdale, NJ: Lawrence Erlbaum Associates.

Loftus, E.F. (1979) *Eyewitness Testimony.* Cambridge, MA: Harvard University Press.

Marshall, B. and Alison, L. (under review) A Structural Analysis of Genuine vs. Simulated Sexual Assault Statements.

Meehl, P.E. (1956) 'Wanted – A good cookbook', *American Psychologist*, 11: 262–72.

Mischel, W. (1968) *Personality and Assessment.* New York: John Wiley and Sons.

Mischel, W. (1999) *Introduction to Personality* (6th edn). Fort Worth, TX: Harcourt Brace College Publishers.

Mokros, A. and Alison, L. (2002) 'Is profiling possible? Testing the predicted homology of crime scene actions and background characteristics in a sample of rapists', *Legal and Criminological Psychology*, 7: 25–43.

Ormerod, D. (1999) 'Criminal profiling: Trial by judge and jury, not criminal psychologist', in D.V. Canter and L.J. Alison (eds), *Profiling in Policy and Practice. Offender profiling series volume II* (pp. 207–261). Aldershot: Ashgate.

Pinizzotto, A.J. and Finkel, N.J. (1990) 'Criminal personality profiling: An outcome and process study', *Law and Human Behavior*, 14: 215–33.

Porter and Alison (in press) 'Behavioural coherence in violent group activity: An interpersonal model of sexually violent gang behaviour', *Aggressive Behavior*.

Proulx, J., Aubut, J., Perron, L. and McKibben, A. (1994) 'Troubles de la personnalité et viol: Implications théoriques et cliniques' ('Personality disorders and violence: Theoretical and clinical implications'), *Criminologie*, 27: 33–53.

Proulx, J., St-Yves, M., Guay, J.P. and Ouimet, M. (1999) 'Les aggresseurs sexuels de femmes: Scénarios délictuels et troubles de la personnalité' ('Sexual aggressors of women: Offence scenarios and personality disorders'), in J. Proulx, M. Cusson and M. Ouimet (eds), *Les Violences Criminelles* (pp. 157–185). Quebec: Les Presses de l'Université Laval.

Ressler, R.K., Burgess, A.W., D'Agostino, R.B. and Douglas, J.E. (1984) *Serial Murder: A new phenomenon of homicide*. Paper presented at the annual meeting of the International Association of Forensic Science, Oxford, England.

Ressler, R.K., Burgess, A.W., Douglas, J.E., Hartman, C.R. and D'Agostino, R.B. (1986) 'Sexual killers and their victims: Identifying patterns through crime scene analysis', *Journal of Interpersonal Violence*, 1 (3): 288–308.

Sears, D.J. (1991) *To Kill Again: The motivation and development of serial murder.* Wilmington, DE: Scholarly Resources.

Shye, S. (1985) 'Nonmetric multivariate models for behaviour action systems', in D. Canter (ed.), *Facet Theory: Approaches to social research*. New York: Springer-Verlag.

Toulmin, S. (1958) *The Uses of Argument*. Cambridge: Cambridge University Press.

Wilson, M., Jack, K. and Butterworth, D. (1997) *The Psychology of Rape Investigations: A study in police decision making* (Unpublished internal document). Liverpool, UK: University of Liverpool, Department of Psychology.

Witkin, G. (1996) 'How the FBI paints portraits of the nation's most wanted', *U.S. News and World Report*, 32.

Chapter 2

Jack the Ripper and the Whitechapel murders: a very Victorian critical incident

Jonathan Ogan and Laurence Alison

The Whitechapel murders

The Whitechapel murders were a series of homicides that occurred in a relatively small section of London's East End. The victims were all commercial sex workers living in the back streets of Whitechapel (more specifically, Spitalfields). One victim fell in the jurisdiction of the City of London Police, and a small group of police officers were charged with the task of policing London's 'square mile'. Thus, a different investigative team were tasked with working on this case. Consequently, the Eddowes murder was investigated separately from the murders of Nichols, Chapman, Stride and Kelly. Despite great efforts from both police forces, the offender remained unidentified. Indeed, the name 'Jack the Ripper' still excites a strong interest in the crimes over 100 years later. Walk into any high-street bookshop and the 'True crime' section will have a number of books on the subject, most of which offer an array of interesting suspects. These include: a depressed barrister, an insane hairdresser, an impressionist painter, a cotton broker, a 'quack', Queen Victoria's physician, a Russian secret agent and a Royal-Masonic conspiracy. This chapter avoids the 'name game' of providing yet another candidate as to the identity of Jack the Ripper, regardless of any particular merits that the candidate may have. Instead, it takes a different tack, focusing on the work of the police, set within the context of the complexity of managing critical incidents, including the pressures faced when investigating these types of high-profile crimes. The 'Ripper' case is, in many ways, particularly illustrative of key issues in critical incidents, combining as it does the involvement and scrutiny of the press, the complexity of multiple murders, contradictory and competing information, concerns around the worries of the local community and the information overload involved in the case. Thus, the chapter sets out the sequence of events from the senior investigators' perspective, highlighting those issues that recur as themes throughout the rest of the book and that illustrate how concerns in detective work have remained relatively stable over the last 100 years.

Grievous injuries

The first recognized crime in the Whitechapel murders occurred on 31 August 1888. A car man going to his work found the body of a woman lying where she had been killed, on Buck's Row in Spitalfields. She was found at 3.40 am by George Cross, who then called over another passing workman, Robert Paul. Cross thought she had been sexually assaulted, since the woman's clothing was disarranged. He pulled her dress back down in order to cover up the lower half of her body. They both decided that they would leave the woman where she lay and find help. Afterwards, they left Buck's Row to summon the police. A PC on his beat, John Neil, independently came across the woman, but with the aid of a regulation 'bull's eye' lantern he saw that she was dead. Her throat was severely cut and some blood lay at the site of the injury. His whistle soon attracted the attention of his police colleagues from the surrounding 'beats'.

The police surgeon, Dr Ralph R. Llewellyn, made a perfunctory examination *in situ*, pronouncing 'life extinct' and death due to the incised neck wound. He estimated her time of death as being at around thirty minutes since he made his examination of the victim a short time after 4.00 am. It was only when the victim was stripped and about to be washed at the mortuary that the full extent of her injuries was revealed. The clothing had been disarranged due the offender stabbing and cutting her lower abdomen and genital area. It appeared that the stays in her corset had prevented an even more severe set of injuries.

Her identity was soon established due to the workhouse stamp on her undergarments. She was Mary Ann Nichols, locally known as Polly. She was a sex worker and occasional habitué of London workhouses. There appeared to be no tangible suspect. The police report estimated her age to be 45 years. The murder made the London and regional press due to the ferocity of the injuries inflicted by the killer. This murder was different from the alcohol-fuelled dispute between intimates, or a quarrel over the fee for sexual transaction. However, this was not the only brutal murder in the Whitechapel area that month. Earlier in August, another sex worker, Martha Turner or Tabram, was found murdered. She was found with multiple neck, chest and abdominal stab wounds on the morning of 7 August 1888, after the previous bank holiday night. Her female companion of that night's carousing was one 'Pearly Poll' Connolly. She had been with Tabram, but had separated when they both went off with soldiers to complete a sexual transaction. They parted company near Angel Alley, close to where the body was found in George Yard Buildings, George Yard, Whitechapel. Despite attempts to identify the soldiers, the police were unable to do so.

The man who found her, John Reeves, brought a local PC to the crime scene, a first-floor stairway into a block of apartments. She was found lying on her back, in a pool of blood, with her clothing disarranged. In all there were 39 stab wounds about her body. The examining physician estimated her age as being about 36–37 years. It was assumed that the murder occurred sometime between 2.00 am and 3.30 am. The press coverage of the crime became a crucial factor in the case. The murders and later crimes were both nationally and internationally reported. Both murders, due to the grievous injuries, made the pages of *The Times*, a newspaper not normally involved with detailed reporting of such sensational crimes or events. Moreover, *The Times* continued coverage of the subsequent inquests. The early involvement of the press in such enquiries has, historically, played a major part in the evolution of murder enquiries and has left an enduring legacy on many cases since the Ripper enquiry. Indeed, this component appears to be one of the defining features of 'criticality'.

Criticality = Impact + Difficulty

Crego and Alison (2004) identified media coverage, as well as a variety of other issues connected with 'external' perceptions of the enquiry, as highly influential factors on the success or otherwise of a 'critical incident'. They developed a generic model of critical incident management based on the joint combination of incident managers' perceptions of *impact* and *difficulty*. Officers engaged in an electronic focus group in which they generated free narrative accounts of the issues they felt were pertinent features of the enquiry that they had to manage. Several of these sessions have since been run on different types of enquiries (siege incidents, child abductions, serial rapes) with similar outputs on each occasion (see Crego and Alison, 2004). In each session, information from the participants is distributed simultaneously to all delegates on an LCD display and is non-source attributable (i.e. no one knew which delegate had made which comment). This process of facilitative free-recall enquiry has proved effective in generating candid views of difficult-to-manage incidents and has been used on several occasions subsequently as a debriefing tool. Once delegates have generated the initial material, they break out into a plenary session and begin to synthesize the large corpus of qualitative material into elements (summary statements that capture the key components of the rich detailed material). In the first session by Crego and Alison, delegates generated 15 elements. The generic model is then formed from two criteria, on which delegates rate the elements: impact (the degree to which the theme impacts on the successful outcome of the critical incident) and ease (how difficult each element is to get right). The basic model results in four possible combinations, as illustrated in Table 2.1. Crego and Alison argued that the elements within each quadrant represented different levels of management skills, ranging from the more narrow aspect of managing the incident itself, through to the increasingly broader issues of managing the team, the cultural context of policing and managing the public.

The table illustrates how critical-incident managers must deal with a very wide range of issues. These include features directly connected with the enquiry (managing the complexity of the enquiry, keeping accurate records), issues associated with the effective management of the team (assigning roles and responsibilities, team skills, team atmosphere), managing the culture of the police environment (race and diversity, culture, Association of Chief Police Officers), managing political issues and managing the public and public response (local community, race and

Table 2.1 Schematic representing elements and synthesized themes and facets (impact and ease) with proposed relevant psychological/sociological components.

	High-impact	Hyper-impact
Difficult	External advice, team atmosphere, roles and responsibilities	Record-keeping, character of SIO (managing the incident)
	Post-incident management, ACPO (managing the team)	
Extremely difficult	Managing a team, racism and diversity, politics, culture (managing the culture)	Family liaison, media, managing complexity, community (managing the public)

diversity, family liaison). Thus, the effective management of a critical incident is likely to require significant cognitive and interpersonal skills that must be employed across a wide range of circumstances and people, and which must constantly be reviewed in terms of standing back and observing the 'big picture'. The joint functions of, on the one hand, having to bear responsibility for success or failure while, on the other, being unable to influence a whole range of individuals that are likely to have a very significant impact on the enquiry must place very considerable stress on the individual.

The Ripper murders provide an early, Victorian, example of a critical incident. The case required senior officers making difficult decisions in complex, uncertain and dynamic environments, in which the police, as well as having to manage the incident itself, found themselves involved in local community issues, managing the media and involvement with local government. Moreover, officers had to work in teams that crossed constabulary boundaries, adhere to strict legal and organizational priorities and policies and carefully manage the impact of the offences on other aspects of policing. Although in the modern era in UK policing, with the legislative requirement of the Local Government Act of 1999, the Best Value regime central to police management and governance at the beginning of the 21st century (Dobson, 2000) has led to the generation of a culture of naming, shaming and blaming, such 'finger pointing' was also popular over 100 years ago. Doubtless, Investigating Inspector Frederick George Abberline and his colleagues (at the 'coal face') and Warren (as Commissioner of the Metropolitan Police) would have felt the over-whelming burden of media, public and governmental scrutiny. The Ripper investigation was carried out under intense public and media evaluation, with the impetus for the examination as perceived failure on the investigative team or, more drastically, on the organizational shortcomings of a particular individual. Criticism can be levelled at any 'layer' of managerial shortcoming, namely errors in managing the incident, the team, the culture and/or the public.

Managing the incident: placing the blame and individual responsibility

Two elements were rated as hyper-impact and not easy – characteristics of the SIO and record-keeping. Relatively speaking, most participants considered these elements as easier to deal with than managing the external perceptions of external forces ('managing the public'). This may be a function of the perceived greater control elements directly associated with the incident, since they concern individual responsibilities rather than the perceptions and actions of others external to the enquiry team. For example, in these enquiries and in the Ripper case, record-keeping is the direct responsibility of the officer in charge and is, therefore, relatively uninfluenced by anyone other than the immediate enquiry team. Nevertheless, these features do relate to the direct and immediate concerns of the incident itself and, consequently, have a significant impact on the enquiry. In the Ripper enquiry, as with all subsequent incidents of this nature, the enquiry team would have felt overwhelmed by the volume of information. Thus, delegates in our focus group, and doubtless Abberline in the Ripper enquiry, will have recognized that the responsibility ultimately lay with him as the critical incident manager. This was captured in our focus group comments in, 'If decisions are characterized as right or wrong (absolutes), then blame will soon be apportioned when new info emerges'. In defending these decisions, delegates realized the importance of comprehensive and accurate note taking, 'SIOs (and others where appropriate) MUST appoint a dedicated loggist to be at their side – in a very busy schedule many decisions and the rationale are not being captured,' and, 'Keep policy/decision logs of all your considerations – you cannot write too much!' This theme appears to relate to the idea that internal features of the enquiry and the day to day running of the service are absolutely crucial – in particular, having the right person for the job and ensuring that what is found is captured and logged effectively. For example, 'We must have officers trained to identify critical incidents and to respond appropriately.'

Inspector Abberline's involvement with the Ripper murders perhaps featured most prominently in relation to the last of the canonical five victims, Mary Kelly, though he had been called in to assist with the enquiry after the earlier murders of Nichols and Chapman because of his extensive knowledge of the East End's criminals. Newspaper coverage celebrating his retirement outlined Abberline's 'cv' as an active detective working in Whitechapel and the Metropolitan Police force in general. During his career, he investigated a wide variety of crimes, ranging from pick-pocketing, burglary, forgery, terrorism and, of course, murder (both adult and child victims). This eclectic casebook, while providing a solid grounding in general criminal investigation, did not relate to any particular form of specialism. In total, Abberline worked for 30 years as a police officer in both West and East London. He started his career as a PC in Islington in 1862 and three years later, he was promoted to the rank of police sergeant. He also worked 'plain clothes' and was involved in a number of investigations, from the mundane investigation of breaking up a pick-pocketing ring to the positively dramatic political sphere of Fenian extremists. His first homicide investigation involved the arrest of a fugitive in London, later found guilty for the murder of a Manchester police sergeant called John Brett. Shortly afterwards, Abberline became an acting Inspector for Kentish Town and later became a permanent Divisional Sergeant for that district. He went to Whitechapel as a uniformed Inspector and remained there until 1887, a year before the Jack the Ripper killings. He then left H Division to join New Scotland Yard as a Senior Chief Inspector. His retirement celebration in 1892 saw a troop of detectives paying him their respects at the Three Nuns Hotel. Frederick Abberline had retired from Scotland Yard service in the previous year. The celebrations in the Three Nuns were for his former colleagues from H Division to say their farewells. The evening culminated in a silver coffee service being presented to him – testimony to his 30 years' service in the metropolis' police as 'Bobby' and detective CID, and for the esteem in which he was held.

Despite the depiction of Abberline (at least in the fictional portrayals) as being the lead detective in charge of the Ripper murders, an analysis of the extant police and Home Office files demonstrates that a number of officers were involved in the investigation. Inspectors Spratling and Keating jointly handled the Nichols crime, while Inspector Chandler investigated the Chapman murder. Later, in the series of murders (the so-called 'double event'), Inspector Edmund Reid investigated the Berner Street murder. Reid also worked on a number of other murders in Whitechapel, attributed rightly or wrongly to Jack the Ripper (such as Tabram and McKenzie, among others). The Mitre Square murder, outside of the Metropolitan Police jurisdiction, meant that City of London Police became involved in the hunt for Jack the Ripper. However, it was always Abberline's name that appeared in press accounts and police files during the investigation of the Nichols and Chapman murders and the resulting suspects. He also played a prominent role in the Kelly enquiry. It remains the case that it is Inspector Abberline who is now most associated with the crimes (highlighting again the prominent media strategy of apportioning responsibility on a key individual).

What sort of men were Reid and Abberline? A man perhaps best placed to comment on both detectives was their junior colleague Walter Dew. He claimed later fame by arresting Crippen in 1910. As a junior detective in Whitechapel, he knew both men. He commented on Abberline as being:

Portly and gentle speaking. The type of police officer who might easily have been mistaken for the manager of a bank or a solicitor. He was also a man who had proved himself in many previous big cases. His strong suit was his knowledge of crime and criminals in the East End, for he had been for many years the detective-inspector of the Whitechapel Division, or as it was called then the 'Local Inspector'.

No question at all of Inspector Abberline's abilities as a criminal hunter.

Again this comment reinforces the contemporary police thinking that the offender would be most likely found among the typical East End criminal classes. Abberline himself drew pleasure from the high number of commendations he had received during his career as police constable and detective. Begg *et al.* (1994) cited the number as 84, which is clear testimony to his effectiveness and professionalism as a 'thief catcher'.

One interesting point of note is that Abberline, unlike his contemporaries, did not publish his memoirs. Although later he did write up some of the investigations that he had been involved with, the Ripper case did not feature. It is perhaps this discretion that led his superiors to task him with the investigation of the Cleveland Street affair. In essence, this was the raiding of a male brothel in that street. One of its patrons was the heir presumptive, Prince Albert Victor, son of Edward VII. Rather ironically, the Prince was named as a Ripper suspect in the 1970s. However, the theory can easily be refuted by an examination of the court circulars over the murder dates. On a number of occasions the Prince had well documented alibis.

Abberline's peer, Edmund Reid, appeared to be something of a character. Dew remarked: 'At 5 feet 6 inches Reid was the shortest officer in the Metropolitan Police. After a myriad of careers including hotel waiter, ship's steward and pastry cook Reid had joined the police in 1872.' In fact before he became a policeman he was an early parachutist. To add to this colourful past, Connell and Evans (2000) wrote that Reid had become the template for the fictional detective, Dier, created by his friend Charles Gibbon. But his 'boy's own' life was not without its price, as his first wife died in a lunatic asylum.[1]

Reid's involvement in the Tabram and McKenzie murders suggests that he was well placed to give an informed opinion on the case, and what the police knew. However, both Reid and Abberline were adamant that there was never a definite identification of the offender. Sadly, a number of contemporary police files are 'missing', presumed destroyed. This leaves the scant surviving police files and newspaper interviews with the investigating officers as the only source of information to identify their investigative actions and reasoning processes around the development of the case. The press interviewed both Reid and Abberline during their retirement, enabling us to gain an insight into their investigative strategies and conclusions about the series of murders. Reid provided his opinion as to the likely offender responsible for the Jack the Ripper killings to the *Sun* (31 May 1901). This interview was set in the context of another vicious stabbing of a commercial sex worker earlier that month, in Dorset Street, a street that would later feature in the last of the canonical five Whitechapel murders. The *Sun* sought to pool the experience of two ex-detectives to summarize their opinions. In today's slant on forensic expert opinions, fuelled by films like 'Silence of the Lambs', this might now have been labelled an 'offender profile'. However, it is merely a subjective, though no doubt honestly given, account of their opinions on the Whitechapel murders. As such it lacks the objective, statistically derived models of offenders' actions and characteristics that comprise the scientific approach to 'profiling' or, as it is now termed, 'behavioural investigative advice'. Nevertheless, Reid's interview presents the reader with a set of potential characteristics in so far as it gives an indication of the thinking behind the case at the time. Reid concluded that the offender: 'Was a man with no skilled knowledge – not even the skill of a novice in butchery. In every instance the mutilation was clumsy in the extreme – was the hacking and tearing of a man in a frenzy, increasing as his work proceeded.' Reid denied that any organs were missing. Reid also debunked the left-handedness theory. Reid deduced, 'In the throat cutting the fiend has shown cunning. The position of the body showed that he stood face to face with the woman and had slashed her throat, with his right hand from right to left, causing blood to spurt away from him.' He concluded that the perpetrator was mentally ill, showing the 'Maniac's cunning, outwitting reason's methods'. Yet, Reid's memory did prove faulty, as he further argued the lack of missing body parts during an interview for the *Morning Advertiser* (30 March 1903). This conflicted with known evidence, both in the public domain via inquest reports and the closed police files. This shows how faulty memory can be over a period of time. It should also read as a cautionary tale for modern 'Ripperologists' who might rely too heavily on extempore comments given by the police when reviewing their role in what proved to be the most infamous of all unsolved murders. Reid's views also hint at the direction that the police enquiry may have taken. It is clear that both he and Frederick Abberline had generated particular narrative accounts of the type of offender that they were dealing with and it is possible that these perspectives shaped early lines of enquiry. Certainly, preliminary evidence from small-scale studies of the relationship between starting-point hypotheses and recommended lines of enquiry suggest that the investigating officer's view does steer the course of the enquiry (Barrett and Alison, in press), further illustrating the importance of the skills and knowledge of the Senior Investigating Officer (SIO). Now, as then, senior officers would benefit from an understanding of the host of psychological/behavioural aspects of offending relevant to assisting them with decision-making. These include, as we have already hinted at, developing an appreciation of the 'type(s)' of offender that they may be dealing with, the extent to which an offence is likely to be repeated and the issue of whether a series of offences has been committed by a single offender. Certainly, in the Ripper case, Reid and Abberline (among others) would have had to closely consider which murders were connected and could be attributed to the same offender.

In total, the Home Office case papers on the murders identified 11 homicides as the Whitechapel murders.[2] This list comprized, Emma Smith, Martha Tabram, Mary Ann Nichols, Annie Chapman, Elizabeth Stride, Catherine Eddowes, Mary Kelly, Rose Mylett, unidentified victim in Pinchin Street, Alice McKenzie and Frances Coles. Thus, Abberline and Reid would have had to consider series linkage. The murders were dubbed the 'Whitechapel murders' simply by virtue of the time frame in which they occurred and because of the relatively small geographical area within which they were committed. The list was not based on any behavioural criteria (such as *modus operandi*). Indeed, geographical and temporal facets have now been recognized as the most reliable and robust methods for linking offences and based on these more recent observations (Goodwill and Alison, in press; see also Chapter 4 of this volume) there would be reasonable grounds to consider all the cases as potentially committed by the same offender. The actual number of victims remains contentious, and, indeed, the controversy among today's 'Ripperologists' was rife in the Victorian era. For example, some investigators, notably Frederick Abberline, concluded that Tabram's murder was committed by the Ripper. It was left to Sir Melville Macnaghten to place some operational definition on what constituted a 'Ripper' murder. Macnaughten set Tabram's murder apart from the other Ripper victims due the lack of throat-cutting and lack of the abdominal/genital mutilations. However, this two-item behavioural set of indicators is less robust than Abberline's conclusions (at least in terms of contemporary research). Indeed, these two factors (or lack thereof) neglect an appreciation of the interrelated factors of victim availability, time constraints, location of the crime, and the risk the offender felt in being disturbed (Alison *et al.*, 2000).

Moreover, Macnaghten did not base his conclusions on any personal involvement with the investigation, since he took up post at Scotland Yard sometime after the murders. Nevertheless, his comments formed a central plank in a document now known by so-called Ripperologists as the 'Macnaghten memorandum'. In this document, three possible suspects are named: 'Kosminski', Montague Druitt and Michael Ostrog. He summed up their prospects as, 'I may mention the cases of 3 men, any one of whom would have been more likely than Cutbush to have committed this series of murders.' Clearly, their brief biographies were cited only to illustrate that any of these men were more likely than another suspect named in the press in 1894, one Thomas Cutbush. It is a point well worth remembering since contemporary Ripperologists often cite one of these three men as the police suspect, ignoring the simple fact that these 'suspects' were named to show the lack of proof positive against any chief suspect and to note the distinctly low probability of Cutbush as Jack the Ripper. The case against Cutbush was very unsatisfactory. He came to the public attention courtesy of the *Sun* newspaper (14 February 1894), which featured him as the culprit in a series of stabbings. In these offences the mutilations were mercifully slight. The *Sun* asserted that Cutbush had stabbed a number of women in their buttocks. This offence was enough to convince the paper that they had got their man and that the identity of Jack The Ripper was finally determined. However, Macnaghten's memorandum revealed how the *Sun* was totally in error. Cutbush led a very solitary life and was involved in mocking up a number of pornographic sketches. But in any case, he was no serial stabber: the *Sun* had confused Cutbush with the true culprit Colicitt.

One major feature in any high-profile murder case is information, or more accurately, the deluge of data that floods the investigating team. A critical issue involves efficient and accurate processing of the information. Abberline himself lamented this state of affairs, noting that, 'Theories ... we were lost almost in theories, there were so many of them.'[3] Clearly, there was no shortage of data coming into the enquiry and, in fact, volumes of information overwhelmed the police, much of which proved inaccurate, irrelevant or positively misleading. This was further illustrated by the street intelligence collated by Inspector Reid. He was able to gain the trust of the local commercial sex workers. The (Portsmouth) *Evening News* (2 0ctober 1888) commented that these women had approached Reid with information on the likely culprit. But this information was far from clear cut. One described him as tall; one as shortish but thick set. Yet another described the suspect as well dressed, while another as shabby. It was not surprising that the newspaper referred to the description as practically useless. But they do show that the women were prepared to approach the police, Reid particularly, and offer what help they could; whereas normally, the police would be their enemy on the streets, now they joined forces to combat a common, if unknown, enemy.

This nebulous corpus of data presents one of the major factors in establishing a need for research in police decision-making, notably what data to use and which to prioritize. Further, in homicide enquiries, information gradually filters into the enquiry and it is unlikely to all be relevant to the case. The role of the senior investigating officers (SIOs) and their colleagues is to determine which piece is significant and which information is worthless. What appeared to be crucial for delegates in Crego and Alison's study was accurate recording of information, prioritizing of said information and 'hot debriefs' in order to keep all relevant parties involved: 'It would be useful to cascade to all DSs the concept of a structured "hot debrief". At all scenes/incidents Detectives should then co-ordinate such a debrief of all staff at the scene PRIOR to them going off duty.' Further, many comments were directed at enhancing professional standards and developing leadership skills among the new cadre of officers in training. This appears to be a significant 'needs' gap, both in terms of identifying what constitutes leadership as well as how the service should train and select leaders:

> Leadership – we have spoken a lot about leadership but with little explicit acknowledgement of what it actually is and how to bring it about. How do we encourage our current leaders to develop our leadership and how do we develop our future leaders? I think it is more than just training and it also involves mentoring, rewards, and personal development.

A major problem in investigating the Whitechapel murders was the lack of previous experience among the detectives in this type of murder. Contrary to Hollywood depiction of the serial killer phenomenon, it remains a rare crime and in Victorian England, one may argue, it was even rarer. However, Abberline's 'casebook' did include 'unusual' murders. One case featured the death of a young child, Elizabeth Lazarus, who disappeared for a couple of days. Apparently, she had been drowned, but she was found lying on a doorstep near to where her parents lived by three young men. Interestingly, one of the young men was called Joe Barnett, but whether this was the same man to be involved with the last of the canonical five victims requires further research. The Lazarus case remained unsolved, despite the arrest of an elderly night watchman. Thus, while Frederick Abberline would have gathered some investigative experience in dealing with robbery, theft and some limited knowledge of murder, the aspects of this particular set of crimes, which involved extensive mutilations, would have been alien to him. This may have led him, and others, to the assumption that the offender must be insane. This lack of experience may impact on an officer's effective decision-making capabilities. Klein (1997), for example, had noted in a study on fire officers that their decisions were formed on the basis of a mental construction of a set of scenarios retained in their memory. Klein termed this process 'recognition-primed decision-making' (RPDM) theory. This model acknowledged the difference between experienced and novice practitioners. According to RPDM there are two main areas of decision-making. Each area is distinct from the other, but in both cases the situation needs to be identified and then a suitable decision can be actioned. Firstly, a simple matching situation may be encountered. This may enable the decision-maker to act very quickly in comparing the problem at hand with a range of problems and drawing on solution models stored in long-term memory. This is achieved by contextual cues that enable a comparison to be drawn with prototypes stored in long-term memory, with the individual retrieving the optimal strategy. If this is applied to detective decision-making, we can see that the detective would construct a narrative account of the crime, with the mental simulation of the event enabling the investigator to understand how all the information to hand will fall into place. For example, Abberline's view on the case appears to have been influenced by his lay theories on murder and murderers. He hypothesized that the poisoner, George Chapman, possessed the requisite psychological traits likely to be exhibited by the killer. Abberline believed that, since Chapman could bear to watch his wives die horribly through poison, then he could quite easily kill and mutilate the five victims.

Managing the team: effective use of the group

In major incidents officers must manage large teams and, as a case gathers momentum and, in this case, claims more victims, other jurisdictions can become involved. This places considerable demands on the ability of the team to work as a cohesive unit. A week after the Nichols murder, on 8 September, another body was found, just before 6.00 am. The police would have known that the prospect of a serial murderer operating in Whitechapel was likely to exert great pressure on an already strained police force. John Davis, a tenant of number 29, Hanbury Street, was entering the house's backyard, and found the female victim lying on the ground in front of him. The woman lay on her back, face nearest the step into the yard, her body parallel to the fence separating the yard from its neighbour, number 27.

This time the victim had been visibly mutilated. Her throat was cut deeply, her dress had been pulled up to reveal abdominal mutilations and her small intestines had been pulled out of the body cavity and placed over the victim's shoulder. Part of the vagina was cut away, and the uterus had been removed and taken away by the perpetrator. The victim's belongings appeared to be laid out at her feet. The time of death was given as some two to three hours before the doctor's examination, made at 6.30 am. However, a witness came forward to say she thought that she saw the victim and a man enter a passageway leading into the yard at approximately 5.30 am. Moreover, a tenant of the house, John Richardson, said he went into the yard at 4.45 am and the body was not there at that time.

Lesser injuries on the woman's fingers indicated that her rings had been recently removed. Chief Inspector Donald Swanson's report, outlining the police investigation of both the Nichols and Chapman murders, identified one investigative strategy: 'A special inquiry to find rings was made at all pawnbrokers, jewellers, dealers'. Sadly, their enquiries yielded no results. This attempt to grasp at a tangible motive, that of robbery, reveals the problems faced in investigating these forms of crimes. This 'functional fixedness', represented by the reliance on the solid, familiar motives such as financial gain during a robbery, may have inhibited other potential lines of enquiry. Could the murders represent an expressive outburst against women, or could the victims be representing a substitute for another, particular woman in the offender's mind? As with Tabram and Nichols, the victim, now identified as Annie Chapman, was also a commercial sex worker. A friend of the victim had seen her on the night of the murder looking for the price of her bed. However, Chapman looked very weak and had recently been involved in a fight with another woman in a public house. Another witness, Mrs Long, who lived in the locality, saw a man and woman go into the passageway that led into the yard, although she could not be absolutely sure it was the murdered woman as she made her identification by her clothing. The man was described as a little taller than the victim, who was 5 ft, and looked to be over 40 years of age. He appeared to be dressed in a 'shabby genteel' fashion. As we have indicated previously (Barrett and Alison, in press), initial hypotheses do appear to have an impact on the first lines of enquiry, so it may be important for the enquiry team to ensure that they have an individual heading the enquiry who has the requisite experience and ability to formulate plausible accounts of the motives for the offence. Indeed, Abberline was drafted into the enquiry due to his in-depth knowledge of the local criminal classes. However, even in this selection of an Officer in Charge, the choice of Abberline perhaps reveals that the police remained fixed in generating suspects from a certain cross-section of Whitechapel's criminal classes.

After the Nichols murder the press coverage of the crimes became increasingly widespread and took the interest in the crimes outside London. However, press amplification of the murders would reach a new height during the next set of murders. This time two women were found murdered on the same night. The press dubbed this as a 'double event'.

On 30 September, just before 1.00 am, Louis Diemshutz' pony made its way into a yard alongside the Working Man's Club on Berner Street, St Georges in the East. The horse appeared to shy at something lying in the yard. Diemshutz saw what he presumed to be a drunken woman. One story suggests that Diemshutz thought that this was his wife, so left her lying there. It was when he found his wife sober and fully conscious, inside the club, that he became concerned. When the crowd inside heard of his find they left to investigate and found the woman lying on her back, with her throat cut. A scarf around her neck was pulled tight. The police believed that the scarf had been pulled tight to one side, so the throat could be cut. There were no other mutilations to the victim. It was calculated that the murder occurred between 12.46 and 12.56 am.

Managing the culture: infrastructure

At around 1.45 am, PC George Morris of the City of London Police found the body of the second victim that night, in Mitre Square. She lay on her back, her clothing disarranged, with her throat deeply cut. In this case, the intestines had been placed around the body and a kidney had been removed and taken away by the perpetrator. One point of interest was that a piece had been cut away from her apron and was not present at the crime scene. But the activities of that night were not complete. Another PC, Alfred Long, found a piece of cloth at the foot of a doorway to the model dwellings on Goulston Street. The piece of apron corresponded to that missing from the dead woman's clothing. Above the cloth was a chalk written message, 'The Juwes [sic] are the men that will not be named for nothing'. The apartment block was inhabited mainly by Jewish folk, a sizable proportion of the inhabitants of the greater Whitechapel district. At the time, anti-Semitic feeling was a major concern to the police. The press had earlier named a possible culprit for the Nichols and Chapman homicides, Jack Pizer.[4] Pizer was a Jewish bootmaker, and was considered because of the allegation that he had threatened to 'rip women up'. Because of the misplaced initial attention on Pizer and the current climate of concern over perceptions of police anti-Semitism, the message was deemed to be so inflammatory that the Commissioner of the Metropolitan Police, Sir Charles Warren, present at the scene early in the morning, personally ordered its removal. This 'message' in the Ripper enquiry, which has always drawn the attention of Ripperologists, probably because of its tantalizing ambiguity, is perhaps more interesting because, again, it highlights how the police are influenced by concerns beyond the immediate enquiry – in this case, impact on the local community. This feature of the enquiry is a prominent concern within our focus group studies on critical incident management.

In contrast to the 'incident managment' theme, elements within the 'managing the culture and public' themes involve aspects that relate to issues beyond the immediate enquiry. While they have an impact upon immediate features, arguably, they relate more to general features of political and cultural aspects of the service. Because of the perceived lack of control, they are seen as particularly difficult to manage. This perceived difficulty appears to relate to the complexity of dealing with so many individuals from many diverse backgrounds and cultures, all of whom may have competing agendas. For example, 'A part of my experience has been that the complexity of the context here is about the fragmentation, diversity and diffusion of previously distinct tasks and roles in society. This is one of the causes of the institutional racism or incompetence that has been uncovered. Things have become blurred.' In some cases, delegates felt that this difficulty was compounded by the perception that individuals outside of the service may have a naïve understanding of what is involved in managing critical incidents: 'Lots of people think they can do the police or the detectives' job, in fact they think they actually do it. To engage in immersive learning allows them to explore their true roles and the contribution and advice that they can give ...'

Of particular concern was the delegates' need to express the view that the resources were not always adequate for particular enquiries and that judgments were being made on unjust comparisons against unreasonable criteria. For example, one delegate noted their frustration at, 'Having to continuously fight for staff or running an enquiry on a shoestring and often being blamed for the force's performance against targets'. In Long's (2003) 41 interviews with managers, he established that while many believed that the UK's Best Value (BV) reform[5] was, on the whole, necessary and progressive, especially around objective setting and performance indicators, most felt that the Audit Commission were perceived as illegitimate by middle managers. Further, they questioned the view that BV would lead to the sharing of good practice because performance indicators and the nature of comparisons inherent within the BV scheme meant that forces would be protective over best-practice issues. Further, they questioned the transference of best practice across different constabularies with diverse needs. Despite the fact that BV reviews are conducted at individual police service level, the whole emphasis on police performance is placed on delivery at local or basic command level. Most felt it was repackaging of old ideas like zero-based budgeting, total quality management or compulsory competitive tendering (Keenan, 2000). These findings, alongside Long's analysis, indicate that there is some considerable dissatisfaction, or at the very least concern, about some of the political constraints that the service has to work under. Delegates were keen that the service recognized the difficulties associated with resources and that there are considerable pressures in running such enquiries without adequate support: 'I want the force to accept that investigating the death of an individual(s) carries enormous pressure with it.'

Managing the public: the enduring legacy of external perceptions

The victims of the 'double event' were identified as Elizabeth Stride, or 'Long Liz' as she was nicknamed, aged 44 years, in Berner Street and Catherine Eddowes, occasionally using the name May Ann Kelly, as the victim in Mitre Square. Her age was estimated as being 43 years. Both women were commercial sex workers, and as with the other victims, there appeared to be no obvious suspects. As Eddowes was killed within the City of London, a different police force became involved in the investigation. Earlier that evening, a City police constable arrested Eddowes for being drunk and disorderly and, as she sobered up, she was released. A group of men had seen a woman they identified as Eddowes by her clothing, enter Mitre Square with a man who was described as being around 30, with a peaked cap and scarf around his neck, though they only glanced at the couple, so no firm description could be made. The post-mortem on the victim, conducted by Dr Gordon Brown, concluded that the offender was used to handling a knife but did not consider that this necessarily implied surgical skill, so we should not dwell too long on the image of a top-hatted doctor, carrying a Gladstone bag full of surgical instruments. Brown went on to to suggest that the offender's skill could have been that possessed by a slaughterman, butcher or the like. Her murder would have occurred sometime between the time she was seen entering Mitre Square with the unidentified man at 1.30 am and the time of the discovery of the body at around 1.45 am. A number of people came forward to say that they had seen Long Liz in the company of a man aged around 30. One witness, PC 252 H Smith, estimated the age as being 28 years. Before the 'double event' the Central News Agency received a letter on 27 September 1888. It was purportedly written by the offender and read:

25 Sept. 1888

Dear Boss
I keep on hearing the police have caught me but they wont fix me just yet. I have laughed when they look so clever and talk about being on the right track. That joke about Leather Apron gave me real fits. I am down on whores and I shant quit ripping them till I do get buckled. Grand work the last job was, I gave the lady no time to squeal. How can they catch me now, I love my work and want to start again. You will soon hear of me with my funny little games. I saved some of the proper red stuff in a ginger beer bottle over the last job to write with but it went thick like glue and I cant use it. Red ink is fit enough I hope ha. Ha. The next job I do I shall clip the ladys ears off and send to the police officers just for jolly wouldn't you. Keep this letter back

till I do a bit more work then give it out straight. My knife's so nice and sharp I want to get to work right away if I get a chance, good luck.

Yours truly
Jack the Ripper

Don't mind me giving the trade name.
Wasnt good enough to post this before I got all the red ink off my hands curse it. No luck yet. They say I'm a doctor now ha ha.

After the Stride and Eddowes homicides, the police decided to publish the letter in the hope that the handwriting could be identified. It appeared in a facsimile format in several newspapers. Following on from the 'Dear Boss' letter, George Lusk, a local man who aided in forming the Whitechapel Vigilance Committee, received a package containing a piece of what the medical school at the London Hospital later identified as a human kidney, with the following note.

From hell
Mr Lusk
     Sir
         I send you half the
Kidne I took from one woman
prasarved it for you. Tother piece I
fried and ate it was very nise. I
may send you the bloody knif that
took it out if you only wate a whil
longer
       signed Catch me when
          you can
      Mishter Lusk

However, later press coverage suggested that the package and accompanying letter were a hoax. Many years after the murders, one junior police investigator at the time, Walter Dew, remarked in his memoirs, that the letter signed 'Jack the Ripper' was not long assumed to have been written by the offender. Whether or not Dew was right in his conclusion, both the letters only added to the furore surrounding the murders. Indeed, the first letter gave the offender a name synonymous with all murderers of commercial sex workers. Other letters soon followed and an extensive file was built up and still remains, containing the letters received at the time of the murders claiming to be from Jack the Ripper.

The letters added further confusion to an already increasingly complex enquiry and, with little effort, one can readily see the overlap between this event and other, modern enquiries in which hoax letters, phone calls and tapes have further frustrated enquiries, strained resources, further encouraged extensive media involvement and piqued the interest of the public.

A delay occurred between the 'double event' and the next murder in the series. On the morning of 9 November, 1888, a rent collector was collecting rents for his employer's tenants. He reached room 13 Miller's Court and knocked at the door, but received no answer. He went to a window where there was a broken pane stuffed with clothing, pulled it back and looked inside, hoping to catch the tenant and get back some of the arrears owed. Instead he saw the body of a woman, grossly mutilated, lying on the bed.

Joseph Barnett, the victim's common-law husband, identified her as Mary Jane Kelly, although the victim preferred the romanticized Gallic version of Marie Jeanette. Kelly was younger than the previous victims, aged about 25. The state of the body was horrific: her face, torso and thighs had been skinned. Some of her internal organs lay around the body and her uterus had been placed under her head.

The time of death given is contentious. Officially, death occurred between 2.00 am and 4.00 am of that morning, although a neighbour, Caroline Maxwell, was convinced that she had seen Kelly alive much later that morning and had even spoken to her at 8.30 am. Half an hour later, she saw her with a man aged about 30, dressed as a market porter, around 5 ft 5 inches tall. Thus, the actual time of this murder was a moot point.

One possible witness of the murderer, George Hutchinson, saw Kelly enter Miller's Court with a man at 2.30 am. Hutchinson described him as around 35, dressed quite smartly with a gold watch chain across his waistcoat. He wore a long coat trimmed with fur and a wide-awake hat. He also carried a small parcel in his hand. Barnett, Kelly's common-law husband, was eliminated after close questioning by Inspector Abberline. In this case, as with the other victims, there were no likely suspects apparent to the police. Despite the ink spilt on writing up these murders, and presenting new and increasingly unlikely suspects, the investigating officers were candid in their summation that they had no idea who had killed these women.

Significantly, the Kelly murder also claimed a political victim. The ever-increasing public interest and the detrimental press coverage over the lack of any tangible results and the culmination of Kelly's murder, had led to Sir Charles Warren's resignation. His resignation demonstrates the impact that the crimes had on the public confidence in the police. In our focus group studies, delegates' consistent view was that elements relating to external parties' views of the case appeared to be both the most difficult to deal with and had the most significant impact on the enquiry. This perceived significance may be a joint product of (i) perceived lack of control over the views of individuals not immediately connected as part of the enquiry team, alongside the fact that (ii) these same individuals are directly relevant to the enquiry and can leave an enduring legacy on the senior officer, the team and the force. Delegates recognized that careful and sensitive attention to these individuals was the key to successful critical incident management and that poor performance in this regard would inevitably result in criticism and pointing the finger of blame later. Thus, while the immediate aim of the enquiry may be to solve the offence, the way in which this process was executed and the sensitivity with which the police dealt with relevant individuals was seen as central. Delegates also appreciated that poor performance at this stage was likely to leave an enduring legacy, particularly in crimes of this nature. For example: 'The Force may be criticized for missing a target for vehicle crime or burglary, but this will pale into insignificance when compared to the loss of public confidence that will occur if we make a mistake on a high profile murder investigation.'

In particular, the press coverage of Ripper murders held the country in a mixture of curiosity and panic and would have significantly pressurized the police for a result. The *Star* (10 September 1888) helped to ferment unrest by their by-line: 'Whitechapel is panic-stricken'. They continued:

> London lies under the spell of great terror. A nameless reprobate – half beast, half man – is at large, who is daily gratifying his murderous instincts on the most miserable and defenceless classes of the community. Hideous malice, daily cunning, insatiable thirst for blood – all these are the marks of the mad homicide. The ghoul-like creature who stalks through the streets of London, stalking down his victims like a Pawnee Indian, is simply drunk with blood and he will have more.

Melodramatic though this quote is, our contemporary press is frequently eager to catalyse extant public feelings of horror by providing the most salacious of details. This curiosity fermented by the press in the Ripper case led to a number of people advancing ideas on how to catch the offender from the more prosaic searching of the city's sewer to the more bizarre suggestion (à la 'Murders in the Rue Morgue') to look for an escaped ape. The panic resulted in any strange-looking individuals being arrested, whether in London, Portsmouth, Liverpool or anywhere else where they appeared to be acting strangely. So significant were the murders that regular updates were also reported on the continent and America. Similar wide-scale searching in major investigations occurs in the modern era, despite the fact that the overwhelming number of offenders who commit rapes and murders are local men. However, the media can encourage large numbers of individuals to come forward with possible lines of enquiry, potentially overwhelming police resources. In Crego and Alison's (2004) focus group interviews with critical incident managers, one of the central key themes (alongside family liaison, managing complexity and managing the local community) was handling the media and its potential impact on an enquiry. Incident managers defined this as follows: 'Anticipate the worst (including leaks), recognize the media as a resource, be aware of its potentially overwhelming impact. Be honest and direct and if there is a need to apologize for errors ensure that you are the person that acts on this first (not the media).'

One delegate in the Crego and Alison study stated, 'An unresolved critical incident affects the community and its relationships with statutory agencies for years'. In the Ripper case, the legacy of these murders and the fact that the case was never resolved have left a very significant mark. Long (2003) has argued that the performance culture in contemporary UK policing represents 'the culmination of a censorious political culture where blame predominates' (p. 33) and has resulted in the threat of hit-teams to replace inefficient public-sector management as well as the very public 'naming and shaming' that takes place when the media report on league tables. It appears that the delegates in our focus group study are well aware of the 'blamestorming' culture and viewed these elements as the most significant and most difficult to control. In particular, reference was made to improving the relationship with, and training in how to deal with, the media:

> It is critical that SIOs, ACPO and investigation teams recognize the impact and importance of media input in a major investigation at the earliest possible stage. As with an investigation, media strategy will change in line with circumstances, and should also be reviewed, health-checked, and challenged in order to ensure that it is robust. Intensive media training should form part of SIO/investigators' training packages.

Summary

The case illustrates how far removed fictional portrayals are from the facts, with multi-jurisdictional responsibility and a whole team of investigators involved. However, then, as now, the media's thirst to attribute direct responsibility to one or two key individuals does reflect the power of the press. Despite the recurring nature of critical cases, in which one or two key individuals ultimately must take responsibility, there is very little consideration of how such cases emerge, the multivariate nature of police investigation and the impact that such enquiries have on the officers in charge. Indeed, as far as we are aware, despite the plethora of books on the Ripper case, the majority of which are devoted to singling out the author's preferred suspect, very little attention is devoted to the officers investigating the case.

In the Jack the Ripper killings, it can be seen that the police would have very little previous experience in dealing with the media spotlight. In those days their only concern was the newsprint. Even so, the hostile press aided in the removal of the Commissioner of the Metropolitan Police. One can only imagine the situation now, with 'twenty four-seven' news coverage on the radio, printed and television media, how these diligent detectives would have faced even more scrutiny and criticism. Such hindsight does not credit the police as it should. It is a sad reflection that now as then, the police will be open to criticism, but now for very different reasons such as aiding and abetting in a Royal Masonic conspiracy, or will be portrayed as a 'psychic' substance abuser as in the recent movie 'From Hell'. Both images belittle the work of the diligent police officer.

Notes

1 Reid's life and career as detective is well documented in the biography by Connell and Evans (2000). See recommended texts.
2 This chapter concentrates on what modern theorists (notably, Begg, Fido and Skinner) term the 'canonical five'. These are: Nichols, Chapman, Stride, Eddowes and Kelly.
3 See *Cassell's Saturday Journal* (22 May 1892) for a full account of Abberline's career.
4 Sometimes referred to as Piser.
5 An audit commission tasked with evaluating the extent to which the service is providing 'best value' in the way it conducts its business.

Suggested reading for the Whitechapel murders

Readers are directed to the following excellent texts for further information on the Jack the Ripper murders.

Evans S.P. and Skinner, K. (2001) *The Ultimate Jack the Ripper Sourcebook: An Illustrated Encyclopaedia*. London: Robinson.

This text contains transcription of extant police and Home Office files, alongside newspaper transcripts of the victims' inquests. This book does not bias the reader towards a particular suspect and makes an excellent starting point to study these crimes.

The following two books are recommended to give a deeper socio-cultural history of the Whitechapel murders, providing an account of press coverage and police actions.

Sugden, P. (1994) *The Complete History of Jack the Ripper*. London: Robinson Books.

Rumbelow, D. (1987, 2nd edn) *The Complete Jack the Ripper*. London: W. H. Allen.

The following books give an insight into the police officers' thoughts during the investigation.

Dew, W. (1938) *I Caught Crippen*. Blackie: London.

This book is very rare and difficult to obtain other than by specialised book dealers.

Connell, N. and Evans, S.P. (2000) *The Man who Hunted Jack the Ripper: Edmund Reid and the police perspective*. Cambridge: Rupert Books.

This book has very good coverage of the 'Ripper' crimes alongside Reid's thoughts and impressions when investigating the crimes.

References

Alison, L.J. and Barrett, E.C. (2004) 'The interpretation and utilisation of offender profiles: A critical review of "traditional" approaches to profiling', in J. Adler (ed.), *Forensic Psychology: Concepts, Debates and Practice*. Cullompton: Willan.

Alison, L.J., Bennett, C., Mohros, A. and Ormerod, D. (2002) 'The personality paradox in offender profiling: A theoretical review of the process involved in deriving background characteristics from crime scene actions', *Psychology, Public Policy and Law*, 8: 115–35.

Barrett, E. and Alison, L. (2004) *Situational Awareness in Detective Decision Making*. Sarmac Conference, New Zealand.

Begg, P., Fido, M. and Skinner, K. (1994) *The Jack the Ripper A to Z*. London: Headline Books.

Connell, N. and Evans, S.P. (2000) *The Man who Hunted Jack the Ripper: Edmund Reid and the police perspective*. Cambridge: Rupert Books.

Crego, J. and Alison, L. (2004) 'Control and legacy as functions of perceived criticality in major incidents', *Journal of Investigative Psychology and Offender Profiling*, 1 (3): 207–25.

Dobson, N. (2000) *Best Value, Law and Management*. Bristol: Jordan.

Goodwill, A. and Alison, L. (in press) 'Sequential angulation in profiling', *Psychology Crime and Law*.

Keenan, J, (2000) 'Just how new is "best value?"' *Public Money and Management*, 20 (3): 45–9.

Klein, G. (1997) 'The current status of the naturalistic decision making framework', in R. Flin, E. Salas, M. Strub and L. Martin (eds), *Decision Making Under Stress*. Aldershot: Ashgate.

Long, M. (2003) '"Naming, shaming and the politics of blaming": best value as censorius mode of police governance', *Policing Futures*, 1 (3): 33–41.

Chapter 3

Psychological research and police investigations: does the research meet the needs?

Emma C. Barrett

Psychology and policing – the current picture

In this chapter, I offer some personal observations on how students and other academic researchers might improve their understanding of the problems that matter to law enforcement professionals, and of the contribution that academic research could make in these areas. A diverse range of research is carried out on issues of relevance to the police. Since 2003 the journal *Police Practice and Research* has published annual reviews of the policing research literature (Beckman *et al.*, 2003, covering 2000; Beckman *et al.*, 2004, covering 2001). The several hundred pieces of literature included in these reviews (335 and 424 published in 2000 and 2001 respectively) include articles and books from researchers in disciplines such as psychology, criminology, sociology, law and social policy. Topics of research range from occupational and organizational issues to police attitudes and citizen satisfaction to the development and use of new technology (Beckman *et al.*, 2003; Beckman *et al.*, 2004; see also Reiner, 2000, for an overview of the history and scope of police research). The present focus, however, is on the more specific contribution of psychology to supporting law enforcement investigative practice.

As Nietzel and Hartung (1993: 152) pointed out, many of the key questions about police practice are psychological, requiring 'an understanding of the perception, thinking, discretion, expectancies, attitudes, emotions and overt behaviour of the police'. Despite this, Nietzel and Hartung argued, academic psychology was failing to address many of these issues, instead demonstrating a 'preoccupation with a few pet topics – eyewitness behaviour and lineup procedures, the reliability and validity of polygraphy, and the psychological assessment of candidates for police work' (1993: 152). In the decade since Nietzel and Hartung's assessment, the contribution of psychology has broadened in a number of areas, most notably police interviewing (e.g. Milne and Bull, 1999; Gudjonsson, 2002), forensic applications of deception research (e.g. Vrij, 2000) and offender profiling (e.g. Ainsworth, 2001; Canter and Alison, 1999). Nevertheless, some crucial areas of police investigative practice remain lamentably under-researched. Investigative decision-making is an example of an area in which psychological research could make a critical contribution, yet which has been virtually untouched by researchers.

Investigative decision-making

At the 2003 International Psychology and Law Conference (jointly organized by the American Psychology-Law Society and the Australian and New Zealand Association of Psychiatry, Psychology and Law, and European Association for Psychology and Law), there were more than 50 presentations on eyewitness issues and a similar number dealing with interrogations, confessions and deception, but only five that could be considered relevant to police investigative decision-making. While this is a relatively crude method of gauging the extent and type of ongoing police-relevant psychological research, it is suggestive of a serious research deficit in a critical area of concern to the police service.

The effective acquisition of investigative information from witnesses, victims and suspects is an important element of a successful investigation. Much is now known about the costs and benefits of the so-called 'cognitive interview', for example, and its usefulness when interviewing witnesses of all kinds, including older witnesses, children and individuals with learning difficulties (Milne and Bull, 1999). Cognitive interviewing is now widely taught in the UK and elsewhere and is considered best practice in police interviewing of eyewitnesses, although as Alison and Howard (this volume) point out, there are still a number of areas in which guidance to officers could be improved, particularly in relation to unco-operative interviewees. In relation to suspect interviewing, the issue of false confessions and individual suggestibility has also received systematic and rigorous attention, leading to recommendations for evidence-based good practice (e.g. Gudjonsson, 2002). All of this is important research, with far-reaching implications.

However, we still know very little about how this and other investigative material, once acquired, is interpreted, processed and used in the course of police investigations. Investigative decision-making, and associated issues such as the nature and development of investigative expertise, are critical issues in the UK and beyond (Police Skills and Standards Organisation, 2003). These concerns are important not just for the police, but also for a range of other investigative and law enforcement agencies, some of which will recruit non-police officers to investigative positions, such as the Independent Police Complaints Commission in the UK and the proposed UK Serious and Organised Crime Agency. Officers involved in the management and investigation of critical incidents such as police corruption, terrorist attacks, murder, rape and child abuse are faced with complex, uncertain and dynamic environments in which meaningful decisions must be taken. Their task is often made more difficult by the need to lead and motivate a large team and to work effectively with a range of other agencies with differing and often competing agendas. Furthermore, decisions must be taken with due regard to the law and to organizational priorities and policies. These complex tasks are carried out under intense public and peer scrutiny, and where mistakes happen they often have extremely serious consequences. In recent years, a series of public inquiries into high profile cases (for instance, the deaths of Stephen Lawrence (Macpherson, 1999) and Victoria Climbié (Laming, 2003)) have forced the police service to scrutinise how investigations are managed, conducted and recorded, and to consider what can be done to enhance the ability of detectives to make considered, effective and defensible decisions in the course of complex, ambiguous, stressful investigations. Steps are being taken to address crucial issues such as identifying best practice in investigation, and selecting and training expert investigative officers (Police Skills and Standards Organisation, 2003), but many of these initiatives are currently taking place largely without the support of systematic, academic research. Having the ability to investigate crimes is an important part of being an 'effective detective' (Smith and Flanagan, 2000), but there remains little understanding of what, psychologically, is involved in the process of 'investigation'; the contextual, social and cultural factors that influence the ways in which investigators comprehend complex investigative problems; how this process is influenced by individual differences in expertise, cognitive style, intellectual ability, and so on; and the means by which investigators select and implement investigative actions with the aim of solving these problems.

Being able to give a coherent account of the influences on the psychological mechanisms underpinning the process of investigation would be of immense benefit in many areas of policing (Barrett, 2002). If, for instance, expert investigators use particular strategies or focus on particular issues that help them solve a crime more quickly than less competent detectives, this may enable us to begin to specify means of accelerating the development of investigative decision-making expertise. If there are particular characteristics of some individuals that make them 'naturally' better at making investigative decisions, then specifying what these characteristics are has important implications for selection and recruitment of detective officers. Finally, it may be that features of the task environment, for instance the type of decision being made, or the domain in which it is being made (e.g. burglary versus rape investigation; a decision relating to witness treatment versus one relating to forensic strategy), have a more significant effect on the quality of the decisions made than characteristics of individuals. If so, this has implications both for training and for the development of decision support systems.

Why has this important area, where psychology potentially has so much to offer, been so ignored? One reason may be a perception, not entirely unjustified, that it is difficult to negotiate access to the domain (Horn, 1996; Reiner, 2000). Research on other policing issues has been carried in conjunction with police organizations (Beckman et al., 2003; Beckman et al., 2004), so access cannot be the only reason for this neglect. However, studying police decision-making sometimes requires access to sensitive data (e.g. case files, observations of ongoing investigations), and practitioners can, understandably, be reluctant to allow non-law enforcement personnel access to details of sensitive cases or techniques. In my experience, and that of colleagues, law enforcement agencies are sometimes prepared to grant this sort of access, but only if researchers can demonstrate that they are aware of the importance of confidentiality, have measures in place to deal with sensitive data, and agree in advance a strict protocol governing the handling and dissemination of such data.

Another possibility is that researchers avoid investigative decision-making because it can be hard to see where to start. Researchers working on witnessing and deception issues, for instance, have a significant and (for the most part) coherent body of traditional research on which to build. There is, however, no established body of research on law enforcement decision-making, and previous psychological research on aspects of decision-making more generally has itself been so broad that it can perhaps be difficult to see exactly from which angle to approach the problems of police decision making. For instance, research on inference generation and argumentation (Schum, 1993), heuristics and biases (Tversky and Kahneman, 1974), problem-solving (Davidson and Sternberg, 2003), expertise (Chi et al., 1988) and naturalistic decision-making (Zsambok and Klein, 1997) are just a few of the bodies of research potentially relevant to (but as yet barely applied to) the study of police decision-making.

The lack of a coherent research base, coupled with the inherent complexity of the topic, suggests that an exploratory and descriptive approach might be the best starting point for developing investigative decision-making research. One example of such an approach is Innes' excellent qualitative study of the investigation of homicide (Innes, 2003), which offers a compelling illustration of the complexity of law enforcement decision-making. However, conclusions about causal mechanisms underlying detective decision behaviour on the basis of this sort of study are inevitably somewhat tentative. In a competitive research funding climate, it may be easier to secure research funding, and, indeed, the support of law enforcement agencies, for projects that offer the prospect of relatively rapid results that are directly applicable to law-enforcement policy and practice.

Detecting deception in a forensic context

The lack of research on investigative decision-making issues is one example of the unbalanced contribution of psychological research to policing concerns. However, there are also areas in which psychological research on issues of interest to police investigations appears plentiful yet, arguably, promises rather more than it can actually deliver. The study of deception is one such issue.

Police and other law enforcement officers are regularly faced with situations in which members of the public may attempt to deceive them. Suspects (both guilty and innocent) may lie in an attempt to escape police scrutiny (Gudjonsson, 2002). Witnesses and victims may lie to protect themselves or others, or in order to frustrate an investigation for some other reason (Parliament and Yarmey, 2002). Informers may lie to their police handlers for personal benefit, to protect others, or in order to appear helpful and thereby maintain what may be a beneficial relationship to themselves, when in truth they have little, if anything, to offer. Being able accurately to assess the credibility of investigative information, some of which may be critical to the progress of a criminal investigation, is clearly an important skill for law enforcement officers.

Although the practice and detection of deception has been the subject of several decades of empirical psychological research, it is only relatively recently that researchers have endeavoured to address and enhance the forensic relevance and generalizability of such research (e.g. Ekman and O'Sullivan, 1991; Frank and Feeley, 2003; Granhag and Strömwall, 1999; Mann et al., 2002; Vrij, 2000). For instance, it has been assumed that the success of lie-catchers depends on an accurate reading of the verbal and non-verbal cues that might betray a liar (Vrij et al., 2000), and the pursuit of such signs has been the focus of numerous studies over the last few decades. However, the findings of a recent meta-analysis demonstrate how problematic this body of research is when applied to police work. DePaulo et al. (2003) analysed 120 deception studies dealing with verbal and non-verbal cues to deception. Of these, 101 were carried out using student participants. Of the others, only three featured genuine police suspects as lie- or truth-tellers (most of the rest used members of the public). Only 16 studies dealt with deception relating to a mock or real crime, or cheating, and only eight with a full interaction between interviewer and interviewee (as opposed to viewing video recordings of individuals making statements that may or may not have been deceptive).

While the work of DePaulo et al.'s and similar analyses demonstrate that there are a small number of relatively reliable cues to deception, and, importantly, that these cues are not generally those commonly believed to indicate deceptive behaviour (such as, for instance, gaze aversion – Vrij, 2000; Strömwall and Granhag, 2003), it is arguable how much confidence we can have in generalizing these findings to the typical situations in which police officers may have to deal with deception. It may be that these cues are consistent indicators of deception and that other cues are genuinely unreliable indicators that should not be depended upon in interview situations, but without a set of studies examining cues to deception in ecologically valid police interview situations such assertions necessarily remain speculative (Mann et al., 2002). The study of deception in real-life cases of individuals accused of serious crimes is still at an early stage, although initial results have been intriguing and sometimes surprising (Vrij and Mann, 2001; Mann et al., 2002; M. Davis, personal communication, 24 June 2004). Mann et al. (2002), for instance, revealed that only two behaviours distinguished suspects' lying from truth-telling: they tended to blink less often and pause more often when lying than when telling the truth. In the case of blinking, this finding contradicts the commonly held assumption that liars are more nervous than truth-tellers: nervous individuals tend to exhibit an *increase* in blink rate (DePaulo et al., 2003; Mann et al., 2002; Navarro, 2003). As Mann and her colleagues note, their results suggest that, for the individuals in this particular sample, lying was a cognitively demanding, rather than an emotionally taxing, activity. This has important implications: it suggests, for instance, that police officers might be able to increase their deception-detection ability by focusing on behaviours that suggest that their interviewee has to think hard about the answers to questions, rather than on nervous behaviours. Indeed, one study has already suggested that police officers are more accurate at detecting lies when they are asked 'does the person have to think hard?' than when they are asked 'is the person lying?' (Vrij et al.,

2001). However, although in this study the lie-catchers were police officers, their targets were nursing students, not real suspects. Again, further work is necessary to discover if the 'are they thinking hard?' instruction enhances officers' real-world deception-detection ability.

There are several other major gaps in the research on deception, and although it is beyond the scope of this chapter to go into all of them, I will briefly touch on a few areas of law enforcement practice where additional guidance from empirical research would be welcome. Dealing with informers, for instance, raises numerous deception-related issues. Deception in an informer's relationship with his or her police handler may potentially be systematic and long-term. However, most research thus far has tended to concentrate on relatively short interactions between strangers, or situations in which the lie-catcher views video recordings of potential liars (Vrij, 2000). It may be, for instance, that over a long-term relationship, an informer may become more effective at deceiving their handler, particularly if the handler perceives the relationship to be productive, in which case it might not be in his or her interests to disrupt it by accusing the source of lying (cf. Ekman, 1996). If true, this would have practical implications, perhaps for the length of time any handler is allowed to maintain a relationship with their source, or suggesting a need for an 'unbiased' outsider to attend or otherwise monitor informer–handler meetings occasionally.

Another gap in forensically relevant deception research is on the long-term effects of practising deception, for instance in an undercover context. The question of how police officers (and, indeed, informers) deal with sustaining long-term deceptive cover, particularly if switching back and forth between legitimate and deceptive identities, has both operational and welfare implications (cf. French, 2003).

Another key under-researched issue is whether cues to deception are universal or culturally specific. The vast majority of the studies analysed by DePaulo and her colleagues used participants who were from North America or Western Europe, and in most cases the ethnicity of the potential liars and the targets of their lies was not reported, making it impossible to make any comment on this potentially important influence (DePaulo et al., 2003). Given that law enforcement agencies deal with an ethnically diverse pool of witnesses, victims and suspects, the issue of whether true or misleading cues to deception have cross-cultural validity is an important one (Vrij, 2000). There is some preliminary evidence that lies can be detected across cultures (Bond and Atoum, 2000), but far more research is needed before psychologists can offer empirically based advice on this issue.

Finally, research on behavioural and verbal cues to deception is of limited value to law enforcement unless there is some evidence that the ability of officers to detect lies can be enhanced. At first glance, the literature suggests that training can have a modest but positive effect on lie-detection ability (Frank and Feeley, 2003; Vrij, 2000). However, as Frank and Feeley note, there are several gaps in this research. They conclude that 'we have not yet fairly examined the extent to which one can train professionals to improve their abilities to distinguish truths from lies' (2003: 72).

As with investigative decision-making, one of the key reasons for the lack of forensically relevant types of study is probably the difficulty in securing access. However, law enforcement organizations may become more receptive to proposals as more academics become involved in work on real cases and demonstrate that they can be trusted to act within the bounds of confidentiality stipulated by practitioner agencies. Even if access to forensic populations is not possible, Frank and Feeley argue that although it is 'impossible to recreate exactly some of the conditions found in the real world' (2003: 63), much can be done to increase the generalizability of deception studies to real-world contexts by creating laboratory situations that are structurally similar to real-world conditions.

In summary, I have suggested that despite many decades of research on deception, much still remains to be done to enhance the quality of advice and training given to law enforcement officers on deception detection. Nevertheless, the progress in this field over the past few years has demonstrated that it is possible to build effectively on existing research, gradually enhancing forensic relevance.

Picking the right problems

I have argued that although in some areas empirical psychological research has made a significant contribution to police practice, there are many other important areas, such as investigative decision-making, which have been unjustly neglected by academia. Furthermore, there are other topics, such as deception detection, where, despite a considerable body of empirical research, it is sometimes impossible to draw any more than tentative conclusions when seeking to apply these findings to law enforcement practice. I turn now to how researchers might identify other under-researched issues and develop research that genuinely addresses practitioner concerns.

Many graduate students, and even perhaps more established researchers, feel daunted by the thought of trying to carry out psychological research directly with the police or other law enforcement agencies: they may feel that they do not have relevant expertise, but more often, the reality of trying to break into what may seem a completely closed shop is what puts researchers off this field. Instead, students and young researchers interested in applying psychological research to policing matters may end up working on a relatively established area of forensic or legal psychology, carrying out controlled experimental studies, often using student participants. I do not mean to suggest that such studies are trivial or that they fail to make an important contribution to the field. On the contrary, this sort of rigorous approach can help a field to progress from the level of descriptive understanding of a phenomenon of interest towards the explanatory level (Brewer *et al.*, 1995; Silke, 2001). However, if most researchers concentrate only on established areas, other important issues remain sadly under-researched, and while participants in such research are drawn largely from a student population results often remain of limited generalizability to law enforcement practice.

The argument that psychologists must pay attention to what matters to law enforcement agencies and develop an understanding of the many and varied concerns that impact on them is in line with a pragmatic approach to police research (Fishman, 2004; Alison *et al.*, 2004). Pragmatic researchers seek answers to practitioners' research problems by carrying out studies that aim as far as possible to take account of the full range of practitioners' concerns. In the remainder of this chapter I suggest some steps that a researcher new to this area could take to ensure that their research identifies and allows for these concerns.

I Get interested in the politics and practice of law enforcement

If you are serious about a career in police psychology, you should be prepared to invest some time in finding out and monitoring what is going on in the world of law enforcement and the criminal justice system more generally. Having an awareness of these issues will help you to recognize research needs and areas in which psychological research can have an impact on law enforcement and to identify the practical implications of your research (Brewer *et al.*, 1995). On a more general level, it will also enhance your credibility when talking to law enforcement officers if you can show a basic understanding of key concerns.

A number of widely available sources provide information on law enforcement developments (a few examples are provided at the end of this chapter). Key sources will be government departments whose respon-sibilities include policing and security matters (for instance, the Home Office in the UK, or the US and Canadian Departments of Justice). Press releases and material from their websites provide important information about current concerns, and the research-aware psychologist will quickly spot the psychological issues involved and opportunities for developing research projects.

In some cases, there may already be a wealth of psychological research available on a topic of current interest, in which case there may be a place for a thorough and well-crafted review of existing relevant research. A striking example of this is Darbyshire's report, 'What can the English legal system learn from jury research?' (Darbyshire *et al.*, 2001). In 2001, the UK government commissioned a report on the reform of the English legal system from Lord Justice Auld and, as is customary in such consultations, Auld asked for comments from interested parties. Darbyshire, who had spent some time working on jury research in the US, suggested to Auld that she and her colleagues be commissioned to prepare a report on jury research. The legal profession had hitherto neglected the significant body of psychological and legal research on jury decision-making, and Darbyshire proposed that 'before we spend yet more public money on re-inventing the wheel, we should take the trouble to find out what we can learn from existing research from England and Wales, the rest of the common law world and elsewhere' (Darbyshire *et al.*, 2001: 1).

Although this example pertains to jury research, Darbyshire's approach is one that could be used in a number of other areas. For instance, the Home Office has published several papers in recent years setting out proposals that will have a direct impact on policing and criminal investigation, including ideas for reform of the police service (e.g. Home Office, 2001), tackling organized crime (Home Office, 2004) and dealing with domestic violence (Home Office, 2003). These papers are littered with issues that demand the type of review provided by Darbyshire, and that could also provide the impetus for original empirical research.

In the domestic violence proposals, for instance, one aim that has a direct bearing on police procedure is 'ensuring an effective police response when victims report domestic violence' (Home Office, 2003: 25). There is little doubt that in the sympathetic and serious treatment of victims of domestic violence, UK policing has improved markedly in recent years. However, a recent police review revealed that:

> while all officers spoken to were clear about the fact that domestic violence was a priority within their force … few had any real understanding of the dynamics of domestic violence. In addition, effective understanding of policy was found to be variable, resulting in differing standards of response being applied which were often dependent on the knowledge, and experience, of individual attending officers. (Her Majesty's Inspectorate of Constabulary, 2004: 33)

The causes of shortcomings in the investigation of domestic violence are open to empirical research. The above comment suggests that ineffective investigation may have a cognitive or attitudinal basis: it is possible that police officers fail to record crimes of domestic violence because they rely on a set of false or stereotypical 'cues' to classify an event as benign rather than a potential crime. Officers may also be constrained in their investigation of domestic violence incidents by force policy or legislation, or their perception of it: officers may correctly recognize and classify an event as a potential domestic violence crime, but feel unsure of their powers. For instance, the Home Office noted that where an alleged domestic violence offender is no longer present at the scene of an alleged crime, and, as is common, the victim does not wish to press his or her complaint, 'police officers are often uncertain about their powers of arrest for a common assault that they have not witnessed' (Home Office, 2003: 26). Such research questions could be tackled through surveys or structured interviews of officers, or by examining officers' perceptions of ambiguous potential domestic violence incidents using card-sort exercises or 'pen-and-paper' studies.

Research that has psychological relevance can often turn up in apparently unlikely places. Although interesting and relevant issues are most likely to arise in government departments that have a specific responsibility for law enforcement issues, bear in mind that some forensic issues can be approached more peripherally. As an example, the UK's Office of the Deputy Prime Minister (ODPM), which has responsibility for fire service policy, established the Arson Control Forum (ACF) to co-ordinate and drive forward efforts to tackle arson. Around 100 people die each year in England and Wales as a result of fires caused by arson, and this crime costs the UK economy more than £2 billion each year, yet the conviction rate for these crimes is only around 2.5 per cent (Young, 2003). As well as devising intervention and prevention strategies, the ACF, via the ODPM, commissioned an overview of research on arson, arsonists and arson prevention strategies (Canter and Almond, 2002). Drawing on existing psychological research on the motivations, characteristics and behaviours of arsonists (e.g. Canter and Fritzon, 1998), the authors showed that 'the sorts of people who commit the different forms of arson can be distinguished from each other and their targets will be different, [meaning that] … agencies that can contribute to the reducing of each form of arson can be distinguished' (Canter and Almond, 2002: 18). However, Canter and Almond's review also revealed a number of important gaps in existing research, including the need for more rich data on the nature and circumstances of arson events, and for thorough evaluation of treatment programmes for arsonists. Many other forensic psychological issues would benefit from the same kind of comprehensive review focusing on problems of interest to policy-makers and practitioners, high-lighting the relevance of existing research and pointing out critical gaps.

Another good source of information about developments in law enforcement is the trade press: publications that are aimed specifically at law enforcement officers and contain news and features on issues of current relevance. In the UK, for instance, *Police Review*, a weekly magazine available on subscription to individuals, in larger newsagents and in some university libraries, will keep you informed of developments, controversies and opportunities for police-related research, and often features articles by academics engaged in police research. The Federal Bureau of Investigation (FBI) monthly *Law Enforcement Bulletin*, available online from the FBI's website, and the Royal Canadian Mounted Police (RCMP) *Gazette* also feature short items and more detailed features covering current and ongoing issues in law enforcement in the US and Canada respectively. Monitoring the news pages and features will allow you to judge whether a particular issue is a passing fad or recurring theme that may be worthy of research attention. For example, over the last two years, the issue of investigative expertise and detective training has featured consistently in *Police Review*, both in news articles and in longer features. As discussed above, this issue raises a wealth of psychological issues, relevant to investigators worldwide, that are as yet hardly touched by academic researchers.

A further source of information on policing is law enforcement and related websites (see examples at the end of this chapter), which often highlight issues of concern where empirical research may have something to offer. Local websites may throw up gems, but it is probably most profitable to start with regional or national policing sites and search through press releases and publications areas first. Examples are the FBI site in the US, the Association of Chief Police Officers' site in the UK, the RCMP site in Canada and the Australasian Centre for Policing Research site.

2 Network with individuals who already work with the police

As with research in most areas, one of the best ways to get your police research career onto a good footing is to work with people who are already doing it: they can offer valuable insights to the processes and practices of working with law enforcement, will often have useful contacts and are likely to have an awareness of current and future developments in the criminal justice system that may guide your choice of research project. They will also be able to let you know whether your proposals are worthwhile, or hopelessly naïve, and whether collecting the data you need is going to be feasible, difficult or outright impossible.

Until relatively recently it has been somewhat unusual to find academic psychologists engaged in research with the police, but this situation is changing rapidly, reflecting an increasing openness by the police and other law enforcement agencies to working with academics, and a mushrooming growth in forensic psychology courses in the UK and elsewhere. But your mentors and advisors do not all necessarily have to be academics: many psychology departments now have current or former law-enforcement officers on Master's degrees programmes, working towards PhDs, and, increasingly, in academic positions (Mulraney, 2003). All these individuals can be invaluable sources of advice and information about the practicalities of doing research in a law enforcement environment. Seek these people out, either in your own department or in other departments that offer forensic psychology courses. If possible, look for individuals who have actually worked with law enforcement agencies, rather than those whose forensic research has been largely with student populations, with results extrapolated to criminal justice applications.

Attending as many conferences and seminars as you can find funding for, particularly in the early stages of your career, is another way of making contacts who may be able to advise on your research proposals or even facilitate access to data. It is often worth looking beyond the traditional academic conference circuit: conferences and seminars that relate directly to law enforcement work will also highlight issues of concern to practitioners, which may in turn generate ideas for potential research projects. Lectures may be fascinating, but the most useful business at conferences and seminars often happens outside the formal presentations. Every conversation you have with an academic engaged in police research or a law enforcement officer interested in what academia has to offer will enhance your understanding of the way in which law enforcement works and the contribution psychological research can make to it. You can use the delegate list, if there is one, to develop a 'hit-list' of people you want to talk to, or simply take any opportunity to talk to a fellow delegate: they are likely to be interesting themselves, but they may be able to introduce you to other useful contacts. One strategy is strike up conversations with other delegates at lunches, dinners and coffee breaks, rather than sticking solely with people you know. Approaching established academics and practitioners can seem daunting, and there is always the chance you may be rebuffed. But most researchers and practitioners are happy to be engaged in conversation, if you can show that you are genuinely interested in and have some understanding of their areas of interest (see step 1 above).

3 Don't ignore current police practice

As well as proposals under consideration by governments and law enforcement agencies, there remain many aspects of current police practice that would also benefit from empirical scrutiny. It is worth investing some time in finding out as much as you can about how police work is actually carried out, by speaking to law enforcement officers or perhaps by skimming through police textbooks to get a feel for policing theory. Probably the best way to begin to get a feel for the range of day-to-day policing concerns, however, is to spend some time on attachment to a police or other law enforcement agency. Although a handful of Masters courses offer placements with criminal justice agencies, outside these more formal arrangements it can often be difficult to set up an attachment. However, if you have contacts already working in or with law enforcement (see step 2 above), it may be worth exploring with them whether you can spend even just a day or two with a police team.

Exposure to the day-to-day work of practitioners is a good way to get a feel for aspects of their work which they might not see as problematic, but which you, as an outside observer, might recognize as worthy of further scrutiny. An example is the police caution that was introduced to England and Wales with the passing of the Criminal Justice and Public Order Act 1994 and which is supposed to alert a suspect to the possibility that although they have the right to remain silent during questioning, their silence may in some circumstances have an adverse impact on their defence if their case comes to court. Police officers administer the three-sentence long caution every time they arrest a suspect, generally followed by asking the suspect if they understand it. An affirmative answer is usually taken at face value to mean that the suspect understands his or her rights.

Fenner et al. (2002) explored public comprehension of the caution, using a forensically relevant population (suspects at a police station and, as controls, job-centre attendees). Fenner et al. revealed that the three-sentence caution, when presented in its entirely, was very poorly understood by this population. This is of crucial importance because, as Fenner et al. point out, 'suspects who do not understand their rights will not be able to make informed decisions regarding their situation: they may give unreliable statements to the police, falsely incriminating themselves' (Fenner et al., 2002: 85). Furthermore, although actual understanding was poor, participants nevertheless tended to claim that they did understand the caution, highlighting the need to develop a better means of judging comprehension than the current practice of simply asking 'do you understand?' at the end of the caution. The value of this sort of research is in taking an everyday policing issue that has wide-ranging and potentially significant consequences and subjecting it to rigorous scrutiny, and demonstrating that psychologists are able to make empirically based recommendations for future changes to policing practice.

4 Don't forget you're a psychologist

One of the most important things to consider when developing police research is what other, perhaps more traditional, psychological research might have a bearing on the topic of interest (Alison and Canter, 1999). Developing research in police psychology does not necessarily mean developing a whole new set of theories and methods. In fact, it is often more productive to apply existing work in a novel context. Work on eyewitness testimony, for instance, is built on almost a century of more general psychological research on human memory (e.g. Baddeley, 1996; Sporer et al., 1996), and the cognitive interview technique was devised by psychologists applying traditional memory research to the issue of how to enhance an interviewee's recall (Fisher and Geiselman, 1992). Similarly, Canter's research on the psychogeography of crime has its roots in his early career as an environmental psychologist, exploring the effects of space and surroundings on people. Canter had always been committed to the concept of applying psychological theory and research to real-world problems (Canter, 1996), and when he was approached by Surrey Police to assist in the investigation of a serial rapist in the 1980s he was able to use the insights gained in his previous work to understand the behaviour and geographical pattern of offending by the rapist (a full account is provided in Canter, 1994).

Where 'traditional' psychological research and theories are applied to problems faced by the police, the results have often made an important contribution to the work of law enforcement: work on eyewitness testimony has led to recommended changes in line-up procedures (e.g. Kebbell, 2000; Kebbell and Wagstaff, 1999; Wells et al., 1998); the cognitive interview is now taught widely in the UK and elsewhere and used to enhance the elicitation of information from victims and witnesses (Powell, 2002; Milne and Bull, 1999); and work on geographical aspects of offending has led to the ongoing development of geographical profiling systems to support police investigations of prolific offenders (Ainsworth, 2001).

In sum, then, much of the most useful psychological research carried out on problems faced by the police has involved considering relatively well-understood psychological issues in a novel context (Brewer et al., 1995). Viewed in this way, it is unsurprising that psychologists who have never worked with law enforcement before but who nevertheless have a solid understanding of psychological research are able to make significant and worthwhile contributions to the understanding of law enforcement problems. These individuals have a good sense of what theories can be applied to the particular issue under consideration and of the strengths and limitations of different methods of exploring these issues. The key message here is not to neglect existing theoretical work, which will inform both the development of your own theories and the methods you use in your research.

5 Don't expect miracles

Research with law enforcement can also be difficult and frustrating. On a practical level, you may often find that what you were assured were solid plans to interview police officers, administer questionnaires or observe training exercises have to be cancelled at short (or no) notice because your participants have been deployed on urgent, last-minute operational commitments. If you are likely to be up against a deadline (for instance, for an assignment or a dissertation), it is worth making contingency plans: students often learn the hard way never to assume that they will have data until they are actually in their hands.

More generally, you should not expect major changes to police policy and practice on the basis of a few (or even many) studies. Such changes do not happen overnight, and usually require a critical mass of studies before changes to policy are even considered. However, you may increase the impact of your own research by submitting articles to trade publications (such as *Police Review*) and journals that are likely to be read by practitioners (such as *Police Practice and Research*, *Police Quarterly* and *Policing*) as well as psychology journals. If, as suggested in step 1, you have kept yourself informed of developments in police policy and practice, you will be well placed to highlight the practical implications of your research in such articles.

Concluding remarks

Despite its frustrations, psychological research with law enforcement can be exceptionally rewarding and can contribute to practice and policy. The consequence of not focusing research effort on some of the critical issues in policing today is that policy is made and practice developed without a grounding in reliable, verifiable research (Murphy, 1999). Indeed, Murphy maintains that 'a research environment that actively produces research "about, on, for and by" the police' (Murphy, 1999: 206) is crucial to effective, efficient and accountable policing. Bowling recently argued that academics have a duty to contribute to public debates on security, policing and other issues of public concern: 'for those working in applied fields ... it is part of our role to contribute to policy development' (Bowling, 2004). The turning point in Bowling's thinking was during the public inquiry into the racist murder of the teenager Stephen Lawrence (Macpherson, 1999). Bowling wrote that, initially,

> although I was putting the finishing touches to a 400-page book based on a decade of scholarly research on issues central to the Lawrence Inquiry, I had somehow failed to realise that I was qualified to contribute. It was over lunch with a senior colleague that the idea took root. 'If you don't submit research evidence,' he asked, 'who will?' (Bowling, 2004).

It is always going to be more straightforward to carry out research on well-established issues where controlled experimental studies are possible, and student participants relatively plentiful. But I hope that more researchers will take up the challenge of seeking out under-researched but important issues and developing innovative, practitioner-focused research. If we don't, who will?

Acknowledgements

Support for the preparation of this chapter was provided by Economic and Social Research Council Grant PTA-030-2002-00482. Many of the ideas in this chapter developed as a result of discussions with a number of academics and practitioners involved in the application of psychology to police work, to whom I am indebted, although, of course, I take full responsibility for any errors of fact, scholarship or judgment. I would like to thank Laurence Alison for his comments on an earlier draft of this chapter.

References

Ainsworth, P.B. (2001) *Offender Profiling and Crime Analysis*. Cullompton: Willan Publishing.

Alison, L. and Canter, D. (1999) 'Professional, legal and ethical issues in offender profiling', in D. Canter and L. Alison (eds), *Profiling in Policy and Practice* (pp. 21–54). Aldershot: Ashgate Publishing.

Alison, L.J., West, A. and Goodwill A (2004) 'The academic and the practitioner: Pragmatists' views of offender profiling', *Psychology, Public Policy, and Law*, 10 (1–2): 71–101.

Baddeley, A.D. (1996) *Human Memory: Theory and Practice* (revised edition). Hove: Psychology Press.

Barrett, E. (2002) *Towards a theory of investigative situation assessment: An examination of the psychological mechanisms underlying the construction of situation models in criminal investigations.* Unpublished Masters Dissertation, Department of Psychology, University of Liverpool, UK.

Beckman, K., Lum, C., Wyckoff, L. and Larsen-Vander Wall, K. (2003) 'Trends in police research: A cross-sectional analysis of the 2000 literature', *Police Practice and Research: An International Journal,* 4 (1): 79–96.

Beckman, K.A., Wyckoff, L., Groff, E.R. and Beatty, P.D. (2004) 'Trends in police research: A cross-sectional analysis of the 2001 literature', *Police Practice and Research: An International Journal,* 5 (2): 165–89.

Bond, C.F. and Atoum, O.A. (2000) 'International deception', *Personality and Social Psychology Bulletin,* 26 (3): 385–95.

Bowling, B. (2004) 'Why I think academics should take part in public inquiries', *The Times Higher Education Supplement,* 13 February.

Brewer, N., Wilson, C. and Braithwaite, H. (1995) 'Psychological research and policing', in N. Brewer and C. Wilson (eds), *Psychology and Policing* (pp. 395–412). Hillsdale, NJ: Lawrence Erlbaum Associates.

Canter, D. (1994) *Criminal Shadows.* London: Harper Collins.

Canter, D. (1996) *Psychology in Action.* Aldershot: Ashgate Publishing.

Canter, D. and Alison, L. (1999) *Profiling in Policy and Practice.* Aldershot: Ashgate Publishing.

Canter, D. and Almond, L. (2002) *The Burning Issue: Research and strategies for reducing arson.* Office of the Deputy Prime Minister. London: HMSO.

Canter, D. and Fritzon, K. (1998) 'Differentiating arsonists: A model of fire-setting actions and characteristics', *Legal and Criminological Psychology,* 3: 73–96.

Chi, M., Farr, M. and Glaser, R. (1988) *The Nature of Expertise.* Hillsdale, NJ: Lawrence Erlbaum Associates.

Darbyshire, P., Maughan, A. and Stewart, A. (2001) 'What can the English legal system learn from jury research?', www.kingston.ac.uk/~ku00596/elsres01.pdf (accessed 24 July).

Davidson, J. and Sternberg, R. (2003) *The Psychology of Problem Solving.* Cambridge: Cambridge University Press.

DePaulo, B.M., Lindsay, J.J., Malone, B.E., Muhlenbruck, L., Charlton, K. and Cooper, H. (2003) 'Cues to deception', *Psychological Bulletin,* 129: 74–118.

Ekman, P. (1996) 'Why don't we catch liars?', *Social Research,* 63 (3): 801–17.

Ekman, P. and O'Sullivan, M. (1991) 'Who can catch a liar?', *American Psychologist,* 46: 913–20.

Fenner, S., Gudjonsson, G.H. and Clare, I.C.H. (2002) 'Understanding of the current police caution (England and Wales) among suspects in police detention', *Journal of Community and Applied Social Psychology,* 12: 83–93.

Fisher, R.P. and Geiselman, R.E. (1992) *Memory-enhancing Techniques for Investigative Interviewing: The cognitive interview.* Springfield, IL: Charles Thomas.

Fishman, D.B. (2004) 'Pragmatic psychology and the law: Introduction to Part II', *Psychology, Public Policy and Law,* 10 (1–2): 3–4.

Frank, M.G. and Feeley, T.H. (2003) 'To catch a liar: Challenges for research in lie detection training', *Journal of Applied Communication Research,* 31 (1): 58–75.

French, N. (2003) *Profiling reassimilation experiences of undercover police officers.* Paper presented at the Psychology and Law: Second International Interdisciplinary Conference, Edinburgh.

Granhag, P.A. and Strömwall, L.A. (1999) 'Repeated interrogations – stretching the deception detection paradigm', *Expert Evidence*, 7: 163–74.

Gudjonsson, G. (2002) *The Psychology of Interrogations and Confessions.* Chichester, John Wiley and Sons.

Her Majesty's Inspectorate of Constabulary (2003) *Violence at Home: A joint inspection on the investigation and prosecution of cases involving domestic violence.* London: HMSO.

Home Office (2001) *Policing a New Century: A blueprint for reform.* London: HMSO.

Home Office (2003) *Safety and Justice: The government's proposals on domestic violence.* London: HMSO.

Home Office (2004) *One Step Ahead: A 21st century strategy to defeat organised criminals.* London: HMSO.

Horn, R. (1996) 'Negotiating research access to organisations', *The Psychologist*, 9 (12): 551–54.

Innes, M. (2003) *Investigating Murder: Detective work and the police response to criminal homicide.* Oxford: Oxford University Press.

Kebbell, M.R. (2000) 'The law concerning the conduct of lineups in England and Wales: How well does it satisfy the recommendations of the American Psychology-Law Society?', *Law and Human Behavior*, 24 (3): 2000.

Kebbell, M. and Wagstaff, G. (1999) *Face Value? Evaluating the accuracy of eyewitness information.* Home Office Police Research Series. London: HMSO.

Lord Laming (2003) *The Victoria Climbié Inquiry.* London: HMSO.

Macpherson, W. (1999) *The Stephen Lawrence Inquiry.* London: HMSO.

Mann, S., Vrij, A. and Bull, R. (2002) 'Suspects, lies and videotape: An analysis of authentic high-stake liars', *Law and Human Behavior*, 26 (3): 365–76.

Milne, R. and Bull, R. (1999) *Investigative Interviewing: Psychology and practice.* Chichester: John Wiley and Sons.

Mulraney, S. (2003) 'With honours', *Police Review*, No. 5729, 20 June.

Murphy, C. (1999) 'The current and future state of police research and policy in Canada', *Canadian Journal of Criminology*, 41 (2): 205–16.

Navarro, J. (2003) 'A four domain model for detecting deception', *FBI Law Enforcement Bulletin*, 72 (6): 19–24.

Nietzel, M.T. and Hartung, C.M. (1993) 'Psychological research on police: An introduction to a special issue on the psychology of law enforcement', *Law and Human Behavior*, 17: 151–55.

Parliament, L. and Yarmey, A.D. (2002) 'Deception in eyewitness identification', *Criminal Justice and Behavior*, 29 (6): 734–46.

Police Skills and Standards Organisation (2003) *Identifying the current and future skills needs of the Police Sector: A report on the Skills Foresight programme.* PSSO.

Powell, M.B. (2002) 'Specialist training in investigative and evidential interviewing: Is it having any effect on the behavior of professionals in the field?', *Psychiatry, Psychology and Law*, 9 (1): 44–55.

Reiner, R. (2000) 'Police research', in Roy D. King and Emma Wincup (eds), *Doing Research on Crime and Justice* (pp. 205–235). Oxford: Oxford University Press.

Schum, D.A. (1993) 'Argument structuring and evidence evaluation', in R. Hastie (ed.), *Inside the Juror* (pp. 175–191). Cambridge: Cambridge University Press.

Silke, A. (2001) 'The devil you know: Continuing problems with research on terrorism', *Terrorism and Political Violence*, 13 (4): 1–14.

Smith, N. and Flanagan, C. (2000) *The Effective Detective: Identifying the skills of an effective SIO*. Home Office Police Research Series Paper 122. London: HMSO.

Sporer, S., Malpass and Köhnken, G. (1996) *Psychological Issues in Eyewitness Identification*. Hillsdale, NJ: Lawrence Erlbaum Associates.

Strömwall, L.A. and Granhag, P.A. (2003) 'How to detect deception? Arresting the beliefs of police officers, prosecutors and judges', *Psychology, Crime and Law*, 9 (1): 19–36.

Tversky, A. and Kahneman, D. (1974) 'Judgement under uncertainty: Heuristics and biases', *Science*, 185: 1124–131.

Vrij, A. (2000) *Detecting Lies and Deceit: The psychology of lying and its implications for professional practice*. Chichester: John Wiley and Sons.

Vrij, A. and Mann, S. (2001) 'Telling and detecting lies in a high-stake situation: the case of a convicted murderer', *Applied Cognitive Psychology*, 15 (2): 187–203.

Vrij, A., Edward, K. and Bull, R. (2001) 'Police officers' ability to detect deceit: The benefit of indirect deception detection measures', *Legal and Criminological Psychology*, 6 (2): 185–96.

Vrij, A., Edward, K., Roberts, K.P. and Bull, R. (2000) 'Detecting deceit via analyses of verbal and non-verbal behavior', *Journal of Nonverbal Behavior*, 24 (4): 239–63.

Wells, G., Small, M., Penrod, S., Malpass, R.S., Fulero, S.M. and Brimacombe, C.A.E. (1998) 'Eyewitness identification procedures: Recommendations for lineups and photospreads', *Law and Human Behavior*, 22 (6): 1–39.

Young, N. (2003) 'Detecting and convicting the arsonist: Lessons from the United States', www.arsonpreventionbureau.org.uk/Publications (accessed 24 July 2004).

Zsambok, C.E. and Klein, G. (1997) *Naturalistic Decision Making*. Mahwah, NJ: Lawrence Erlbaum Associates.

Useful websites

Government departments

UK Home Office: www.homeoffice.gov.uk/
UK Home Office, Research Development and Statistics:
  www.homeoffice.gov.uk/rds
Criminal Justice System Online (UK): http://www.cjsonline.org/home.html
US Department of Justice: www.usdoj.gov
US National Criminal Justice Reference Service:
  www.ncjrs.org/index.html
Canadian Department of Justice: http://canada.justice.gc.ca

Police sites

UK Police Service portal: www.police.uk
Association of Chief Police Officers (UK): www.acpo.police.uk
Her Majesty's Inspectorate of Constabulary (UK):
    www.homeoffice.gov.uk/hmic
Police Training and development (UK): www.centrex.police.uk
Federal Bureau of Investigation: www.fbi.gov
Royal Canadian Mounted Police: www.rcmp-grc.gc.ca
Australasian Centre for Policing Research: www.acpr.gov.au

Other useful sites

UK Criminal Justice Weblog: www.ukcjweblog.org.uk/
Psychology and Crime email information list:
    http://groups.yahoo.com/group/crime-psych

Chapter 4

Suspect prioritization in the investigation of sex offences: from clinical classification and profiling to pragmatism

Georgia Wilson and Laurence Alison

Research has shown that approximately half of all sexual assaults are stranger sexual offences. For example, Mulvihill *et al.* (1969) reported that 53 per cent of rapes reported in the US were committed by a stranger to the victim. In the UK, Lloyd and Walmsey (1989) reported that stranger rapes accounted for 49 per cent of recorded rapes in 1973, and 40 per cent of recorded rapes in 1985. While not confirmed, this decrease in the proportion of stranger rapes is thought to be due to an increase in the reporting of acquaintance and so called date-rape offences. In contrast, however, in Eastern Europe, Kocsis (1982) reported that while 55 per cent of victims were known to the offender, a further 40 per cent of victims had come into contact with the offender prior to the assault, resulting in only a small minority of offences being defined as stranger rapes.

Stranger sexual assaults are also particularly difficult to solve. Where should investigators start looking when initially there is no suspect? Should they be looking for a particular type of person? It appears not. Prentky and Burgess (2000: 26–27) concluded that 'one of the few indisputable conclusions about sexual offenders is that they constitute a markedly heterogeneous group', arguing that 'the childhood and developmental histories, adult competencies, and criminal histories of sexual offenders differ considerably. The motives and patterns, moreover, that characterize their criminal offenses differ considerably.'

In order to reduce this diversity, researchers have devised classification systems in an attempt to differentiate between types of sexual offender, types of child molester and types of rapist. Classification systems have potential use in gaining an understanding of the aetiology of the offending behaviour, devising treatment programmes for offenders, assessing the risk of recidivism and informing decisions in the criminal justice system. In addition, classification systems have been applied to, and devised for use within, criminal investigations. The premise behind this is that if different types of sexual offender can be differentiated and linked to different types of sexual offence, then these classification systems could be used to prioritize suspects in the investigation of stranger sexual offences. In this chapter, various approaches to the classification of sexual offenders will be described and evaluated in relation to their application and usefulness in prioritizing suspects in the investigation of stranger sexual offences.

Early clinical classification systems: a lack of empiricism

The earliest classifications of sex offenders were typically proposed by clinicians working with sex offenders in a therapeutic environment. Recognizing, or assuming from the outset, a difference between child molesters and rapists, classification systems were typically proposed for one or other of these groups of offenders. For example, several different classification systems for child molesters have been proposed (e.g. Fitch, 1962; Kopp, 1962; McCaghy, 1967; Swanson, 1971; Cohen et al., 1969; Howells, 1981; Groth, 1981). Furthermore, research has shown that incest offenders are as heterogeneous as non-incest offenders (e.g. Rist, 1979; Summit and Kryso, 1978) and thus separate classification systems have been proposed for this group (e.g. Weinberg, 1955; Summit and Kryso, 1978). Similarly, several classification systems for rapists have been proposed (e.g. Guttmacher, 1951; Guttmacher and Weihofen, 1952; Kopp, 1962; Gebhard et al., 1965; Amir, 1971; Rada, 1978; Cohen et al., 1969; Groth et al., 1977).

Cohen et al. (1969), for example, proposed separate classification systems for child molesters and rapists. In the former system, three types of paedophile were described. The *paedophile-fixated* type has a longstanding and exclusive preference for children as social and sexual companions, and will often have a platonic relationship with the victim prior to the offence, which will involve minimal force and typically nongenital sexual acts. In contrast, the *paedophile-regressed* type will exhibit normal development in terms of adult sexual relationships, but in the face of stress will turn to an inappropriate object. Finally, in contrast to the previous two types, in which the primary motive is said to be sexual, the primary motive for the *paedophile-aggressive* type is aggression, and offences will contain both sexual and aggressive features. Later Cohen *et al.* (1979) described a fourth, *exploitative*, type who uses the vulnerable child to satisfy his own sexual needs. These offences typically involve victims unknown to the offender, will include genital sexual acts and, if necessary, instrumental violence to ensure the victim's compliance.

In addition, Cohen *et al.* (1969) described four types of rapist based on the relative emphasis of sex and aggression in the offence. For the *compensatory* rapist, the motive is said to be more sexual than aggressive. The offender is preoccupied by rape fantasy and aroused by the rape, but aggression is only used to attain the victim's compliance. It is argued that the sexual offence compensates for the rapist's pervasive feelings of inadequacy. In contrast, for the *displaced aggression* rapist the aggressive assault is an expression of anger, with the intent being to physically harm and humiliate the victim. The assault is said to follow a precipitating event involving a significant female in the offender's life, where the offence is a displacement of the offender's anger at this female onto an innocent victim. For the *sex-aggression-diffusion* rapist, feelings of sexual arousal and anger are said to coexist such that one cannot be experienced independently of the other. As a result, this type of rapist commits sadistic offences involving both sexual and aggressive elements that reinforce each other, so that as sexual arousal increases, anger increases and vice versa. Finally, for the *impulsive* rapist the motive is neither sexual nor aggressive; rather the offence is predatory and opportunistic and represents part of a more general pattern of antisocial and criminal behaviour.

In contrast, Groth *et al.* (1977) have argued that it is not sex and aggression that best describe rapists' motivations, but the use of sexuality to express power and anger. Their typology, therefore, emphasizes the psychological function of the rape for the offender, rather than the behaviour exhibited within the rape. The resulting classification system bears some similarity to the classification proposed by Cohen *et al.* and consists of four types of rapist, two of which use sexual aggression to satisfy their need for power (*power-assertive* and *power-reassurance*) and two of which use sexual aggression to express anger (*anger-retaliation* and *anger-excitation*).

The power-reassurance rapist uses the sexual assault to alleviate his feelings of sexual inadequacy and to increase his sense of masculinity. The power-assertive type, however, has more pervasive and generalized feelings of inadequacy, which are alleviated by expressing his potency and dominance within the sexual assault. The anger-retaliation rapist seeks revenge and expresses his rage towards the women in his life by degrading and humiliating his victim. Finally, the anger-excitation rapist is a sadist who obtains sexual gratification from the pain and suffering of his victim.

It can be seen that these early classification systems, or typologies, combine descriptions of types of sexual offender with motivation and the psychological significance of the offence in order to predict the type of offence each type of offender is likely to commit. Thus, it is clear how these classification systems might be applied within the context of an investigation: if the type of offence is known, it should be possible to predict the type of offender who committed it.

However, while the pioneering nature of these classification systems is acknowledged, their originators have been heavily criticized for not empirically testing the reliability and validity of the systems proposed. Furthermore, independent research by third parties has failed to find support for the reliability or validity of such systems (e.g. Prentky *et al.*, 1988). As Grubin and Kennedy (1991: 126) put it:

> All these typologies have a certain logic and face validity to them. They tend to distinguish the sexually deviant from the socially deviant and add in a few other distinctions depending on the author's prejudices. [However] there is no real reason why one should be preferred to another; nor is it clear how to decide to which class a particular rapist belongs.

MTC classifications: empirical, but inappropriate for use within criminal investigations

In 1978, in response to these criticisms and the need for a valid classification of sexual offenders, Knight, joined by Prentky in 1980, commenced a programme of empirical research at the Massachusetts Treatment Center (MTC). The outcome of this ongoing research, which was based on the previous work of Cohen, Groth and their colleagues, has been the development and refinement of two empirically driven typologies, both of which are currently in their third iteration: the MTC:CM3 classification for child molesters and the MTC:R3 classification for rapists.

The MTC:CM3 (Knight *et al.*, 1989; Knight, 1989) distinguishes offenders on a number of factors, including sexual preoccupation with children (high/low), social competence (high/low) and contact with children (high/low). Further distinctions are drawn between inter-personal high-contact offenders who are interested in children as social as well as sexual companions, and narcissistic high-contact offenders who are exclusively interested in gratifying their sexual needs. Low-contact child molesters are distinguished based on the degree of physical injury (high/low) and the degree of sadism (high/low) within their offences.

The MTC:R3 typology for rapists (see Knight and Prentky, 1990) is a motivation-driven system consisting of four primary motivations: opportunity, pervasive anger, sexual gratification and vindictiveness. Additional dimensions are used to discriminate between nine types of rapist proposed by the classification system: expressive aggression, juvenile and adult antisocial behaviour, social competence, global or pervasive anger, sadism, sexualization and offence planning (Prentky and Burgess, 2000). The individual subtypes are defined in part by the relative importance of these dimensions for each type, with each subtype having its own criteria for assigning cases, or its own 'profile' of features and characteristics against which new cases can be assessed.

In contrast to previous classification systems, these two typologies for child molesters and rapists have been refined and revised by iterative research (see Knight and Prentky, 1990). Furthermore, they have been empirically validated by research conducted within and outside the MTC (see Prentky and Burgess, 2000). Despite the progress inherent in these empirically derived typologies, criticism has been levelled against them for their emphasis on offenders' motivation, which, it is argued, cannot be objectively assessed from the scene of a crime. As Grubin and Kennedy (1991: 125) argue, motivation 'is something that can never be known, only guessed at and argued over [and thus] its incorporation fatally weakens the structures it is meant to support'.

Canter and Heritage (1990), on the other hand, concede that an analysis of motivation may be relevant in a clinical context where the patient is present and available, and may contribute to an understanding of why certain types of rapist will commit certain types of offence. However, they argue that the use of these classification systems within the context of a criminal investigation is inappropriate because 'most published conceptualizations of variations in offender behaviour have tended to combine accounts of actions in an offence with explanations of the intentions, motivations and inferred offender characteristics' (Canter and Heritage, 1990: 187) in a way that reduces the possibility for inferring one from the other, as is the aim of psychological profiling.

Indeed, studies have addressed whether the MTC:R3 classification can be used to classify rapists from an analysis of crime-scene data. For example, Knight et al. (1998) used an FBI dataset on 254 rapists incarcerated within the MTC and attempted to predict rapist classification from crime-scene behaviours that they had already shown are consistently exhibited by offenders across different offences. However, although Knight et al. reported that crime-scene behaviours were good predictors of expressive aggression and adult antisocial behaviour, variables indicative of the other dimensions that make up the MTC:R3 (e.g. sadism, offence planning and relationship with victim) did not work well at predicting classification. This research, therefore, highlights the problems inherent in attempting to use the MTC:R3 to classify an unknown suspect based on limited crime-scene data.

Criminal profiling at the FBI: progress, but lacking in scientific rigour

The problems with applying clinical classification systems to crime-scene analysis have led to the development of several classification systems designed specifically for use within the context of criminal investigations.

Agents at the FBI (Ressler *et al.*, 1986), for example, analysed 118 offences committed by 36 incarcerated sexual murderers and concluded that crime scene and offender characteristics could be divided into an organized/disorganized dichotomy. *Organized* offences were more likely to be premeditated, planned offences committed by mature, resourceful offenders who were likely to be in skilled employment. In contrast, *disorganized* offences were random, haphazard offences committed by immature, opportunistic offenders with unstable family backgrounds.

Hazelwood (1987), also at the FBI, proposed that rapists can be classified as selfish or unselfish. The *selfish* rapist uses the victim as a prop, is physically and verbally abusive, uses moderate or excessive force to achieve his aims, and is unconcerned as to the welfare or feelings of his victim. In contrast, the (pseudo) *unselfish* rapist attempts to involve the victim in the sexual act, may be complimentary, reassures his victim, and only uses minimal force in order to fulfil his fantasy of the victim's willing compliance.

Hazelwood and Burgess (1987) subsequently modified and interpreted the early Groth *et al.* (1977) typology of rapists to create a fourfold typology specifically designed for use within criminal investigations. Warren *et al.* (1991) tested the validity of this classification using data from 73 offences committed by 41 offenders, and 33 verbal, sexual and behavioural scales. They concluded that these scales could successfully be used to classify rapes according to the typology. However, Hazelwood and Burgess (1987: 176) did issue a word of warning: 'Seldom will a rapist commit a crime in a manner that will allow the analyst to classify him clearly or simply as one of the types set forth ... More commonly the investigator will be confronted with a mixture of types. It is at this point that common sense is to be applied.'

As a result, but despite this caveat, this fourfold system has become the foundation of the investigative analysis of rapists conducted by the FBI's National Center for the Analysis of Violent Crime (NCAVC). Law-enforcement agencies across the US submit unsolved rape cases to NCAVC where investigative analysts examine the case and 'supply local investigators with demographic, offence-related and lifestyle information that often proves valuable in the identification of the offender' (Warren *et al.*, 1991: 56).

More recently Hazelwood and Warren (2000) have presented a paradigm of serial sexual offenders that delineates two major categories of sexually violent offenders, although they do not describe the sample on which this paradigm is based, simply stating that it is 'derived from our criminal investigative analysis experience and research' (Hazelwood and Warren, 2000: 267). The *impulsive* offender is described as being criminally unsophisticated and opportunistic, and is characterized by his broad criminal history, high levels of physical violence and his generic sexual interests. In contrast, the *ritualistic* offender has a carefully developed set of crime-scene behaviours, a pervasive fantasy life, and a variety of paraphilic interests.

Despite the progress inherent in the development of classification systems specifically for use within criminal investigations, these criminal profiling typologies have come under severe criticism (Ainsworth, 2001). Firstly, it is argued, they are often based on clinical or intuitive classification systems, like Groth's, which themselves have been criticized for lacking in reliability and validity. Secondly, they are based only on limited samples of offenders, with no systematic procedures defined for the collection of data or classification of offenders. Thirdly, critics have questioned the scientific rigour of these classification systems, arguing that they lack reliability and validity.

For example, in relation to Ressler *et al.*'s (1986) organized/disorganized dichotomy, Muller (2000: 225) states that 'there have never been any published empirical studies on the difference between various subtypes of serial offenders'. Furthermore, Canter *et al.* (2004) tested the model by conducting an empirical analysis of 39 behaviours derived from the crime scenes of 100 serial murders in the US and reported no distinct subsets of offence characteristics related to organization or disorganization. Rather, their analysis showed that there appear to be a subset of organized behaviours that are typical of most serial murder, while disorganized behaviours occur more rarely and not simultaneously. This finding has therefore raised serious doubts about the possibility of systematically assigning serial killings to organized or disorganized types.

As a consequence of the criticisms of the FBI typologies, a scientific approach has been applied to criminal profiling resulting in the development of two alternative empirical techniques: item-to-item correlation analysis and thematic behavioural analysis.

Item-to-item correlation analysis

Rather than try to identify types of offender, item-to-item correlation studies have examined the possibility of links between single offence behaviours and offender characteristics. For example, Davies *et al.* (1998) analysed the offence behaviours and criminal records of 210 British rapists and reported some success in developing odds ratios linking specific offence behaviours with specific offender characteristics. For example, offenders who attempted to destroy traces of semen were reported to be four times more likely to have a previous conviction for a sexual crime than those who did not; offenders who took precautions not to leave fingerprints were four times more likely to have a previous conviction for burglary than offenders who took no such measures; offenders who had broken into the victim's house to commit the rape were over five times more likely to have a previous conviction for burglary than those who did not break in; and an offender who exhibited extreme violence at the crime scene was almost three and a half times more likely to have a previous conviction for a violent offence than an offender who did not exhibit extreme violence. Finally, taking a group of crime-scene actions together, Davies *et al.* reported that an offender who took precautions not to leave fingerprints, stole from the victim, forced entry and had imbibed alcohol was more than 90 per cent likely to have a previous conviction for burglary.

Salfati and Canter (1999), however, have pointed out a number of problems with the application of these findings. Firstly, offenders may not behave in a consistent manner and may instead exhibit different behaviours within different offences, which may result in different and perhaps conflicting inferences being made from the different behaviours. Secondly, item-to-item correlation analysis ignores the complex interplay between different behavioural variables, focusing only on a single behaviour at a time and ignoring the relationship between behaviours. Canter and his colleagues have therefore advocated a multidimensional analysis of the themes of offender behaviour within offences.

Thematic behavioural analysis

Thematic behavioural analysis involves examining and classifying offence behaviour at a general level, in terms of broad psychological themes, in an attempt to enable predictions of general information about an offender's background (Alison *et al.*, 2002). The premise behind this approach is that offenders exhibiting the same theme within their offences are likely to have similar background characteristics. Thus, if an analysis of solved crimes can reveal links between broad themes of offence behaviour and types of offender, an unsolved crime can be compared with this model to predict the characteristics of an unknown offender. For example, Canter and Fritzon (1998) have been successful in demonstrating how particular themes of behaviour within arson are associated with different themes within offenders' backgrounds, such as a history of psychiatric problems or a long history of criminal convictions.

Studies of sexual offences have also supported this aggregate level of research. Canter and Heritage (1990), for example, conducted a multi-variate analysis of 33 offence variables for 66 sexual offences committed by 27 offenders in the UK. As well as reporting the existence of a group of core behaviours that are common to sexual offences, they also found support for the existence of five behavioural themes (intimacy, sexuality, violence, impersonal, criminality). The *intimacy* pattern was characterized by the offender trying to establish intimacy with the victim. The *sexuality* pattern featured sexual intercourse as a crucial element of the assault. The *violence* pattern was characterized by violent treatment of the victim, while in the *impersonal* pattern the offender treated the victim as an object. The *criminality* offence pattern included criminal behaviours that were not overtly sexual in nature.

More recently, Canter *et al.* (2003) have used the same multidimensional scaling technique to investigate whether there exists a scale of differing levels of violation of the victim by the offender within a sample of 112 first offences committed by British rapists. They reported that there is a scale of violation of the victim that ranges from personal violation, through to physical violation, and finally to sexual violation of the victim. Further-more, they reported that, within these levels of violation, offences could be differentiated into 'hostile', 'controlling', 'stealing' or 'involving' themes of behaviour.

Beauregard and Proulx (2002) have also investigated whether themes of behaviour exist within sexual murder using cluster analysis to investigate the behavioural themes exhibited in the offences of 36 sexual murderers incarcerated in the province of Quebec, Canada. They reported two themes of behaviour. The *sadistic* sexual murderers planned their offences, used physical restraints, mutilated and humiliated their victims and hid their bodies. In contrast, the *anger-oriented* sexual murderers did not plan their offences, which were less likely to entail mutilation, humiliation or physical restraints and often involved the body being left at the crime scene.

While these studies have made progress by demonstrating the existence of core behaviours that are common to sexual offences and the possibility of identifying themes of offence behaviour, they failed to address the issue of linking these offence styles with offender characteristics. Häkkänen *et al.*

(2004) have taken this crucial next step in their analysis of a sample of 100 Finnish stranger rapes. First, they examined whether their sample would reveal the same thematic distinctions as Canter *et al*. (2003), but reported only three themes of offence style (hostility, theft and involvement) and not the fourth controlling theme. Second, they attempted to establish whether these themes could be linked to themes of offender characteristics. Categorizing the offender characteristics revealed four themes: conventional, psychiatric/elderly, criminal/violent and criminal/property. However, Häkkänen *et al*. were only successful in linking the theft offence style with the criminal/property offender characteristic.

Kocsis *et al*. (2002a) also attempted to link offence styles with offender characteristics in their multivariate analysis of 62 incidents of serial sexual assault committed in Australia. They reported the existence of a central cluster of behaviours that are common to all patterns of sexual rape, along with four distinct offence styles that they labelled brutality, intercourse, chaotic and ritual. Crucially, Kocsis *et al*. (2002a) were also able to identify distinct offender characteristics that were associated with each of these offence styles. For example, offenders exhibiting the *brutality* style tended to be 'relatively older, have scars and a criminal record, and they are typically in some form of conjugal relationship'. The *ritual* offenders were 'highly rational, well groomed, and mobile in the commission of their offences'. In contrast, the offender who exhibited an *intercourse* style of offending was described as 'an almost diminutive, meek individual'. Finally, offenders exhibiting the *chaotic* pattern of offending had a criminal lifestyle and 'are typically young and consequently are unlikely to have any identifiable features or social patterns that come with age' (Kocsis *et al*., 2002a: 162–164).

Kocsis *et al*. (2002b) conducted a similar analysis of the crime-scene and offence characteristics relating to 85 cases of sexual murder committed across Australia. Again, using non-linear multidimensional scaling procedures they identified a central cluster of behaviours common to sexual murder that were characterized by the three themes of intercourse, violence and premeditation. In addition, Kocsis *et al*. (2002b) identified four distinct outlying patterns of offence style (predator, fury, rape and perversion) that were each related to distinct offender characteristics. The behaviour exhibited in the *predator* offence style was violent, suggesting deliberate cruelty, and was associated with offenders who were typically older, white, well groomed, mobile, living with a partner and who collected crime literature and sexual materials. The *fury* pattern represented an unfocused, explosive obliteration of the victim, perhaps motivated by revenge or anger. While a proportion of these offenders were identified as being of a violent, mentally ill orientation, an equal proportion did not suffer from these disorders. The *rape* style of offence was less violent, with death perhaps not intended, and was often committed by an impetuous younger, non-white offender who was acquainted with his victim, or perhaps discovered a victim and acted on impulse. The *perversion* pattern was typified by extreme paraphilic and perverse activity, against younger victims who were often male, and was committed by offenders who tended to be older with bisexual or homosexual tendencies.

Further studies have reported links between particular themes of offence behaviour and personality disorder. For example, studies have reported an association between the level of physical violence exhibited within an offence and different facets of personality disorder. In particular, more violent offenders have been found to score significantly higher than less violent offenders on histrionic, narcissistic, antisocial and paranoid subscales (Proulx *et al.*, 1994; Langevin *et al.*, 1985).

Similarly, a more recent study categorized rapists as sadistic, opportunistic or anger type rapists according to their *modus operandi*, and reported substantial differences between the sadistic and the opportunistic types with respect to personality disorders. The sadistic offenders were more likely to have avoidant, schizoid and dependent tendencies, whereas the opportunistic offenders were characterized as narcissistic, paranoid and antisocial (Proulx *et al.*, 1999).

Some success has also been achieved in linking offence themes with offenders' criminal histories. House (1997), for example, used a multi-dimensional scaling technique to analyse the offence themes of 50 rapists and compared these with their criminal antecedents. The four offence themes – aggression, criminality, pseudo-intimacy and sadism – were identified, and House reported different criminal backgrounds for offenders exhibiting different themes. For example, those offenders whose crime-scene actions were primarily of a criminal nature (for example, stealing some of the victim's belongings) had the highest likelihood of previous convictions (88.9%). Perhaps surprisingly, but based only on a small sample size, a lower proportion of sadism-type rapists (55.6%) than pseudo-intimacy type rapists (69.0%) had previous convictions for violent offences. However, House notes that across the four categories of offence theme the criminal histories of the corresponding individuals varied within close boundaries only. The highest difference in percentage was found for previous deception-type offences between aggressive (26.9%) and pseudo-intimacy (51.7%) type rapists.

Thematic behavioural analysis: are its assumptions robust?

While the above studies show that thematic behavioural analysis has had some success in linking themes of offence behaviour with offender characteristics, its critics have argued that this aggregate level of analysis of offence behaviours and offender backgrounds does not provide a prediction of offender characteristics specific or narrow enough to be of use to investigations. Others have criticized the sample selection and data-collection methods used within these studies, arguing that because these profiles are averaged and generalized from limited data collected from known, apprehended criminals, they ignore those criminals who are most skilful at avoiding detection and therefore may not reflect the characteristics of offenders at large (Turvey, 2000). Most crucially, some critics have questioned the validity of the underlying assumptions of this approach to offender profiling.

Offender profiling has two underlying assumptions (Mokros and Alison, 2002; Alison et al., 2002): consistency in offender behaviour across offences, and the existence of a homology between crime-scene actions and offender characteristics. The first assumption is that an offender will exhibit similar behaviour across separate offences of the same type, or at least that the variation between the crimes of a serial offender are less than between a random selection of offences. The second assumption, homology, is that the more similar two offenders are, the more closely their crimes will resemble each other. That is, the degree of similarity of the background characteristics of two offenders will be matched by the degree of similarity of their styles of offending. Both of these assumptions have been questioned.

Several studies have found support for the assumption that offenders exhibit consistent behaviours across offences of the same type, and have shown how this consistency can be used to link crimes to a single offender (Green et al., 1976; Canter, 1995; Craik and Patrick, 1994; Grubin et al., 2001; Bennell and Canter, 2002). However, despite these successes, Alison et al. (2002) have criticized the reliance of offender profiling on the naïve trait approach to understanding personality, which assumes that 'individuals are characterized by stable and broadly generalized dispositions that endure over long periods of time and that generate consistencies in their social behaviour across a wide range of situations' (Mischel, 1990: 112).

Indeed, Alison et al. cite research that demonstrates that global trait constructs fail to accurately predict behaviour over time and across situations (Bem and Allen, 1974; Mischel, 1968). Instead, they argue that behaviour is not stable, but is influenced by the complex interplay between person and situation, which will affect an offender's behaviour from one offence to the next. Thus, discarding the context-free traditional trait approach to offender profiling, Alison et al. propose the development of a framework that takes into account the context of the offence, the role and reaction of the victim, the interaction between the person and situation, and the probabilistic relationships between behaviours and offender characteristics.

Alison *et al.* (2003) also question the homology assumption that similar types of offenders will commit offences in similar ways, citing Mokros and Alison's (2002) analysis and comparison of the crime-scene actions, demographic characteristics and criminal histories of 100 British male stranger rapists. Mokros and Alison tested whether increased similarity in offence behaviour coincided with increased similarity in background characteristics and reported that rapists who offended in a similar fashion were no more similar with respect to age, socio-demographic features or criminal record.

It appears, therefore, that while some research supports the use of thematic behavioural analysis to construct a profile of an unknown offender, other research questions the very assumptions on which it is based. While researchers continue to develop this technique and investigate the validity of its use, new approaches to suspect prioritization have been developed.

Suspect prioritization: a move towards pragmatism

New approaches to suspect prioritization have drawn on the complementary frameworks of pragmatism and research in naturalistic decision-making. In a pragmatic approach to research the goal is to address particular practical problems within a specific context; for example, the problems and issues faced by investigators within the context of a stranger sexual assault. The approach has two main emphases. Firstly, that the experience of practitioners is 'central and crucial in developing and informing the research programme' (Alison and Barrett, under review). Secondly, the importance of developing a large corpus of context-bound experiences that can be drawn upon by practitioners and academics in the face of subsequent problems. For example, a well-developed corpus can be used to extract general trends in information, and allow experienced practitioners to compare current cases with the archive and, where appropriate, apply previous experience to a current case (Fishman, 1999, 2003).

Fishman (1999) has also recommended that pragmatic research programmes are carried out using the standards of utility, feasibility, propriety and accuracy. That is, that research provides results which are realistic, useful and capable of being implemented; legally appropriate, and conforming to appropriate moral and ethical guidelines; and technically accurate and appropriate within the context of the research.

Naturalistic decision-making (NDM) research has been identified as a classic example of a pragmatic approach to practical problems (Alison and

Barrett, under review). Indeed one of its main proponents has argued that NDM research programmes are 'often informed by practical problems, as opposed to testing hypotheses derived from theories' (Klein, 1997: 12). NDM is a pragmatic approach in that it studies decision-making in the field in an attempt to understand how individuals and teams use their experience to make meaningful decisions in dynamic, uncertain and often time-pressured situations (Zsambok, 1997). In the past NDM research has focused on decision-making in contexts such as the military (Drillings and Serfaty, 1997), fire-fighting (Klein, 1999), the nuclear industry (Roth, 1997) and with commercial airlines, their pilots and crew (Orasanu, 1997). Recently however, researchers in the UK have turned their attention to an examination of police decision-making within an NDM framework (Crego and Spinks, 1997; Crego and Harris, 2002; Barrett, 2002), which has culminated in the recent establishment of the International Centre for the Study of Critical Incident Decision Making at the University of Liverpool in the UK.

Much of this research is based on Gigerenzer and Todd's (1999) proposal that much of human real-world decision-making can be modelled using fast and frugal heuristics that allow inferences to be made under constraints of limited time and knowledge. Clearly, in the context of a criminal investigation, where time is of the essence and information is scarce, such fast and frugal decision-making models that can help focus the search for an unknown offender would be extremely useful. Recent research has demonstrated a number of ways in which a pragmatic approach can be applied to suspect prioritization.

Alison et al. (2003) have discussed how Toulmin's (1958) philosophy of argument might be applied to the construction of reports for criminal investigations. 'The strength of a "Toulminian" approach lies in its ability to deconstruct arguments into their constituent parts, thus allowing for close scrutiny of the strengths and weaknesses of various aspects of the argument' (Alison et al., in press). Based on a large corpus of historical offence data, it might be claimed that an unknown offender is likely to live within 5 km of the crime scene, for example. However, with a Toulminian approach, in order to substantiate this claim, the conditions on which the claim has been developed (the *grounds*) must be stated, along with the justification for relying on these grounds (the *backing*) and the strength or certainty of the claim (the *modality*). In this example, therefore, a report using a Toulminian approach would state that the offender was likely to live within 5 km of the crime scene (*claim*) because generally rapists do not travel more than 5 km from home to offend (*grounds*) as reported by Wilson and Alison (in prepraration) (*backing*), who reported that 73.8 per cent of sexual offences were committed within 5 km of the offender's home (*modality*).

The advantages of this approach over a traditional offender profiling approach are clear. Investigators are now informed of the probabilistic nature of the offender characteristic and can assign resources accordingly, perhaps focusing their efforts on suspects living within 5 km of the crime scene, but remembering that while less likely, the offender might live outside this range. Furthermore, this fast and frugal heuristic is simple, clear and could easily be applied to assist in the prioritization of suspects within an investigation.

In his research, House (1997) used a heuristic based on the spatial and behavioural characteristics of offenders recorded in the computerized Criminal Suspect Prioritization System (CSPS) at the Criminal Behavior Analysis Unit of the Royal Newfoundland Constabulary (RNC) in Canada. This system holds details of over 10,000 arrests made between 1978 and 1997, and allows a user to search for or filter suspects based on personal information (such as age, gender or ethnicity), spatial location and criminal antecedents (such as whether the offender has previous convictions for a specified type of offence).

House (1997) illustrated the use of the CSPS to assist in the investigation of a stranger rape, reporting the existence of four behavioural themes within rape offences (aggression, criminality, pseudo-intimacy and sadism), each having links to different types of previous conviction. House therefore argued that any new rape case could be assigned to a thematic region based on the behaviours exhibited within the offence, allowing inferences to be made about the likely previous convictions of the perpetrator. The CSPS could then be used to generate a list of suspects who have the expected previous convictions, and who live within a specified geographic radius of the offence location.

Notwithstanding the criticisms levelled at the homology assumption, this study demonstrates the potential of combining geography and previous convictions to provide a heuristic for prioritising suspects. Snook et al. (in press) have argued that it would further benefit from the addition of a systematic process to allow it to be empirically tested. This process, they say, should include a definition of both the size of the search radius and the sequence in which shortlisted suspects should be prioritized.

Snook et al. developed and refined this technique of suspect prioritization using a sample of commercial armed robbery offences extracted from the CSPS. First, Snook et al. examined the previous convictions of their sample of 197 armed robbers and found that the most prevalent type of previous conviction was for property offences, with 86 per cent of offenders having this type of previous conviction, compared with 90 per cent who had a previous conviction of any sort. Next, they filtered the offenders in the CSPS by criminal career. Filtering by previous convictions for property offences reduced the number of suspects to 25 per cent of the total sample of suspects (from 10,000 to 2,597). Finally, they took a sub-sample of 36 commercial armed robberies from the CSPS, mapped each geographically, and prioritized or ranked the 2,597 suspects according to the proximity of their home address to each offence.

Snook *et al.* reported that in a third of offences the offender responsible for the robbery was identified in the first 35 ranked suspects; in two-thirds of offences the offender was ranked within the first 255 suspects, and for nearly all the offences (91 per cent) the offender was ranked within the top 771 prioritized suspects. It appears therefore that this approach to suspect prioritization has great potential for helping the police with their investigations, first by narrowing down the pool of potential suspects, and then by specifying the sequence in which the remaining suspects should be checked. Clearly, applying this particular approach to the investigation of sex offences would be of great interest.

Finally, Wilson and Alison (in preparation) applied a pragmatic approach to improving decision-making with respect to suspect prioritization in the investigation of sex offences. Drawing on Swets' (2000) proposals on enhancing diagnostic decisions, they analysed the likelihood of specified offender characteristics for a sample of 63 stranger sexual offences. First, a decision tree was constructed indicating the frequencies of certain offender characteristics, chosen because they are overt and available to a police investigation, including whether the offender: (i) lived within 5 km of the offence, (ii) had any previous convictions, (iii) was prolific, had (iv) sexual or (v) violent preconvictions, (vi) had served a custodial sentence, and (vii) was over 25 years old. The route taken through the decision tree therefore determined the resulting 'offender profile', with the base rates for these characteristics providing an indication of the route most likely to be correct. For example, they reported that 73.8 per cent of offences were committed within 5 km of the offender's residence, and 49.2 per cent of offences were committed by an offender with preconvictions who lived within 5 km of the offence. Of those offences committed by an offender with preconvictions, they report that 68.4 per cent were committed by prolific offenders who had been convicted of more than four offences previously, 56.8 per cent were committed by offenders who had a preconviction for a violent offence and 81.0 per cent were committed by offenders who did not have a preconviction for a sexual offence.

Already, these results could clearly be used as the basis for fast and frugal decision-making about the likelihood that an unknown offender lives within a certain distance from the crime scene and has certain preconvictions. However, Wilson and Alison also used logistic regression analyses to establish whether the presence of particular offence behaviours could provide further support for particular decisions regarding the likely characteristics of the perpetrator of an offence. They reported that an offender using a 'con' approach towards his victim was four times more likely to live further than 5 km from the crime scene than an offender not using a con approach. In relation to previous convictions, Wilson and Alison reported that an offender making sexual comments was four times more likely to have previous convictions, and an offence in which there was evidence of planning was up to ten times (depending on the sub-sample and regression model used) more likely to have been committed by a prolific offender. Furthermore, an offence involving vaginal or anal penetration was between three and 21 times more likely to have been committed by a prolific offender than an offence not involving penetration. Looking at specific preconvictions, it was reported that an offender uttering words to the victim prior to the attack was five to ten times more likely to have sexual preconvictions than an offender not speaking prior to the attack, and an offender subjecting his victim to anal intercourse was six times more likely to have a preconviction for a violent offence than an offender not committing anal intercourse.

Wilson and Alison also looked at whether behaviours exhibited within the offence could indicate whether the offender was likely to have served a custodial sentence. They reported that an offence that appeared to have been planned was three to four times more likely to have been committed by an offender who had served a custodial sentence. Further, an offence in which a con approach was used towards the victim was four to five times more likely to have been committed by an offender who had not served a custodial sentence.

Finally, addressing the question of the age of the unknown offender, Wilson and Alison reported that an offence in which the offender had been drinking was approximately six times more likely to have been committed by an offender over the age of 25. Further, an offence in which the offender spoke words to the victim prior to the attack was three to five times more likely to have been committed by an offender over the age of 25. Conversely, an offence in which the victim had been drinking was four to five times more likely to have been committed by an offender who was under 25 years old.

Suspect prioritization: the future?

This chapter has shown how approaches to suspect prioritization in the investigation of stranger sex offences have developed over the past 50 years: from the use of clinical classification systems to the development of criminal profiling techniques and typologies, to the recent emphasis on pragmatism.

Along the way, much has been learnt about the essential features of any classification system designed to assist in the prioritization of suspects. First, the system must be specifically designed for use within investigations, not borrowed from another discipline. Second, it must be based on large and comprehensive samples of offenders and offences. Third, it must be based on crime-scene and offender data that is overt, reliable and available to an investigation; for example, age, sex, location, criminal record, but not motivation or fantasy. Fourth, a classification system must be supported by empirical evidence of its reliability and validity. Fifth, it should be transparent, indicating the premise on which it is based, and the probabilistic nature of its predictions. Finally, it must be practical, easy to use and intuitive, designed specifically for use within investigations by investigators.

These requirements highlight a need for academics and practitioners to engage in a collaborative approach to the collection of offence and offender data, and the construction and application of classification and decision-making systems within police investigations (Alison et al., 2004). Indeed, recent research based on a pragmatic approach has demonstrated the practical application and usefulness to an investigation of fast and frugal decision-making techniques, providing assistance both with suspect prioritization and the concomitant issue of the organization and allocation of police resources.

References

Ainsworth, P.B. (2001) Offender Profiling and Crime Analysis. Cullompton: Willan.

Alison, L.J. and Barrett, E.C. (under review) Pragmatic research in criminal investigative decision making: Projects from the International Centre for the Study of Critical Decision Making.

Alison, L.J., Bennell, C., Mokros, A. and Ormerod, D. (2002) 'The personality paradox in offender profiling: A theoretical review of the processes involved in deriving background characteristics from crime scene actions', Psychology, Public Policy and Law, 8: 115–35.

Alison, L.J., Smith, M.D., Eastman, O. and Lee, R. (2003) 'Toulmin's philosophy of argument and its relevance to offender profiling', Psychology, Crime and Law, 9 (2): 173–83.

Alison, L.J., West, A. and Goodwill, A. (2004) 'The academic and the practitioner: Pragmatists' views of offender profiling', Psychology, Public Policy and Law, 10 (1–2): 71–101.

Amir, M. (1971) Patterns in Forcible Rape. Chicago: University of Chicago Press.

Barrett, E.C. (2002) *Towards a theory of investigative situation assessment: An examination of the psychological mechanisms underlying the construction of situation models in criminal investigations.* Unpublished Master's dissertation, University of Liverpool, Liverpool, UK.

Beauregard, E. and Proulx, J. (2002) 'Profiles in the offending process of nonserial sexual murderers', *International Journal of Offender Therapy and Comparative Criminology*, 46 (4): 386–99.

Bem, D.J. and Allen, A. (1974) 'On predicting some of the people some of the time: The search for cross-situational consistencies in behavior', *Psychological Review*, 81: 506–20.

Bennell, C. and Canter, D. (2002) 'Linking commercial burglaries by modus operandi: Tests using regression and ROC analysis', *Science and Justice*, 42 (3).

Canter, D.V. (1995) 'Psychology of offender profiling', in R. Bull and D. Carson (eds), *Handbook of Psychology in Legal Contexts* (pp. 343–355). Chichester: Wiley.

Canter, D.V., Bennell, C., Alison, L.J. and Reddy, S. (2003) 'Differentiating sex offences: a behaviorally based thematic classification of stranger rapes', *Behavioral Sciences and the Law*, 21: 157–74.

Canter, D.V. and Heritage, R. (1990) 'A multivariate model of sexual offence behaviour: developments in offender profiling', *Journal of Forensic Psychiatry*, 1 (2): 185–212.

Canter, D.V. and Fritzon, K. (1998) 'Differentiating arsonists: A model of firesetting actions and characteristics', *Journal of Criminal and Legal Psychology*, 3: 73–96.

Canter, D.V., Alison, L.J., Alison, E. and Wentink, N. (2004) 'The organized/ disorganized typology of serial murder: Myth or model?', *Psychology, Public Policy and Law*, 10 (3): 293–320.

Cohen, M.L., Seghorn, T.K. and Calmas, W. (1969) 'Sociometric study of the sex offender', *Journal of Abnormal Psychology*, 74 (2): 249–55.

Cohen, M.L., Seghorn, T.K., Boucher, R. and Mehegan, J. (1979) *The sexual offender against children.* Paper presented at the meeting of the Association for Professional Treatment of Offenders, Boston.

Craik, M. and Patrick, A. (1994) 'Linking serial offences', *Policing*, 10: 181–87.

Crego, J. and Harris, C. (2002) 'Training decision making by team based simulation', in R. Flin and K. Arbuthnot (eds), *Incident Command: Tales from the hot seat*. Aldershot: Ashgate.

Crego, J. and Spinks, T. (1997) 'Critical incident management simulation', in R. Flin, E. Salas, M. Strub and L. Martin (eds), *Decision Making Under Stress*. Aldershot: Ashgate.

Davies, A., Wittebrood, K. and Jackson, J.L. (1998) *Predicting the criminal record of a stranger rapist.* Special Interest Series: Paper 12. London: Home Office, Police Research Group.

Drillings, M. and Serfaty, D. (1997) 'Naturalistic decision making in command and control', in C.E. Zsambok and G. Klein (eds), *Naturalistic Decision Making*. Mahwah, NJ: Lawrence Erlbaum Associates.

Fishman, D.B. (1999) *The Case for Pragmatic Psychology.* New York: New York University Press.

Fishman, D.B. (2003) 'Background on the "Psycholegal Lexis Proposal": Exploring the potential of a systematic case study database in forensic psychology', *Psychology, Public Policy and Law*, 9 (3–4): 267–74.

Fitch, J.H. (1962) 'Men convicted of sexual offences against children', *British Journal of Criminology*, 3: 18–37.

Gebhard, P., Gagnon, J., Pomeroy, W. and Christenson, C. (1965) *Sex Offenders: An analysis of types*. London: Heinemann.

Gigerenzer, G. and Todd, P. M. (1999) *Simple Heuristics that Make us Smart*. New York: Oxford University Press.

Green, E.J., Booth, C.E. and Biderman, M.D. (1976) 'Cluster analysis of burglary M/Os', *Journal of Police Science and Administration*, 4: 382–88.

Groth, A.N. (1981) *Sexual Offending against Children*. Distributed by Forensic Mental Health Associates, Webster, MA 01570.

Groth, N., Burgess, A. and Holmstrom, L. (1977) 'Rape, power, anger and sexuality', *American Journal of Psychiatry*, 134: 1239–243.

Grubin, D., Kelly, P. and Brundson, C. (2001) *Linking serious sexual assaults through behaviour*. Research Study 215. London: Home Office.

Grubin, D.H. and Kennedy, H.G. (1991) 'The classification of sexual offenders', *Criminal Behaviour and Mental Health*, 1: 123–29.

Guttmacher, M.S. (1951) *Sex Offenses: The problem, causes and prevention*. New York: Norton.

Guttmacher, M.S. and Weihofen, H. (1952) *Psychiatry and the Law*. New York: Norton.

Häkkänen, H., Lindlöf, P. and Santilla, P. (2004) 'Crime scene actions and offender characteristics in a sample of Finnish stranger rapes', *Journal of Investigative Psychology and Offender Profiling*, 1: 17–32.

Hazelwood, R.R. (1987) 'Analyzing the rape and profiling the offender', in R.R. Hazelwood and A.W. Burgess (eds), *Practical Aspects of Rape Investigation: A multidisciplinary approach* (pp. 169–199). New York: Elsevier.

Hazelwood, R.R. and Burgess, A.W. (1987) *Practical Aspects of Rape Investigation: A multidisciplinary approach*. New York: Elsevier.

Hazelwood, R.R. and Warren, J. (2000) 'The sexually violent offender: Impulsive or ritualistic?', *Aggression and Violent Behavior*, 5 (3): 267–79.

House, J.C. (1997) 'Towards a practical application of offender profiling: The RNC's criminal suspect prioritization system', in J.L. Jackson and D.A. Bekerian (eds), *Offender Profiling: Theory, research and practice* (pp.177–190). Chichester: John Wiley and Sons.

Howells, K. (1981) 'Adult sexual interest in children: Considerations relevant to theories of aetiology', in M. Cook and K. Howells (eds), *Adult Sexual Interest in Children* (pp.55–94). New York: Academic Press.

Klein, G. (1997) 'The current status of the naturalistic decision making framework', in R. Flin, E. Salas, M. Strub, and L. Martin (eds), *Decision Making Under Stress: Emerging themes and applications* (pp. 11–26). Aldershot: Ashgate Publishing.

Klein, G. (1999) *Sources of Power: How people make decisions*. Cambridge, MA: MIT Press.

Knight, R.A. (1989) 'An assessment of the concurrent validity of a child molester typology', *Journal of Interpersonal Violence*, 4 (2): 131–50.

Knight, R.A. and Prentky, R.A. (1990) 'Classifying sexual offenders: The development and corroboration of taxonomic models', in W.L. Marshall, D.R. Laws and H.E. Barbaree (eds), *The Handbook of Sexual Assault:*

Issues, Theories and Treatment of the Offender (pp. 23–52). New York: Plenum Press.

Knight, R.A., Carter, D.L. and Prentky, R.A. (1989) 'A system for the classification of child molesters: Reliability and application', *Journal of Interpersonal Violence*, 4: 3–23.

Knight, R.A., Warren, J.I., Reboussin, R. and Soley, B.J. (1998) 'Predicting rapist type from crime-scene variables', *Criminal Justice and Behavior*, 25 (1): 46–80.

Kocsis, L. (1982) 'Posudzovanie sexualnych delikventov', in *Forenzne Aspekty Sexuality, Sexualita zeny*. Zbornik referatov: Kosice, September: 186–94.

Kocsis, R.N., Cooksey, R.W. and Irwin, H.J. (2002a) 'Psychological profiling of offender characteristics from crime behaviors in serial rape offences', *International Journal of Offender Therapy and Comparative Criminology*, 46 (2): 144–69.

Kocsis, R.N., Cooksey, R.W. and Irwin, H.J. (2002b) 'Psychological profiling of sexual murders: An empirical model', *International Journal of Offender Therapy and Comparative Criminology*, 46 (5): 532–54.

Kopp, S.B. (1962) 'The character structure of sex offenders', *American Journal of Psychotherapy*, 16: 64–70.

Langevin, R., Paitich, D. and Russon, A.E. (1985) 'Are rapists sexually anomalous, aggressive, or both?', in R. Langevin (ed.), *Erotic Preference, Gender Identity, and Aggression in Men: New research studies* (pp. 17–38). Hillsdale, NJ: Erlbaum.

Lloyd, C. and Walmsey, R. (1989) *Changes in Rape Offences and Sentencing*. Home Office Research Study: Number 105. London: HMSO.

McCaghy, C.H. (1967) *Child Molesters: A study of their careers as deviants*. New York: Holt, Rinehart and Winston.

Mischel, W. (1968) *Personality and Assessment*. New York: Wiley.

Mischel, W. (1990) 'Personality dispositions revisited and revised: A view after three decades', in L. Pervin (ed.), *Handbook of Personality: Theory and research* (2nd ed, pp. 111–134). New York: Guilford Press.

Mokros, A. and Alison, L.J. (2002) 'Is offender profiling possible? Testing the predicted homology of crime scene actions and background characteristics in a sample of rapists', *Legal and Criminological Psychology*, 7 (1): 25–43.

Muller, D.A. (2000) 'Criminal profiling: Real science or just wishful thinking?', *Homicide Studies*, 4 (3): 234–64.

Mulvihill, D., Tumin, M. and Curtis, L. (1969) *Crimes of Violence*. Staff report submitted to the National Commission on the Causes and Prevention of Violence (Volumes 11–13). Washington DC: US Government Printing Office.

Orasanu, J. (1997) 'Stress and naturalistic decision making: Strengthening the weak links', in R. Flin, E. Salas, M. Strub and L. Martin (eds), *Decision Making Under Stress: Emerging themes and applications*. Aldershot: Ashgate.

Prentky, R. and Burgess, A. (2000) *Forensic Management of Sexual Offenders*. New York: Kluwer Academic/Plenum Publishers.

Prentky, R.A., Knight, R.A. and Rosenberg, R. (1988) 'Validation analyses on the MTC taxonomy for rapists: Disconfirmation and reconceptualization', in R.A. Prentky and V. Quinsey (eds), *Human Sexual Aggression: Current perspectives* (pp. 21–40). New York: New York Academy of Sciences.

Proulx, J., Aubut, J., Perron, L. and McKibben, A. (1994) 'Troubles de la personnalité et viol: Implications théoriques et cliniques' ('Personality disorders and violence: Theoretical and clinical implications'), *Criminologie*, 27, 33–53.

Proulx, J., St-Yves, M., Guay, J. P. and Ouimet, M. (1999) 'Les aggresseurs sexuels de femmes: Scénarios délictuels et troubles de la personnalité' ('Sexual aggressors of women: Offence scenarios and personality disorders'), in J. Proulx, M. Cusson, and M. Ouimet (eds), *Les Violences Criminelles* (pp. 157–185). Sainte-Foy, Quebec, Canada: Les Presses de l'Université Laval.

Rada, R.T. (1978) 'Classification of the rapist', in R.T. Rada (ed.), *Clinical Aspects of the Rapist* (pp. 117–132). New York: Grune & Stratton.

Ressler, R.K., Burgess, A.W., Douglas, J.E., Hartman, C.R. and D'Agostino, R.B. (1986) 'Sexual killers and their victims: Identifying patterns through crime scene analysis', *Journal of Interpersonal Violence*, 1 (3): 288–308.

Rist, K. (1979) 'Incest: Theoretical and clinical views', *American Journal of Orthopsychiatry*, 49, 680–91.

Roth, E.M. (1997) 'Analysing decision making in process control: Multi-disciplinary approaches to understanding and aiding human performance in complex tasks', in C.E. Zsambok and G. Klein (eds), *Naturalistic Decision Making*. Mahwah, NJ: Lawrence Erlbaum Associates Inc.

Salfati, C.G. and Canter, D.V. (1999) 'Differentiating stranger murders: Profiling offender characteristics from behavioural styles', *Behavioral Sciences and the Law*, 17: 391–406.

Snook, B., Wright, M., Alison, L.J. and House, J.C. (in press) 'Searching for a needle in a needlestack: Combining criminal careers and journey-to-crime research for criminal suspect prioritization'.

Summit, R.C. and Kryso, J. (1978) 'Sexual abuse of children: A clinical spectrum', *American Journal of Orthopsychiatry*, 48: 237–51.

Swanson, D.W. (1971) 'Who violates children sexually?', *Medical Aspects of Human Sexuality*, 5: 184–97.

Swets, J.A. (2000) 'Enhancing diagnostic decisions', in T. Connolly, H.R. Arkes and K.R. Hammond (eds), *Judgement and Decision Making: An interdisciplinary reader* (2nd edn). Cambridge: Cambridge University Press.

Toulmin, S.E. (1958) *The Uses of Argument*. Cambridge: Cambridge University Press.

Turvey, B.E. (2000) 'Deductive criminal profiling: Comparing applied methodologies between inductive and deductive profiling techniques', *Policja: Kwartalnik Kadry Kierowniczej Policji* (*Quarterly of Police Management*, Poland), 4.

Warren, J.I., Reboussin, R., Hazelwood, R.R. and Wright, J.A. (1991) 'Prediction of rapist type and violence from verbal, physical, and sexual scales', *Journal of Interpersonal Violence*, 6 (1): 55–67.

Weinberg, S. (1955) *Incest Behavior*. New York: Citadel Press.

Wilson, G.E. and Alison, L.J. (in preparation) Suspect Prioritisation: Improving decision making in the investigation of sex offences.

Zsambok, C.E. (1997) 'Naturalistic decision making: Where are we now?' in C.E. Zsambok and G. Klein (eds), *Naturalistic Decision Making*. Mahwah, NJ: Lawrence Erlbaum.

Chapter 5

The range of issues in crime analysis

Nina Cope[1]

What does crime analysis mean in the police?

Increasingly, the analysis of information and intelligence has become routine in the police, influenced by a number of reform agendas, policing styles and strategic interventions, which require crime problems to be identified so that resources can be allocated effectively. In order to meet this demand, the role of the crime analyst has developed, somewhat inconsistently, across police forces and law-enforcement agencies. If analysis is defined as the process of deconstructing problems in order to understand them, it follows that crime analysis refers to the application of this process to crime data. A plethora of definitions of analysis varyingly refer to the function of detecting patterns and linkages in data (Canter, 2000; Osborne and Wernicke, 2003), while also stressing the importance of the interpretation of information (Cope, 2003) so that analysis is better able to support police or judicial interventions (Gill, 2000), and the development of operational or preventative strategies (Tilley, 2002*a*). O'Shea and Nicholls (2003), based on their study of crime analysis in the United States, describe three functions of police crime analysis: firstly, to assess the nature and distribution of crime in order to efficiently allocate resources and personnel; secondly, to identify crime–suspect correlations to assist investigations; and finally, to identify the conditions that facilitate crime and incivility so that policy-makers may make informed decisions about prevention approaches. This highlights the extent to which crime analysis supports both reactive and proactive policing, where *reactive* refers to analysis that supports police activity after an incident has occurred. This includes analysis through to profiling, which is developed to support an investigation. *Proactive* refers to analysis which is developed to support 'strategic, future-orientated, targeted approaches ... [which focus] upon the identification, analysis and "management" of persisting and developing "problems" or "risks"' (Maguire, 2000: 316).

Is what we do crime analysis?

Analysts will frequently work within analytical or intelligence units and support operational sections by researching information, analysing data and disseminating intelligence for police officers' use. An analyst will be required to read crime and intelligence reports in order to track and link patterns in the data to identify persistent problems or offenders and link series of crimes. Information technology and software packages, including geographical information systems, support crime analysts in retrieving and presenting information. The complexity of defining crime analysis in an increasingly multifaceted law-enforcement environment emerges when considering the variety of functions to which analysis is applied, and the range of outcomes it is expected to deliver in the context of policing. Fundamentally, analysis in policing is not simply about analysing information about crime, but rather the term 'crime analysis' is used more generically to refer to the process of researching, sorting, reviewing, presenting and interpreting information and intelligence about a range of policing problems. Analysts who work in the police may have a number of different titles, including: intelligence, performance, investigative or strategic, that aim to capture the full scope of their role or the purpose to which their work is applied.

Researching the variety of types of crime analysis reveals the complexity of its function in supporting police work. Osborne and Wernicke (2003) refer to six types of crime analysis: tactical, involving analysing current crime problems; strategic, focusing on longer-term problems; administrative, providing summary data on statistics and trends; investigative; profiling suspects and victims; intelligence, focusing on organised crime where problems are already known; and operations, which examines the use of resources. Analysis is defined by both its function and outcome, such as strategic analysis where the aim is to support the development of strategy, and by the type of information used, such as intelligence analysis. This chapter introduces five approaches in analysis:

- Strategic analysis. Reviews the trends and patterns of crime in context to support planning and policy decisions.

- Tactical analysis. Reviews current crime problems to support pro-active operational activity; can include crime pattern analysis or network analysis.

- Investigative analysis. Reviews information and intelligence associated with an investigation; can include profiling of suspects and victims.

- Performance analysis. Reviews performance data, in relation to crime and the operation of the organization to highlight areas that require further focus.

- Operational [business] analysis. Provides analysis of the use of resources in the organization; can include information on deployment and resource allocation.

These approaches are interdependent on one another. For example, strategic analysis will draw on intelligence developed by all the approaches, as it will require an understanding of current crime problems and the nature of investigations that have been undertaken to review the trends in crime. The use of performance and business analysis will also be critical as information on where resources need to be allocated to achieve targets, and how resources are currently used, will be crucial for making informed planning decisions.

Recently I was involved in a meeting attended by a number of practising analysts who worked for various law-enforcement agencies in the UK. The discussion moved to the development of academic literature in the field of crime analysis and a general consensus emerged that the literature did not capture the role they and their colleagues actually performed – something was missing. In developing this chapter I revisited this discussion, along with my own experiences of working and researching in the police, to consider what current academic debates fail to address in relation to analysts in the police. My thoughts focused on the extent to which the literature captures the rationale, scope and function of analysis in policing. I also considered the factors which influence the current and future demand for the role of the analyst, and how the role is currently operationalized in police forces. Finally, my attention turned to a vision for analysis in policing, and the factors that might support analysis achieving its potential.

This chapter discusses current and potential future developments in crime analysis in order to provide an introduction to crime analysis in police work. The first section introduces intelligence-led policing, which is widely associated with creating the foundation for the development of systematic crime analysis in police forces. The chapter moves on to outline the reforms in law enforcement which are responsible for sustaining the demand for crime analysis in policing. In light of these developments, I offer my thoughts on potential developments in crime analysis to contribute to a vision for the future.

Crime analysis and intelligence-led policing: a current view

The development of intelligence-led approaches to police work offered an alternative to the traditional 'reactive' model of investigation, where the police implemented strategies to identify suspects after an offence had been committed. The number of offences that remained unsolved raised questions about the effectiveness of such an approach for reducing crime. A seminal report undertaken by the Audit Commission (1993) acknowledged inefficiency of so-called 'fire brigade' approaches to policing (Maguire, 2000) and laid the foundations for a more proactive style of intervention. It emphasized the potential benefit to the police of focusing resources on the small proportion of recidivist offenders who committed a high proportion of offences. To enable this approach, intelligence-led policing advocates the targeting, gathering, analysis, and dissemination of information (Gill, 1998a), which is used to inform decisions about the prioritization of problems and allocation of resources. Unlike other approaches to policing, such as community policing or problem-solving, an intelligence-led approach does not focus on developing a philosophy of policing. However, its proactive emphasis is associated with the requirement on criminal justice agencies to develop approaches to managing risk, especially within the late modern society, where fear and insecurity about crime is increasingly endemic (Maguire, 2000; Garland, 2001; Johnston and Shearing, 2003). Intelligence-led policing substitutes debates about the function of policing with a focus on the delivery of efficient and effective police services (Tilley, 2003).

The National Intelligence Model (NIM) (National Criminal Intelligence Service, 2000) has provided a framework for the implementation of intelligence-led policing in the UK. The NIM has also supported the development of a more systematic process of crime analysis. The NIM aims to 'rationalise and systematise the ways in which the police service handles information and makes key decisions about the deployment of resources' (John and Maguire, 2003). Fundamentally, the NIM organizes policing into three levels:

- level 1: local, covering a basic command unit;
- level 2: cross-border and force level;
- level 3: national and international.

The aim of the process is not only to develop smarter policing within the levels, but also to ensure that the intelligence exchange and resource allocation are managed between the level. The core components of the NIM address the key stages of the intelligence cycle: data collection, analysis, prioritization and dissemination, to enable the police to manage resources at both a tactical and strategic level. Data collection and development are covered by the guidelines on *system products*, including the information technology that stores intelligence; *knowledge products*, including the legislation that governs the collection and use of intelligence; *source assets*, which include the protocols for gathering and managing covert intelligence; and *people assets*, which outline standards for those who work in the intelligence field, including crime analysts.

Crime analysts will use a range of techniques to produce reports or products for use by the police. The techniques are powerful methodologies for exploring patterns in data, frequently supported by the development of information technology, including geographic information systems, which enable analysts to represent data patterns in a mode that can be easily communicated and understood. The strengths and limitations of information technology and analytical techniques have been discussed elsewhere (for example, Cope, 2003; Peterson, 1994) and are not the focus of this chapter. A core aim of the NIM is to support standardization of analytical and intelligence products across police forces and other associated law-enforcement agencies. It aims to provide guidance on core analytical products and techniques which inform standard intelligence products that are developed to support decision-making (see summary in Table 5.1).

The intelligence products inform the tasking and co-ordinating group (TCG) which is responsible for prioritizing, actioning and disseminating the outcome of crime analysis. The TCG process operates at both a strategic and a tactical level. The strategic meeting is convened every three or six months and is informed by the strategic assessment. It focuses on developing the priorities in line with local and national objectives. The outcome of the meeting is the *control strategy*, which in simple terms acts as a plan to capture the activities of the policing level in relation to intelligence, prevention and enforcement. The tactical meeting is convened more regularly. It is informed by the tactical assessment and aims to target offenders, manage hot-spots, investigate linked series offences and apply preventative measures.

Table 5.1   Summary of NIM analytical techniques and products and intelligence products

NIM analytical techniques and products	Description
Crime pattern analysis	The analysis of patterns of crime, either spatial, linked series, or general trends.
Network analysis	The analysis of offenders and their activities and relationships
Criminal business profile	A profile of the *modus operandi* of criminal business enterprises
Demographic and social trend analysis	A review of the broader contextual factors and how they impact on crime
Market profile	A profile of a crime market, including details of the offenders, geography and assets exchanged
Operational intelligence assessment	To an ongoing review of intelligence throughout an operation
Target profile	A profile of an individual, including activities and associates
Results analysis	An assessment of the impact of activity to understand what works to inform decision-making
Risk analysis	A review of the risks associated with individuals or problems to assess the imperative to intervene

NIM intelligence products	Description
Strategic assessment	A strategic overview of performance and policing problems in context that forecasts trends to inform planning and policy development. Informs the development of a control strategy.
Tactical assessment	A short-term review of problems with recommendations for activity based on the tactical menu
Problem profile	A detailed analysis of a problem, either crime series or hot-spot, to inform targeting decisions
Subject profile	A detailed analysis of an individual, developed to inform targeting decisions

Sources: NCIS, 2000; Cope, 2003; John and Maguire, 2003).

Case Study 1
Some Analytical Techniques in Action

The Technique/Product: Network Analysis
This is a widely used technique for assessing the association between suspects and victims.

The Example: Telephone Network Analysis
During a house search the police retrieved both Class A drugs and firearms. Three men were found residing at the property. The police also found substantial telephone paraphernalia at the address. The analyst was commissioned to explore possible linkages between eight suspects, from both the UK and abroad, based on their use of telephones in the preceding year. Based on the analysis of 19 phones the analyst inferred ownership of five phone numbers and proved an association between suspects based on the calling patterns. All call schedules were accepted as evidence in the conviction of the suspects.

The Technique/Product: Subject Profile
A subject profile case uses a range of different analytical techniques but aims to capture the relevant information associated with intervals.

The Example
Source information highlighted an identified threat from an individual who was a member of an organization which held politically extreme views. The intelligence was evaluated as reliable. The individual has threatened to undertake an organized attack on a religious centre. The intelligence was passed to an analyst who was instructed to develop a more detailed profile of the individual and known associates. The analyst undertook a detailed search of all intelligence databases to develop a profile of the suspect. This included detailed network analysis of known associates who were affiliated with the political group and were suspects in the attack. The analyst continued to develop the profiles as intelligence was developed by covert sources. The suspect was apprehended prior to the incident.

The Impact of Analysis
Case study 1 highlights the extent to which analysis can:

1. demonstrate linkages and association between suspects

2. support the detailed profiling of individuals to support proactive interventions

3. provide a scanning function to identify crime series, where previously incidents were perceived as discrete.

The National Criminal Intelligence Service (NCIS) has supported the implementation of the NIM by providing minimum standards to be attained by police forces. The standards focus on both the infrastructure and the processes required to support intelligence-led policing. While the impetus and impact of the NIM in the longer term has yet to be evaluated, currently implementation is driven by the UK Home Office and the Association of Chief Police Officers (ACPO), establishing it as a national programme of police reform. This centralized approach to implementation is critical if the NIM is to realize its aim of standardising practice and facilitating the management of intelligence information at local, force, regional and national levels.

Despite the national commitment to the NIM, its implementation has met with key challenges. John and Maguire (2003), in their evaluation of the roll-out of the NIM, found that the detailed definitions and guidance necessary for supporting the model's standardization agenda were not fully developed beyond the initial publication of the model, which simply provided a conceptual framework. Furthermore, understanding of the core processes of the model was limited and frequently confined to those working directly in the intelligence field. This lack of engagement in intelligence-led policing was also reflected in a study of intelligence-led policing in two UK police forces, where Cope et al. (2001) found the perception of intelligence units as 'black holes', where information went in but little of benefit came out, reinforced a lack of understanding about the processes of the NIM. Broader issues associated with the operation of policing also contributed to the difficulty associated with implementing an intelligence-led approach, including the priority of informal information sharing over the formal recording of intelligence (Gill, 1998b), which in turn influenced the potential for information systems to store quality data that could be retrieved and analysed (Ratcliffe, 2002). A further critical issue relates to the extent to which the policing environment supports analysis or understands the role of the analyst and is ready to accept the implications it may have on police practice, including testing the validity of experiential knowledge, and through the tasking process, limiting officers' discretion to take action (Cope, 2004).

Despite the difficulties associated with developing an intelligence-led approach, the explicit role for analysts and the framework for analytical products within the National Intelligence Model has assured the role for analysis in police work. Arguably, as a number of police reforms demand analysed information, there will be a need for the scope of intelligence and analysis to be broadened. The next section explores how developments in the police continue to support the demand for analysis and influence the scope and the range of uses to which it is applied.

Analysing demand: the impact of developments in policing on crime analysis

The future demand for analysts in the police is integrally linked to reform agendas that have increased the flow and reliance on information in order to 'get the job done'. All policing approaches, from community, neighbourhood or reassurance policing (e.g. the COPS programme), problem-solving (e.g. POP) and COMPSTAT, rely on information to progress effectively, as Grieve (2004: 34) succinctly notes: 'intelligence development has been a positive evolution … designed to produce evidence in specific cases but also in recognition of the value of routinely gathered information'. This chapter does not have space to allow for a detailed discussion of the definition or elements of each of the models;[2] however, I argue that all the approaches are driven by a similar impetus for change which was basically 'a call on the police to be less reactive and more proactive … and … were based on a premise that policing can be and needs to be improved' (Tilley, 2003: 311). Furthermore, the changes share core characteristics, and this in turn influences the demand for analysis to support police work. I will focus on three factors which continue to provide the impetus and infrastructure to support the development of analysis. The first relates to the rationalization of police resources and a requirement to understand what works. A further issue is a more acute emphasis on performance, which has increased the need for clearly defined objectives and improved accountability for the delivery of police services and performance. Finally, the development of information technologies and system packages which facilitate the storing, searching and retrieval of information has been crucial in supporting the development of analysis.

Rationalized resources and understanding what works

A sustained demand for analysed information to inform the allocation of resources can be related to the ongoing 'rationalization of policing', which asserts that the police do not have sufficient resources to deal with the demand for their services (Manning, 2001). Furthermore, criminal justice agencies are increasingly under pressure to provide 'best value' in providing their delivery of services to the public. Crime analysis assists this agenda by enabling large volumes of data to be processed. Analysis also supports the visualization of crime problems to provide an evidence base to inform tasking decisions, as fundamentally, 'the analyst's role is to construct an image of the criminal environment and convey that picture to decision-makers' (Ratcliffe, 2004: 9).

Implicit in the agenda to rationalize resources and deliver services which are value for public money is the need to build an understanding of policing problems and the impact of police resources. The development of evidence-based approaches is essential if the delivery of policing is to become more effective. Sherman (1998: 3–4) summarizes evidence-based policing as 'the use of the best available research on the outcomes of police work to implement guidelines and evaluate agencies, units and officers. Put more simply, [it] uses research to guide practice and evaluate practitioners.' While the requirement for evaluation is not contested, the complexity of developing rigorous evaluations in the context of crime and policing (Tilley, 2002b) and the skills and ability of police organizations to develop research (Ratcliffe, 2002) and systematically integrate the knowledge derived from it (Ekblom, 2002) is more debatable. Crime analysis can certainly contribute to the development of research in police forces because, in its simplest form, the process provides the opportunity to define problems and monitor the impact of interventions.

Performance-focused, clarity of objectives and accountability for delivery

An increased pressure on the police to enhance performance can be tracked over a number of decades and is associated with a number of inquiries into police practice and police reforms which have given the government the authority to set national objectives and targets for police forces (Hallam, 2000). An increasingly centralist-driven performance agenda has coincided with a focus on crime control and reduced autonomy across criminal justice agencies, requiring the police to be more responsive to political and community concerns in terms of focus and policy development (Garland, 2001).

The focus on performance is demonstrated by the development of the Policing Performance and Assessment Framework and the Police Standards Unit, as part of the Home Office in the UK. In the US, the approach of COMPSTAT articulated an explicit relationship between gathering statistics to inform the allocation of resources, where effectiveness relied on knowledge of crime problems and how resources were being used. Criticisms of this performance approach have focused on the narrowness of its scope, in that what was measurable became measured (Garland, 1996), leading targets to be essentially quantitative in nature. Furthermore, there was evidence that a focus on performance indicators had a negative impact on service delivery, as police forces concentrated on achieving targets, rather than the quality and outcomes of policing (Hallam, 2000).

However the performance culture may develop to capture the qualitative elements of policing, the demand for measuring performance is unlikely to decline as governments aim to justify the costs of delivering services to the public. Analysis is crucial for understanding performance

Case Study 2
Reactive to Proactive: Analysis and the Investigation
of Serious Crime

Intelligence Development
Throughout 2000 an increase in violent crime was developing among
an ethnic community. Analysts were tasked to produce a problem
profile. However, as the problem was emerging, an initial scan of the
available information highlighted the extent to which the computer
systems were not organized to capture intelligence on the community or the suspects. No intelligence was available. The first stage
of analysis produced recommendations to develop an intelligence
strategy. Crime and intelligence flags, which facilitate the searching
and retrieval of relevant information, were developed. The analysis
also suggested the targeting of open and closed intelligence sources,
to improve the information so that the scale and nature of the
problem could be better understood.

Linking the Issues
The severity of violence gradually increased, so that within a period
of 18 months, the police had responded to seven murders. The
investigations indicated the extent to which the escalating violence
was gang related. As the intelligence developed, the relationships
between suspects and victims were clarified. Detailed network
analysis, which linked victims, suspects and other known associates,
indicated the extent of the 'gangs' within the community. Some six
gangs were identified, and the analysis sought to understand both
rivalries and affiliations to provide a more detailed understanding of
the violent incidents. Crime pattern analysis also indicated the extent
to which the gang activity was geographically concentrated in
particular localities, which supported targeted deployments.

Analysing the Interventions
Based on the detailed analysis of the reactive investigations and
further intelligence, a proactive response to target the associated
gang members was developed. The aim was to ensure the analytical
input was sustained throughout the operational interventions, both
to appraise incoming intelligence (thereby assessing the extent to
which activity may have undermined the networks that had been
identified), and to assess the impact of the interventions more
generally. The operation aimed to pioneer an analysis of the results,
both in terms of outputs (for example, the arrest of suspects, seizure
of weapons), and outcomes, including the extent to which

perceptions of the problem and fear of violence among the community had changed. The aim was to extend analysis to include the progress of cases through the criminal justice system and to identify any areas of improvement for the proactive team in the future.

The Impact of Analysis
Case study 2 highlights the extent to which crime analysis provides more than an understanding of crime. The analysis in the case:

1. identified areas where intelligence needed to be developed

2. developed a detailed understanding of the critical drivers to violent incidents

3. monitored the impact of police interventions and the process of cases through the criminal justice system to support the development of strategies for improvement.

as it provides the ability to monitor performance trends, so that police forces can anticipate and respond to areas where they may not be achieving their targets. Perhaps a more significant contribution is developing an understanding of why the police may be successful or otherwise in their approach. It is only by developing a more detailed interpretation of performance data that police forces are able to develop the appropriate responses to problems. For example: police forces may be failing on targets because of factors external to the police; the training provided to officers in a particular field may not support effective interventions; the target may not be an appropriate measure of activity, or the data collected could be inaccurate. Therefore, analysis provides an opportunity to develop a detailed understanding of statistical data, and supports the identification of variables which may affect the outputs and outcomes of police activity.

The continued development of information technologies

Technology plays a significant role in how the police services are organized, by supporting the drive to improve the efficiency and effectiveness of the police, offering the potential to satisfy the demands of external agencies for information, and providing an infrastructure that can meet the requirements of new forms of police management and accountability (Chan, 2001). The constant advancement of information technology continues to support the development of analysis in policing. Studies on the police and police culture highlight the extent to which police work is mundane, administrative and information-based, demonstrating that despite the powerful action imagery with which it is often associated (see Bowling and Foster, 2002, for a summary), the police are 'knowledge workers' (Ericson and Haggerty, 1997). Therefore, crime analysts play an integral role in the management and prioritization of information for the police by analysing information that is routinely stored on police computer systems. The development of analytical software supports this. For example, crime-mapping software has influenced the range of uses to which police data are applied, including crime profiling, strategic fore-casting and developing policy (Weisburd and McEwen, 1998).

While the theory supporting the development of information technologies would suggest that their impact on policing would be significant, in practice the evidence is more equivocal (Manning, 1992; Ericson and Haggerty, 1997; Chan, 2001). Primarily, this is because officers' interpretation and understanding of technology is a critical factor in influencing its development in practice (Chan, 2001). Information quality and overload, which severely impact on the ability of the police to sort relevant information from irrelevant 'background noise'; increases in bureaucracy; habitual demands for data, both internally and externally, combine to limit the impact of information technologies (see Chan, 2001; Cope *et al.*, 2001; Sheptycki, 2003).

Trends in the globalization of crime indicate more co-operation between police forces will be demanded, suggesting that the police are experiencing only the beginning of technology's influence, and currently may be understood as relative novices who have yet to internalize and normalize the use of information technologies. Further development of information technologies also assures the position of analysis in policing, as the need for information to be evaluated, analysed and disseminated is likely to increase. However, what is clear is that to realize the potential for information technologies involves more than simply making computers available (Chan, 2001, 2003) as the importance of the cognitive element must not be underestimated or overlooked. As Buslik and Maltz (1998: 123) note:

> a canny analyst … doesn't need a computer to analyze the data so much as he or she needs to present the data in a suitable form for pulling out patterns … highlighting the extent to which analysis is not simply a matter of computer competence, but exploiting the opportunities provided by computers and software in the process of thinking about crime, performance or strategic issues.

Case Study 3
Linking the Crime Series: Getting at the Intelligence

An analyst, after attending a discussion about crime committed towards the homosexual community, undertook an intelligence search for related offences to explore the potential extent of the problem. The search revealed three locations where incidents were prevalent. A more detailed search indicated that a number of the victims were attacked within one location which was identified as a homosexual 'cruising' area. The victims of the robberies were frequently subjected to extreme violence. A detailed analysis of the incidents identified through the initial review revealed similarities in *modus operandi* of the offender, suggesting this was a linked series of crimes, undertaken by the same suspect. The victims also provided a clear description of the suspect which reinforced this inference. As a result of the analysis an operational command structure, which included partnership groups, was developed. Police deployments were focused in the locality and all officers were briefed about the nature of the incidents and the description of the offender. The suspect was identified by a patrolling officer and arrested.

The analysts working on the case suspected that given the profile of the offences it was likely the suspect was a persistent offender who was known to the police. However, despite a clear description, which included identifiable marks, a suspect name could not be found. On arrest of the suspect, a search on the database revealed that the suspect was identified by the intelligence. However, poor data standards meant the report could not be accessed by the searches.

The Impact of Analysis
Case study 3 highlights the extent to which the identification of problems emerges during the scanning and review of information. It highlights the importance of the analysts reading all the information about crime. This is an onerous task if information flow is high but quality of intelligence is low.

The case study also highlights the extent to which analysis relies both on receiving the right information to support the development of an intelligence picture, but also that intelligence is inputted correctly so that it can be searched and retrieved.

Where intelligence can be accessed and linked, the case study clearly demonstrates the value of linking data to inform operational activity.

Developing the potential of crime analysis: a strategic view

Crime analysis has been required to develop fairly rapidly to support an exponential increase in demand for timely, reliable, analysed information by the police. The longevity of the demand for analysts in the police is undeniable as all approaches to policing and reform agendas, as discussed in this chapter, require analysis for problem identification, evaluation, and intelligence to support the allocation of limited resources. However, the revolutionary potential of analysis on police work may not be fully realized as analysis remains focused on providing intelligence to support tactical activity. There is now an opportunity to consider how to support the development of analysis in policing to ensure it is able to meet the current and future needs of the police. In this section I outline two critical areas for development. The first area relates to the professionalization of crime analysis as a discipline within police work. The second area focuses on the development of strategic intelligence and analysis.

Professionalization: creating the right environment for analysis

Recent research begins to provide some insight into the professional structure and management of crime analysts across police forces in both the UK and US. For example, in a qualitative study of two police forces in England, Cope *et al.* (2001) and Cope (2004) reported that 14 of the 16 crime analysts in the research were civilian staff; two were police officers ('sworn crime analysts'). The demographics and the backgrounds of the analysts varied: 11 were female; six had transferred from other administrative roles within policing, and five were educated to degree level. While the line management and career opportunities for analysts varied, both forces offered limited opportunities for promotion. The analysts were managed by police officers, at either a Police Sergeant or Inspector level, within the intelligence unit in which they worked. A study of crime analysts working in police departments across the United States found similar variations. O'Shea and Nicholls' (2003) research was based on two national surveys (65 per cent of 859 agencies responded), site visits and interviews with 49 analysts across nine large departments within the country. The research found that in relation to human resources, formal job descriptions were either not drafted or appeared to lack any grasp of the skills required to fulfil the function of an analytical role. Furthermore, selection procedures for civilian and sworn staff members in the analysts' role appeared to differ. In terms of career structure, there was little opportunity for either vertical or lateral moves. Finally, both the UK and US studies found a limited emphasis on training and development. Training, when available, was principally based on the information technology used to support analysis, or basic tactical analysis, rather than focusing on subject areas which could support analysts' ability to understand problems.

Studies of crime analysis in police departments highlight the need to address the profession for analysts (John and Maguire, 2003; O'Shea and Nicholls, 2003; Cope, 2004). At a basic level, this involves the implementation of good practice in human resource management. Recruitment practice and the skill profile required to perform the role of analysts; training and professional development to ensure that the personnel in the role are able to realize their potential; and career development are critical areas that need to be addressed.

As crime analysis develops in policing there is an increasing demand for a range of products to inform decision-making at all levels of police management. As a consequence, analysts are required to be competent communicators, and able to engage with a range of personnel to explain the outcomes of their research. This can create tensions for analysts who have found that in practice their role lacked legitimacy, their products were not routinely integrated into police activity, and their knowledge and experience were frequently challenged or received sceptically (Cope, 2004). Addressing these problems requires police forces to readily accept a range of information to inform their activity. However, there is also a need to assess whether current job descriptions and skill profiles for analysts accurately describe their responsibilities, both in terms of their expertise in data management and development, but also the ability to communicate their findings. Without these recruitment and selection processes police forces will not attract personnel able to fulfil the considerable demands and potential for the analysts' role.

Crime analysis needs to take stock of its role in policing and consider itself as a source of expert advice, rather than a source of aggregated information. In their useful support manual for crime analysts, Clarke and Eck (2003) include 'rethinking the job' as a critical stage in becoming an effective problem-solving analyst. Part of rethinking the job involves being a crime expert, knowing what works in policing, promoting problem-solving, learning about environmental criminology, developing research skills and communicating effectively. This approach to crime analysis demands that analysts not only understand the information technology and techniques of analysis, but that they are able to engage with and apply relevant theory to enable and enhance interpretation. In the absence of theory, analysis remains descriptive, lacking the cognitive input that makes it truly informative and able to support decision-making (see Cope, 2003; Manning, 2001; Eck, 1998). A crime expert who is able to engage effectively with the police requires a range of skills on top of competence in technology and the ability to manage information. Developing the theoretical elements of crime analysis will require inputs from other relevant disciplines, such as criminology, psychology and geography, which may require a fundamental reorganization in the emphasis of current training and continued professional development programmes for analysts. The view that an analyst becomes an expert after training will also require modification, as a range of analytical skills will be developed as an individual matures in the role and develops an appreciation for the context and problems they need to understand.

Police forces will also be required to address the career opportunities for analysts. Providing an opportunity to develop in terms of management or, equally as important, the opportunity to develop as a specialist will be necessary to retain crime experts in post. However, the extent to which the culture of police forces which emphasize rank and, albeit inadvertently, reinforce divisions between police officers and civilian support staff, has the flexibility to accommodate a professional analyst career structure needs to be considered. Police forces that are too cumbersome to respond to market pressures will find it difficult to recruit and retain personnel.

While developing the professional structure is crucial, for analysts to fully realize their potential requires the police to create the right environment for analysis to flourish. Developing a supportive environment for analysts in policing can only really be achieved through developing a culture of analysis, where all personnel are encouraged to ask critical questions during the course of delivering policing services, not only about the evidence for action, but the quality of data and the impact of activity. The real challenge is to create a milieu in police forces that is able to integrate and respond to the advice provided by analysts.

Strategic analysis: understanding problems and planning

A high level of appreciation for the tactical elements of analysis means analysis has tended to focus on the crime-control model of policing, rather than developing a more strategic view or detailed understanding of problems (O'Shea and Nicholls, 2003; Cope, 2004). However, analysis has a crucial role in supporting strategic development, not least because a good strategic review will involve analysis across a number of issues, including crime, internal resource management, demand for services and perceptions of the quality of service provision. The development of strategic analysis has the potential to impact on strategy as it considers crime in context to forecast trends that in turn support planning and policy development (Olligschlaeger, 2003; Ratcliffe, 2004).

Strategic analysis has some core features which develop the use of intelligence in police work. Fundamentally, strategic analysis aims to provide an understanding of the context of emerging threats and policing problems in order to develop the predictive element of analysis, thereby enhancing the ability of the police to forecast trends (Quarmby, 2004). To facilitate this, strategic analysis includes an overview of crime trends to explore patterns in terms of increases and decreases in crimes, the profile of offenders and victims, and concentration of crime in particular spaces, places or at certain times. A strategic review will also assess issues that influence the context of crime, which can include socio-demographic analysis, and analyses of other political, environmental, social, techno-logical, legal and organizational issues which may impact on policing problems.

Understanding the context in which crime trends emerge allows strategic analysis to develop predictions of anticipated threats, thereby providing police forces with an opportunity to develop preventative or enforcement strategies, or even plan the training and development of the workforce to meet the expected demand. To use a simple example, a review of crime trends may show that a significant number of low-level disorders are committed by young men between the ages of 13 and 17 years. A review of the contextual factors highlights a political agenda to tackle antisocial behaviour, which suggests this area of crime will receive an increased focus in terms of performance targets. Furthermore, socio-demographic analysis suggests a changing dynamic in the population, and the number of youths in the local population will increase, largely as a result of new family housing developments in the locality. However, an overview of the social environment has shown that the facilities for young people are underdeveloped, which means young people are likely to travel to schools within or outside the locality (increasing their presence on public transport, a critical area for youth disorder). Furthermore, the absence of organized recreational amenities indicates that many young people will congregate in public spaces, increasing the potential for disorder and the public's fear of crime. Highlighting these factors provides an opportunity to develop a plan to prevent crime or build the capacity to respond to the projected problem. The plan may address consultation with developers to provide facilities for young people, through to training youth and community officers to engage with the problem and implementing CCTV in vulnerable areas to support enforcement.

As the example indicates, strategic analysis is informed by a range of information and intelligence, beyond covert sources which have been traditionally associated with intelligence-led approaches. Rather, it needs to include intelligence which is better equipped to inform on the contextual factors that contribute to crime (see Tilley, 2003). However, because strategic intelligence requires information from the community and partnership agencies to be shared, protocols need to be developed to resolve issues of data compatibility, legality of sharing, confidentiality of personal data, politics between partnership agencies, social expectations of privacy and security of data exchange (Wartell, 2003). Nevertheless, it is crucial that strategic analysis engage relevant stakeholders so that it is 'capable of identifying problems that are of most concern to the community, [and] solutions that are acceptable to the community and the agencies and organizations that are capable of achieving these functions' (Fletcher, 2000), as the outcomes of the process are unlikely to be resolved by relying on police interventions.

Strategic analysis could also have profound implications on other areas of policing where currently the analysis adopted is more on a case-by-case basis. For example, in the field of murder investigations, investigative analysis is frequently relied upon to support a reactive investigation. In theory, analysts support investigators by exploring the patterns of the actions of the offenders in order to understand the crime and seek out suspects. The development of geographic profiling further reinforces the role of the analysts in capturing and representing critical intelligence to help solve the crime (see Canter, 2003; Rossmo, 2000, for further discussion). The techniques of analysis, because they enable investigators to make information more manageable and understandable, are also used to present data in court proceedings. However, the impact of analysis on homicide should not be limited to individual cases. Analysing trends in murder, and exploring why any changes in the trends have occurred, provides the police with an opportunity to prevent escalating problems. White *et al.* (2003), found that the police could employ problem-solving techniques to positively impact on the trend in homicides, after a review of crimes between 1985 and 1998 in Richmond, California, demonstrated changes in the pattern and nature of offences as a result of a suppression strategy that employed a problem-solving approach. The potential for this strategic approach is significant and may provide police forces with a more detailed understanding of the nature of violence. The age, gender and ethnic profile of the offenders and the victims, the relationship between the offender and victim, the location, the time, the motivation for the offence, the weapon used (if any), through to the type of forensics captured from the crime scene, can provide a strategic picture of homicide and suggest the priority area for the implementation of police suppression resources, or highlight areas where training and skills can be developed to ensure investigative and forensic opportunities are being realized. Furthermore, strategic analysis, by providing an assessment of the risk factors associated with homicide, facilitates an understanding of emerging threats. The exciting potential for strategic analysis is how it can support differentiated policing strategies for tackling crime and provide an opportunity for the police to begin to realize the potential for proactive problem-solving techniques in a field more readily associated with reactive crime investigation.

Intelligence-led policing and principles of strategic analysis could initiate change in the working practices of a range of traditional areas of police work. For example, there is considerable potential for linking crime scenes by combining forensic data within geographical information. Ribaux *et al.* (2003: 58) highlight the potential for applying analytical techniques to forensic data, noting that:

> forensic case data are still poorly integrated into crime analysis and the investigative process. There is a lack of theoretical framework in which to classify problems and experiences ... [however] the adaption of crime analysis methods in a forensic intelligence context are adequate dimensions to start building such a framework.

Crime analysis provides the opportunity to extract and develop patterns in intelligence, which offers a different approach to identifying crime hot-spots or linking crime series through forensic identifications. Reviewed strategically, forensic intelligence will also provide an insight into trends in crime. For example, exploring the changing *modus operandi* of burglars as understood by patterns in forensic data in the context of crime-prevention strategies, may offer an insight into potential tactical displacement in terms of how offences are committed, which could inform the further development of crime-prevention interventions.

Despite the potential for strategic analysis, it has yet to be fully integrated into the field of intelligence. Sheptycki and Ratcliffe (2004) suggest strategic analysis suffers because it is not regarded as having the same 'day-to-day' relevance as tactical or operational approaches. Furthermore, a lack of support from officers and a difficulty of measuring the impact and outcomes of strategic analysis can make it difficult to justify maintaining the approach. The lack of support may also exemplify the extent to which the police are not yet comfortable with working strategically, preferring to use analysis to support the reactive approaches. Without doubt the outcomes of strategic analysis will require a different approach from police managers. Firstly, rather than working in an environment of the known, where crimes have been committed and problems are reported, strategic analysis provides a framework for assessing priorities based on inferential forecasts and predictions where there is less certainty. Secondly, while the police are currently used to undertaking risk assessments in the management of cases, strategic analysis will potentially highlight a range of corporate risks which can be anticipated and need to be managed organizationally. Such an approach may be less developed in police forces that frequently respond to prob-lems. The process and outcomes of strategic analysis offer fundamentally different ways of working for the police, which may indicate why the approach currently lacks legitimacy. However, it has the ability to provide a sound foundation for the development of techniques of crime control.

Conclusion

Crime analysis refers to the process of exploring the patterns and trends in data with a view to impact on crime and judicial practice (Gill, 2000). The initial demand for crime analysis is most closely associated with advancement of intelligence-led policing, which aims to develop a more proactive style of policing. The continued development of analysis in policing is associated with reforms in the delivery of policing services within an environment of rationalized resources and an increasingly focused performance agenda, all of which sustain the demand for reliable, analysed information, and a detailed understanding of policing problems.

My own strategic analysis suggests that the demand for analysts will remain in the increasingly complex environment of police work. Nevertheless, while the future of crime analysts in policing appears assured, questions remain about how the profession of analysis should develop. There is little doubt that demand has, and will continue to also broaden the scope of analysis to support operational policing and strategic development, although there is some way to go before it realizes its full potential. While the role of the analysts may have been employed somewhat haphazardly to meet the immediate demands of the police, the time is ripe now to determine the skills, training and professional development required to ensure an analytical workforce is appropriately supported. Fundamentally, police forces need to create the right environment for analysis to flourish, where intelligence processes are valued and understood and there is an appetite to use evidence, rather than intuitive or experiential information, to inform decision-making. The police must be ready to respond to the outcomes of analysis and recognize that this may require a different approach to the allocation of police resources and management of planning and strategic development.

Notes

1 The views of the author are not necessarily those of the Metropolitan Police Service. The details of examples have been changed to maintain anonymity. The author would like to thank the analysts within the MPS who discussed their work to support the development of this chapter.
2 For further discussion see Tilley (2003) for community, problem solving and intelligence-led policing; John and Maguire (2003) and Maguire (2000) for intelligence-led policing and NIM; Trojanowicz and Bucqueroux (1998) and

Skogan and Hartnett (1997) for community policing; Goldstein (1990) for problem oriented policing; and Goldsmith *et al.* (2000) and Dennis (1997) for COMPSTAT.

References

Audit Commission (1993) *Helping with Enquiries: Tackling Crime Effectively*. London: HMSO.

Bowling, B. and Foster, J. (2002) 'Policing and the Police', in M. Maguire, R. Morgan and R. Reiner (eds), *The Oxford Handbook of Criminology* (3rd edn). Oxford: Oxford University Press.

Buslik, M. and Maltz, M. (1998) 'Power to the people: mapping and information sharing in the Chicago Police Department', in D. Weisburd and T. McEwen (eds), *Crime Mapping and Crime Prevention*. Monsey, NY: Criminal Justice Press.

Canter, D. (2003) *Mapping Murder. The Secrets of Geographical Profiling*. London: Virgin Books.

Canter, P. (2000) 'Using a Geographic Information System for tactical crime analysis', in V. Goldsmith, P. McGuire, J.H. Mollenkopf and T. Ross (eds), *Analyzing Crime Patterns, Frontiers of Practice*. Thousand Oaks: Sage.

Chan, J. (2001) 'The technology game: how information technology is transforming police practice', *Criminal Justice*, 1: 139–59.

Chan, J. (2003) 'Policing and new technologies', in T. Newburn (ed.), *Handbook of Policing*. Cullompton: Willan.

Clarke, R. and Eck, J. (2003) *Become a Problem-Solving Crime Analyst*. Cullompton: Willan.

Cope, N. (2003) 'Crime analysis principles and practice', in T. Newburn (ed.), *Handbook of Policing*. Cullompton: Willan.

Cope, N. (2004) 'Intelligence-led policing or policing-led intelligence? Integrating volume crime analysis into policing', *British Journal of Criminology*, 44: 188–203.

Cope, N., Innes, M. and Fielding, N. (2001) *Smart Policing? The Theory and Practice of Intelligence-led Policing*. Unpublished. London: Home Office.

Dennis, N. (ed.) (1997) *Zero Tolerance: Policing a free society*. London: IEA Health and Welfare Unit.

Eck, J. (1998) 'What do those dots mean? Mapping theories with data', in D. Weisburd and T. McEwen (eds), *Crime Mapping and Crime Prevention*. Monsey, NY: Criminal Justice Press.

Ekblom, P. (2002) 'From the source to the mainstream is uphill: the challenge of transferring knowledge of crime prevention through replication, innovation and anticipation', in N. Tilley (ed.), *Analysis for Crime Prevention*. Monsey, NY: Criminal Justice Press.

Ericson, R.V. and Haggerty, K. (1997) *Policing the Risk Society*. Oxford: Oxford Clarendon Press.

Fletcher, R. (2000) 'An intelligence use of intelligence: developing locally responsive information systems in the post-Macpherson era', in A. Marlow and B. Loveday (eds), *After Macpherson: Policing after the Stephen Lawrence Inquiry*. Dorset: Russell House Publishing.

Garland, D. (1996) 'The limits of the sovereign state: Strategies of crime control in contemporary society', *British Journal of Criminology*, 36: 445–65.

Garland, D. (2001) *The Culture of Control*. Oxford: Oxford University Press.

Gill, P. (1998a) 'Making sense of police intelligence? The use of a cybernetic model in analysing information and power in police intelligence processes', *Policing and Society*, 8: 289–314.

Gill, P. (1998b) 'Police intelligence process: a study of criminal intelligence units in Canada', *Policing and Society*, 8: 339–65.

Gill, P. (2000) *Rounding up the Usual Suspects? Developments in Contemporary Law Enforcement Intelligence*. Aldershot: Ashgate.

Goldsmith, V., McGuire, P., Mollenkopf, J. and Ross, T. (2000) *Analyzing Crime Patterns Frontiers of Practice*. Thousand Oaks: Sage.

Goldstein, H. (1990) *Problem-Oriented Policing*. New York: McGraw-Hill.

Grieve, J. (2004). 'Developments in UK criminal intelligence', in J. Ratcliffe (ed.), *Strategic Thinking in Criminal Intelligence*. Sydney: The Federation Press.

Hallam, S. (2000) 'Effective and efficient policing: some problems with the culture of performance', in A. Marlow and B. Loveday (eds), *After Macpherson: Policing after the Stephen Lawrence Inquiry*. Dorset: Russell House Publishing.

John, T. and Maguire, M. (2003) 'Rolling out the National Intelligence Model: key challenges', in K. Bullock and N. Tilley (eds), *Crime Reduction and Problem-Oriented Policing*. Cullompton: Willan.

Johnston, L. and Shearing, C. (2003) *Governing Security Explorations in Policing and Justice*. London: Routledge.

Maguire, M. (2000) 'Policing by risks and targets: some implications of intelligence-led crime control', *Policing and Society*, 9: 315–36.

Manning, P. (1992) 'Information technologies and the police', in M. Tonry and N. Morris (eds), *Modern Policing*. Crime and Justice 15 (pp. 349–99). Chicago: University of Chicago Press.

Manning, P. (2001) 'Technology's ways: information technology, crime analysis and the rationalizing of policing', *Criminal Justice*,1: 83–104.

McGuire, P. (2000) 'The New York Police Department COMPSTAT Process: Mapping for analysis, evaluation and accountability', in V. Goldsmith, P. McGuire, J.H. Mollenkopf and T. Ross (eds), *Analyzing Crime Patterns, Frontiers of Practice*. Thousand Oaks: Sage.

National Criminal Intelligence Service (2000) *The National Intelligence Model*. London: The National Criminal Intelligence Service.

Olligschlaeger, A. (2003) 'Future direction in crime mapping', in M. Leipnik and D. Albert (eds), *GIS in Law Enforcement: Implementation Issues and Case Studies*. London: Taylor and Francis.

Osborne, D. and Wernicke, S. (2003) *Introduction to Crime Analysis: Basic Resources for Criminal Justice Practice*. New York: Haworth Press.

O'Shea, T. and Nicholls, K. (2003) *Crime Analysis in America*. Washington: US Department of Justice.

Peterson, M. (1994) *Applications in Criminal Analysis: A Sourcebook*. Westport: Greenwood Press.

Quarmby, N. (2004). 'Futures work in strategic criminal intelligence', in J. Ratcliffe (ed.), *Strategic Thinking in Criminal Intelligence*. Sydney: The Federation Press.

Ratcliffe, J. (2002) 'Intelligence-led policing and the problems of turning rhetoric into practice,' *Policing and Society*, 12: 53–66.

Ratcliffe, J. (2004) 'The structure of strategic thinking', in J. Ratcliffe (ed.), *Strategic Thinking in Criminal Intelligence*. Sydney: The Federation Press.

Ribaux, O., Girod, A., Walsh, S., Margot, P., Mizrahi, S. and Clivaz, C. (2003) 'Forensic intelligence and crime analysis', *Law, Probability and Risk*, 2: 47–60.

Rossmo, K. (2000) *Geographic Profiling*. Boca Raton, FL: CRC Press.

Sheptycki, J. (2003) *Review of the Influence of Strategic Intelligence on Organised Crime Policy and Practice*. London: Home Office.

Sheptycki, J. and Ratcliffe, J. (2004) 'Setting the strategic agenda', in J. Ratcliffe (ed.), *Strategic Thinking in Criminal Intelligence*. Sydney: The Federation Press.

Sherman, L. (1998). *Evidence-Based Policing*. Washington: The Police Foundation.

Skogan, W. and Hartnett, S. (1997) *Community Policing, Chicago Style*. Oxford: Oxford University Press.

Tilley, N. (ed.) (2002a) *Analysis for Crime Prevention*. Monsey, NY: Criminal Justice Press

Tilley, N. (ed.) (2002b) *Evaluation for Crime Prevention*. Monsey, NY: Criminal Justice Press.

Tilley, N. (2003) 'Community policing, problem-oriented policing and intelligence-led policing', in T. Newburn (ed.), *Handbook of Policing*. Cullompton: Willan.

Trojanowicz, R. and Bucqueroux, B. (1998). *Community Policing*. Cincinnati, OH: Anderson Publishing.

Wartell, J. (2003) 'Crime mapping and data sharing', in M. Leipnik and D. Albert (eds), *GIS in Law Enforcement Implementation Issues and Case Studies*. London: Taylor and Francis.

Weisburd, D. and McEwen, T. (eds) (1998) *Crime Mapping and Crime Prevention*. Monsey, NY: Criminal Justice Press.

White, M., Fyfe, J., Campbell, S. and Goldkamp, J. (2003) 'The police role in preventing homicide: Considering the impact of problem-oriented policing on the prevalence of murder', *Journal of Research in Crime and Delinquency*, 40 (2): 194–225.

Chapter 6

The interpersonal dynamics of police interviewing

Laurence Alison and Joanne Howard

In the following studies, the research team worked alongside officers from Australia, Canada, Norway and the UK. Our purpose was to begin with some basic evaluation of their work with suspects and witnesses. Much of this work involved simple 'bean counting' of the use (or lack thereof) of particular tactics. However, in tracking the *evolution* of particular tactics over time (in evaluations 1 and 2) and in assessing *perceptions* of the use of tactics against actual use (in evaluation 3), we found a number of interesting issues pertinent to the way in which these officers conducted their interviews. Principally, it became clear that many social/interpersonal aspects are relevant in police interviews, from the emergence of socially constructed narratives of the case, as expressed by constructing and then confirming preconceived ideas; through to perceptual difficulties in assessing what qualities discriminate acceptable persuasion from unacceptable coercion.

Evaluations 1 and 2: witnesses and suspects

Both evaluations 1 and 2 are modest in their scope, with the Canadian sample represented by 19 interviews with adult witnesses, collected from two Canadian law enforcement agencies, and the Norwegian sample represented by just 11 interviews conducted with children.

In order to protect the anonymity of the individuals involved, few demographic details about either the interviewers or interviewees will be provided; suffice to say that over 30 interviewees and over 40 different interviewers from diverse backgrounds participated in the interviews analysed (further details can be found in Wright and Alison, 2004; and Mykelbust and Alison, 2000). Before discussing the results of these studies, in which we coded the presence or absence of cognitive interviewing strategies, it is worth reviewing some of the foundation studies that have formed the basis of the argument for cognitive interviewing.

In Kebbell and Milne's (1998) survey, 159 British officers stated that witnesses 'usually' (51 per cent) or 'almost always' (33.1 per cent) provide the major leads in an investigation. The most rigorously tested and widely accepted method of conducting such interviews in the UK is the cognitive interview (CI) (Fisher *et al.*, 1987). Although this technique is regularly discussed in purely cognitive, 'memory capacity' terms, with the original version consisting of four distinctly cognitive components, it is arguably the case that the central components of its effectiveness reside in active listening and rapport building, from which many of the other aspects flow. These include asking the interviewee to report everything – the recall of seemingly unimportant, or partially remembered, details may trigger the recall of others which are more salient (Memon and Kohnken, 1992); mentally reinstating the context of the witnessed event – it is generally recognized that individuals are better able to remember information if they are in the same place/context as that in which the information was originally encoded (see Fisher, 1995, for review; Milne and Bull, 1999); recalling information from a variety of different perspectives or in different orders – asking individuals to 'shift' their perspective, and recall a story from the point of view of someone else or in 'reverse order' facilitates retrieval by minimizing the effects of prior knowledge and expectations/schema (Memon, 1998; Fisher, 1995; Geiselman and Callot, 1990).

Both laboratory and field studies have revealed that inclusion of the above strategies can lead to 30–35 per cent more information, without a substantial increase in the number of incorrect details reported (Fisher, 1995; see Milne and Bull, 1999, for review). As noted, at the heart of the CI are strategies that incorporate a distinctly social element. Indeed, Fisher (1995) recognized this in the so-called 'enhanced' cognitive interview in which he highlighted rapport building and the use of supportive behaviour, as well as witness-compatible questioning and focused retrieval. Rapport is fostered when the interviewee is given the opportunity to select the order in which s/he describes events and is allowed to proceed at his/her own pace (Memon and Kohnken, 1992). Similarly, forming individualized questions, specifically with the abilities and nuances of the interviewee's background and interpersonal style in mind, facilitates effective rapport. Finally, focused retrieval involves encouraging adequate focus within an appropriate environment and thus interviewers should do everything possible to ensure that the interviewee is committed to the interview process (Milne and Bull, 1999), is comfortable, does not feel pressed for time, and is distracted as little as possible. The enhanced CI has been shown to elicit 35–70 per cent more details from the interviewee than the original version of the CI, and again, most studies reveal that this extra information is either just as accurate as, or more accurate than, the information reported by control groups (Fisher, 1995; see Milne and Bull, 1999, for review).

The most popular method of assessing police interactions with witnesses has considered interviewers' performance in controlled laboratory conditions. Fisher (1995) claims that while such methods have their place in the research, designs of this sort may not represent an accurate account of police interviewing in the field. According to Fisher (1995), such experimental manipulations are insufficient devices for replicating the sense of urgency and motivation in a real investigation, represent low-fidelity simulations and fail to provide the extensive background information about the witnessed event (as was the case in Geiselman et al., 1985). As such, these studies may present less opportunity for officers to make certain errors, such as asking leading questions. Further, monitoring may (either consciously or inadvertently) alter officers' regular interviewing style (Fisher, 1995). In contrast, very few studies have considered how police officers interview witnesses during the course of a real investigation. Exceptions are Fisher et al.'s (1987) small-scale study of 11 US interviews, George's (1991) study of 45 witness interviews conducted by British police officers, and Davies et al.'s (2000) examination of 36 police interviews with British children who were the suspected victims of sexual abuse.

Field studies suggest that investigators tend to make several common mistakes. These include interrupting the interviewee, monopolizing on the amount of time spent talking, asking leading and/or closed questions and making assumptions about the interviewee's claims. Interruptions have the immediate effect of stopping an interviewee before s/he has the chance to add potentially valuable information, as well as potentially causing him/her to expect to be interrupted in the future. If the latter occurs, the witness may begin to shorten his/her responses in order to 'fit the time constraints apparently set by the interviewer' (Kohnken, 1995; Milne and Bull, 1999, p.3), thereby eliciting less detailed information (Milne and Bull, 1999).

Closed, multiple and repeated questioning also inhibits the amount of information available. Subtypes of closed question include 'selections' (presenting the interviewee with at least two responses, from which s/he is expected to choose one option), 'identifications' (requires the respondent to identify a person, place, object, time, etc.), 'Yes/No questions' (any question that can adequately be answered with a 'yes', 'no', or 'I don't know') (Hargie *et al.*, 1987; Gudjonsson, 1992; Milne and Bull, 1999). The effects of closed questions may be especially problematic in cases where the interviewee is vulnerable (Milne and Bull, 1999). However, these negative effects can be eliminated or at least inhibited if the interviewee is told that s/he does not have to respond if uncertain of the correct answer (Koriat, 1993), though this rarely happens in practice (Fisher, 1995).

Although closed questions present numerous difficulties, they may prove effective in certain circumstances. Closed questions are easy to answer, can be helpful if an interviewee is having difficulty discussing a particular topic and may enhance details if provided after effective open-ended questioning (Hargie *et al.*, 1987; Gudjonsson, 1992), on the understanding that they should not be used simply to confirm the interviewer's beliefs.

Leading questions suggest, 'by [their] form or content, what the answer should be, leads (the respondent) to the desired answer, or indicates the questioner's point of view' (Hibberd and Worring, 1981, quoted in Milne and Bull, 1999: 25). This, of course, proves especially problematic in cases where questions are based on underlying assumptions or knowledge that is inaccurate (Gudjonsson, 1992). Leading questions may interfere with individuals' ability to correctly recall events, particularly in relation to peripheral details and when the interviewer is perceived as a highly credible authority (Smith and Ellsworth, 1987; Fisher, 1995).

While some studies reveal that repeating open-ended questions within and between interviews does not affect the accuracy of a witness's account, and may in fact help interviewees recall more information (Poole and White, 1991; Warren and Lane, 1995, for review), other research suggests that interviewees who are asked repeated open questions invent details after they have recounted all they can remember (Warren and Lane, 1995). Poole and White (1991) demonstrated that 9 per cent of a sample of 47 adults changed their answer at least once when asked three repeated questions about an event.

Many of these findings were replicated in our studies of the Canadian and Norwegian samples. For example, on average, the Canadian interviewers spoke roughly 33 per cent of the time, whereas interviewees and lawyers spoke 67 per cent and 0.37 per cent of the time, respectively. On average, interviewers were found to interrupt interviewees once every 4 minutes and 36 seconds. Similarly, distracting or disruptive noises from the environment (e.g. a pager went off; it was possible to hear an intercom or voices in the hallway) occurred once every 5 minutes and 48 seconds on average.

None of the 19 interviews included efforts to make the witness recall events from the perspective of someone else who was (actually or imagined to be) present at the time, and few interviewers incorporated instructions that would help the witness mentally reconstruct the physical/emotional context experienced. However, the majority of investigators (over 60 per cent) verbally signalled that they were listening, gave the interviewee an opportunity to contribute information that the interviewer had not specifically asked about, and used a questioning sequence that was compatible with the interviewee's recollections. In addition, over 20 per cent encouraged the witness to report any detail s/he could remember, and to recall the incident, or aspects of the incident, in a different order.

The total number of questions, multiple questions, instructions and paraphrases used by investigators from each law-enforcement agency were identified for each of the interviews that were accompanied by audio-tapes (N=15). On average, a question was asked once every 16 seconds and a multiple question was asked once every 4 minutes and 21 seconds. Similarly, an instruction was given once every 1 minute and 53 seconds, while paraphrasing occurred once every 7 minutes and 8 seconds.

Further, on average, one clarification question was asked every 2 minutes and 29 seconds; one leading question was asked every 3 minutes and 35 seconds; a closed yes/no question was asked every 49 seconds; a closed identification question was asked every minute; and a closed selection question was asked once every 6 minutes and 13 seconds. A closed question of some variety was therefore asked, on average, once every 42 seconds. In addition, repeated questions were asked every 10 minutes and 32 seconds, while in contrast, open questions were asked, on average, every 6 minutes and 15 seconds.

Time reveals all: dynamic features of police interviews

Interviews were divided into ten intervals, such that each interval was equivalent to 10 per cent of the interview's complete length in minutes. This allowed for a standardized means of comparing the distribution of instructions, open and closed questions across interviews, which were of different lengths. It was felt that ten intervals would be sufficiently sensitive to retain the original nature of the data, yet still practical for performing analyses.

Instructions peak at the beginning and end of interviews. During the initial phase of interviews (time interval 1), the mean number of instructions was found to be higher than either the mean number of open or closed questions, with the interviewer usually providing the following information:

- the date, time and location of the interview
- his/her name, and that of the second interviewer (when present)
- the reason for the interview,
- the interviewee's legal rights.

Instructions given during intervals 2 through 9 typically consisted of directions to 'carry on' after an interruption, or to draw certain features on a geographical representation of the crime scene. Those given at the end of interviews (interval 10) were less extensive than initial instructions, and typically included an acknowledgement that the interview was being concluded, a statement of the current time and, occasionally, information about what the interviewee could expect to happen next in the legal proceedings.

Investigators asked very few open-ended questions at any point. However, as was the case with instructions, when open questions were asked, they were usually found at the beginning (interval 1) and end (interval 10) of interviews. Interviews were dominated by closed questions from interval 2 onwards. Most of these were of the identification and yes/no types. Further, as interviews progressed, the mean number of yes/no and selection questions gradually increased (peaking at intervals 8–9), whereas the mean number of identification questions declined (after peaking in time intervals).

Interviewers' discourse comprised just over 30 per cent of the talk time. Though this figure is not as large as the interviewer talking times reported in other studies (Myklebust and Alison, 2000, observed that children suspected of being sexually abused spoke only 2 per cent more than their interviewers), the figure is still rather high. Further, some of the investigators achieved talking times as low as 10 per cent, 11 per cent and 13 per cent, suggesting that much lower rates are possible.

Alongside frequent interruptions, the fact that officers gained nearly a third of the dialogue suggests that in at least some cases officers had a preconceived idea of the events and were simply seeking to confirm these beliefs. However, of those officers who initially invited the witness to give a free-recall description of events, the majority were careful to ensure that this initial account was not disrupted. Given that research indicates that most of the information a witness provides is generated in his/her opening narration, this does suggest that many officers did at least present interviewees with an opportunity to express their views (Fisher, 1995).

In reconfirming this, it was observed that several investigators allowed other distinct periods of free-recall narration, in which interviewees were not disturbed. However, another consistent finding was the fact that these free-recall periods were frequently followed by a series of closed questions. Although it may on occasion be appropriate to follow an interviewee's answer to an open question with specific closed questions (Hargie *et al.*, 1987), by moving directly to a 'probing' stage, rather than attempting to expand an interviewee's reflections with further open-ended questions, investigators must be careful not to miss a potentially valuable chance to elicit further information, nor should they be using the probe stage simply to confirm their own version of events. One way of eliminating such bias from an interview is to reduce the interviewer's prior knowledge of the case by providing him/her with only the most general background information (Fisher, 1995). Of course, many officers may resist this because the trade-off is that investigators are unable to make valuable preparations for the interview (Fisher, 1995).

The use of excessive introductory instructions may inhibit more natural dialogue and foster poor communication for the rest of the interview. The fact that many instructions were designed to inform the interviewee about the legal consequences of providing false testimony may have further contributed to the development of such a negative atmosphere. Although such warnings are essential, it may be worth considering whether one interviewer is used to introduce these to the interviewee, thereby allowing the other to enter into a more natural dialogue directly.

Finally, many cognitive interview techniques were applied infrequently and on the rare occasions that they were, they were often oversimplified, and compromised by the investigator's rapid return to a more standard questioning approach. For example:

INT: *You can visualize the scene afterwards. After ... all the cars have come to a stop. Do you recall that? Do you have a visualization of that?*
WIT: *Yea.*
INT: *Ok. So is your car at the rear of ...?*

This interviewer's guidance was so brief that it was unlikely to enable the witness to formulate a detailed mental representation of the scene. Additionally, in asking a closed yes/no question as soon as the witness began to concentrate, the investigator may have prematurely disrupted his/her recall efforts. Milne and Bull (1999) state that effective context reinstatement is demanding for the interviewer, since the interviewer must be thorough when developing contextual cues, and s/he must leave pauses between each of the mini-questions/statements to allow an interviewee enough time to picture the event.

Similarly, few of the investigators in this study asked the interviewee to report everything s/he knew about the witnessed event in detail and without editing. Again, those who did use this technique were not as explicit as they might have been, and failed to emphasize that the interviewee should mention everything that came to mind, even if it seemed unimportant or trivial.

It was also observed that after the interviewee gave a free-recall account of the event, few investigators invited him/her to re-describe it later in the interview. None of these attempted to reduce the potentially obstructive effects of a witness' mental script by having him/her recall the event, or certain aspects of it, in reverse order. As Geiselman and Callot (1990) observed, however, witnesses who recalled a crime in forward order, followed by reverse order, remembered more (correct) information than did those who simply went through the event twice from beginning to end.

Further, none of the interviewees was asked to recall the crime scene from the perspective of someone else who was present at the time. It is possible that this technique was omitted because it is too time-consuming to explain properly, or because it is perceived as a form of speculation or hearsay evidence that would not be admissible in court (Boon and Noon, 1994). According to George (1991, quoted in Kebbell and Wagstaff, 1999: 32), it is also 'not an easy concept to ask someone to put themselves in someone else's shoes to review an event asking them to say what they think they would have seen'. People rarely encounter such exercises in their day-to-day lives, and might feel slightly confused and/or uncomfortable when either giving or receiving this type of instruction.

On the other hand, investigators did demonstrate a relatively high use of supportive listening, and made a special point of asking the witness if s/he had any information to contribute that had not already been discussed in the interview. In part, this may reflect the fact that such devices are easier to implement than the other cognitive techniques, as they require little extra time or mental processing on the part of the interviewer.

In addition, a large proportion of interviewers employed a questioning sequence that was compatible with the witness's mental representation of the event. It is often challenging for the interviewer, who has only a limited amount of time, to tailor his/her questions to the interviewee's retrieval process, and to ask questions in a sequence that minimizes the number of times the interviewee must access a mental image (Kohnken, 1995). Nevertheless, such efforts are worthwhile, as they enable a witness to fully concentrate on one thought at a time, thereby facilitating a focused and thorough retrieval attempt.

Although the CI has been proven to be an effective and beneficial investigative tool, it does have several practical limitations. It is possible that these were sufficient to discourage interviewers from consistently incorporating all of the recommended cognitive components into their interviews. Firstly, several studies suggest that the CI takes longer to conduct than a standard interview and is more mentally challenging for the investigator, since s/he must be able to make on-line decisions and demonstrate greater flexibility than in a regular police interview (Fisher, 1995). Secondly, any benefits of the CI are likely to be diminished if interviewers fail to use it in the earlier phases of an investigation, before the witness has had time to mentally rehearse the event and prepare a set account (Fisher *et al.*, 1988).

Finally, as Fisher (1995: 753) notes, the CI is intended for use with co-operative witnesses, but in many investigations, 'witnesses ... may have a vested interest in not divulging information or they may be unmotivated to participate because of the time commitment or fear of "getting involved"'. Despite the many studies on eyewitness testimony and cognitive interviewing, there is surprisingly little research devoted to interviewing recalcitrant or difficult witnesses and precious little on interviewing suspects (other than the plethora of studies devoted to the dangers of oppressive interviewing).

The second study was conducted by a serving police officer of the South Australian Police (SAPOL) in order to make some headway into under-standing the extent to which officers accept that coercive strategies may lead to false confessions. The aim was to examine interviewing tactics used by police and further explore their attitudes towards interviewing suspects for any possible discrepancies between their comments on 'unacceptable' interviewing strategies and the extent to which they themselves used (or did not) use those strategies.

Evaluation 3: Suspect interviewing in South Australia: confession culture or search for the truth?

The confession culture has deep roots in police history. Psychological ascendancy over suspects was often achieved through 'deception, intimidation and on occasion, physical violence' (Davies, 1999). Similarly, Baldwin's 1989–1990 study, based on 600 audio and video-tapes of police suspect interviews, showed that 'many officers clearly approached the interview anticipating a confession' (1993: 340). In Softley's study (1980), it was noted that in 60 per cent of cases interviewers used at least one tactic to encourage suspects to part with information. Tactics used included: pointing out contradictions; bluffing or hinting that other evidence would be forthcoming and the truth would inevitably emerge; stressing the overwhelming evidence against the suspect, making denial seem pointless and minimizing the offence or the suspect's part in it.

A study by Moston and Engelberg (1993) of over 400 taped suspect interviews demonstrated an emergence of a confrontational style of questioning, with 15 per cent of interviewers directly asking the suspect about their guilt or innocence ('Did you steal the car?'); a further 5 per cent used a questioning style that allowed the suspect to provide an explanation but implicit was an assumption of wrong doing ('You were found in possession of a hammer; would you like to tell me what you were doing'?) and finally 5 per cent of interviewers presented suspects with evidence that implicated them and then asked them to comment on it.

Moston suggests the confrontational style questioning is an indication that 'present-day interrogators are seeking self-incriminating admissions rather than information of a more general kind … [and] that interrogators commonly lack the necessary skills to cope with suspects who do not readily come forward with a confession' (Gudjonsson, 1992: 47).

Kalbfleisch's (1994) typology of questioning describes tactics designed to obtain confessions and to search for the truth. Intimidation tactics consist of directly accusing the suspect of being a liar; delivering a negative evaluation to indicate disagreement or disapproval of a statement, for example questioning the suspect's judgment and faculties and telling the person they are unworthy. Delivering a rapid fire of accusations and criticisms, referred to as 'hammering', serves to have an unnerving effect on the suspect. Futility tactics espoused by Kalbfleisch focus on the impending danger associated with continued deceit. Emphasizing that the truth will eventually be known, that nothing the suspect has to say can change history and stressing the vulnerability of the suspect that they are all alone in their deception, are tactics designed to prompt suspects to confess. Creating discomfort for the suspect through the magnification of lies told and then providing truth as the only avenue of relief is another tactic reported by Kalbfleisch. The belief that 'confession is good for the soul' epitomizes this tactic.

Bluffing a suspect by fabricating evidence or suggesting 'an imminent uncovering of evidence might impeach [the] deceivers' credibility' (Buckwalter, 1983: 477) are confession tactics that rely on fear of discovery.

Kalbfleisch's typology accounts for minimization tactics as similarly documented by Kassin and McNall (1991). Providing face-saving excuses by making lies less reprehensible, softening or downplaying the seriousness of the crime, stating that anyone else would have acted the same in the given circumstances and shifting the blame onto another, are all tactics that seek to reduce the responsibility the suspect may feel, encouraging them to confess.

Pointing out contradictions made by a suspect, either as they appear or presenting all inconsistencies at the end of the interview, is a tactic designed to fluster and expose 'slip-ups' in the suspect's story (Tierney,

1970). Kalbfleisch describes the tactic 'a chink in the defence' as requiring the interviewer to obtain an admission about one small part of the suspect's story and then infer that they could have lied about everything else. Disclosing information about one's self with the expectation that the suspect will reveal personal, possibly incriminating, information is a tactic that relies on the norm of reciprocity.

Admonishing a suspect to be truthful consists of two further tactics that, firstly, prey on what others may think of the suspect if they continue in their deceit; and directly instructing the suspect to tell the truth because it is the most morally desirable thing to do: 'Surely you have no objection to discussing the truth about this occurrence ... with me' (Buckwalter, 1983: 106). The final tactics selected from Kalbfleisch's typology represent showing concern and empathy for the suspect, by indicating they are someone special, reminding the interviewer of a friend or family member, and that the feelings of the suspect are shared by the interviewer.

The selection of confession-orientated interview tactics described above are by no means exhaustive; however, they are common tactics that are replicated in the works of many other authors (Oxford, 1991; Merrill, 1995; Hess, 1997).

Interview strategies designed to search for the truth have been referred to as ethical interviews and inquisitorial strategies (Moston, 1990). The aim is to move away from the psychological and deceptive interview strategies used to obtain confessions. The emphasis on seeking the truth through information gathering has risen from the gradual loss of credibility associated with confessions and questionable police conduct during suspect interviews (Gilbert, 1998).

In Softley's 1980 study of 218 interviews held with criminal suspects, officers were asked what they hoped to gain in the interview. Eighty-six per cent said they interviewed to 'simply find out what has happened or to get the suspect's side of the story' (1980, p. 31). Baldwin suggests that planning, rapport building and social skills are necessary for a successful interview. Kohnken (1995) stresses the importance of rapport building so to create a relaxing atmosphere that facilitates conversation. Kalbfleisch (1994) concurs by stating that 'people are more likely to disclose information when they trust and feel comfortable with the person with whom they are conversing' (p. 478). This idea is replicated in many bodies of literature that investigate interviewing strategies designed to seek the truth (Balinsky, 1978; DeLaduranty and Sullivan, 1980; Rich, 1968; Stewart and Cash, 1974).

The truth tactics incorporated in Kalbfleisch's typology reflect this premise. Encouraging suspects to continue giving or discussing information is advocated by Kalbfleisch through the use of positive exclamations, such as 'Yes', 'I hear you', 'Aha!' (p. 479). Requesting the suspect to elaborate on topics under discussion is another truth tactic that promotes information collection and exchange. The tactic of diffusing responsibility is suggested for negative questions that may dissolve established rapport. This tactic is achieved by prefixing such questions with 'people are saying that you ...', thereby inferring that the interviewer is no longer asking the question, rather an interested public (Brady, 1976; Kalbfleisch, 1994).

Additional tactics of playing the devil's advocate, suggested for neutralizing potentially harsh questions and praise, whereby questions are prefixed with praise for the suspect, 'Hi Slim, everyone says that your horses are the best ... but Joe says that your horses were never officially registered ... What are the grounds for his claim?', are presented (Kalbfleisch, 1994: 480). Praise can also be given to encourage a suspect to expand on a topic of discussion.

Kalbfleisch points out that the tactics included in the typology are primarily techniques learned from colleagues and field experience and are not the result of scientific study. However, their existence is evident from the works of scholars (Irving, 1980; Irving and McKenzie, 1989) who have studied tactics used in police interrogations. An important consideration is that the above-mentioned tactics must be used in concert with an open mind and genuine interest in searching for the truth.

We were interested in the extent to which a confession or search for the truth culture had been embraced within the South Australian Police Department (SAPOL). The notion of securing a confession at all costs has been dispensed with by the South Australia legislature and the police hierarchy. Police conducting interviews in South Australia are now legally bound to follow rigid procedures for recording suspect interviews on video or as a secondary source, on audio tape. The legislation applies to all interviews conducted with suspects for indictable offences (Summary Offences Act, 1953).

Suspects are furnished legal rights that permit a friend, relative or solicitor to be present during an interview, interpreter services are made available and suspects have the right to refrain from answering questions, with no inference being derived from their silence. Officers are obliged to give suspects a certain amount of information about the nature of the inquiry or why he or she has been arrested. Failure to comply can result in any subsequent interview being 'at risk of being excluded on the basis that the suspect was prevented by lack of information from doing justice to his/her own position' (Brebner and Mulligan, 1998: 1). Therefore, given the lack of research within SAPOL and the surrounding 'search for truth' context encouraged by current legal requirements, we wanted to examine the attitudes towards suspect interviewing, explore the levels of satisfaction with training and gain some insight into the tactics actually used in recent suspect interviews.

The data were acquired from sworn serving SAPOL police officers. To collect data for this study a submission was made to SAPOL's Officer in Charge of Policy and Project Services. The submission outlined the aims of the study, detailed what data would be necessary and how it could be collected. The data request consisted of a proposed sample comprising 200 SAPOL officers who would each be a voluntary participant and would be operational members with no restrictions placed on minimum years of police service. Each participant would complete a questionnaire pertaining to their length of service, attitudes about interviewing suspects, interview training and performance indicators. Approval was granted by SAPOL's Policy and Project Services Branch after a series of correspondence regarding questionnaire approval, additional information and confirmation of confidentiality matters.

The response rate cannot be accurately measured, as members were not targeted to participate; rather the invitation was made public throughout the 3,500 members of SAPOL requesting those with operational experience to respond. It is unknown how many operationally experienced members were exposed to the opportunities to participate through email, word of mouth and the dissemination of faxed information within the time frame. It is further unknown how many officers were not exposed to the study due to annual leave, sick leave, court commitments and interstate/ international secondments.

The 51 participants involved in this study were sworn serving SAPOL police officers. Male officers accounted for 82 per cent (42 officers) of the sample with nine female officers representing the remaining 18 per cent. The average age of the sample was 37 years, with a minimum age of 25 years and a maximum age of 48 years. Forty-five per cent of officers held the rank of Detective Senior Constable, 27 per cent were qualified Senior Constables. The remaining officers were distributed between the ranks of Constable (22%), First Class Constable (2%) and Sergeant (4%). The average length of service among the officers was 17 years, with a minimum service of 5 years and a maximum service of 29 years.

The 102 interviews were conducted between 1990 and 2000, with 92 per cent conducted between 1995 and 2000. Sixty-three per cent of the sample consisted of offences committed against property and 37 per cent represented offences against the person. As no information was given about the specific focus or design of the study, participants were not aware what factors were being measured in the interviews or why. Participants were asked why they selected particular records of interview. Twenty-one officers responded to this question, with 80 per cent stating, 'It was the first one (interview) I came across that fitted the criteria (serious/minor/ transcribed)'. The remaining four officers gave other reasons: 'because it was a long interview', 'it was a funny one', 'it was an important case to me' and 'I had others in hard copy but I sent these two because I had them electronically transcribed' (4.8 per cent).

The time duration was recorded for 85 interviews, with an average interviewing time of 36 minutes, a minimum of 3 minutes and a maximum of 128 minutes. Seventy-nine per cent of interviews were recorded by audio and/or video tape and 21 per cent were handwritten. The interviews resulted in 32 per cent of suspects making admissions and 15 per cent making confessions. Forty-eight per cent of suspects made no admissions and 5 per cent refused to answer questions.

Sixty-four of these interviews were conducted with suspects of minor offences. Seventy-seven per cent of these were for offences committed against property and 23 per cent represented offences against the person. The average time length of minor offence interviews was 29 minutes, with a minimum of 3 minutes and a maximum interviewing time of 111 minutes. Seventy per cent were recorded by audio and/or video tape and 30 per cent were hand written. The interviews resulted in 31 per cent (20 cases) making admissions and 9 suspects (14 per cent) making confessions. Fifty-two per cent made no admissions and 3 per cent refused to answer questions.

The remaining 38 records were with suspects of serious offences. Forty per cent of the sample consisted of offences committed against property and 60.5 per cent represented offences against the person. The average time length of serious offence interviews was 48 minutes, with a minimum of 10 minutes and a maximum interviewing time of 128 minutes. Ninety-five per cent of serious offence interviews were recorded by audio and/or video tape and 5 per cent were handwritten. The interviews resulted in 34 per cent of suspects (13 cases) making admissions and 6 suspects (16 per cent) making confessions. Forty-two per cent of suspects (16 cases) made no admissions and 8 per cent refused to answer questions.

Questionnaire design and content

The questionnaire the participants completed was a three-page document designed to collect information on three areas. The first area involved demographic information. The second area involved opinions and actions undertaken in relation to self-directed and departmental interviewer training, feedback received of interviews conducted, self-assessment of interview competency and beliefs concerning the purpose of interviewing and the likelihood of false confessions. This section allowed participants to write open answers to five questions, without being restricted to closed 'yes or no' answers. The final area required that, from a set of 30 interviewing tactics, the participants indicated the ones they had ever used in interviewing suspects.

Content analysis dictionary of interviews

A content analysis dictionary was designed to analyse the interview transcripts. Thirty-eight variables were selected and are defined in the content dictionary. Variables numbered 1 to 8 are descriptive categories that classify background information about the type of offence committed, and the format, length and result of the interview. The remaining 30 variables were selected as they are well represented in the literature describing common police interview strategies. Variables numbered 9 to 30 represent a theme of interviewing to obtain a confession. Variables numbered 31 to 38 describe a theme of interviewing to search for the truth. Interview tactics that rely on audio or visual observations and the fabrication of evidence have not been included in this study, as these tactics could not be measured from the data sample. Variables were coded simply for presence or absence. The aim of the study was to analyse what interviewing tactics were used by the sample, not how often they were used by individual officers in specific interviews. Fifteen interview transcripts were randomly selected from the data sample and analysed using the content analysis dictionary constructed for this study. The method of analysis was found to be reliable with an average inter-rater reliability score of .87.

Table 6.1 below outlines the responses to the first set of questions and Table 6.2 shows the percentage results of techniques 'ever' used by the sample.

As can be seen from Table 6.3, the majority had received some form of training, commonly in terms of a specific detective training course or in advanced detective workshops. However, in the majority of cases, the time since the last training period was several years. Just over half of the sample had undertaken some form of self-initiated training and the over-whelming majority stated that they had learnt many skills from watching colleagues. However, although the majority felt they had sufficient interviewing skills, most stated they had never received feedback on their interviews and 90 per cent stated they would like more training. In total, 60 references were made to the evidential importance of suspect interviews, 21 to the importance of obtaining the suspect's version of events, 13 to the importance of obtaining the truth and 12 references were made to the importance of obtaining a confession. Nearly 60 per cent stated that suspects could falsely confess to a crime that they did not commit.

Table 6.1   Interviewer training

Question	Response
Since cadet training have you received training in interviewing suspects?	Yes = 71 per cent (36) No = 29 per cent (15)
What interviewer training have you received?	Detective training course = 21 Advanced detective workshops = 9 Specific crime investigation courses = 5 Lectures on legal requirements = 4 One day vocational seminars = 4 Workplace lectures = 4
How long since you have received interview training?	Mean = 9 years (range 2 months – 22 years)
Have you undertaken any self-initiated training?	Yes = 51 per cent (26) No = 49 per cent (25) Literature = 16, study = 13, practical = 10, work experience = 1, television = 1
Have you learnt any interviewing skills from watching colleagues	Yes = 94 per cent (48) No = 16 per cent (3) Questioning skills = 13, procedural skills = 29, manipulation skills = 13, other skills = 9
Have you received feedback from superiors about your interviewing skills?	Yes = 37 per cent (19) No = 63 per cent (32) 23 highlighted positive, constructive feedback.
Do you feel you possess sufficient interviewing skills?	Yes = 77 per cent (39) No = 13 per cent (12)
Would you like to receive more suspect interview training?	Yes = 90 per cent (46) No = 10 per cent (5)
Are interviewing skills an important part of policing?	Yes = 100 per cent (51)
In your view what is the purpose of suspect interviewing?	Evidential = 60 (facts and information, obtain evidence, etc.) Suspect's version = 21 (tie the suspect down to a story, ascertaining why the suspect committed the offence) Truth = 13 Confessions = 12
Do you believe a suspect may confess to a crime s/he didn't commit?	Yes = 59 per cent (30) No = 41 per cent (21)

Table 6.2 Questionnaire text box 'Which interview techniques have you ever used?'

Confession	%	N	Truth	%	N
Inconsistencies	100	51	Encouragement	100	51
Direct	92	47	Elaboration	94	48
Chink in defence	88	45	Rapport	92	47
Empathy	86	44	Background	88	45
Unkept secret	84	43	Collect	80	41
Hammering	80	41	Praise	71	36
Concern	74.5	38	Diffuse	63	32
Liar	72.5	37	Cushioning	55	28
Bad situation worse	72.5	37			
Pride	71	36			
Excuses	59	30			
Imminent discovery	57	29			
Reputation	55	28			
Blaming	53	27			
Discomfort/Relief	51	26			
Body language	51	26			
Play down	45	23			
Indifference	41	21			
Act same	35	18			
Self-disclosure	33	17			
Criticism	27.5	14			
All alone	20	10			

In terms of attitudes to tactics used, analysis of the results, utilising Fisher's Z transformation test and Wilcoxon's T-test, show there is a significant difference ($Z = -2.521$, $p = .012$) between the average number of confession tactics (mean = 31.27) and truth tactics used (mean = 41) (see Table 6.2). These results indicate the sample believed the latter techniques to be used more commonly throughout their interviewing careers. All officers claimed to have used the 'truth' tactic of *encouragement* and the 'confession' tactic of *highlighting inconsistencies*. Other popular tactics in the 'confession' tactics were a *direct approach* (e.g. 'simply tell me the truth, let's be honest here'), finding a *chink in defence* (i.e. getting them to admit that they have already lied about one thing, so what about the truthfulness of the rest of the account?), feigning *empathy*, pointing out the futility of deceit because eventually the truth will be known (*unkept secret*) and *hammering* (a relentless pursuit of the suspect through consistent, rapid fire questioning). In terms of the 'search for the truth', in over 50 per cent of all cases officers claimed they used such tactics. Especially prominent was praise and *encouragement*, asking the suspect to *elaborate* on a particular issue and trying to build *rapport*.

Table 6.3 summarizes the frequency of the various tactics used across all interviews and, more specifically, within the serious and minor offence subsets.

In terms of an analysis of the interviews provided by officers in relation to confession tactics, *highlighting inconsistencies* (22%), *criticizing the suspect* (8%), *addressing the suspect as a liar* (7%), directly *admonishing* the suspect to share the truth (7%) and providing *excuses* (8%) are the most common 'confession' interviewing tactics displayed by the sample.

'Search for the truth' interview tactics are characterized by the *collection of information* without cross-examination (95%), *elaborate* on answers given (77.5%), *encouraging* the suspect to answer questions (69%) and developing a *rapport* (67%). Analysis of the results, utilizing Fisher's Z transformation test and Wilcoxon's T-test, revealed no significant difference ($Z = -1.69$, $p = .866$) between the number of confession tactics (mean = 7.85, sd = 6.62) and truth tactics used (mean = 51.57, sd = 35.94).

An exclusive use of confession tactics was not present in any interview. Rather, when they did exist, they were used in conjunction with truth tactics in 33 interviews, with a minimum of one tactic (present in 16 cases) and a maximum of five tactics (present in one case) with an average of 1.8 confession tactics per interview. Truth tactics were used in all 102 interviews and in 69 cases truth tactics were used exclusively. The results show an average of four truth tactics used per interview. Analysis of the mean scores, utilizing Fisher's Z transformation test and Wilcoxon's T-test, show that where both confession and truth tactics were used in an interview, no significant difference was found between the number of different tactics used ($Z = -.081$, $p = .936$).

Minor offence interviews

The frequencies representing interview tactics used to interview minor offences show that highlighting *inconsistencies* (27%), addressing the suspect as a *liar* (8%), providing *excuses* (8%) and directly *admonishing* the suspect to share the truth (8%) are the most common confession interviewing tactics displayed by the sample. Search for the truth interview tactics are characterized by the *collection of information* (100%), *encouraging* the suspect to answer questions (77%), *elaborate* on answers given (58%) and developing a *rapport* (58%). The confession variable *pride* was not used in the minor interview transcripts examined.

Analysis of the results, utilizing Fisher's Z transformation test and Wilcoxon's T-test, revealed no significant difference ($Z = .000$, $p = 1$)

Table 6.3 Content coding of interviews

Confession	% score for ALL N=102	% and raw score for MINOR N = 64	% and raw score for SERIOUS N = 38
Inconsistencies	22	27 (17)	13 (5)
Criticism	8	8 (5)	8 (3)
Liar	7	8 (5)	5 (2)
Direct	7	8 (5)	5 (2)
Excuses	6	8 (5)	3 (1)
Discovery	3	3 (2)	3 (1)
Empathy	2	2 (1)	3 (1)
Indifference	1	2 (1)	0
Self disclosure	1	2 (1)	0
All alone	1	2 (1)	0
Unkept secret	1	2 (1)	0
Pride	1	0	3 (1)
Bad situation worse	0	0	0
Discomfort/Relief	0	0	0
Hammering	0	0	0
Play down	0	0	0
Act same	0	0	0
Blaming	0	0	0
Body language	0	0	0
Concern	0	0	0
Reputation	0	0	0

Truth	% score for ALL	% and raw score for MINOR	% and raw score for SERIOUS
Collect	95	100 (63)	87 (33)
Elaborate	76	77 (49)	79 (30)
Encourage	69	58 (37)	87 (33)
Rapport	67	58 (37)	82 (31)
Diffuse	38	39 (25)	37 (14)
Background	7	3 (2)	13 (5)
Praise	3	3 (2)	3 (1)
Cushioning	0	0	0

between the number of confession tactics (mean = 5.7, sd = 5.25) and truth tactics used (mean = 30.7, sd = 22.87).

Confession tactics were not exclusively used in any interview, though they were used in conjunction with truth tactics in 24 interviews, with a minimum of one tactic (present in 11 cases) and a maximum of five tactics (present in one case). The results show that an average of 1.8 confession tactics per interview.

Truth tactics were used in 64 interviews. In 40 cases (62.5%) truth tactics were solely present and in the remaining 24 cases (37.5%) there was a combination of confession and truth tactics. The results show that an average of 3.9 truth tactics used in the combination style interviews.

Analysis of the mean scores, utilizing Fisher's Z transformation test and Wilcoxon's T-test, show that where both confession and truth tactics were used in interviews, no significant difference was found between the number of different tactics used ($Z = -.744, p = .457$).

Serious offence interviews

The frequencies representing interview tactics used to interview serious offences show that highlighting *inconsistencies* (13%), *criticizing* the suspect (8%), directly *admonishing* the suspect to share the truth (8%) and addressing the suspect as a *liar* (5%) are the most common confession interviewing tactics displayed by the sample. Search for the truth interview tactics are characterized by the *collection of information* (87%), *encouraging* the suspect to answer questions (87%), developing a *rapport* (82%) and *elaborating* on answers given (79%). Analysis of the results, utilizing Fisher's Z transformation test and Wilcoxon's T-test, show a significant difference ($Z = -2.028, p = .043$) between the number of confession tactics (mean = 2.14) and truth tactics used (mean = 21). Confession tactics were not exclusively used in any interview; they were used in conjunction with truth tactics in nine interviews. The results show an average of 1.7 confession tactics used per interview.

Truth tactics were used in all 38 serious interviews. In 29 cases (76%) truth tactics were solely present and in the remaining 9 cases (24%) there was a combination of confession and truth tactics. The results show an average of 4.3 truth tactics used in the combination tactic interviews. However, analysis of the mean scores, utilizing Fisher's Z transformation test and Wilcoxon's T-test, show that where both confession and truth tactics were used in interviews, no significant difference was found between the number of different tactics used ($Z = -.059, p = .953$).

Truth tactics (where used in combination with confession tactics) in minor and serious offence interviews were compared using Fisher's Z transformation and Wilcoxon's T-test. No significant difference was found between the numbers of truth tactics used ($Z = -.534, p = .594$).

Confession tactics (where used in combination with truth tactics) in minor and serious offence interviews were compared using Fisher's Z transformation and Wilcoxon's T-test. A significant difference was found as more confession tactics were used in minor interviews ($Z = -1.974$, $p = .048$).

Confession culture or search for evidence?

This study both challenges and reinforces past trends in police interviewing. Operating in an environment of limited feedback and lacking in recent training, officers conducted interviews within a framework developed mainly through detective and self-initiated training and learning skills from fellow colleagues. While officers declare they possess sufficient interviewing skills, further training was ardently welcomed. The majority of officers perceived obtaining evidence to be the main purpose of conducting suspect interviews. In their interviewing careers, officers attest to using both truth and confession tactics. While truth tactics were predominant in the current interviews examined, and used with greater frequency in serious crime interviews, a portion of interviews nevertheless consisted of both truth and confession tactics. The latter tactics tended to be used more frequently in more minor than serious crime interviews, despite officers' awareness that false confessions can occur.

The current study sheds new light on the perceived purpose of suspect interviews, with 'evidential matters' being cited as the most common reason. Police appear to be focused on the collection of evidence, rather than strictly obtaining a confession or searching for the truth. Even obtaining the suspect's version of events rated more highly than the two aforementioned factors. This welcome shift in focus might be attributed to several factors.

Firstly, in Stockdale's study of 145 records of interview conducted by 208 officers (1993), police reported 'the importance of interviews with suspects was diminishing with respect to the investigative process' (p. 6). With increased scrutiny of police practices, and the perception that interviews are 'getting harder (and) many suspects … more professional' (p. 7), perhaps the role that 'frustrated police' (p. 7) choose to play in the accusatorial system is that of an evidence collector for the court, whose role it is then to find the truth.

Several officers interviewed only to cover the elements of the alleged offence. Many questions were asked often with no corresponding direct answers from suspects and police failed to follow up lines of questioning. Secondly, the importance placed on evidence, forensic or otherwise, has been heightened within SAPOL with the introduction of Criminal Law

(Forensic Procedures) Act 1998. The act stipulates police practice in requesting, ordering and conducting forensic procedures and, among other factors, the act requires evidence collection from suspects to be videotaped. With all operational SAPOL officers having received mandatory training in these legal requirements and procedures of evidence collection, it is possible that the concentration and importance placed on evidence has filtered into these study responses.

These interviews were characterized by collecting information, elaboration, encouragement and rapport, as supported in the studies and literature identifying common truth tactics. The emergence of SAPOL officers primarily using truth tactics to conduct suspect interviews signifies a positive shift towards ethical investigative interviewing. However, coupled with the fact that, unlike their British and American counterparts (Baldwin, 1993), 59 per cent of officers in the current study acknowledged that false confessions can occur, it is somewhat surprising that one-third of interviews contained an average of 1.8 confession tactics. Therefore, it would appear that the roots of a confession culture are still somewhat prevalent in South Australia.

The combination interviews were characterized by an average of 3.9 truth and 1.8 confession tactics. While this difference was not found to be statistically significant, it does show that officers are adept at using multiple tactics during the course of an interview at increased rates of those reported by Irving (1980). In the current study the primary confession tactics used consisted of: highlighting inconsistencies, criticizing the suspect, addressing the suspect as a liar, directly telling the suspect to tell the truth, and providing the suspect with excuses. Previous studies reveal a more concentrated use of minimization and maximization tactics, emphasizing the seriousness of the crime, increasing the suspect's anxiety, and bluffing with forthcoming evidence (Baldwin, 1993).

We established that truth tactics were significantly more frequently employed in serious crime interviews. However, 24 per cent of the serious crime interviews were conducted using a combination of tactics. While a majority of truth tactics characterized the combination interviews, the difference was not significant.

Interview training

All of the officers in this study agreed that interviewing skills are an important part of policing. Researchers in this field concur and further advocate that effective interviewing can be mastered through training and recognizing the effects of police culture (Baldwin, 1993). The current study clearly highlights a need for improvement in SAPOL's commitment to interview training, since 29 per cent of officers had received no further training since graduating from the police academy. Of those who had, the time passed since training averaged at 9 years, with one officer last being trained 22 years previously. Of the 71 per cent of officers who received interview training, detective training courses were the most common source. Despite detectives representing 45 per cent of the sample, there are indications that SAPOL's interview training resources are directed to a select category of officers, namely detectives. Research reveals that officers of varying ranks are involved in conducting interviews, not just detectives. (Stockdale, 1993; Beck and Wilson, 1997; Gudjonsonn, 1992; Milne and Bull, 1999; Plimmer, 1997). It must not be overlooked that SAPOL also invests in basic interviewing skills for police cadets. However, upon leaving the police academy as probationary police, studies show that officers associate with co-workers who often have negative views of the organization (Beck and Wilson, 1995). The effect of 'pairing naïve but committed police recruits with experienced, credible and cynical senior officers is likely to be powerful and possibly destructive' (Beck and Wilson, 1997, p. 176). Therefore only training a select group of officers, such as cadets and detectives, can have detrimental effects on the quality of interviewing throughout the police.

While SAPOL's dedication to interviewing was found to be wanting, half of the officers were motivated enough to undertake self-initiated training, reading articles and undertaking external academic studies. Consistent with other findings (Stockdale, 1993; Gudjonsson, 1992), officers in the current study (94 per cent) learnt interviewing skills from watching fellow colleagues. The practice of police learning skills and techniques from their partners is not new. However, in an environment that does not facilitate regular training for all officers, the dangers of poor tactics being observed and adopted becomes very real. Stockdale (1993: 9) acknowledged the danger, as young officers can learn from 'out of date officers, who have never learnt how to interview appropriately or have forgotten the fundamental principles – a case of the blind leading the blind'. This practice is one explanation of how interview tactics designed to obtain confessions can continue to be used by junior and senior police. This current study reveals that the impetus needs to shift from officers taking responsibility for their interviewing training, to police agencies developing an all-encompassing interview training programme. Perhaps not surprisingly, 39 officers (76.5 per cent) in the current study indicated they possessed sufficient interviewing skills. However, contrary to Baldwin's findings, 94 per cent of this sample stated they wanted to receive more interview training.

Learning from this current study, SAPOL has acknowledged the self-motivation and eagerness of officers to learn more about interviewing. With a view to avoid officers learning from untested colleagues, SAPOL has implemented a new investigative interviewing skills training course which all General Duty (operational) police officers are obliged to complete. Investigative interviewing training is also included at the recruit level and comprises a significant component on specialist investigators' courses. By providing an updated and compulsory interview training package the use of confession tactics by SAPOL officers may become a practice of the past.

Limitations

Due to the sample size (51 officers, 102 records of interview) the collective results of the study should not necessarily be viewed as representative of SAPOL practice or necessarily generalizable to the wider police population. It should also be noted that 21 per cent of the interviews were not electronically recorded, thereby not affording the same opportunity to verify the quality of the data. Further to this point, using transcripts of electronically recorded interviews prevented analysis of non-verbal behaviours and audio inflections.

Hollin (1989) espouses the view that police display reserved attitudes when their work practices and performance come under scrutiny. However, this effect may have been decreased for a variety of reasons. Firstly, the contributions made by officers involved in this study did not appear to be reserved, as controversial information was received through questionnaire responses and officers disclosed past questionable interviewing methods. In addition, the elected study co-ordinator and the primary researcher of this study were both SAPOL officers, therefore perhaps expelling some of the suspicion and reluctance that officers may feel in being open and candid with unfamiliar researchers (Leonard and Alison, 1999). However, our results should be cast in cautionary tones since we have no real way of knowing the response rate or how representative this sample was.

Similarly, we do not know what happened directly before or after these interviews. McConville's (1992) study of videotaped suspect interviews revealed that when police were aware of the video they used a 'soft style' of interviewing, not challenging the suspect, and acting impeccably. However, this study revealed 'conversations' taking place between officers and suspects both before and after the formal recorded interview. McConville recognizes that official records do indicate that fewer coercive tactics are being used in interviews; however, he raises an important point that it gives no insight into the 'cases in which police, off camera, resort to interrogation techniques' (1991: 546). This is, however, a feature of the overwhelming majority of interview research and there is no easy answer.

Summary of Evaluation 3

The interview tactics displayed by this sample of South Australia police exemplify an encouraging, albeit not exclusively embraced, shift away from interviewing in order to obtain a confession. The majority stressed the importance of searching for evidence, rather than obtaining a confession. Further, analysis of the interviews revealed an emphasis placed upon 'truth tactics'. However, a large percentage of officers admitted to having, at some point in their career, used a variety of confession-seeking tactics. Even in observation of recent interviews such tactics were still being used in a significant minority of cases. While the content analysis dictionary for this study clearly demarcates 'truth' from 'confession' tactics in the real world, the line between interviewing to search for truth and interviewing to obtain a confession may not be so clear. Some interviewing tactics may blend with and complement other inappropriate tactics, making the distinction between a coercive and a non-coercive interview more difficult to establish. The subtleties that interviewers bring to an interview setting cannot always be accounted for and are often difficult to measure. Virtuous aim or not, a set of rules, not guidelines, that explain acceptable and legal interviewing tactics would be a positive step in breaking down the confession culture and encouraging police interviewers to search for the truth.

Conclusion

Though modest in scope, these three evaluations present a range of research studies, from checklist counting, to the analysis of the dynamic structure of interviews, through to officers' self-perceptions of performance in interviews. The studies illustrate that, despite the very large corpus of knowledge on police interviewing there remain many unanswered questions. These include the following:

What is the effect of interviews with suspects where partial silence, partial answers are given?
Why do suspects exercise their right to silence?
What if anything can be done to influence the suspect to answer questions?
What are the skills required to conduct interviews with suspected offenders?
What are 'specialist' interviews?
Do interviewers require specialist skills to conduct 'specialist' interviews and if so what are these skills?
How effective is an interview plan?
How should officers defend their use of various tactics in court?

Are different individuals more suitable for interviewing different types of
suspect/witness? If so, what qualities are we looking for?
What is coercion? When does persuasion become coercion?
Are women better interviewers than men? In what circumstances?[1]

(Moseley, personal communication)

Interestingly, many of these have little, or anything, to do with enhancing
memory but, rather, concern a number of interpersonal qualities that have
gone relatively unexplored. We believe that contributions to these areas
will generate significant theoretical developments in our understanding of
these intense interpersonal events and serve to enhance the professional
standards of police interviewing.

Note

1 The authors are grateful to Gavin Moseley (Kent Police), who provided much
   of the interest in these and related questions.

References

Baldwin, J. (1992) *The Conduct of Police Interrogations*. London: HMSO.

Baldwin, J. (1993) 'Police interview techniques, Establishing truth or proof?',
British Journal of Criminology, 33: 325–51.

Balinsky, B. (1978) *Improving Personnel Selection through Effective Interviewing:
Essential for management*. Baltimore, MD: Williams and Wilkins.

Beck, K. and Wilson, C. (1995) *The Development of Organizational Commitment Across
the Career Span of Police Officers*. National Police Research Unit, January.

Beck, K. and Wilson, C. (1997) 'Police officers' views on cultivating organizational
commitment: Implication for police managers', *Policing: An International Journal
of Police Strategy and Management*, 20 (1): 175–95.

Boon, J. and Noon, E. (1994) 'Changing perspectives in cognitive interviewing',
Psychology, Crime and Law, 1: 59–69.

Brady, J. (1976) *The Craft of Interviewing*. Cincinnati, OH: Writers Digest.

Brebner, P. and Mulligan, (1998) 'Judicial discretion', in M. Lyons, *SAPOL Criminal
Investigation Branch Bulletin*, 87 (July). South Australia: SAPOL.

Buckwalter, A. (1983) 'Interviews and interrogation', in P.J. Kalbfleisch (1994) The
language of detecting deceit. *Journal of Language and Social Psychology*, 13:
469–96.

Davies, G. (1999) 'Series Preface', in R. Milne and R. Bull (eds), *Investigative
Interviewing. Psychology and Practice*. Chichester: John Wiley.

Davies, G.M., Westcott, H.L. and Horan, N. (2000) 'The impact of questioning style
on the content of investigative interviews with suspected child abuse victims',
Psychology, Crime and Law, 6 (2): 81–97.

DeLaduranty, J. and Sullivan, D. (1980) 'Criminal investigation standards', *Enforcement Bulletin*, October: 11–14.

Fisher, R.P. (1995) 'Interviewing victims and witnesses of crime', *Psychology, Public Policy and Law*, 1 (4): 732–64.

Fisher, R.P. and McCauley, M.R. (1995) 'Improving eyewitness testimony with the cognitive interview', in M. Zaragoza, J.R. Graham, G.C.N. Hall, R. Hirschman and Y.S. Ben-Porath (eds), *Memory and Testimony in the Child Witness*. Thousand Oaks, CA: Sage.

Fisher, R.P., Geiselman, R.E. and Raymond, S.E. (1987) 'Critical analysis of police interviewing techniques', *Journal of Police Science Administration*, 15 (3): 177–85.

Geiselman, R.E. and Callot, R. (1990) 'Reverse versus forward order recall of script-based texts', *Applied Cognitive Psychology*, 4: 141–44.

Geiselman, R.E., Fisher, R.P., MacKinnon, D.P. and Holland, H.L. (1985) 'Enhancement of eyewitness memory with the cognitive interview', *American Journal of Psychology*, 99: 385–401.

George, R. (1991) 'A field and experimental evaluation of three methods of interviewing witnesses/victims of crime.' Unpublished manuscript. Polytechnic of East London, London.

Gilbert, J. (1998) *Criminal Investigation* (4th edn). New Jersey: Prentice Hall.

Gudjonsson, G.H. (1992) *The Psychology of Interrogations, Confessions and Testimony*. Chichester: Wiley.

Hargie, O., Saunders, C. and Dickenson, D. (1987) *Social Skills in Interpersonal Communication*. London: Routledge.

Hess, J. (1997) *Interviewing and Interrogation for Law Enforcement*. USA: Anderson.

Hollin, C. (1989) 'Psychology of crime. An introduction to criminological psychology', in *Criminal Law Review*, August, London: Sweet and Maxwell, pp. 532–48.

Inbau, F.E., Reid, J.E. and Buckley, J.P. (1986) *Criminal Interrogation and Confessions* (3rd edn). Baltimore, MD: Williams and Wilkins.

Irving, B. (1980) *Police Interrogation. A case stody of current practice*. Royal Commission on Criminal Procedure. Research Studies No. 2. London: HMSO.

Irving, B.L. and McKenzie, I.K. (1989) *Police Interrogation: The effects of the police and criminal evidence act*. London: The Police Foundation.

Kalbfleisch, P.J. (1994) 'The language of detecting deceit', *Journal of Language and Social Psychology*, 13: 469–96.

Kassin, S.M. and McNall, K. (1991) 'Police interrogations and confessions', *Law and Human Behavior*, 15: 233–351.

Kebbell, M. and Milne, R. (1998) 'Police officers' perceptions of eyewitness factors in forensic investigations', *Journal of Social Psychology*, 138: 323–30.

Kebbell, M. and Wagstaff, G. (1999) 'The effectiveness of the cognitive interview', in D. Canter and L. Alison (eds), *Offender Profiling Series I – Interviewing and Deception* (pp. 23–39). Aldershot: Ashgate.

Kohnken, G. (1995) 'Interviewing adults', in R. Bull and D. Carson (eds), *Handbook of Psychology in Legal Contexts* (pp. 215–33). Chichester: John Wiley.

Koriat, A. (1993) 'How do we know that we know? The accessibility model of the feeling of knowing', *Psychological Review*, 100: 609–39.

Leonard, R. and Alison. L. (1999) 'Critical incident stress debriefing and its effects on coping: Strategies and anger in a sample of Australian police officers involved in shooting incidents', *Work and Stress*, 13 (2): 144–61.

Memon, A. (1998) 'Telling it all: The cognitive interview', in A. Memon, A. Vrij and R. Bull (eds), *Psychology and Law: Truthfulness, Accuracy and Credibility* (pp. 170–87). London: McGraw-Hill.

Memon, A. and Kohnken, G. (1992) 'Helping witnesses to remember more: the cognitive interview', *Expert Evidence*, 1 (2): 39–48.

Merrill, W. (1995) 'The art of interrogating rapists', *FBI Law Enforcement Bulletin*, 64: 8–13.

Milne, R. and Bull, R. (1999) *Investigative Interviewing: Psychology and Practice*. Chichester: John Wiley.

Moston, S. (1990) *The ever-so-gentle art of police interrogation*. Paper presented at the British Psychological Society Annual Conference, Swansea University, 5 April.

Moston, S. and Engelberg, T. (1993) 'The effects of social support on children's testimony', *Applied Cognitive Psychology*, 6: 61–75.

Myklebust, T. and Alison, L. (2000) 'The current state of police interviews with children in Norway: How discrepant are they from models based on current issues in memory and communication?', *Psychology, Crime and Law*, 6: 331–51.

Oxford, T. (1991) 'Spotting a liar', *Police Review*, 15 February, 328–329.

Plimmer, J. (1997) 'Confession rate', *Police Review*, 7 February, 16–18.

Poole, D.A. and White, L.T. (1991) 'Effects of question repetition on the eyewitness testimony of children and adults', *Developmental Psychology*, 27 (6): 975–86.

Rich, J. (1968) *Interviewing Children and Adolescents*. London: Macmillan.

SAPOL, (1997) *Basic Psychology for Police Officers*. South Australia: SAPOL.

SAPOL, (1998) *OperationTraining Manual, Interviewing*. Book 12, South Australia: SAPOL.

Smith, V.L. and Ellsworth, P.C. (1987) 'The social psychology of eyewitness accuracy: misleading questions and communicator expertise', *Journal of Applied Psychology*, 72 (2): 294–300.

Softley, P. (1980) *Police Interrogation*. Home Office Research Study No. 61.

Stewart, C. and Cash, W. (1974) *Interviewing: Principles and practices*. Dubuque, IL: W.C. Brawn.

Stockdale, J. (1993) *Management and Supervision of Police Interviews*. Police Research.

Tierney, K. (1970) *Courtroom Testimony: A policeman's guide*. NewYork: Funk.

Vrij, A. (1998) 'Interviewing suspects', in A. Memon, A. Vrij and R. Bull (eds), *Psychology and Law, Truthfulness, Accuracy and Credibility* (pp. 105–19). New York: McGraw-Hill.

Warren, A.R. and Lane, P. (1995) 'Effects of timing and type of questioning on eyewitness accuracy and suggestibility', in M. Zaragoza, J.R. Graham, G.C.N. Hall, R. Hirschman and Y.S. Ben-Porath (eds), *Memory and Testimony in the Child Witness* (pp. 44–63). Thousand Oaks, CA: Sage Publications.

Wood, R. (1990) *Police Interrogation*. Toronto: Carswell.

Wright, A. and Alison, L. (2004) 'Questioning sequences in Canadian police interviews: Constructing and confirming the course of events?', *Psychology, Crime and Law*, 10 (2): 137–54.

Chapter 7

Policing the police: theoretical and practical contributions of psychologists to understanding and preventing corruption

Louise E. Porter

Given the very serious repercussions of highlighting incidents of corrupt behaviour, there is often disagreement in the literature regarding: (i) what constitutes corruption, (ii) what causes corrupt behaviour, and (iii) how such behaviour can be investigated sensitively with a view to (iv) prevention.

This chapter seeks to offer insight into the potential range of contributions that psychologists can make in addressing these four key areas. While many elements have been linked with both the causes and prevention of corruption, there are two recurring themes in the literature, which reflect the organizational culture of the police service and social pressures placed upon those involved. This chapter aims to assimilate the existing literature on police corruption in light of the organizational and social psychological dimensions.

The first section will deal with the first two areas, which relate to deepening our theoretical understanding of corrupt behaviour. In particular, this section will discuss both definitions and causes. In this endeavour, psychologists can produce theoretical models, rooted in pragmatic evidence and informed by psychological theory, to describe the various forms of corrupt behaviour that are evident within the police as well as shedding light on how they occur. The second section will focus on the latter two issues of investigating incidents of corrupt behaviour and recommending strategies for future prevention.

Theoretical examination of police corruption: defining and researching corrupt behaviour

High-profile incidents of organized police corruption have been uncovered in many countries, including the USA (Knapp, 1972; Mollen, 1994), Australia (Fitzgerald, 1989; Wood, 1997a, b) and the UK (McLagan, 2004). While some take this to suggest that corruption is both serious and widespread throughout police culture, a 2003 UK Home Office study suggests that organized corruption is rare (Miller, 2003). However, any form of corrupt police behaviour, particularly when made conspicuous by media attention, can have serious negative impacts upon the police service, both in terms of internal officer morale and external public perception that can decrease the effectiveness of the police service.

In 1999, Her Majesty's Inspectorate of Constabulary (HMIC)[1] reported that cases of corruption in UK policing were rare, with only 0.1 per cent (153 of 136,285 officers) of police officers serving in England, Wales and Northern Ireland having been suspended for alleged corruption and similar matters (HMIC, 1999). Similarly, Miller (2003), in a study of Professional Standards Unit (PSU) intelligence published by the Home Office, examined police corruption in the UK and concluded that between about 0.5 and 1 per cent of police staff (both officers and civilians) had potentially, though not necessarily, engaged in corrupt behaviour. Kiely and Peek (2002), in their interview-based study of British police officers, report one participant as remarking that 'there are still some officers who believe their priority is solving crime, but how they go about it takes second priority' (p. 174).

It is difficult to assess the extent of the problem of police corruption without first recognizing what the problem is and why it occurs. This chapter suggests that psychologists are in a unique position as scientific researchers of human behaviour to produce theoretical models, rooted in pragmatic evidence and informed by psychological theory, to define and explore police corruption.

Definition

There are difficulties in assessing the extent of corruption through reviews of existing literature since there are differences in opinion between researchers as to how 'corruption' should be defined. Authors seeking to define police corruption tackle the issue from two perspectives: those who seek to define behaviour that can be described by the term 'corrupt' (and how that may differ from other types of behaviour), and those who seek to distinguish different types of corruption under this umbrella term.

Many suggest that corruption must involve a 'corruptor', an abuse of power, and personal, organizational or group gain; that is, doing or not doing something for an external or internal 'corruptor' for some kind of gain. This can include breaking rules to achieve results (Punch, 2000; Newburn, 1999). As Skogan and Meares (2004) describe, corruption involving personal gain can include such behaviour as receiving 'police discounts' (for example, for meals), the sale of inside information, accepting bribes not to enforce the law or to testify falsely, and even payoffs to secure their own career advancement. Corruption can also involve organizational gain in so-called 'noble-cause' corruption. This could include the planting of evidence and lying in court so as to secure convictions against those who are viewed as 'deserving' of punishment.

However, others argue that much of the behaviour that is often described as 'corrupt' should be regarded as unethical or criminal behaviour. For example, Punch (2000) draws a distinction between three broad categories of police deviance: (i) *corruption* is described as the conventional understanding of taking something (such as a bribe), against your duty, to do or not to do something, as an exchange from an external corruptor; (ii) *misconduct* involves police breaking their own internal rules and procedures; and (iii) *police crime* describes such behaviour as using excessive violence, drug dealing, theft and burglary, sexual harassment, and violating a person's rights.

Roebuck and Barker (1974), however, offer a looser definition, which involves any form of 'deviant, dishonest, improper, unethical or criminal behaviour by a police officer' (p. 423). For the review purposes of this present chapter, a similarly loose definition will be utilized in order to allow discussion of the variety of corrupt and 'unethical' behaviour that exists among the police, including both officers and civilian staff.

Within the realms of behaviour that is considered 'corrupt', there are further distinctions to be made. Skogan and Meares (2004) suggest that corruption may be *proactive*, for example when officers seek out and rob street drug dealers; or *reactive*, to offers or bribes from community members. Miller (2003) also identified and distinguished between two main forms of corruption based upon those involved. These are individual and internally networked. Miller (2003) suggests that organized, networked corruption is actually rare in the UK, although somewhat more likely in the Metropolitan Police Service (MPS), where it typically involved CID or special squads operating together and often involved corrupt relationships with informants. The higher incidence of corruption could reflect a particular problem within the MPS, with a higher concentration of crime within London providing greater associated risks of corruption in terms of opportunities for corrupt behaviour. However, as Miller also highlights, the higher incidence may reflect a higher success rate in the investigation and uncovering of such cases. Indeed, the MPS have established several initiatives concerning tackling corruption, including an Anti-Corruption Group (formerly known as CIB3).

However, according to Miller (2003), the most common form of corruption among police in the UK involves information compromise/ leaking. This typically involves individuals acting in isolation from their colleagues and can include obtaining information for personal purposes, passing information to friends/family, leaks to the media and deliberate leaks to offenders. Such leaks can cause serious problems in the investigation and conviction of criminals in terms of undermining proceedings against offenders, tip-offs to offenders, the intimidation of witnesses, etc.

Recommendation: psychologists as 'corruption reviewers'

Miller (2003) suggests that many standard research methods, such as the use of surveys or interviews with those directly involved, are simply not practical in studying corruption. Due to its deviant nature and the seriousness of its repercussions, Miller states that even those who have been exposed as corrupt tend to deny their activities. Skogan and Meares (2004) agree that corruption is difficult to study systematically and that self-report surveys are unlikely to uncover anything but the least serious misconduct.

As independent experts, psychologists have a variety of methodologies at their disposal. For example, in order to uncover more effectively the prevalence of corrupt behaviour and study its nature, a psychological redefinition of the problem may be helpful. Klockars et al. (2000) have demonstrated success in surveying corruption by use of measures of the 'culture of police integrity' rather than directly surveying corrupt behaviour. Klockars et al. produced a survey that asked police for their general opinion regarding the seriousness of certain corrupt behaviours, their awareness of the rules governing unacceptable behaviour, their support for disciplinary procedures for misconduct, and their (hypothetical) willingness to internally report various kinds of misconduct. It was argued that the hypothetical, opinion-related structure of the questionnaire allowed officers to answer questions freely without implicating themselves or colleagues in corrupt acts, thus ensuring a more honest response.

Psychologists have a range of scientific skills at their disposal to assimilate and explore information, collect and analyse data and make sense of complex real-world phenomena. In the context of police corruption, psychologists can offer an objective review of the 'problem' that can be used for subsequent exploration of the causes, or contributing factors, of such behaviour.

Contributory factors in police corruption

A scientific approach to the study of corruption will aid the production of both descriptive and explanatory models that will ultimately inform prevention strategies, since different forms of corruption are likely to have different roots that require different reforms.

While there are points of disagreement between authors, most contemporary research into corruption tends to agree that police corruption is not defined by corrupt individuals (so-called 'bad apples'), but that it is particular behaviour that is corrupt. A number of factors have been cited as contributing to the causes of corrupt behaviour, including personal problems and attitudes and the increased opportunities for corrupt behaviour that present themselves in particular areas of police work. However, there are two recurring themes in the literature that reflect ordinary processes of social and organizational psychology. These are: the organizational culture of the police service and social pressures placed upon those involved. Table 7.1 summarizes these factors, which will be discussed in detail below.

Organizational factors

Many authors have blamed both specific and general elements of police culture for encouraging and/or tolerating police corruption. The issues

Table 7.1 Contributory factors to police corruption

Contributing factors	
Organizational	
Organizational culture	Emphasis on performance and clear-up rates
Policy/rules	Insufficient guidelines on corruption
Leadership	Lack of supervisory presence
Opportunities	Undercover work, informant handling, vice
Ineffective investigation/consequences	Knowledge of difficulties in proving and convicting for corrupt acts
Social	
Social culture	Solidarity and silence, pressure not to report, negative attitude towards investigators and those who co-operate
Colleague influence	Influence from peers to conform, influence of observing supervisor's bad example
External influence	Pressure from family/friends or criminals

discussed here connect directly with principles of organizational psychology that may aid in this process.

According to Punch (2000), corruption and police misconduct are persistent and constantly recurring hazards generated by the organization itself. Bayley (1995) offers a similarly critical view by stating that the police service involves an occupational culture that 'excuses and encourages abuses of power' (Bayley, 1995: 95). There are a number of aspects to this argument that cover all levels of the organizational structure, affecting all levels of the staff hierarchy. Specifically, aspects relating to performance culture, policy and rules, leadership, opportunities for corruption in police work and the impact of ineffective investigations of corruption will be discussed.

Organizational culture

Fleming and Lafferty (2000), in their discussion of police corruption in Australia, examine the changing internal culture of Australian organizations. They note that, during the 1980s, the Australian public sector endeavoured to apply the 'private sector solution to the public sector problem' (Dixon et al., 1998: 1); that is, they viewed increases in operational performance and efficiency as paramount for an effective police service. These techniques were implemented in the police service, not only in Australia, but also in most English-speaking countries (Dixon et al., 1998; McLaughlin and Murji, 1997).

Traditionally, in the UK, police performance indicators have placed considerable emphasis on detection rates. Where police 'success' is measured by results, officers may be encouraged to cut corners or bend the rules to achieve such outcomes. Here, police officers may believe that the 'ends justify the means' in their desire to perform well. Indeed, evidence has emerged that the pressures placed upon police through this demonstrable performance culture is a major factor affecting integrity, with the boundaries sometimes being pushed too far and unethical practices employed to 'improve' their figures (HMIC, 1999). Examples of such behaviour include not recording crimes that are unlikely to result in detection, the inaccurate classification of crimes and encouraging convicted criminals to admit crimes that they did not commit. However, Her Majesty's Inspector reported that, in general, there is little evidence that these practices are in any way widespread, but 'pockets' of unethical crime recording were still in existence at that time (HMIC, 1999).

This emphasis on performance has seen the beginnings of change in recent years to an emphasis on professional standards, rules and integrity (Miller, 2003). This is particularly relevant to the police service's increasing recognition of the importance of community 'impression management'; that is, being seen to serve the community and build a trusting and mutually rewarding relationship between themselves and the public that they serve. However, a similar 'ends justify the means' argument is also relevant to those officers who indulge in corrupt behaviour to achieve results due to their own negative beliefs surrounding the criminal justice system and a desire to protect the community. For example, Sherman (1985) states that police officers may perceive agencies or practices to be ineffective, or that dubious prosecutorial decisions may cause them to believe that 'justice' is not being done. Under such circumstances, police officers may be tempted into such practices as the planting of evidence on suspected criminals or lying in court to secure a conviction.

Linked to the idea of performance culture is the possibility that the organization itself may wish to cover up incidents of corruption in order to prevent negative effects of an investigation. Miller (2003) points out that investigations into incidents of police corruption can cause demoralization of forces in terms of low morale and distrust among officers, as well as bad publicity. In a study by Kiely and Peek (2002), police officers who were interviewed regarding their views of police culture did indeed note that corrupt behaviour served to discredit the police service, reducing public confidence in the police. HMIC (1999) notes that community support is an essential part of providing an effective police service; therefore media reports of corruption or corruption investigations may reduce this effectiveness through a decreased willingness of the public to co-operate in future police work.

Policy/rules

While the issues discussed above suggest that police officers 'choose' to bend or break the rules in order to do their job, it has also been suggested that underlying problems based on inadequate policy and performance measures facilitate and contribute to corrupt behaviour. For example, both HMIC (1999) and Miller (2003) reported that there were insufficient rules governing what behaviour is acceptable and what is considered unethical or, indeed, corrupt within the police service. Without more strongly defined guidelines, officers are less able to judge either their own behaviour or that of their colleagues. Indeed, many officers and support staff demonstrated poor security awareness in terms of the sensitive information that they were dealing with in their work. Miller concluded that officers were insufficiently trained in the sensitivities and the negative effects of behaviours such as the leaking of information and, as a consequence, were far too open with others, both within and outside the police force, about such information.

Leadership

In 1999, the HMIC reported that the most prominent of all the factors that could lead to a lack of integrity in the police service was an absence of good supervision, management and leadership. Leadership can impact upon corruption and unethical behaviour in a number of ways.

In Australia, in response to media allegations of criminal activity within Queensland's Police Force (QPF), a Commission of Inquiry, chaired by Tony Fitzgerald, QC, was established in 1987. The report arising out of the Fitzgerald Inquiry (Fitzgerald, 1989) identified QPF's highly centralized, rigid and hierarchical structure as a major factor in police corruption, which adversely affected both communication between ranks and decision-making processes. HMIC (1999) identified a similar lack of communication between leaders and subordinates in the UK police service in that staff were unaware of the views of their chief officers with respect to guidelines of acceptable behaviour, since superior officers had not set out common standards and were not keen to be the first to do so. Indeed, the HMIC reported that leadership of staff and the management of day-to-day operations were being increasingly neglected. Further, Sherman (1985) suggests that supervisors may willingly turn a blind eye to corrupt behaviour if they, themselves, share in the 'ends justify the means' attitude, or are similarly unaware of the potentially negative impact of the behaviour.

Overwhelmingly, though, police work often tends to involve a general lack of supervisory presence. Many police officers conduct their work on their own or with a partner, with much of the decision-making on the methods and tactics that they adopt in the field made by officers on the spot with few witnesses. Skogan and Meares (2004) state that police work combines high discretion with low-visibility decision-making. The lack of supervision in activities makes this discretion hard to monitor and control. At the very least, weak management and low control over staff will fail to pick up inappropriate behaviour that arises from insufficient training, and may be seen to silently condone it. Further, as Miller (2003) states, there is often a tendency not to closely examine those officers who perform well, despite the fact that this performance may, as discussed above, be indicative of corrupt behaviour to achieve surface results. Skogan and Meares (2004) also argue that lack of supervision in police field work can lead to increased opportunities for corrupt behaviour in 'an environment that can be awash with tempting opportunities and an ample supply of "regular" citizens willing to offer up even more' (Skogan and Meares, 2004: 75).

Opportunities for corruption
Many authors agree that the occupation of policing is intrinsically vulnerable to misconduct (Newburn, 1997; Wood, 1997a, b) since numerous rewarding opportunities exist. Fleming and Lafferty (2000) note

that public servants, particularly police officers, are rarely praised, but often criticized, for their efforts to provide a public service. Such a lack of public praise may lead officers to seek rewards elsewhere and, as Marx (1980) remarks, 'the financial rewards from police corruption, particularly in gambling and narcotics, can be great and chances for avoiding detection rather good' (Marx, 1980: 426).

Indeed, certain areas of police work are more prone to corruption than others, such as where officers are likely to work with informants, under-cover, unsupervised and are exposed to potentially high rewards for corrupt behaviour. For example, Skogan and Meares (2004) state that narcotics units are especially prone to corruption owing to the large sums of money and drugs that they deal with, the willingness of both buyers and sellers to offer bribes to officers, and the low visibility of the decisions that are made in the field by investigators (US General Accounting Office, 1998, cited in Skogan and Meares, 2004). Further, the nature of the crimes investigated means that those whom they deal with are unlikely to be trusted or taken seriously should they complain about any aspect of police behaviour (Newburn, 1999).

Undercover police work is particularly difficult to supervise (Marx, 1980) and the very secrecy that aids police in dealing with offenders can also aid them in breaking the law themselves. Marx (1980) points out that police who have infiltrated groups sometimes become converted to, or sympathize with, the perspective of the group and may develop guilt and apprehensions over their deception.

Another high-risk area of police work in terms of a potential for corruption is the use of informants. Since the publication of the report *Helping with Enquiries: Tackling Crime Effectively* (1993) by the Audit Commission[2] there has been an increasing reliance on intelligence-led policing, which involves the use of informants (HMIC, 1999). Police officers who handle informants are exposed to offenders far more fre-quently and in a less controlled environment. While guidelines have been issued by ACPO[3] (1997) that advise on the way that informers should be managed, they primarily concern the procedure and do not address the ethical dilemmas that can arise. Indeed, HMIC (1999) found that in some cases the guidelines used by police forces for informant handling were inadequate and often not employed for practical reasons.

Dunnighan and Norris (1998) report that officers often have their own, highly individualized, 'lines' that they draw for informant handling rather than agreed norms. This results in a wide variety of opinions between officers regarding what constitutes acceptable or unacceptable behaviour. Thus, Dunnighan and Norris (1998) report that informant handlers often keep details of their dealings secret in order to avoid crossing someone else's line. This promotes secrecy and unsupervised behaviour. Further,

Dunnighan and Norris also report that the majority of officers see rule-bending as an essential element of running informants.

A further problem in informant handling, highlighted by HMIC (1999), involves the possible development of a close relationship between the informant and the handler. This is increasingly likely the more 'exclusive' the relationship (for example, an informant who will only deal with one particular officer) and where the relationship runs for a number of years. Here the handler may be more sympathetic towards the informant, more likely to turn a blind eye to the informant's own criminal activity, or likely to offer high or unethical rewards for information. The Inspectorate highlights the policy of one agency in dealing with this, whereby an informant can be handled by the same individual for a maximum of two years only.

Investigation and consequences

Individuals may also be tempted to engage in corrupt behaviour indirectly through the knowledge that such behaviour is often difficult to investigate and detect. Further, where investigations are successful in uncovering incidents of corruption, there are still further problems in proving and punishing such behaviour. Skogan and Meares (2004) note that few cases are actually brought forward by internal inspectors and that intent is often difficult to document. Punch (2000) agrees that the difficulty of prosecution for corruption lies in proving that bribes or gifts were offered in the expectation of a service and that the officer responded by abusing his or her authority. Thus, it involves interpreting the motivations and proving the nature of the exchange. Further, Miller (2003) reports that it is difficult to convince judges and juries to convict and the few sentences that are actually imposed tend to be light. Miller notes that officers know how to present themselves well in court and often gain sympathy from the jury in terms of the 'noble cause' neutralizations that 'justify' the corrupt means in terms of the achieved ends.

Social factors

According to Punch (2000), police corruption does not simply involve individuals seeking personal gain. It involves:

> group behaviour rooted in established arrangements and/or extreme practices that have to be located within the structure and culture of police work and the police organization. Police officers have to be initiated into these practices, rationalizations have to be produced to accept them, supervisors have to collude or turn a blind eye, justifications have to be sought to continue them, and

organizations have either in some way to condone or encourage these activities – or else fail to tackle them.

(Punch, 2000: 304)

This implies various levels of involvement, from the organization (as discussed above), but also influence from superiors and colleagues. Contrary to this, Miller (2003) concluded that the majority of corruption in UK police forces is conducted by individuals and predominantly concerns leaking information. However, even in such cases, social factors can play an influential role; for example, through solidarity and silence of colleagues that condone such behaviour, pressure and influence from peers and superiors within the police force and also social networks (including criminal associations) outside of the police force.

Social culture: solidarity and silence

Police culture has been discussed above in terms of its occupational factors. However, there are also strong social factors that define the culture of policing. Sherman (1985) states that the policing culture fosters solidarity, secrecy and cynicism among officers. Police officers are in a unique position in their relationship to the public that may promote feelings of social isolation, causing them to rely heavily on colleagues for support (Fleming and Lafferty, 2000). This sense of solidarity can be powerful and can also extend to an apparent gulf between 'street cops' and 'management cops' (Reiner, 2000). Within these social groupings there is often a sense of 'sticking together' or 'looking after your own' and, therefore, reporting wrongdoings of colleagues is seen as breaking the 'code'. As Skogan and Meares (2004) note, corruption is very much facilitated by tolerance, or at least passive unresponsiveness, by peer officers in the organization. Such tolerance not only reinforces corrupt behaviour by giving the impression that it is acceptable, but it also reassures those involved that, since they will not be reported, they are unlikely to be caught and disciplined for their behaviour. ACPO has acknowledged the influence of such a culture on the behaviour of officers and has been quoted as stating that 'Police culture is extremely powerful and overlooking its importance is frequently the cause of failed attempts at organizational change' (*Police Review*, 1994: 13).

The 'code of silence' creates particular pressure upon staff not to report corrupt behaviour. As has been mentioned, there often exists a close bond between police officers, perhaps caused by the perceived gap between themselves and the public that they serve. This creates difficulties for staff to expose wrongdoing (HMIC, 1999). Crank (1999) reports the existence of protection of corrupt staff by colleagues and that honest officers learn to keep quiet about deviant behaviour, thus demonstrating corrupt behaviour themselves. There is typically negative behaviour towards those who co-operate in internal investigations, as well as the investigators themselves when they return to their ordinary police work. In light of the existence of such hostile behaviour, there is a strong need for support to be set in place in the police service for those who do report corrupt activity. Absence of such support may send the message to staff that the organization does not support those who report corruption.

Inside influence: peers and superiors

Social influence inside the organization may also be more direct, arising out of relationships with, and observation of, both peers and superiors. Punch (2000) argues that corrupt behaviour is learned socially in small groups within the context of police culture. He reports that, in some cases, new recruits are gradually introduced into corruption and learn to accept it as normal. Punch goes on to suggest that these individuals will conform to deviant behaviour to be part of the group. Sherman (1985) agrees that group dynamics are crucial, with young officers relating primarily to small, cohesive units upon joining and having to conform to informal norms to be accepted. Such social pressure is well documented in social psychology, where individuals will conform to group norms through fear of being singled out as different and rejected by the group (Asch, 1951; Barbuto, 2000). Further, the group provides social support for behaviour, allowing group members to rationalize and neutralize their behaviour (Barbuto, 2000; Grosser et al., 1951). To go against the group is not only seen as an act of betrayal that may incur social sanctions from those involved but also may mean facing prosecution and prison.

Apart from peer pressure, a strong source of internal influence is likely to stem from superior officers. In hierarchically structured organizations, such as the police force, there are many levels of leadership and management through the ranks. HMIC emphasizes that senior ranks carry a great deal of respect and that staff perceptions of senior officers significantly influence how those staff behave. HMIC highlights the importance of senior staff setting high standards and 'being seen to practise what they preach' (HMIC, 1999: 66). Junior staff, particularly those new to the organization, are often likely to look to role models for information on professional conduct. Further, if senior officers are seen to 'break the rules' or ignore policy guidelines, then those rules and policies are seriously undermined in the eyes of junior staff in the organization.

Outside influence

In addition to possible influence from within the police service, police officers may also be exposed to external influences encouraging corrupt behaviour. Such external influences are likely to promote *reactive* corruption; for example, where police perform corrupt behaviour in response to external bribes.

Miller (2003) highlighted the influence of family and friends on the act of leaking information and also social networks with criminals as an important basis for corruption. Such influences are most likely where officers live and work in the same force area. Police staff can be targeted specifically by those involved in organized crime and offered bribes to co-operate by turning a blind eye, or helping to cover criminal activity. Marx (1988) further points out that police engaged in undercover work or informant–handler relationships can come to share the views of the criminals that they are trying to police and be drawn into co-operating in criminal activity. Conversely, Sherman (1985) suggests that such close relationships with criminals can foster hostile feelings towards such individuals, which can lead to either 'noble-cause' corruption or tackling criminals by committing a crime against them in retaliation.

Recommendation: psychologists as 'corruption analysts'

As outlined above, there are many varieties of corrupt behaviour and many contributing factors. Exploration of these from a psychological perspective has revealed particular themes that relate to particular organizational and social factors, which in turn may require differing initiatives to tackle these problem areas.

The use of analytical research techniques to identify police corruption has been highlighted by Quinton and Miller (2003), in their summary of findings from their individual research on police misconduct procedures and corruption (Miller, 2003; Quinton, 2003). Specifically, Quinton and Miller draw attention to the approach of the UK's Merseyside Police, which has been successful in significantly reducing the number of recorded complaints against their officers. The approach employed techniques to centrally monitor complaints data to identify underlying problems. This highlights the importance of detailed and continuous analysis of police intelligence that identifies both the extent and nature of misconduct. Such an approach not only informs specifically within police constabularies of particular problems or problem officers (therefore making officers more accountable), but also allows for general analysis and theory building of corruption as a wider national, or indeed international, phenomenon. Psychologists, as social scientists, may be particularly well placed to conduct objective analysis of this type and integrate findings with psychological theory. Such theory is of particular use for underpinning initiatives for targeted investigation and prevention of corruption. This will be the subject of the next section of this chapter.

Practical strategies for uncovering and preventing corruption

The problems and contributory factors outlined above in relation to organizational and social psychological dimensions of police corruption now warrant two further practical recommendations for which psychologists can offer advice. It will be argued that psychologists can offer a service of external investigation of corrupt behaviour to the police service, which has the advantage of being both objective and scientific. Further, psychologists can be used in an advisory capacity to tailor initiatives for preventing corrupt behaviour within the police service, as well as the possibility of actually providing some of these initiatives, such as administering training courses to police personnel. Such involvement would be subject to the psychologist negotiating a contract of confidentiality of information with the police service.

Investigating corruption

In the UK, the Home Affairs Committee (1998a) concluded that the police complaints and disciplinary procedures were inadequate, a view shared in the Stephen Lawrence Inquiry (Macpherson, 1999). The Home Secretary (Home Affairs Committee, 1998b) then announced changes to the disciplinary process, implemented in April 1999, which included a new code of conduct, fast-tracking of cases, a reduction in the standard of proof necessary at disciplinary hearings and the introduction of written warnings and tribunal panels.

However, Quinton's (2003) review of these reforms demonstrated that, while the use of written warnings gained strong support among staff, in general the new procedures have not led to an overall increase in the number of investigations or number of charges brought against officers, and provisional evidence also suggested no significant change in the outcome of cases.

There are several suggestions in the literature for improvements to all levels of the detection of corruption and misconduct, beginning with issues surrounding the initial reporting of behaviour. Miller (2003) stresses the need to encourage the reporting of corrupt behaviour and for support strategies to be in place to aid those who do wish to report corruption. For example, a confidential helpline could relieve much of the stress experienced by officers contemplating reporting their colleagues and long-term support should be available throughout the course of the whole investigation.

Generally officers tend to be somewhat insecure about, and distrustful of, the investigation process (Quinton, 2003). This demonstrates a need for openness and fairness in the investigation process rather than officers feeling they are being, or could potentially be, unfairly targeted. Many police forces in the US, Australia and indeed the UK (Prenzler and Ronken, 2001), have used 'integrity tests' to investigate corruption both proactively and reactively, where individuals are faced with 'sting' operations that simulate misconduct opportunities and test how the officer responds. While targeted integrity testing is used to reactively investigate those officers who are already under suspicion of corruption, random integrity testing may be used as a proactive measure to dissuade officers from engaging in corrupt behaviour through fear that they may be the subject of such a test, since, potentially, any officer could be (randomly) chosen.

However, any change in behaviour brought about by the threat/ knowledge of integrity tests is ultimately a result of compliance through fear rather than internalization of morals, ethics or values, and is likely to foster feelings of unfairness and mistrust of investigators and their operations. Such feelings are likely to make officers less co-operative with corruption investigators and less likely to report corrupt behaviour. Integrity testing also raises many serious issues regarding privacy, deception, entrapment, provocation and the legal rights of individuals (Prenzler and Ronken, 2001).

Recommendation: psychologists as corruption investigators

As Miller (2003) argues, many standard investigative methods will be ineffective in cases of police corruption since those under investigation are likely to be aware of these methods and so can evade detection. Further, information regarding internal investigations may circulate within the police force or surveillance teams could be recognized: both could compromise the investigation.

The capacity of psychologists to act as external reviewers of police corruption has been discussed above in relation to analysis of police intelligence, as well as a range of survey methods for uncovering the prevalence of corrupt behaviour. However, it is argued that intelligence-led approaches require both proactive and reactive investigation, monitoring of possible problem areas or individuals and significant analysis of such data in a rigorous, scientific way. Further, such investigations and reviews should be handled objectively.

The Home Office case study review report of Operation Lancet (2002) discusses whether investigations should be managed internally or whether an 'outside force' should be brought in. A number of considerations that should be made in such a decision are offered. First, there may be a requirement for specialist skills and techniques, particularly in intelligence gathering and analysis, where specialist knowledge of research and analytical methods is essential. Such skills may not be available in internal staff members. Further, internal investigations may encounter problems arising from past or present associations between the officer(s) under investigation and the officer(s) appointed as investigator(s). Related to this is a perception that the force may not be able to demonstrate true independence, both in terms of directives from senior staff and also in terms of their own objectivity of investigation, since the investigation team may also be affected by any bad publicity stemming from the uncovering of corrupt individuals.

Such issues can be overcome through external reviews, for example with the use of police officers from another force. In the UK, the Independent Police Complaints Commission (IPCC) has been established under the Police Reform Act. Further, Professional Standards Units (PSUs) were established in order to proactively investigate police corruption through the gathering and analysis of intelligence. However, Chan (1999) points out that external investigations can actually be counterproductive since they are typically resented by police staff, who hide behind a wall of silence.

Preventing corruption

As mentioned above, new misconduct procedures were implemented within the police force in 1999. These included a reduction in the standard of proof necessary in disciplinary hearings, a new Code of Conduct, fast-tracking cases with clear evidence of misconduct and the introduction of written warnings for less serious incidents. Quinton (2003) evaluated these organizational changes within the police service and concluded that the perception among the majority of staff within the Complaints and Discipline department was that the changes to the disciplinary process had little practical impact. While most believed that the new misconduct procedures were relatively effective at dealing with incidents of misconduct, they were not necessarily seen to be any more effective than the old discipline procedures, with the perception being that they had failed to resolve the problems that existed with the old procedures.

Much of the procedures in place in the past have tended towards reactive investigation of complaints and guidelines for dealing with corruption. However, more recently there has been a shift towards proactive investigations, intelligence gathering and targeting sources of learning of corrupt behaviour through strong leadership and ethics training (Miller, 2003). Once again, as both organizational and social factors contribute to the causes of corruption and create difficulties in its detection, so similar factors can be used to inform practices for preventing and dealing with corrupt behaviour. Table 7.2 summarizes a specific set of

Table 7.2 Police corruption prevention recommendations associated with organizational and social contributing factors.

Contributing factors	Prevention
Organizational	
Performance culture	Shift to professional standards
Insufficient policy/rules	Clear rules with definitions and working examples
	Training from external personnel – communicate rules, ethics and risks and implications of corruption
Lack of leadership presence	Visible leadership, fair appraisal and feedback. Transformational leadership
Police work opportunities	Vetting, rotation, levels of access to data
Ineffective investigation/ punishment	Encourage reporting, helpline, openness and fairness, external reviews
Social	
Social culture: solidarity and silence	Intolerance to harassment – protect their own
Colleague influence	Use solidarity to encourage integrity, good leadership (set good example)
External influence	Combination of above, particularly those associated with policy and opportunities

recommendations relating to each of the contributing factors outlined earlier. These recommendations are discussed in detail below.

Organizational factors

The organizational factors that impact upon the prevention of corruption include the police culture, rules and policy, leadership, opportunities for corruption and investigation. Each of these will be discussed in turn with recommendations for improving ethical behaviour within the police service and decreasing misconduct.

Culture

Police culture has been discussed above in terms of its powerful influence over the behaviour of police officers. Thus, many agree that changes in the behaviour of police staff must begin with changes to the organizational culture. Kiely and Peek (2002), from their interviews with police officers, concluded that police culture is slowly but surely evolving, with the police increasingly incorporating agendas that are more similar to the private sector than to the public sector. These private sector agendas now reflect issues of quality of service, professional standards and integrity more than performance measures that reflect clear-up rates (Miller, 2003).

While challenges to the existing police culture are generally a move in the right direction, such efforts will need to be persistent (Punch, 2000) and care is needed in how to implement such changes. Fleming and Lafferty (2000) give caution that unwelcome organizational changes may push police officers further together for support and generate pockets of resistance. Values such as loyalty to fellow officers are deeply rooted in police cultures and there may be resistance to new management techniques that promote individual performance and accountability or strict policies over reporting on colleagues' behaviour. Such policies may negatively affect officer morale and, in Australia, have been reported to produce a management division between senior and junior police officers (Fleming and Lafferty, 2000). Thus, there is a danger of new policy implementation actually exacerbating issues of solidarity among officers, rather than discouraging it, as well as widening the communication gap between the ranks.

Clearly, since the solidarity aspect of police culture seems so ingrained, organizational change will be most effective if it can harness this influence and exploit it to change the focus of its power. For example, rather than solidarity being viewed as a negative influence that prevents officers from reporting unethical conduct, solidarity can be utilized to promote a positive feeling of shared accountability, where the misconduct of one officer is perceived to impact negatively upon the whole group. This will be discussed in more detail below. However, the starting points for change, from an organizational perspective, are clear rules that are effectively communicated through formal training programmes and strong, unambiguous leadership.

Rules/policy
HMIC (1999) acknowledges that there is a difficulty in changing organizational culture and highlights the importance of communicating more explicitly what constitutes acceptable and unacceptable behaviour. Mastrofski (2004), referring to the Committee to Review Research on Police Policy and Practices (2003) in the US, reports that the research reviewed by the committee suggests that formal rules and guidelines and strong disciplinary procedures reduce corrupt practices. For example, the Inspectorate (1999) points out that corrupt behaviour would be more difficult if all gifts, gratuities and perks were totally unacceptable within the police service. The Inspection Team also highlight the importance of clarity over issues surrounding confidentiality and information sharing, particularly in light of the move towards multi-agency working.

As mentioned above, following concerns raised by the Home Affairs Committee (1998a), significant changes were made to the system for dealing with police misconduct. These changes included a new Code of Conduct that sets out standards of behaviour that are expected from police officers. However, in reviewing the effects of these changes on the police service, Quinton (2003) reported several problems encountered with the new Code. First, there was a great deal of uncertainty among officers about how misconduct was actually defined. Indeed, Quinton (2003) points out that there is no discrete definition of what constitutes misconduct in either the old discipline procedures or the new misconduct procedures: both simply provide frameworks against which officer conduct can be judged. However, while the framework in the old discipline code gave specific examples of offences, the framework of the new code sets out ethical standards for behaviour. Quinton (2003) found that many officers believed the old discipline code to be clearer and more specific than the new Code of Conduct. In light of this, many officers had developed their own definitions of misconduct, which, much like the old discipline code, tended to consist of examples of behaviour that the officers considered to be unacceptable, such as threatening, aggressive or unnecessarily forceful behaviour and swearing and use of racist language.

Police officers in Quinton's (2003) review described the principles set out in the Code as imprecise, open to interpretation and lacking clarity. They encountered fundamental problems of having to apply positive standards of conduct to allegations of negative behaviour and found that the Code required a greater degree of interpretation in formulating misconduct charges since it was too abstract. Quinton remarks that this degree of interpretation in the use of the Code may, potentially, result in cases being handled inconsistently. It is, therefore, important that rules of conduct are seen to be relevant and grounded in police practice as well as being clear and unambiguous. It seems that codes of conduct, in order to be effective, should include definitions and working examples of both acceptable and unacceptable behaviour.

While having clear rules and policies is a starting point, these will only be effective if they are communicated throughout the organization. The officers interviewed in Quinton's (2003) study demonstrated little knowledge of the specific changes implemented to the misconduct procedures, indicating that the new procedures had not been communicated widely or effectively.

Many authors agree that education and training are a major factor in promoting integrity and ethical policing. Training programmes can communicate the code of conduct and ethical standards in an operational context, with a trainer on hand to settle any queries that the officers may have. Training programmes can also educate staff about the risks of corruption that they may be exposed to, both inside and outside the organization, how to minimize these risks and the consequences of engaging in corrupt behaviour (Miller, 2003; Quinton, 2003).

Staff training can also be employed to promote intolerance of corrupt behaviour and an ethos of supporting those who report misconduct. This may help reduce the negative labelling and hostility that occur towards those who do report their colleagues. Once again, how this training is administered is of importance if the correct information is to be communicated effectively. The Fitzgerald Report in Australia recommended that police trainers should be replaced by external qualified personnel. It was suggested that this would limit the transmission of the negative aspects of police culture to new recruits and also reduce the insular nature of the police force that can foster negative aspects of solidarity (Fitzgerald, 1989).

Organizational leadership presence

Whilst the hierarchical system within the police service means that officers are required to follow rules set out by their superiors, clearly the existence of corrupt behaviour demonstrates that this will not always be the case, indicating that leadership is not always effective. Most authors agree that leadership is an essential element of promoting integrity and discouraging corrupt behaviour. Principles of leadership from organizational psychology can shed some light on possible pathways that such leadership should take in order to be effective at promoting ethical behaviour in the police service.

Example-setting as influential leadership behaviour has been discussed above in terms of contributing to corrupt behaviour, where superior officers display unethical behaviour themselves that is then observed by junior officers. Indeed, HMIC (1999) suggests that efforts towards positive behaviour change in junior staff will not succeed unless senior officers set the right example. However, to set an example, senior officers must be available as a model; that is, they must be visible in order to be observed. HMIC (1999) criticizes the communication gap between levels of management in the police service and advises that senior staff should ensure that they are accessible in order for their leadership to be effective. This, it is proposed, requires all levels of management to be 'far more involved in day-to-day "hands on" intrusive supervision of their staff' (HMIC, 1999: 6). Such supervision will also allow senior staff to more readily identify and monitor problems of conduct and deal with such behaviour as it arises (Quinton, 2003). The monitoring of behaviour has been demonstrated to be a particularly important element of social influence in terms of the presence of an influencer with the power to both punish unacceptable behaviour and reward good behaviour. However, such monitoring must be seen to be fair, consistent and based on performance.

Komaki (1998) states that effective managers provide constant monitoring and feedback of subordinates' tasks, gathering information about subordinates' performance and giving feedback that is contingent upon that performance. This provides consequences of behaviour in terms of comments and reinforcements. Leaders are seen to show an interest and are present to punish and oversee and, thus, subordinates are aware that how they behave will affect how they are subsequently treated.

Unfortunately, examples have been noted where the police service does not always follow these principles. For example, in Australia, the Fitzgerald Report noted the potential for favouritism in promotions. Fitzgerald (1989) argued that actual officer performance, aptitude or skill held little consequence in the promotion process. In the UK, HMIC (1999) drew similar conclusions regarding the appraisal process in the police service. The Inspectorate noted:

> little evidence that appraisals were conducted with complete honesty and objectivity, most supervisors preferring to be charitable, either to avoid upsetting a member of their staff or because they lack the skills to produce a balanced and evidenced assessment.
>
> (HMIC, 1999)

Like, Komaki (1998), HMIC (1999) endorse the importance of a fair appraisal system in promoting integrity, where police officers can be sure that the consequences for particular behaviour (good or bad) will be fair and consistent and that senior staff acknowledge the behaviour of junior staff, are aware of any potential difficulties and take steps to support their staff where necessary. Such principles also extend to the misconduct investigation process, where such investigations should demonstrate openness and fairness, where possible, and discipline procedures should be contingent upon behaviour and consistent across situations and individuals (Quinton, 2003).

However, while the leadership outlined above generally involves effective influence through rewards or threat of punishment, the most effective form of leadership, it has been suggested, is that which involves internalization of values and rules, or a personal 'transformation' (Smith, 1986). Such 'transformational leadership' means that subordinates follow due to their belief in the legitimacy of rules or behaviour, rather than through fear of, or desire for, particular consequences. Where subordinates believe in the values, such influence is most likely to extend beyond supervised situations, ensuring acceptable behaviour without constant monitoring (Turner, 1991). These individuals are also more likely to promote such behaviour to others, continuing the transmission of the goals and values from the higher levels of the organization down to the lower ranks. Mastrofski (2004) reports that the concepts behind transformational leadership are becoming increasingly endorsed in police management texts, although, he states, there is little empirical research that tests whether and when it is effective in police organizations.

Work opportunities

While the processes above can be set in place, there are still areas of policing that are particularly at risk to opportunities of corruption. These areas, discussed above as those where informants and covert operations are utilized and where large sums of money are involved, need to be highly regulated. Miller (2003) suggests that policies for vetting staff at the recruitment stage for these high-risk posts should be in place, and Quinton (2003) endorses the rotation of staff in these positions, whereby officers occupy such positions for a limited, fixed period of time. Miller also stresses the importance of appropriate levels of access for data systems that contain sensitive information. This will allow easier auditing of the use of such systems and also encourage an appropriate sense of confidentiality regarding the information stored.

Social factors

Social culture

The importance of changing the attitudes of staff and encouraging internalization of moral standards through leadership, training and clear rules has been discussed above in relation to preventing corruption. However, some view the most difficult hurdle in this process as the deep-rooted solidarity between officers that may make them less susceptible to change. In his report on Australia's New South Wales Police Service, Wood (1997a) remarked that

> the significance of the code of silence, which is an incontrovertible and universal product of police culture, cannot be understated. The code of silence and other negative aspects of police culture need to be vigorously addressed as part of the reform process.
>
> (Wood, 1997a: 33)

Punch (2000) agrees, and talks of the vital need to focus on group dynamics and the negative aspects of police culture in the tackling of corruption. However, given the strength of this culture it may be profitable to utilize this solidarity in a positive way to encourage ethical behaviour. Where integrity is the group norm, those officers who engage in corruption will be perceived as deviating from the group and the same negative group pressures that have been focused against those who report corruption will then work against those who engage in it. Thus, the strong social support between officers is used to promote positive behaviour, where the goal of the group is to protect each other from those who engage in corruption, rather than protecting corrupt individuals from detection.

There are specific areas that need to be addressed. Fundamentally, the group norm needs to be one of ethical values. Thus, group pressure will be placed upon those who behave unethically, since this will be against the group norm. Further, Miller (2003) highlights the importance of intolerance to harassment and victimization, including protection of those who report corrupt behaviour. It is necessary to promote a positive group attitude towards reporting corruption, for example, by framing it as having positive consequences for the group as a whole in contrast to the negative impacts that corruption carries, such as damaging the public reputation of the whole police force.

Colleague influence

Peer influence has been addressed in the above section. However, influence within the organization may also come from superior officers. HMIC (1999) reported that, if integrity is to be maintained, all managers, from chief officers down, should set a clear and unequivocally good example, and should not practise double standards (for example, condemning the receiving of perks as unethical but then accepting such offers themselves). The act of providing a 'good example' is a particularly important aspect of leadership, if ethical behaviour is to be promoted throughout the organization. Leading by example is a particularly effective leadership process, especially where guidelines of conduct are vague. Junior staff will look to their superiors for guidance on how to act themselves. This is a process of modelling (Bandura, 1971). Indeed, even where the hierarchy is not overt, individuals will model their behaviour on others when unsure of the situation and those who are perceived to possess higher levels of status are particularly likely to become attractive models (Bandura *et al.*, 1963).

External influence

Many of the recommendations discussed above will combine to guard against outside targeting of police for corrupt behaviour. In particular, educating officers as to the risks of outside influences, the ethical issues involved and the repercussions of such behaviour will serve as a good base precaution. This should be grounded in a police culture that is centred on integrity and ethical policing. Further, the appropriately set levels of access to information and stricter protocols for exposing police to opportunities for corruption that have been outlined above should serve as extra constraints on the prospects of external civilians influencing police personnel into engaging in corrupt acts.

Recommendation: psychologists as corruption-prevention advisors

In light of the points outlined above, there are several facets of corruption prevention for which psychologists could act in an advisory capacity. Based upon the knowledge gained through analysis and application of psychological theory, particular recommendations have been made that relate to specific problems/factors in police corruption. First, psychologists can offer general advice on applying principles of organizational and social psychology to the police service in terms of the development of an ethical culture and effective leadership. Psychologists may also offer a more specific advisory role in terms of vetting, inter-viewing and recruitment procedures of officers in high-risk areas of policing. Further, psychologists may take on the role of an external trainer/educator to run training programmes on codes of conduct and definitions of corruption and also the risks and consequences of corruption. This role can also help to promote ethics within the police service and encourage unity among officers in terms of intolerance to corruption and support of those who report it. These recommendations can be implemented in all or in part: that is, while some forces may wish to set such practices in place in a proactive way, others may wish to tailor initiatives to their specific needs based on the extent and type of corruption evident from analysis of intelligence.

Conclusion: contributions of psychologists to assessing, uncovering and preventing police corruption

This chapter has reviewed the literature on police corruption and misconduct and has integrated findings with principles of occupational and social psychology to explore the definitions and causes of corruption, investigative strategies for uncovering incidents of corruption and also corruption prevention. Specifically the potential role of psychologists has been highlighted at each of these stages in a set of specific recom-mendations. These relate to the roles of psychologists as reviewers, analysts, investigators and advisors. However, the key across all of these services is the role of psychologists as operating in an external capacity and offering advice that is objective and scientific.

Several further observations have been made from this review. Importantly, the current state of policing in the UK seems to involve relatively few cases of corruption, with the majority of incidents involving less serious, individual misconduct associated with the leaking of information. However, there are still problems in that when incidents do arise they have serious negative consequences for the police service as a whole organization, particularly with regards to the public's perception of the police.

As Punch (2000) explains, the police are dependent on the co-operation of the public in tackling and investigating crime. The lack of confidence in the police that can be brought about by high-profile incidents of police misconduct can seriously decrease the willingness of the public to trust the police with information, which can very seriously reduce the effectiveness of their service. Interestingly, however, HMIC's (1999) inspection into police integrity highlighted that poor officer behaviour (for example, rudeness, racism and discriminatory comments) was the issue that caused most public concern.

In conclusion, there is a fundamental need to promote the common goal of ethical policing and highlighting for officers why it is important. The organizational culture needs to embrace this view so that police staff can work together to reduce all levels of misconduct through training to promote awareness of important issues and leadership to set good examples and reward/punish behaviour in a fair and consistent way as well as promote the ideal goals and values of the organization throughout the ranks.

Acknowledgements

I would like to thank Professor Alison for his valuable comments on an earlier version of this chapter.

Notes

1   Her Majesty's Inspectorate of Constabulary (HMIC) are charged with examining and improving the efficiency and effectiveness of the Police Service in England, Wales and Northern Ireland.
2   The Audit Commission is an independent public body responsible for ensuring that public services, such as the police, deliver high-quality service and value for money.
3   ACPO is the Association of Chief Police Officers in the UK whose core activity is in developing policing policies.

References

Asch, S.E. (1951) 'Effects of group pressure upon the modification and distortion of judgements', in H. Guetzkow (ed.), *Groups, Leadership and Men* (pp. 177–90). Pittsberg, PA: Carnegie Press.

Audit Commission (1993) *Helping with Enquiries: Tackling crime effectively*. London: Audit Commission.

Bandura, A. (1971) *Social Learning Theory*. New York: McCaleb-Seiler.

Bandura, A., Ross, D and Ross, S.A. (1963) 'A comparative test of the status envy, social power, and secondary reinforcement theories of identificatory learning', *Journal of Abnormal and Social Psychology*, 67 (6): 527–34.

Barbuto, J.E. (2000) 'Influence triggers: A framework for understanding follower compliance', *Leadership Quarterly*, 11: 365–87.

Bayley, D. (1995) 'Getting serious about police brutality', in P. Stenning (ed.), *Accountability for Criminal Justice: Selected essays*. Toronto: University of Toronto Press.

Crank, J.P. (1999) *Understanding Police Culture*. Cincinnati, OH: Anderson.

Chan, J.B.L. (1999) 'Governing police practice: limits of the new accountability', *British Journal of Sociology*, 50 (2), 251–70.

Dunnighan, C. and Norris, C. (1998) 'Some ethical dilemmas in the handling of police informers', *Public Money and Management*, Jan–Mar: 21–5.

Fitzgerald, G. (1989) *Report on the Commission of Inquiry into Possible Illegal Activities and Associated Police Misconduct*. Brisbane: Queensland Government Printer.

Fleming, J. and Lafferty, G. (2000) 'New management techniques and restructuring for accountability in Australian police organizations', *Policing: An International Journal of Police Strategies and Management*, 23 (2): 154–68.

Grosser, D., Polansky, N. and Lippitt, R. (1951) 'A laboratory study of behavioral contagion', *Human Relations*, 4: 115–42.

Her Majesty's Inspectorate of Constabulary (HMIC) (1999) *Police Integrity: Securing and maintaining public confidence*. London: Home Office.

Home Affairs Committee (1998a) *Police disciplinary and complaints procedures*, Volume 1: *Report and proceedings of the committee*. London: Stationery Office.

Home Affairs Committee (1998b) *Government reply to the First Report from the Home Affairs Committee Session 1997–98: Disciplinary and complaints procedures*. London: Stationery Office.

Home Office (2002) *Operation Lancet: A Case Study Review Report*. London: Home Office.

Kiely, J.A. and Peek, G.S. (2002)'The culture of the British police:Views of police officers', *The Service Industries Journal*, 22 (1): 167–83.

Klockars, C. B., Ivkovich, S.K., Harver, W.E. and Haberfeld, M.R. (2000) *The Measurement of Police Integrity*. Washington, DC: National Institute of Justice.

Knapp, W. (1972) *Report of the Commission to Investigate Alleged Police Corruption*. New York: George Braziller.

Komaki, J.L. (1998) *Leadership from an Operant Perspective*. London: Routledge.

Marx, G.T. (1980) 'The new police undercover work', *Urban Life*, 8 (4): 399–446.

Mastrofski, S.D. (2004) 'Controlling street-level police discretion', *The Annals of the American Academy of Political and Social Science*, 593 (1): 100–18.

McLaughlin, E. and Murji, K. (1997) 'Public policework and the managerialist paradox', in P. Francis, P. Davies and V. Jupp (eds), *Policing Futures: The police, law enforcement and the twenty-first century*. Basingstoke: Macmillan.

Miller, J. (2003) *Police Corruption in England and Wales: An assessment of current evidence*. Home Office Report 11/03. London: Home Office.

Mollen Commission (1994) *Report of the Commission to Investigate Allegations of Police Corruption and the Anti-Corruption Procedures of the Police Department*. City of New York: Mollen Commission.

Newburn, T. (1999) *Understanding and preventing police corruption: lessons from the literature*. Police Research Series Paper 110. London: Home Office.

Police Review (1994) London: Police Review Publishing Company, p.13.

Prenzler, T. and Ronken, C. (2001) 'Police integrity testing in Australia', *Criminal Justice*, 1 (3): 319–42.

Punch, M. (2000) 'Police corruption and its prevention', *European Journal on Criminal Policy and Research*, 8: 301–24.

Quinton, P. (2003) *An evaluation of the new police misconduct procedures*. Home Office Online Report 10/03. London: Home Office.

Quinton, P. and Miller, J. (2003) *Promoting ethical policing: Summary findings of research on new misconduct procedures and police corruption*. Home Office Online Report 12/03. London: Home Office.

Reiner, R. (2000) *The Politics of the Police*. Oxford: Oxford University Press.

Roebuck, J.B. and Barker, T. (1974) 'A typology of police corruption', *Social Problems*, 21: 423–37.

Sherman, L.W. (1985) 'Becoming bent: Moral careers of corrupt policemen', in F.A. Elliston and M. Feldberg (eds), *Moral Issues in Police Work*. Totowa, NJ: Rowman and Allanheld.

Skogan, W.G. and Meares, T.L. (2004) 'Lawful policing', *The Annals of the American Academy of Political and Social Science*, 593 (1): 66–83.

Smith, D.J. (1986) 'The framework of law and policing practice', in J. Benyon and C. Bourn (eds), *The Police: Powers, Procedures and Proprieties*. Oxford: Pergamon.

Turner, J.C. (1991) *Social Influence*. Milton Keynes: Open University Press.

Wood, J.R.T. (1997a) *Final Report of the Royal Commission into the New South Wales Police Service: Volume 1: Corruption*.

Wood, J.R.T. (1997b) *Final Report of the Royal Commission into the New South Wales Police Service: Volume 2: Reform*.

Chapter 8

Working with the courts: advice for expert witnesses

David Ormerod and Jim Sturman QC

Introduction

The study of the interrelationship between law and psychology is increasingly common. Historically such work was conducted by psychologists on legal issues (Memon *et al.*, 2003; Kapardis, 1997; Roesch *et al.*, 1998), particularly witness testimony, false memory and eyewitness identification (Cutler and Penrod, 1995). More recently, scholars in both disciplines have exhibited a mutual interest in broader issues (McEwan, 2003; Kapardis, 2002; Bull and Carson, 2003). This interest may represent an increased willingness on the part of the law to learn from psychology. More cynically, it may represent lawyers' increased wariness about psychology, which they perceive to be trespassing into ever-more sacrosanct territory – both in terms of psychology's acceptance in the courtroom and its potential to challenge hallowed precepts of the common-law tradition, especially those relating to the quality of evidence, the manner of its presentation and the manner of decision-making (McEwan, 2003: Ch. 8). Psychological experts would do well to bear in mind this underlying anxiety of many legal practitioners, which is shared by the judiciary.

In this chapter, we examine controversial uses of offender profile evidence. In doing so, we demonstrate the difficulties that prevent parties in criminal cases relying upon profiles as evidence and highlight the obstacles facing a psychologist seeking to assist the police or give evidence at trial.

Uses of offender profiling in investigation

Fundamental differences exist between criminal investigation and trial and these must be appreciated in order to understand the law's approach to psychological profiles. Investigation might be compared to the diagnosis and treatment of an illness, with the investigation (diagnosis) being an open-ended inquiry with sensitivity rather than specificity as the goal, whereas the trial (treatment) is specific and focused upon ultimately one question: guilty (beyond reasonable doubt) or not (Mair, 1995).

However, the fact that criminal investigations and offender profiling share this emphasis on sensitivity does not mean that the profile will be welcomed unreservedly by the law as a legitimate investigative tool. In the only case in England and Wales in which the prosecution sought to rely on profiling evidence at trial, R v *Stagg*, the judge doubted the admissibility of such evidence and commented critically on its use even in investigations. Ognall J, while accepting the value in certain cases of the assistance of a psychologist, observed that he 'would not wish to give encouragement either to investigating or prosecuting authorities to construct or to seek to supplement their cases' by reliance on profiles.

The anxiety over the extent to which the psychologist, and particularly the 'offender profile', has any part to play in the investigative and trial process in a specific case is due in part to the uncertainty over what the offender profile is – if it is indeed one thing. We acknowledge that many of the methods and techniques have been developed and continue to develop towards a more scientific method (Ainsworth, 2000; McEwan, 2003: Ch. 6; Jackson and Bekerian, 1997). As the types of profile become more specific and scientific, with greater awareness of the limitations in terms of reliability and validity, the law will be required to respond to the different types distinctly.

R v Stagg

The unambiguous rejection of even the investigative uses of the profile in *Stagg* has not deterred profiles from being created in numerous criminal investigations, and there are many reasons for this. In stark contrast to the position relating to trials (discussed below), there are no rigid legal rules about their use in investigation. Provided the police comply with statutory and common-law rules relating to processes of search, arrest and interviewing, etc., and the rules relating to the collection and disclosure of material gathered, there is no prohibition on their employing even the most bizarre detection methods such as consulting psychics and mediums. This relatively unlimited discretion in the choice of investigative techniques has promoted police reliance on profilers, with their popularity being enhanced by numerous other factors. Firstly, they might offer advice which renders the investigation more efficient than it would otherwise have been (by, for example, reducing the time spent on wholly irrelevant suspicions). Given increasing police pressures to meet performance targets, this will always be welcomed.

Secondly, use of such methods demonstrates a force's continuing commitment to intelligence-led policing and the policing of risks. This again is prompted by national policing initiatives. Thirdly, the profiler may well echo the investigator's own views as to the identity of likely suspects and the directions an investigation should take. Furthermore, certain profilers are quick to offer their services to the investigation, sometimes publicly, and a failure to accept that offer could be castigated by the media as 'narrow-minded'.

Police–profiler relations

However, the police should be alert to the risk that in hiring a profiler they may be likely to be provided with information which the profiler perceives them as wanting to hear. Research has demonstrated that police may be unduly influenced by who is advising them as a profiler (Kocsis and Hayes, 2004). In addition, the police should not regard the profiler as a means of clothing illegitimate hunches with a veneer of science. In short, the increasing pressure to meet targets and to engage in 'intelligence-led policing' must not serve as an excuse to abdicate responsibility for policing. It should be noted that the Criminal Procedure and Investigations Act 1996 places the police under specific duties to investigate the crime and not the suspect. This includes an obligation to pursue lines of enquiry that point away from the suspect.

The Colin Stagg case provides a stark example of these dangers. The undercover operation mounted against Colin Stagg was effectively controlled by the profiler, Mr Britton. At trial, Ognall J described the seven-month operation against Stagg and noted that it was 'under the constant supervision and direction of the psychologist', noting that 'Mr Britton – if I may be forgiven for using the phrase – was pulling the strings' (page 6B). Having drafted the initial profile of the 'killer', Britton guided and advised the officers investigating Stagg at every turn of the undercover operation. The profile was based on an examination of the crime scene and what was described as 'victimology', namely the characteristics of the victim, her habits, movements and whether or not she had any 'enemies'. The exact nature of this material on 'victimology' available to Britton was never disclosed to the defence at trial because the investigators asserted that it contained 'errors'. (The judge's rulings meant that the impact of these 'errors' in the 'victimology' on the accuracy of the profile never needed to be examined.) Britton subsequently advised on the appropriate characteristics of the person to be introduced as a confidante and he was consulted on each letter sent to Stagg from the undercover officer as well as offering an opinion on each letter received from the suspect. Mr Britton asserted at the preliminary stages of the case in the committal hearing (where he was cross-examined at length) that as the operation went on, the 'predictions' he had made, based on his profile, came true. Those 'predictions' were in fact written on a whiteboard and erased at the end of meetings with the investigating officers, with no note kept of what the predictions were – a surprisingly unscientific way to proceed.

The subsequent trial never had to determine the admissibility of Britton's 'opinion' but the trial judge stated that the prosecution would have faced 'formidable difficulties' in persuading him that the opinion was admissible (page 7D). Later in the judgment he observed that even if the material generated by the undercover operation could have been regarded as admissible, in arguing that Britton's opinion was admissible the Crown faced 'an even higher mountain to climb' (page 28B).

As with any expert, there is always a danger that a profiler will not in fact respect the standards of his discipline, but with profiling there is a real danger that a profiler might become biased and perceive himself to be a part of the prosecution team. The Canadian courts have recently recognized the risk of this and suggested that in the rare instances in which profilers are permitted to testify (see below) they should be cross-examined by the defence to ascertain any possible bias that has crept into their work (*Ranger* (2003)).

Ethical problems

Serious ethical concerns may arise for a psychologist if the actions involve any conduct that might have a detrimental psychological impact on the suspect (Ainsworth, 1999: 180; Memon *et al.*, 2003: 177). The ethical issues that arose as a result of the operation against Stagg could be said to have dramatically affected not only Stagg, but the undercover officer herself and the relatives of the victim, Rachel Nickell. Stagg spent a year on remand in prison reviled by the public as a murderer (although, happily for him, other inmates were convinced that the police had the wrong man and he was not the subject of the sort of attacks that persons actually convicted of such murders suffer) but also had to bear the emotional cost of the operation itself. The operation preyed on Stagg's weaknesses in an attempt to obtain incriminating material. As Ognall J stated at page 14A to C: 'He (Stagg) was a desperately lonely man and a sexual virgin and a man who longed for a long term sexual liaison with a woman. I am satisfied that from the inception of the operation Lizzie James, no doubt under instruction, played upon that loneliness and those aspirations.'

The manipulation of Stagg at the direction of Britton included offering, in the judge's words: 'an almost irresistible inducement to this solitary man: the prospect of a long-term relationship with a woman' (page 17E). While Mr Britton has always sought to defend himself from suggestions that the operation was 'unethical' (most notably in his books *The Jigsaw Man* (1997) and *Picking Up the Pieces* (2000)), it was significant that the experts instructed by the defence (Professors Alison, Canter and Gudjonnson) roundly condemned the manipulation of Stagg and the methodology employed (Alison and Canter, 1999). The undercover officer, 'Lizzie James', sued for the psychological damage she had suffered, claiming that the operation itself was negligent. She was awarded very substantial damages. The costs to the Nickell family must have been beyond measure. The ethical concerns are obvious, and the costs to the victims of an operation of this type are incalculable.

A further danger also highlighted by the Stagg case is that of the potential for the profiler's actions to breach the pre-trial safeguards for the suspect where the profiler is involved in working on the psychological state of the suspect rather than the offender only. Even if the investigation is otherwise carried out faultlessly, any breach of such a safeguard may be regarded as tainting the whole investigation to such an extent that the prosecution case is also tainted and the admissibility of evidence at trial would be affected. There is a popular misconception that the Crown's case against Stagg included a 'confession' (no doubt because of the media reporting of the case at the time of arrest and in the aftermath of the original acquittal). In fact the suspect repeatedly and persistently denied any involvement in the offence. Britton, however, was of the opinion that once introduced to an appropriate confidante, Stagg would confess within a short space of time: 'the consequent confession of guilt – would be likely to follow within a time bracket as short as two weeks from the inception of the liaison and at the latest within 16 weeks of its commencement' (page 4A).

In fact the operation lasted 28 weeks and as the learned judge noted: 'It is very important to my mind to note that at no stage during this very protracted operation did the accused ever admit that he was the murderer. Indeed, to the contrary, he repeatedly denied it' (page 5C). If there had been a confession the inducements offered to Stagg would almost certainly have rendered it worthless because of the restrictions imposed by the Police and Criminal Evidence Act 1984 on the way in which confessions must be obtained in accordance with strict procedures. The psychologist would have led the police to overstep the boundaries on these rules that in a normal investigation would have been strictly observed.

Further anxieties about the use of the profile in investigation involve European Convention on Human Rights/Human Rights Act 1998 challenges to investigative procedures. Rights of privacy are guaranteed, and there are complex regimes governing the use of surveillance which might form part of an ongoing psychology-led investigation.

Disclosure

An additional danger is that given the acknowledged legal anxiety about profiling, the police or prosecution may be unwilling to reveal fully the extent to which they have relied on the advice of a psychologist and equally unwilling to disclose in full the material from the investigation. If uncovered, this secrecy would be highly likely to prove fatal to the prosecution case. A stark example is provided by the case of *Browning* (1994), where psychological assistance (hypnosis of a witness to the M5 killing in which the evidence related to the defendant driving a silver Renault 25 with a number plate including 'C7') was not fully disclosed to the defence, and the conviction was quashed on appeal. Failings in disclosure continue to arise in expert evidence cases (*Sally Clark* (2003)). The significance for accurate record-keeping by the profiler and clarification of the responsibilities of confidentiality and retention of data are obvious.

Discrimination

More insidious dangers in the use of profiles in investigation include the risk of discrimination, and the perpetuation of a class of suspects who will be targeted for specific types of crime. There are harsh lessons to be learned from US drug courier profiles in this regard (Thompson, 1999; Johnson, 1995; Kadish, 1997). The US courts, while accepting that these courier profiles are legitimate in providing the drug agency/police with sufficient evidence to justify stopping and searching a suspect, refuse to accept the profile as evidence at any subsequent trial (*US* v *Sokolow* (1989); *US* v *Quigley* (1989)). These dangers suggest that a national review of the data produced by profiles and the uses to which they are put would be a valuable safeguard against misuse.

Future uses of profiling in investigation?

There is no doubt that the appropriate use of psychology in policing can be valuable in supplementing and improving existing procedures and techniques, not only in an individual case, but by improving best practice. While acknowledging that investigative psychologists could be used appropriately within police investigations, we suggest that further constraints ought to be imposed on the use of psychological techniques designed to identify likely suspects, offenders and the likely patterns of their behaviour. In particular, we would suggest that profilers ought to be accredited by the Home Office on strict criteria and that the bases of accreditation should be transparent and publicly available. In addition, any accreditation process should ensure that profilers comply with strict guarantees of confidentiality.

Stringent standards for monitoring and review of individual profilers should also be introduced. Arguably, the efficacy of any purported profiler could be subjected to periodic review and monitoring by objective assessment. Old case files in which a conviction has been proved to be accurate (perhaps by both confession and good-quality DNA sample evidence) could be provided to profilers with the relevant information about the defendant removed. From this, an individual profiler's ability to provide accurate and reliable information about the offender and the defendant could be evaluated, provided sufficient information from the files was archived to replicate live investigations. It is clear that leading practitioners are anxious to take proactive steps in this direction (Alison *et al.*, 2004; Kocsis, 2003).

Use of psychology in preparation for trial

An issue that has not received detailed attention in England is the extent to which a psychologist might assist in the preparation for trial once a defendant has been charged. In particular, the question arises as to whether a psychologist might advise counsel on how best to examine and cross-examine particular witnesses, or how to 'get the best from the jury'. Beyond the Bar Council's Code of Conduct relating to the manner in which a barrister must deal with witnesses, perhaps the greatest obstacle to such uses of psychology remains the barrier of the lawyer knowing best. We would anticipate that this would be an insurmountable hurdle at the present time except in the most unusual cases.

Profiles as evidence at trial

Expert evidence

Expert evidence on any topic is received under specific restrictions which have proved increasingly controversial in recent years. It should be noted that the criminal trial is concerned not only with the accuracy of verdict but with due process guarantees: it is not enough that the defendant was convicted on reliable evidence if that infringed some fundamental right to a fair trial. This is an important issue for the scientific expert to bear in mind. However, it should be noted that there are numerous differences between the criminal trial's concern for accuracy and reliability and that in the psychology lab which are all too often overlooked. Scientific research can be conducted by any appropriate method, provided the reliability and validity can be secured, which will be dependent on the research in question and the specificity and sensitivity of the research. The criminal trial will seek to prove guilt beyond reasonable doubt on a single finite question: Did the defendant commit the offence charged? These crucial differences between the quest of the scientist and the lawyer and their impact on the different processes has been recognized by the US Supreme Court:

> Scientific conclusions are subject to perpetual revision. Law, on the other hand, must resolve disputes finally and quickly. The scientific project is advanced by broad and wide-ranging consideration of a multitude of hypotheses, for those that are incorrect will eventually be shown to be so, and that in itself is an advance. Conjectures that are probably wrong are of little use, however, in the project of reaching a quick, final, and binding legal judgment – often of great consequence – about a particular set of events in the past.
>
> *Daubert v Merrell Dow Pharmaceuticals Ltd* (1993))

Although the most common forms of expert evidence are scientific, expert opinion is admissible in the court on a very wide range of topics; there is no closed list.

> Expert evidence is not … limited to the core areas. Expert evidence of fingerprinting, handwriting, and accident reconstruction is regularly given. Opinions may be given of the market value of land, ships, pictures, or rights. Expert opinions may be given of the quality of commodities, or on the literary, artistic, scientific or other merit of works alleged to be obscene … Some of these fields are far removed from anything that could be called a formal scientific discipline. Yet while receiving this evidence the courts would not accept the evidence of an astrologer, a soothsayer, a witch-doctor or an amateur psychologist.
>
> *R v Robb* (1991)

The statement is in fact overbroad. Strictly, astrologers and suchlike are not permitted to give expert evidence of the likelihood of guilt of an accused, etc, as their evidence on such a matter is irrelevant in that it cannot be established to be reliable enough to support any proposition relating to guilt. They could, however, give evidence on, for example, the practices of astrology if they happened to be relevant to a trial.

Before expert evidence of any kind, including the many variants of profiling, can be received by the court, there are three crucial legal tests to be met: (a) relevance, (b) admissibility and (c) the rules governing reception of expert opinion evidence.

Relevance

Essentially this is a question of whether the proposed evidence (the profile) makes one of the issues more probable or not. The courts take a strict approach to relevance – stricter than a merely common-sense understanding of relevance, although rarely articulating what they mean by it. Relevance keeps the jury focused on the issues and filters out irrelevance which serves to maximize efficiency and accuracy. The American Federal Rules of Evidence r. 401 provides a concise and accurate statement: relevant evidence is 'evidence having any tendency to make the existence of any fact that is of consequence to the determination of the action more probable or less probable than it would be without the evidence'.

Whether this rule prohibits the profile being received in the trial depends on a number of issues, including the profiling technique (how scientific it can be demonstrated to be) and on what issue the profile was being admitted at trial (comparative crime-scene analysis, evidence of a defence profile, etc.). The different scenarios are discussed below. It is critical for the profiler to keep in mind what his opinion relates to. Is it a statement about the likelihood of the offender having a certain trait; or the dissimilarity of crime scenes?

Admissibility

The most basic rule of evidence is that all relevant evidence is admissible subject to the exclusionary principles embedded in rules of admissibility. The rules exclude evidence on the basis of its being unfair (as with illegal searches), unreliable (as with false confessions), privileged (e.g. confidential documents), or prejudicial (where the jury reasons that the accused is guilty on inadequate proof). Strict rules of admissibility (are supposed to) protect the accused from potentially unfair evidence and also to guarantee accuracy in the verdict.

Again, these rules will pose a significant problem for the profile depending in particular on whether it is being admitted as, for example, evidence of the defendant's guilt, as comparative crime-scene analysis evidence, or crime reconstruction evidence. These are discussed below.

Experts

Qualification

In addition to the evidence being relevant and admissible, expert evidence must satisfy other criteria. The first group of limitations relates to the witness being suitably qualified. This issue is to be decided by the judge, but there is no clear guidance on what degree of formal training or qualification or practical experience suffices. Clearly, this poses something of a problem for a technique such as profiling which is in its (relative) infancy.

The need for special 'gatekeeping' rules to ensure that only true experts give evidence is necessary because the expert is allowed to give opinion evidence (unlike normal witnesses who are restricted to testifying about fact). Moreover, the expert is granted greater latitude in his reliance on hearsay evidence. In addition, the courts are concerned that the expert has a potentially unwarranted influence on the jury because of his status. Empirical work suggests that typical jurors form impressions of experts stereotypically, based on the occupation of the experts, and superficially on the personal characteristics of the experts (Shuman et al., 1996). This might be a particular concern where a profiler has had a high media profile and is commonly portrayed as 'Cracker' or some other fictional profiling expert.

There is specific research which demonstrates how significantly a jury might be influenced by the status of a profiler as such (Kocsis and Heller, 2004). Indeed, the fact that the evidence is presented as a profile may unduly influence the jury, as has been suggested by practitioners (Alison et al., 2003), and the Canadian courts (Ranger (2003); Clark (2004)). In those decisions the courts deprecated the lengthy introduction given to the profiler, allowing her to testify at length about profiling in general under the guise of establishing her expertise and credentials.

In light of recent miscarriages of justice arising from the misuse of expert evidence (e.g. the evidence relating to Sudden Infant Deaths in Cannings (2004) and ear prints in Dallagher (2002)), the English courts will be especially vigilant against experts with inadequate expertise. There will also be a concern to ensure that accepted experts testify only on matters within their field of expertise. Psychologists should be particularly careful when testifying about the statistical aspects of their work to remain within the bounds of their expertise. The courts have rejected the use of statistical methods when explaining issues to the jury (e.g. Bayes' theorem; Adams (1996)), and following the cases of Sally Clark (2003) and Angela Cannings (2004) are now acutely aware of the hazard of assuming that each item of evidence (in those cases of sudden infant deaths within a family) is statistically independent. However, there is a growing pressure for the courts to take a more receptive approach to statistics since their appropriate use can assist in understanding the accuracy and significance of the figures presented by an expert (Aitken, 2003).

The problems with statistics represent one aspect of the growing concern that the jury must not be too greatly impressed by the nature of the expert evidence. Again, the *Cannings* case presents a clear illustration of the dangers. The jury were presented with seemingly irrefutable odds of 73 million to 1 of successive sudden infant deaths. (See the response of the Royal Statistical Society, www.rss.org.uk/archive/). The conviction was quashed by the Court of Appeal as unsafe.

Helpfulness

The second group of additional rules relating to expert evidence seeks to ensure that expert opinion will be admissible in any criminal trial only 'to furnish the Court with ... information which is likely to be outside the experience and knowledge of a judge or jury' (*Turner* (1975); Redmayne, 2001). This is also an issue to be decided by the judge. Research from Australia reveals that judges tend to have a high opinion of their capacity to understand the expert evidence. Just under half of the judges surveyed were of the view that 'they had "never" encountered evidence that they were not able to evaluate adequately because of its complexity. However, just over half conceded that this had happened "rarely" or "occasionally"' (Freckelton, 1997).

Research in the USA has suggested that in controlled conditions, professional profilers were found not to 'process material in a way *qualitatively* different' from untrained psychologists, detectives and first-year psychology students. Recent Australian research suggest that profilers do demonstrate superior skills in such assessments (Kocsis *et al.*, 2000). But, in comparisons of non-psychologist groups, chemistry students outperformed detectives (Kocsis *et al.*, 2002). Despite these ambiguities, there is little doubt that the courts would conclude that profiling, in all its guises, lies beyond the capabilities of a jury. This is even more clearly apparent where the crime involved is one of particular deviance, as most profiled crimes are.

Reliability

Reliability is important to admissibility in two ways. First, there should be a reliable foundation for the experiences and knowledge on which the evidence is based. Second, the application of the knowledge in the given case must be reliable. These requirements are of general application to lay witnesses and experts giving opinion evidence. With a non-expert testifying about his witnessing events, the reliability of the foundation knowledge, beliefs and experiences on which his perceptions are made is challenged in court by cross-examination. There is no inclination to ascertain how the witness came by his knowledge. With an expert the reliability of the evidence is not merely a matter of weight to be tested in cross-examination, there are also rules of admissibility because the expert is giving opinion evidence to which jurors will attach greater weight than with lay witness testimony. The court will need to be persuaded of the reliability of the scientific foundations for the conclusion about the opinion.

In all cases, the expert must demonstrate that the method he is using is reliable. He will also be subject to cross-examination on its application in the particular case. In many instances there will be no preliminary inquiry as to the underlying reliability of the science since the court would be familiar with the existence of the science in question, e.g. with ballistics or blood grouping. Similarly, where psychological expert evidence is relevant, it may be that evidence of the psychologist can be readily adduced in relation to general issues (o.g the general behavioural traits of battered women syndrome (BWS) sufferers or vulnerable suspects, etc.) or to the issues in a particular case (e.g. the behaviour of this BWS sufferer or vulnerability of this suspect). The same acceptance of reliability will not be true of a psychologist seeking to testify on profile evidence: there will be some inquiry into whether the evidence is reliable. However, what remains unclear is the extent to which the courts will scrutinize the reliability and validity of the science in question, and by which criteria they will measure that reliabilty.

Novel techniques
An additional hurdle for expert evidence arises with novel techniques. Until recently, English law admitted novel techniques as the basis of expert opinion evidence without any special scrutiny. The attitude was that there are 'no closed categories where such evidence may be placed before a jury' and that 'it would be entirely wrong to deny to the law of evidence the advantages to be gained from new techniques and new advances in science' (Clarke (1995)). However, it seems that English law is entering a state of change in this respect prompted by concerns about the expert evidence received in cases such as Clark and Cannings where the appeal court recognized that the evidence of the causes of deaths was 'at the frontiers of knowledge' (para 178).

When faced with expert evidence on activities such as ear prints, the Court of Appeal in Dallagher declined to take a stricter attitude to the admissibility of novel sciences and techniques despite defence sub-missions that the American approach was to be preferred to the traditional English approach (Ormerod, 2002). After the successful appeal, and prior to Dallagher's retrial, DNA analysis of cellular material recovered from the 'earprint' previously stated to be the defendant's demonstrated that the DNA could not have come from Dallagher. Further tests on a 'cheek print' from the same window also revealed that DNA from that print could not be Dallagher's. The Crown ultimately offered no evidence. It may have made a substantial difference to the terms of the Court's judgment in the *Dallagher* appeal if the DNA evidence had been available at the time of the appeal. Dallagher had been convicted largely on the basis of 'expert' evidence from a 'new' area of 'expertise' that was wholly inconsistent with the expert evidence from an established science. Events after Dallagher's conviction was quashed provide an example of the dangers in setting the bar too low for novel and untested techniques.

The lack of clear regulation governing admissibility in England and Wales is in stark contrast to the position in the USA, where the much-discussed criteria derived from the case of *Daubert* (1993) require judges to exert strict control on the admissibility of novel techniques. In particular, Federal Courts are to have regard to whether the technique is falsifiable, subjected to peer review, has published error rates as regards its validity and reliability, and whether the data are capable of replication. The Supreme Court in the US has confirmed that these criteria apply to all experts, not just the purely scientific (*Kumho Tires* 1998). In a number of US cases (e.g. *Distefano* (1990)), courts have ruled that profiling lacked the reliability required to satisfy the *Daubert* test (Ingram, 1998; Slobogin 1998).

Recent English cases signal a growing judicial unease with the relaxed English approach, but it remains unclear whether they would apply a strict *Daubert*-based test to novel techniques such as profiling. For example, in *Gilfoyle* (1996) the Court of Appeal appeared to adopt the old US *Frye* test to the admissibility of novel techniques – asking whether the evidence has general acceptance in the scientific community. In *Gilfoyle* the application of that test led the court to reject Professor Canter's evidence on psychological autopsy. It is impossible to confirm a definite judicial move towards *Frye* or *Daubert* since a subsequent English decision, although quashing convictions based on dubious 'scientific' techniques, declined to apply the *Frye* test, preferring to rely on the orthodox pragmatic position (*Dallagher* (2002)). However, other recent decisions such as *O'Doherty* (2001) on voice identification expertise can be seen as an example of an increased willingness to engage in an assessment of the reliability of novel techniques, which stands in conflict to earlier cases.

In the most recent decision on novel techniques, the Court has shied away from the opportunity to adopt any more stringent evaluation of novel techniques. In the case of *Luttrell* (2004), the court considered the reliability of lip-reading evidence when a prosecution witness, Miss R, a deaf woman who was a skilled and qualified lip reader, gave evidence as to what was said at a CCTV-recorded meeting between the accused and another man. The Court of Appeal held that the evidence was admissible. It had to be shown that the witness's study or experience gave her opinion an authority which the opinion of a person not so qualified would lack. The ultimate weight to be attached to the opinion was for the fact-finding tribunal. The court was prepared to adopt a liberal approach to admitting the evidence, placing emphasis on the judge's obligation to protect against misuse of the expert evidence by issuing a special warning to the jury highlighting both the potential dangers involved in relying on the evidence in question and the need to exercise particular caution. The strength of the warning and its terms would depend on the nature of the evidence, its reliability or lack of it, and the potential problems it posed. For instance, it had been recognized that identification of a suspect by voice was less reliable than visual identification evidence, and accordingly usually required a warning that was couched in stronger terms. In what might seem a surprisingly candid statement, the Court acknowledged that lip-reading evidence required a warning from the judge as to its limitations and the risk of error, not least because it would usually be introduced through an expert who might not be completely accurate.

Irrespective of whether the English courts remain reluctant to declare openly a particular test for the evaluation of the reliability of novel scientific evidence, what recent cases demonstrate is that the present position is prone to lead to miscarriages of justice. It should be noted that whatever test English law finally settles on, the question will not be purely one of whether the technique is 'scientific'. In any event, it remains debatable whether a profile can be described as a scientific endeavour (Copson et al., 1997; Ainsworth, 2000; Jackson and Bekerian, 1999).

Receiving evidence from an investigative psychologist

In this final section we seek to demonstrate that the application of the rules as outlined above renders the admissibility of investigative psychology evidence in the criminal trial in England and Wales unlikely in relation to identity, but technically possible in five limited categories.

I. Profiles identifying the defendant will be excluded as insufficiently relevant, unreliable, prejudicial and unscientific

This assertion is unsurprising given the statements made in R v Stagg, where Ognall J noted that: there was 'no authority in any common law ... jurisdiction to the effect that [profile] evidence has ever been treated as properly admissible in proof of identity'. This attitude is displayed by the US courts in a range of cases involving different offences (*People* v *Robbie* (2001); *Commonwealth* v *Frias* (1999) and *People* v *Avellant* (1997)).

Irrelevant

If all that a profile can do is suggest that in the opinion of a criminal psychologist, the perpetrator will have certain characteristics (age, residence in a certain area, etc.), that will be insufficiently relevant to be received by the court as evidence of the defendant's guilt. Although the profile may well be based upon statistical data, that foundation alone will not make the profile relevant in terms of indicating the likelihood of this defendant being guilty.

Unreliable

As noted above, a ballistics expert would only be allowed to testify about the likelihood of a match between the offender's bullet and defendant's gun because he can demonstrate by reliable means that the tests are accurate within known parameters. This is quite different from the evidence of, say, a crank who believes that, by tossing a coin at the scene of the crime, he can determine whether the offender had a particular trait – say, left-handedness. If the prosecution sought to rely on such evidence to demonstrate that the crank's evidence made it more probable that the left-handed defendant committed the crime, the court would reject the evidence as unreliable. The position is quite distinct from the ballistics expert who can demonstrate that the offender's bullet had a particular pattern shared by the defendant's gun. In contrast, the crank acts on unsubstantiated beliefs about the left-handedness. Nor would it be sufficient that the crank uses a reliable and repeatable technique (e.g. a specially minted coin to guarantee fairness in the toss); there is no science or defensible theory behind the technique.

The investigative psychologist seeking to prove the identity of the offender will be suggesting that his experience and training lead him to conclude from his examination of the materials that the offender had an identifiable trait, that this defendant shares that trait and that therefore the defendant is more likely to be the offender. In *Stagg*, for example, the psychological profile was tendered to support the prosecution case that the offender had certain characteristics and that the accused (Colin Stagg) matched those characteristics. With such a profile, unless there is a reliable method of demonstrating that the technique can identify the specified trait in an offender, the evidence will be insufficiently reliable to be received. Unless a profiler can show that psychology can support with sufficient strength a claim that he can reliably and consistently identify behavioural traits from scenes of crime and related information the evidence would lack a reliable foundation, and the English courts would rule it inadmissible.

Profile evidence is too prejudicial

In *Stagg*, Ognall J noted that 'it was doubtful that evidence is more than merely evidence of propensity'. In simple terms, profiling rests on the assumptions that behaviourial traits or imprints are displayed or reflected in crime scenes, that such imprints are identifiable, that they are unique to the offender, that they remain constant, etc. Even assuming that the trait is imprinted identifiably at the scene, there is unlikely to be proof that it is 'unique' and/or that it can be guaranteed to be identical to each of the crime scenes of that offender. In legal terms it is likely to be evidence of only a type of possible offender. Such information is potentially of value to the investigation, but is too prejudicial to be received at trial. This was one of the most obvious of Ognall J's concerns in *Stagg*. Profile evidence is potentially very prejudicial when it is being used to draw links between the offender and the accused. Evidence of discreditable traits of the offender will be transposed in the minds of the jury to the accused. We know that previous convictions, or other discreditable conduct not amounting to a crime, also create in the minds of the jury sinister prejudices. The most important of these prejudices have recently been described as 'moral prejudice' and 'reasoning prejudice'. The prejudicial effect includes risks that the jurors could: convict a defendant on the basis of the characteristic alone (where it is reprehensible); assign a disproportionate weight to the evidence of the characteristic; deny the accused the benefit of doubt and convict on less than the full standard of proof; and the police could be inclined to 'round up the usual suspects'.

The peculiarity of the behaviour and whether it amounts to a hallmark or signature, i.e. the ability of the person to point to an individual rather than simply a type, is crucial when it comes to the question of avoiding prejudice. Unless the particular technique of the profiler can be demonstrated to be sufficiently accurate in identifying traits to provide more than an indication of the type of offender, it will be inadmissible as evidence of identity of the defendant. The profile identifies a type, but 'there is all the difference in the world between evidence proving that the accused is a bad man and evidence proving that he is *the* man' (*Thompson* (1918)).

Even evidence of a ballistics expert, using impeccable scientific method scrupulously applied, would be inadmissible if it could only demonstrate an unspecified degree of similarity between the firearm in crime A and the defendant's gun. The evidence would be inadmissible because it would create too much prejudice when weighed against the limited probative value that it carries.

Not expert evidence?

In *Stagg*, Ognall J stated that 'a prosecutor wishing to rely upon such evidence would face "formidable difficulties" in proving that such a profile was in fact expert evidence'. As noted, the *Turner* rule limits the reception of expert opinion evidence on material that is not outside the jurors' common understanding. We suggest that the courts should be alert to the potential to use expert evidence not only in relation to material that the jury do not know anything about, but also in relation to the material that jurors (mistakenly) think they know about, and material that they know only a little about. The behavioural traits of a serial arsonist, killer or rapist or other types of crime on which profile evidence is likely to be available are not within the experience of a juror. However, the potential usefulness in explaining the activities of such an individual will not render the otherwise inadmissible profile admissible as evidence of identity.

One of the difficulties with a technique which is so specific and novel is that there are fewer experts to call upon. The danger is that the expert will be subjected to less effective challenge as there are no opponents, and his evidence will be afforded a disproportionate weight.

There is no opportunity for an experienced detective to claim that he is acting as an expert in behavioural science if that is the qualification that is called for to testify on the particular issue (*Mombourquette* v *The Queen Ontario* (2001)). As the court in England has noted in the recent lip-reading case, it has to be shown that the witness's study or experience gives his opinion an authority which the opinion of a person not so qualified would lack.

Not scientific

In *Stagg*, Ognall J also stated that

> it was doubtful that psychological profile evidence is sufficiently well established or 'generally accepted' as a scientific method to be received as expert evidence. And that such a novel technique must satisfy tests such as those in *Frye* v *U.S.* (1923) and *Daubert* v *Merrell Dow* (1993) (see now *Kumho Tires* (1998)).

As noted, English law has not made a firm commitment to the application of any strict rules on the admissibility of novel techniques. If English law adopts the more relaxed *Frye* test, the question would be whether a profiler can show that the technique he is using is one that would be recognized within the psychological community. Even this is doubtful. As Gudjonnson has noted, 'profiling is neither a readily identifiable nor a homogenous entity and its status is properly regarded as a professional sideline, not amounting to a true science' (Gudjonnson, 1984: 80). If the more stringent *Daubert*-type test is adopted, focusing on the reliability of the evidence, the profiler will be obliged to demonstrate a known potential error rate to the activity, recognize the degree of falsifiability of the technique and demonstrate a degree of acceptance in the community.

We suggest that the potential for such a test to be imposed in relation to all scientific evidence is a further reason for the psychological community to consider imposing monitoring and reviews of profiling with blind testing against known case outcomes as described above.

2. Profiler can testify as to crime scene

There has been a spate of recent interest in Canada where the prosecution have sought to call an expert (DI Lines of the Behavioural Science Unit in Ontario) to testify about the likelihood that murder scenes were 'staged' to resemble burglaries. Such evidence of staging has been received in the USA (*NY* v *McDonald* (1996)). The evidence has been scrutinized with great care by the Court of Appeal in Ontario in two separate cases and their conclusion is that an expert opinion on the events at the crime scene is admissible as evidence, but that there are strict limits as to what may be admitted. In particular, the expert is permitted to testify only as to what she believed happened at the scene. Opinion on the possible motivations of the offender (e.g. that he acted in a given way to avoid being recognized as known to the victims) or the possible identity of the offender is strictly inadmissible (*Ranger* (2003); *Clarke* (2003)). The court noted that the profiler's opinions on these issues amounted to no more than 'educated guesses' (*Ranger*, para 82). The court also noted that the evidence was such that limited expertise was necessary to present the facts and that a police officer might adequately perform the task. This should not be used as an opportunity to call a profiler so as to put before the jury her practical experience of criminal profiling when establishing her expertise and experience. Such evidence (i.e. experience of profiling) would be likely to have a very powerful and inappropriate impact on the jury. In England such evidence would almost certainly be excluded on the basis that its prejudicial effect outweighed its probative value.

3. Profiles may be admissible as comparative crime-scene analysis

Some cases require the prosecution to establish that the crimes involved are all the work of the same offender who has a peculiar, yet similar, manner of committing his crime. This involves adducing evidence of the similarity of the group of crimes (and their dissimilarity as a group from the norm) to determine whether they can be clearly attributed as the work of one offender/group. The evidence to allow the court to make this decision is usually presented by police officers or forensics experts. In such cases, it might be possible for the psychologist to testify as to how similar the crimes were, and how peculiar they were. The need for such evidence is particularly important in cases of 'cumulative similar fact', which involve the prosecution proving that two (or more) activities or offences are the work of the same person, based on there being a sufficient peculiarity in the activity or manner of performance. The jury is then invited to combine items of inconclusive evidence (e.g. identifications) from each individual offence to prove that the defendant was the offender on both occasions. In some jurisdictions, a behavioural expert has been allowed to testify as to the distinctive nature of the group of crimes and their similarity to each other. For example in US cases, experts have testified about the distinctiveness of three prostitute murders and the forensic links they shared (*Pennell* v *State* (1991)) and as to the numerous signature links in a unique handcuff ligature in (*State* v *Code* (1999)).

The claim is that this is legally relevant evidence to prove the fact of similarity (which is a different legal issue from direct evidence of this defendant's guilt) provided that the basis on which the factors were arrived at is reliable. Such evidence might be seen as valuable assistance to the jury. Where the jurors are asked as a preliminary question to determining the offender's guilt to assess the likelihood that the offences were all those of the same person, a psychologist might shed light on that likelihood and assist the jury in how they should go about making their decision as to how the crimes relate to each other. If the court is satisfied that there is sufficient foundation for that, and it does not generate too many distracting side issues, it might regard it as sufficiently relevant to be adduced in court.

It is not certain that such evidence would be admissible. A further objection to comparisons of crimes would be that the best that the profiler could do would be to say that the crime scenes belonged to a general 'type'. The more bizarre the case and the less likely that it is a characteristic shared by many, the more likely that this objection would be met. However, if the facts are very bizarre it might be asked why it was then necessary to use a profiler to point that out to the jury (this was a point well taken in *Ranger* (2003)). The real possibility is that there are some bizarre signature-like traits that can be identified by a profiler in his analysis of the crime scenes but not by others lacking psychological expertise.

Even if the comparative crime-scene analysis evidence is relevant and not too prejudicial, it may fall foul of the expert evidence rules. Thus, in *Fortin* v *State* (2000), such evidence linking crimes was regarded as not too prejudicial and was strong evidence because of the similarities – unusual biting and strangling patterns of a sexual murderer. Nevertheless, the court was not prepared to allow the famous FBI profiler Agent Hazelwood to give evidence of this as an 'expert' witness because it was not established that the material would satisfy the 'reliability' test (in *Daubert*) above. It remains to be seen whether the English courts will adopt such a strict test to admissibility of expertise.

4. The accused seeks to establish his own personality and its incompatibility with the police profile

This rather unusual scenario could arise where an accused seeks to call a profiler to prove that although the offender had a profile including certain traits, these are not shared by the accused. There is some support for this stemming from the Canadian Supreme Court case of *The Queen* v *Mohan* (1994), where the court accepted a possibility that an expert could testify that the offences were committed by a paedophile, but that the accused was not a paedophile, he was a sexual psychopath. The Canadian Supreme Court has subsequently confirmed that the defendant can lead such evidence exceptionally if the perpetrator has displayed abnormal behaviour that was so distinctive that they indicated a person of unusual personality traits such that the perpetrator would be a member of an unusual and limited class of person and the accused did not possess the personality traits of that class of persons: *R* v *J-LJ* (2000).

It should be noted that the court is accepting only a possibility in a future case of allowing the defendant (not the prosecution) to use such evidence. On the facts of that case the court rejected the evidence because the expert had such limited experience that his conclusion could not be regarded as sufficiently reliable. In more recent cases the Canadian courts have confirmed that this approach is possible, although it has been denied on the facts of the cases (e.g. *R* v *Perlett* (1999) where the accused was not permitted to rely on expert evidence to suggest that all those who kill usually fall into a category of psychological dysfunction. See also *R* v *Bernier* (1999); *R* v *B* (1997)). The Canadian Supreme Court has emphasized that the profile of the offender must have 'truly distinctive' psychological elements that were present and operating in the offender at the time of the offence. Moreover, it was concerned that the profile should not be one constructed for the case, and should confine the class of potential offenders to useful proportions. Similar concerns about the reliability of the technique and the distinctiveness of the trait have been raised in US cases (*US* v *Banks* (1992); Murphy and Peters, 1992).

5. A profile might be admitted where the question is whether it is more likely that defendant A rather than defendant B committed the crime with which they are both charged

This situation might arise where, for example, A and B are charged with burglary of a house and arson in destroying the evidence. A claims that he has no arsonist tendencies, and that at least one of the offenders had. A might be able to call a psychologist to confirm that the offender was an arsonist (and that the fire was not by accident). There are some broad judicial statements to this effect:

> A defendant is always entitled to call evidence of his good character or other evidence in disproof of his own guilt of the offence charged against him. The test is whether the evidence is relevant or not to the question of guilt. The evidence is relevant if it tended to show that the version of facts put forward by one co-accused was more probable than that put forward by the other. (*Thompson* (1995))

Other examples of this having been used successfully include a Canadian case, *McMillan* (1975), in which a husband charged with killing his child was allowed to call evidence that his wife had a psychopathic personality and was quick to anger.

In the unusual case of *Lowery* v *R* (1974), K was permitted to adduce psychological opinion evidence to establish that he was less likely than L, his co-accused, to have committed the horrific murder with which the two were charged. The test for admitting such evidence was, according to the Court, whether 'it tended to show that the version of facts put forward by one co-accused was more probable than that put forward by the other'.

This was thought to be an exceptional case turning on its own facts; however, the House of Lords has recently returned to it in *Randall* (2003). The House held that where two defendants A and B were jointly charged with murder (in this case kicking or bludgeoning the victim to death in the street), where there were no eye-witnesses, where each blamed the other, and where evidence had been adduced before the jury of the character and convictions of each (B having a much worse record – including violence – than A), it had been a misdirection of the judge to tell the jury that the evidence as to the background of B went only to his credibility; in the particular circumstances, B's antecedent history was relevant not only in relation to the truthfulness of B's evidence but also because the imbalance between B's history and A's 'tended to show that the version put forward by A was more probable than that put forward by B'.

The House of Lords distinguished clearly between the prosecution calling evidence showing no more than the accused's propensity to commit the crime (prejudicial evidence of the type discussed above). In the case of a co-accused seeking to exculpate himself there is no reason of policy or fairness which requires the exclusion of such evidence. Therefore, the propensity to violence of a co-accused might be relevant to the issues between the prosecution and the accused tendering such evidence.

Conclusion

It is well established that psychologists are not always able to provide definitive answers to questions posed by, *inter alia*, academic and practising lawyers, the judiciary, jurors, law-enforcement personnel or the general public. However, the results of their empirical work can throw very useful light on psycho-legal issues that enables informed decisions to be made. At the same time, psycho-legal research enriches the tapestries of contemporary law and psychology (Kapardis, 1997).

The psychological profile has serious limitations: it is practised in an inconsistent manner, often from an unverified base of material by a body of individuals with diverse levels of training and experience, and inadequate independent monitoring and review. For as long as profiling continues to be perceived as little more than educated guesswork it is hard to see circumstances in which it could be regularly used as evidence in the English and wider common-law jurisdictions. An 'art' (as both profiling and earprint identification have been termed by their critics) is too dependent on personal perception to satisfy the degree of certainty required to provide evidence with the degree of safety which is necessary to convict a person of a crime. Psychologists face the struggle of demonstrating the reliability of the technique and of the people who practise it.

References

Ainsworth, P. (2000) *Offender Profiling and Crime Analysis*. Cullompton: Willan.

Aitken, C. (2003) 'Conviction by probability', *New Law Journal*, 153: 1153–54.

Alison, L. and Canter, D. (eds) (1999) *Interviewing and Deception*. Aldershot: Ashgate.

Alison, L., Smith, M. and Morgan, K. (2003) 'Interpreting the accuracy of offender profiles', *Psychology, Crime and the Law*, 9(2): 185–95.

Alison, L., West, A. and Goodwill, A. (2004) 'The academic and the practitioner: pragmatists' views of offender profiling', *Psychology, Public Policy and Law*, 10 (1).

Britton, P. (1997) *The Jigsaw Man*. London: Bantam Press.

Britton, P. (2001) *Picking Up the Pieces*. London: Bantam Press.

Bull, R. and Carson, D. (2003) *Handbook of Psychology in Legal Contexts* (2nd edn). New York: John Wiley and Sons.

Copson, G., Badcock, R., Boon, J. and Britton, P. (1997) 'Editorial: Articulating a systematic approach to clinical crime profiling', *Criminal Behaviour and Mental Health*, 7: 13.

Cutler, B. and Penrod, S. (1995) *Mistaken Identification: The eyewitness, psychology and the law*. Cambridge: Cambridge University Press.

Freckleton, I. (1997) 'Judicial attitudes toward scientific evidence: The antipodean experience', *U.C. Davis Law Review*.

Gudjonnson, G. (1984) 'The current status of the psychologist as an expert within criminal trials', *Bulletin of the BPS*, 37: 80.

Ingram, S. (1998) 'If the profile fits: admitting criminal psychological profiles into evidence in criminal trials', *Washington Uni Journal of Urban and Contemporary Law*, 239.

Jackson, J. and Bekerian, D. (1997) *Offender profiling: Theory, research and practice*. New York: John Wiley and Sons.

Johnson, E. (1995) 'A menace to society: The use of criminal profiles and its effects on black males', *Howard Law Journal*, 38: 629.

Kadish, S.H. (1997) 'The drug courier profile: In planes, trains and automobiles; and now in the jury box', *American University Law Review*, 45: 747.

Kapardis, A. (1997) *Psychology and Law: A critical introduction*. Cambridge: Cambridge University Press.

Kapardis, A. (2002) *Psychology and Law: A critical introduction* (2nd edn). Cambridge: Cambridge University Press.

Kocsis, R. (2003) 'An empirical assessment of content in criminal psychological profiles', *International Journal of Offender Therapy and Comparative Criminology*, 47: 37–46.

Kocsis, R. and Hayes, A. (2004) 'Believing is seeing?: Investigating the perceived accuracy of criminal psychological profiles I', *International Journal of Offender Therapy and Comparative Criminology*, 48 (2): 149–60.

Kocsis, R. and Heller, A. (2004) 'Believing is seeing?: Investigating the perceived accuracy of criminal psychological profiles II', *International Journal of Offender Therapy and Comparative Criminology*, 48 (2): 313–29.

Kocsis, R., Irwin, H., Hayes, A. and Nunn, R. (2000) 'Expertise on psychological profiling: A comparative assessment', *Journal of Interpersonal Violence*, 15 (3): 311–31.

Kocsis, R., Hayes, A. and Irwin, H. (2002) 'Investigative experience and accuracy in psychological profiling of a violent crime', *Journal of Interpersonal Violence*, 17 (8): 811–23.

Mair, K. (1995) 'Can a profile prove a sex offender guilty?', *Expert Evidence*, 139.

McEwan, J. (2003) *The Verdict of the Court: Passing Judgment on Law and Psychology*. Oxford: Hart Publishing.

Memon, A., Vrij, A. and Bull, R. (2003) *Psychology and Law: Truthfulness, Accuracy and Credibility* (2nd edn). New York: John Wiley and Sons.

Murphy, W. and Peters, J. (1992) 'Profiling child sex abusers', *Criminal Justice Behaviour*, 19: 24.

Ormerod, D. (2002) '*Dallagher*' [2002] *Criminal Law Review*, 821.

Redmayne, M. (2001) *Expert Evidence and Criminal Justice*. Oxford: Oxford University Press.

Roesch, R., Hart, S. and Ogloff, J. (eds) (1998) *Psychology and Law: the State of the Discipline*. London: Kluwer Academic/Plenum Publishers.

Shuman, D., Champagne, A. and Whitaker, E. (1996) 'Assessing the believability of expert witnesses: Science in the jury box', *Jurimetrics Journal*, 37: 23.

Slobogin, C. (1998) 'Psychiatric evidence in criminal trials: To junk or not to junk?', *William and Mary Law Review*, 40: 1.

Thompson, A. (1999) 'Stopping the usual suspects: Race and the Fourth Amendment', *New York University Law Review*, 74: 956.

Case list

Adams (1996)
Browning (1994)
Cannings (2004)
Clark (2003)
Clarke (1995)
Commonwealth v *Frias* (1999)
Dallagher (2002)
Daubert v *Merrell Dow Pharmaceuticals Ltd* (1993)
Distefano (1990)
Fortin v *State* (2000)
Frye (1926)
Gilfoyle (1996)
Kumho Tires (1998)
Lowery v *R* (1974)
Luttrell (2004)
McMillan (1975)
Monbourquette v *The Queen (Ontario)* (2001)
NY v *McDonald* (1996)
O'Doherty (2001)
Pennell v *State* (1991)
People v *Avellant* (1999)
People v *Robbie* (2001)
R v *B* (1997)
R v *Bernier* (1999)
R v *L-J* (2000)
R v *Perlett* (1999)
Randall (2003)
Ranger (2003)
Robb (1991)
Stagg (1994)
State v *Code* (1999)
The Queen v *Mohan* (1994)
Thompson (1918)
Thompson (1995)
Turner (1975)
US v *Banks* (1992)
US v *Quigley* (1989)
US v *Sokolow* (1989)

Part Two

Advising on Investigations

Chapter 9

Rhetorical shaping in an undercover operation: the investigation of Colin Stagg in the Rachel Nickell murder enquiry

Laurence Alison and David Canter

Through words we may govern men

(Disraeli)

The Nickell murder

This chapter represents just one aspect of the commentary on the case from the defence experts' point of view, namely the range, the development, the appropriateness and the possible psychological impact of the discourse strategies employed by the undercover officer. Many other factors were considered and can be found in Alison (1998). It is important to emphasize that this chapter develops many of the theoretical approaches utilized by the authors in assisting us in understanding the material rather than directly reflecting the material provided to the courts. Instead, we have presented the theory underpinning this particular enquiry in order to illustrate the application of a rhetorical approach to case studies of this nature.

Rachel Nickell was murdered mid-morning on Wimbledon Common, London, in July 1992 while walking with her son Alex and her dog Molly. The case has been written about quite extensively in several other books from a variety of perspectives: the victim's partner (Hanscombe, 1997), the officer involved in the investigation (Pedder, 2002), the suspect (Stagg and Kessler, 1999) and the clinical psychologist who worked with the enquiry team (Britton, 1997). Britton was asked to provide an offender profile as well as other forms of guidance on the case. It does not fall within the remit of this chapter to consider the problems associated with the profiling methods employed in this case; suffice to say that the process involved in generating the advice remains enigmatic. Britton's profile generally focused on certain demographic features: offender's location, employment history, preconvictions as well as a number of features that merely served to embellish the account but were probably of little practical use to the investigative team. For example, some elements contained the proposed attitudes or fantasies of the individual. Britton (1997) generated a 'picture' of a lonely individual – an outsider, socially and sexually inept, claiming that, 'An image was forming in my mind' (p. 157) as he examined the case material. When the police eventually focused on a suspect two months later (Colin Francis Stagg) who they believed fitted this profile and who had been identified from an E-Fit shown on the BBC's 'Crimewatch UK', four interviews with Stagg were conducted.

Subsequent to detectives' suspicions, based probably, in part, on inconsistencies in Stagg's account and the witness statements of a number of people who had claimed to have seen Stagg near the murder scene that morning and on the profile generated by Britton, the investigating team (again under the direction of the psychologist) decided to set up a covert operation known as 'Operation Edzell'. This involved an undercover officer with the pseudonym Lizzie James befriending the suspect. The pretence was that she wished to develop contact through a lonely hearts club that it was known Stagg had joined prior to the murder. James began by writing to Stagg, claiming to know a previous lonely hearts correspondent that he had written to some years before. The relationship between Stagg and James evolved slowly – beginning with a sequence of letters, progressing to phone calls and finally meetings. Edzell was purportedly designed to establish whether Stagg would divulge sexual fantasies to his 'newly found partner' that corresponded with those predicted in the psychologist's profile of the murderer.

Broadly speaking, the letters began in a rather benign fashion, with exchanges involving discussion of mutual interests, expressions of loneliness and relatively conventional flirting. However, before long, the sexual elements began to dominate the letters, with references to James' 'chequered past' consistently re-appearing in the dialogue. Though at first the details of this constructed background were referred to obliquely, James eventually revealed that she was involved in some bizarre cult rituals that involved group sex, human sacrifice and drinking blood. These details were eventually revealed to Stagg in a meeting. Stagg subsequently expressed concern that he would be unable to live up to James' unconventional expectations. Throughout, James had given hints as to her background and to the desires that ensued, as a product of a past that she claimed would be hard to repeat. Stagg, in a series of letters, wrote increasingly violent sexual fantasies that culminated with a reference to an attractive blonde woman being teased with a knife so that blood was drawn. This scenario, among previous violent fantasies, which was set in the open air near a tree, was enough to convince the enquiry team that Stagg's fantasies were increasingly approximating core features of the murder of Nickell. Moreover, to Britton and the investigation team, they fitted the profile allegedly originally constructed at the beginning of the enquiry.[1]

The material

The material contains a set of four police interviews, 43 correspondences from the undercover officer (12 letters, 27 phone calls and 4 meetings), 21 sexual fantasy letters from the suspect, and a variety of other documents relevant to the case, namely:

- Mr Britton's assessments of the letters

- the document provided to the courts prepared by the present authors

- reports from Gisli Gudjonsson and Glen Wilson regarding psycho-metric tests carried out on Stagg and assessments of the sexual fantasy material

- two sets of pathologists' reports

- statements from witnesses

- the skeleton reports from the defence and prosecution

- Stagg's sexual fantasy correspondence with two other women

- the transcript of the palantype notes of DL Sellers and Co in relation to The Honourable Mr Justice Ognall's summing up in the Central Criminal Court.

The material is very unusual in its breadth and diversity. Firstly, it concerns a single case study in considerable depth. Secondly, it considers the course of events from the murder (15 July 1992) to the Judge's summing up (14 September 1994). Thirdly, apart from certain aspects within the documents provided by Wilson, Gudjonnson and Canter and Alison, in the main it is 'real-world' data – i.e. it has not been collected for the purposes of research. The material may therefore be considered as plotting a two-year narrative of the Stagg enquiry as seen from a variety of perspectives, including the suspect's, the undercover officer's, the enquiry team's, the courts' and the expert witnesses'. As such, the material opens up a diverse range of ways of exploring the rhetorical issues at the heart of the enquiry. However, for the present concerns the main focus lies within the undercover operation.

It should be made clear that the police transcribed the material. Moreover, the material does not exist in its complete form – tapes of the interviews and the undercover operation were not available. This presents the researcher with a number of restrictions on what can be achieved. Firstly, it is highly unlikely that the transcripts are an accurate reflection of what occurred, since it is possible that some phrases were either inaccurately transcribed, misheard or of such a low quality as to be indiscernible. Though this latter point was infrequent (it was only in the last phone call that the transcriber actually admits a section of tape was 'indiscernible'), it is possible that other sections were 'guessed' at. Secondly, it is impossible to examine issues of style and intonation since there is no indication of tone, pauses, etc., from the transcripts. Thirdly, we did not have the luxury of examining the interaction first hand, so notes could not be taken regarding significant features of the transactions. Despite these limitations it is still possible to explore issues relating to the form and evolution of the rhetoric as well as issues relating to content and the development of individual narratives.

Rhetoric and 'shaping' discourse

This chapter only represents one component of the analysis conducted on the material, concentrating principally on the 'relationship' between Stagg and James and, in particular, on the undercover officer's use of persuasive tactics. The approach that we adopted carefully considered the range and combination of rhetorical devices employed by the undercover officer. In part, we viewed this as analogous to operant reinforcement paradigms, with the rhetorician reinforcing desired behaviours (violent sexual fantasies) until closer and closer approximations to pre-specified criteria are achieved (violent sexual fantasies similar to those predicted in the offender profile and 'relevant' to the murder of Rachel Nickell). However, useful though the reinforcement paradigm is, a rhetorical approach furthers our understanding of this transactional process by exploring how social influence is reliant on persuasive tactical stratagems rather than simple reward systems. For example, the model of the 'influencer' as orator renders the reward function of the reinforcement paradigm redundant – actual penetrative sex does not need to be directly offered to the suspect, just the hinted promise of such. Thus, rhetorical tactics are employed to direct behaviour through more subtle social processes than explicit reward functions.

Rhetorical tactics are defined, in part, by their temporal sequencing, the influential power achieved, in part, by the sequencing and combination of devices. Underpinning behaviourist research is the reliance on cause–effect contingencies and the fundamental assertion that behaviour is subject to predictable lawful patterns (Grunbaum, 1952). A consequence of this is the opportunity for creating contexts within which behaviours can be elicited, controlled and shaped. Once the behaviours under examination are precisely specified, what remains is the necessary set of observations upon conditions under which they are commonly produced. As in more familiar processes of reinforcement (where, for example, key pecking results in the administration of food pellets), so too the provision of emotional needs acts as a reward system through which select operants, reinforced by the 'experimenter', become more frequent. However, the contexts that produce behavioural changes in operant repertoires under emotional conditions have not been easy to classify (Michael and Meyerson, 1962). Because of the complexity of emotional responses, as well as the large repertoire of acquired behaviours developed by the individual in the past, the problem of specifying operant contexts is an area fraught with difficulty.

Instead, certain social processes that lie within the grasp of a rhetorical framework may be better equipped to deal with these subtleties. A behaviourist perspective that simply sees each unit of verbal behaviour as a functionally adapted reinforcer neglects the expressive oratorical model of man. Rhetorical tactics do not act in the same way as food pellets. Instead they take on a variety of expressive meanings as a function of the individuals involved and the context within which they occur. In doing so, they remove the need for an explicit reward system. The task is to identify these tactics and examine how they rely on social processes for their various effects. Further, any discussion of the affective components of rhetoric must also take account of the developmental change in the combination of strategies.

In order to develop a theory of the structural change of rhetoric we consider the nature of the tactics used in the undercover operation where attempts were made to elicit specific types of information from Stagg. A central question that needs to be asked then is, 'Can we identify the rhetorical tactics employed?' To examine this one needs to consider the nature of such tactics within the context of processes of interaction.

The joint process of emotional shaping

What the behaviourist and rhetorical perspectives do share in common is the argument that language is part of a behavioural repertoire integral to everyday functioning. Wittgenstein (1958), for example, argued strongly against behaviours as merely symptomatic reactions to external stimuli. Indeed, he was very keen to promote models that dealt with the expressive qualities of language. He viewed them as an integral part of behaviour rather than as an abstract picture of reality that was then mapped onto events. In turning away from the concept of language as a representation of the world he stated that his desire was to 'bring into prominence the fact that speaking of language is part of an activity or a form of life' (Wittgenstein, 1958). Thus, both the behaviourist and rhetorical per-spectives hold a common view that language's power to manipulate is an integral feature of the model of man as an interacting, language-driven organism. However, the rhetorician parts company with the behaviourist in viewing the use of the manipulative properties of language as a process of tactical and meaningful arrangement rather than as a reward contingency process. Where a behaviourist model necessitates some observable form of reward this component can be dropped from the rhetorical equation. Thus the rhetorician can 'shape' behaviour without having to provide rewards as long as the tactician is cognizant of the potential effect that his/her words will have on the target.

A central feature of rhetoric is that the process of engaging the interlocutor emotionally necessitates explicit *involvement* with him/her/them. Successful emotional manipulation literally involves the elicitation of a physiological change in the interlocutor – the rhetorician has to 'move' his/her audience in a predefined direction in order to take the individual from perspective 'a' to perspective 'b':

> The emotions (pathé) are those things through which, by undergoing change, people come to differ in their judgements and which are accompanied by pain and pleasure, for example anger, pity, fear, and other such things and their opposites. (Kennedy, 1991: 121)

Crucial in the process of emotional engagement is the rhetorician's ability to predict the likely emotional response of the interlocutor (Cockroft and Cockroft, 1992). In conditions where prediction is high, the process is likely to bear fruit. Where the needs of the target are known, and can easily be appealed to, encouragement of the desired behaviour becomes a more manageable task. In the case of the undercover operation our concern is not so much with the needs of the target but rather in identifying, through the rhetoric of the undercover officer, what the enquiry team may have thought these were and how those presumed needs were exploited, so we had to ask, 'Is it possible to identify the implicit theory the enquiry team held regarding the suspect's proposed involvement with the murder of Rachel Nickell?'

In instances in which two individuals are closely intertwined but where one is 'in control', the relatively less powerful partner's predicted change of behaviour should be more clear by virtue of the anticipated needs that can be 'played' upon. Thus, the appropriate conditions under which select components of a behavioural repertoire may be shaped are more readily available – i.e. each time the suspect behaves in the desired way, the rhetorician can prompt that behaviour and ignore all others. However, as we have emphasized, these interactions cannot be adequately accounted for within a behavioural perspective since, for example, a tactic such as 'prompting' cannot be explained within a behaviourist's framework. While desired outcomes may be lawful and predictable, the 'operant' becoming more frequent with continual prompts from the source, the nature of those prompts lies within particular tactics and their meaning. Before discussing the definitions of the rhetorical tactics let us consider previous attempts at examining the shaping of verbal behaviour within a behaviourist paradigm.

Verbal shaping

From the behaviourist perspective events in the environment are seen as influencing behaviour in two ways. Firstly, as external consequences of behaviour they act as reinforcers that increase the frequency of a preceding behaviour. Secondly, they act as signalling functions by informing the organism when and where behaviour is likely to be followed by a reinforcing event. Actions that change the environment, that produce consequences for the organism, can be shaped. When consequences are desirable the action that produces them is reinforced and eventually becomes a learned response. When the action is complex and does not come easily it can be shaped. *Shaping* is a learning procedure where the experimenter has, at the origin of the behaviour, very low criteria for the behaviour (i.e. it can very loosely approximate the eventual required response). Response criteria may then be increasingly tightened by only rewarding actions that come nearer and nearer to the required criterion. While such a framework has been employed successfully in a great many studies of behaviour, the paradigm has been less successful in exploring verbal shaping.

However, in the 1950s Verplanck (1955) reported considerable success in exerting strong control over the casual conversations of other people by selectively reinforcing a certain type of opinion-statement and extinguishing all other types of statement. Notably though, Azrin and Lindsley (1956) refer to this experiment as one of the very few successful attempts to reinforce human verbal behaviour in a free operant condition. In a replication of the study they reported success in reducing the number of opinions to one particular type of opinion although one of the problems in the replication was the students' inability to get more involved in the conversation than they were supposed to. In other words, they were told only to reinforce one topic by simple agreement to that sole topic. Thus while Azrin reports that, 'The importance of extending the procedures of operant conditioning to "real life" situations should not be allowed to override the elementary considerations of experimental control' (p. 248), the problem with the experiment illustrates neatly a necessary feature of verbal interaction – namely that it is a dynamic, two-way process. For example, there is a degree of involvement between both parties beyond a simple reinforcing contingency impacting on a single aspect of the target's/interlocutor's discourse. This is a fundamental problem with the behaviourist paradigm since it ignores the levels of meaning in language. Because of the strict requirement for control over specific verbal units within the behaviourist paradigm, any attempt to replicate the real qualities of discourse becomes untenable. Instead we must explore the rhetorical nature of discourse and its impact upon the dialogue generated by both parties.

The identification of the rhetorical tactics employed

According to Schwerin and Newell (1981), behavioural changes cannot occur without attitude change having taken place. 'Attitude change' implies that 'a person's evaluation is modified from one value to the other' (Petty and Wegener, 1998: 324). The basic principles of persuasion research are represented by the independent variable/s relating to the source of the message, the message itself, the recipient of the message and the context, impact on emotions, cognition and/or behaviour, which, in turn, influence the attitude toward an object (Petty and Wegener, 1998). Although the affective, cognitive and behavioural processes of attitude change may be independent (Zanna and Rempel, 1988), they are often linked and a change in one typically leads to changes in the others (Rosenberg, 1960). Of course, the 'Yale approach' (Hovland et al., 1953) represents one of the earliest and most significant studies of the variables that relate to persuasive communication, identifying three central variables: the source of the message, the message itself and the audience. Four distinct steps in the persuasion process were identified: attention, comprehension, acceptance and retention.

In the late 1970s two multi-process frameworks for attitude change were developed: the Elaboration Likelihood Model (ELM) (Petty and Cacioppo, 1981) and the Heuristic-Systematic Model (HSM) (Chaiken, 1987). These models conceptualized the extensive attitude change research from the first half of the twentieth century, and accounted for apparently conflicting findings by exemplifying how the same persuasion variables may have different effects in different situations, and how a given variable could produce the same outcome by different processes. Today the models are seen as being similar and generally account for the same empirical results (Petty and Wegener, 1998).

The variables influencing attitude change have been traditionally classified into source, message, audience and context categories. According to the ELM model, for every variable there are different ways of influencing judgement that depend on the motivation and ability to analyse attitude relevant information (Petty and Wegener, 1998).

Source variables

Trustworthiness

A crucial aspect of the Stagg enquiry involved the credibility of the undercover officer 'Lizzie James' as being trustworthy. The perceived level of trust placed in the source influences overall persuasion as well as the processing of the message (Petty and Wegener, 1998). For example, Eagly *et al.* (1978) found that sources regarded as trustworthy or sincere were more persuasive than sources perceived as untrustworthy. This was particularly influential among individuals who were less critical in assessing information. However, when the source was regarded as untrustworthy, individuals engaged in the same amount of message processing irrespective of 'need for cognition' (Priester and Petty, 1995). Stagg presents as an intelligent individual with the capacity to think critically, and Gudjonsson's assessment indicated that he was not prone to interrogative suggestibility. Further, in discussions with Stagg (Canter and Alison, 1998)[2] it was apparent that he was wary, considered James as 'odd' and claimed not to believe her stories of involvement in ritual and sacrifice.

Power

Powerful sources are generally more persuasive than weak sources (Festinger and Thibaut, 1951; Raven and French, 1958). It appears that Stagg viewed James as a powerful figure and was eager to please her. Moreover, even a cursory examination of the phone calls and meetings reveals that James appears dominant – she occupies a large proportion of the time spent talking and, particularly in the meetings, makes a number of ultimatums regarding the relationship.

Message variables

Issue relevance/importance

How much one cares about an issue will be primarily determined by the extent to which it is personally relevant (Boninger *et al.*, 1995). Using personal rather then impersonal pronouns may enhance this effect (Burnkrant and Unnava, 1989). According to Petty and Cacioppo (1979), an increase in personal relevance would encourage thinking about the message, and therefore would increase the message's persuasive capacity if the arguments were strong, but decrease persuasion if the arguments were weak. Johnson and Eagly's (1989) meta-analytic review supported this hypothesis when the issue was important in terms of personal consequences. Clearly, in Stagg's case, the promise of a sexual relationship was a highly personally relevant issue. Needless to say, the message, 'you can trust me, we can have a relationship, if …' was likely to prove highly persuasive, particularly since Stagg was keen to lose his virginity.

Explicit/implicit

Some studies have supported the notion that explicit messages attract greater persuasive influence (Hovland *et al.*, 1949), while others have suggested that it is preferable if conclusions are drawn by the recipient, i.e. an implicit message (Fine, 1957). The latter accords with Walster's and Festinger's (1962) conclusion that people are more easily persuaded if they think the message is not deliberately intended to persuade them. Often, recipients are unable or unmotivated to draw the conclusion on their own (McGuire, 1969), but when individuals have the ability to process the message and are sufficiently motivated, then the implicit route may be preferable (Stayman and Kardes, 1992). In Stagg's case, it appears as though he was uncertain as to the desired message, with early attempts to impress James falling widely off the mark. Indeed, in the early sexual fantasy letters he offers a series of possible fantasy scenarios (group sex, bondage, bisexual/gay scenes) in an apparent effort to test out which arousal cues James was likely to respond to. However, as we will demonstrate, James' requirements became more and more direct as the sequence of transactions progressed.

Argument quality

According to Petty and Wegener (1991), consequences that are likely and desirable are more persuasive than those that are less likely or desirable. The perceived likelihood of a consequence is enhanced where the source provides an explanation of why this result is likely to occur (Slusher and Anderson, 1996). Several other factors influence argument quality, such as their resemblance to the recipient's view of the world (Cacioppo *et al.*, 1982) or their novelty (Burnstein and Vinokur, 1975). In this case it is unclear as to whether Stagg could see any persuasive reason why James would want 'the sort of man' that could kill a woman. James explained that in the rituals she had been involved with, the experience was a thrill and exhilarating and that she wanted to repeat the same sort of experience. However, in our interview, Stagg claimed 'I was just trying to get my leg over' and thought that James was 'weird', so it is possible that he was unable to find any explanation or justifiable logic in James' reported need for violence and abuse.

Fear arousal

According to Petty and Wegener (1998), appeals that include strong negative consequences if the message is not adopted are very effective. Boster and Mongeau's (1984) meta-analysis of the fear appeal literature indicated that increases in fear are associated with increased persuasion. However, several factors may work against the effectiveness of fear appeals (see review by Petty and Wegener, 1998). For example, if the recipients do not believe they can cope effectively with the threat this will not increase the message's persuasive value (Mullis and Lippa, 1990; Rippetoe and Rogers, 1987). Several researchers have attempted to interpret this relationship between fear and persuasion (see the Extension of the Drive Model (Janis, 1967); the Parallel Response Model (Leventhal, 1970); and the Original Protection Motivation Theory (Rogers, 1983)). In the undercover operation, Stagg repeatedly refers to his fear of losing his relationship with James. The subsequent threat of withdrawal of this relationship on the part of Lizzie James may have led Stagg to moderate and adapt his behaviour accordingly and to satisfy the perceived needs of his newly found relationship. Indeed, Stagg at one point, shortly after some hints that the relationship might be under threat, indicates that he was involved in a murder several years previously. In checking police records, it became clear that this was a fabrication.

Positive feelings

According to Thurstone (1928), attitudes are evaluations of various stimuli. Therefore, commercial messages, for example, involve efforts to make recipients feel positively inclined towards the persuasion object (Hogg and Vaughan, 1998). At select points throughout the discourse, James does positively reinforce Stagg through indications that she has enjoyed what he has written. However, the general tenor is one in which she persistently notes that what he has provided has not gone far enough.

Guilt arousal

Several studies have revealed that when feelings of guilt are aroused, participants are more ready to comply with later requests, such as participate in a future experiment or donate blood (Carlsmith and Gross, 1969; Darlington and Macker, 1966; Freedman *et al.*, 1967). The reasons for this include attempts to expiate the guilt by doing a good deed, punish oneself (Freedman *et al.*, 1967) or bolster self-image (Carlsmith and Gross, 1969). It does not appear that James plays upon this stratagem. Indeed, at the point where Stagg claims to have committed a previous (unrelated) murder, her tone is disappointed disbelief.

The reciprocity principle
Based on the social norm that people should treat others the way others have treated them, it is expected that providing a favour for someone will make that person feel obligated to reciprocate. Regan (1971) has demonstrated that greater compliance was obtained from people who had previously received a favour than from those who did not. Other than the gifts that she gives Stagg (a baseball cap – to make him more conspicuous to the team monitoring them in the park, and a personal stereo), James relies on a *quid pro quo* of fantasy letters throughout her relationship with Stagg. This sequence of alternating letters results in a succession of speedy responses from Stagg.

Context variables

Media type
Several studies have investigated the extent to which messages in written, audiotaped or videotaped form rely on their mode of communication for persuasive effect. It is assumed that the differences between these media types arise from the message being self-paced (written) vs externally paced (face to face). In general, self-paced messages receive greater scrutiny than the externally paced ones, perhaps because they are easier to analyse (Petty and Wegener, 1998). Accordingly, Chaiken and Eagly (1976) found that a written message led to greater persuasion and recall of message arguments than audio- and videotaped messages. However, this is probably contingent on the nature and context within which the message is receieved. In Stagg's case it is clear that significant effort was put into his fantasy letters and that he probably read James' over and over again (indicated by his verbatim reference to many of the phrases used by James). However, in meetings, he appears more submissive and introvert, responding uncomfortably.

We now turn to a closer examination of the actual devices employed by James and illustrate how important the chronological development of these are against the backcloth of the factors that enhance persuasion.

The rhetorical tactics

Mirroring and eulogizing

'Mirroring' is a well known device both to social psychologists and rhetoricians and involves the conveyance of a self-image of similarity in attitude and style to the target. Perceived attitudinal similarity and liking has a long and enduring history, research upon which all points to the fact that perceived similarity is associated with attraction. Crutchfield *et al.* (2003), for example, established that advertisers who perceived high similarity between themselves and those within their agency rated their agency as superior to those who felt they had less in common with agency contacts. Dion *et al.* (1972) found that dating, engaged and married couples are more similar to one another in the degree to which they are physically attractive.

The strength of this effect is so powerful that it exists even where individuals are led to believe that they are similar even where they may not be. For example, Newcomb (1961) established that, in friendships among university students, the more two individuals liked each other, the more they assumed they were similar. Even anticipation of similarity is sufficient to increase liking. Therefore, mirroring involves the source outlining a number of features about him/herself that bear similarities to the target. This may include many of the features that Berscheid *et al.* examined, i.e. preferred form of social participation (loner or socially gregarious) family background and social attitudes and similarities in leisure pursuits. Mirroring takes its effect by convincing the target that s/he is well matched to the source and therefore the pair are compatible. The reinforcing property of this tactic stems from the comfort it provides the target in convincing her/him that s/he will not have to adapt her/his behaviour to an unsuitable partner. The positive aspect of this effect appears then to be partly an issue of consistency (Tesser and Conlee, 1975). Certainly, the issue of consensus agreement over attitudes appears to be very important early on in relationships. Cramer (2001), for example, has noted that, early on in courting couples' relationships, consensus value is of critical importance in determining whether or not a relationship survives. Only later in the relationship can issues of complementariness occur and even then it is controversial whether complementary aspects are more effective than maintaining similarity. It is therefore in the interest of the source to feign similarity to the target.

The tactic is also well known to rhetoricians, with Aristotle urging speakers to 'represent, as existing, that which is honoured by each set of people – as by Scythians, or Lacedaemonians or philosophers' (Kennedy, 1991: 1367b).The process of identification is employed to increase the subsequent probability of successfully manipulating the target. Once achieved it may become more possible to mould attitudes that otherwise would have been immutable. As Billig (1996) points out, however, this transactional process is not an act of brainwashing since the means by which the orator sides with the audience is determined in part by that audience's beliefs. Thus, in the Stagg case, it was important to try and establish the implicit theories that the enquiry had regarding the supposed similarities that they thought could be acted upon. This bears some intriguing similarities to the selection process by which reinforcement theories operate. As Skinner states, 'note that the organism changes our behaviour in quite as precise a fashion. Our apparatus was designed by the organism we study, for it was the organism which led us to choose a particular manipulandum' (Skinner, 1974). Thus, the choice of proposed similarities to the target (the manipulation tactic) helps to identify the implicit theory that the enquiry team had regarding the qualities supposedly matched to the suspect. These, in turn, may vary according to the repertoire of the target. Thus different qualities may be mirrored as they evolve from the suspect. As Hass states, fluctuations of *expression* 'are very probably a frequent ingredient of social interaction' (1981: 140). Conversational participants are therefore engaged in a constantly shifting process of trying to maintain a common ground between themselves and their partner. An associated problem with this is if the target is following a line of rhetoric himself. In other words he may have his own agenda for manipulation that involves a desire to impress. In this hypothetical arrangement, the 'common ground' increasingly deviates from the original, genuine and 'spontaneous' qualities of both partners. The under-cover operative manipulates the target by feigning presumed similarities to the suspect. Paradoxically, these 'similarities' may in fact be the suspect's own attempts to win over the affections of his new-found partner by mirroring her (unbeknown to him) artificial attributes. Both parties become increasingly involved in a process of rhetorical manipulation as they construct identities designed for each other. Increasingly, this leads each partner to a distorted picture of the other.

Encouraging

An additional tactic that is likely to be an enduring characteristic of the transactions is to praise or encourage the target. This is because the source needs to continually prompt for more information. Each time this is occurs, the target needs to be assured that it is welcome and that there will follow a reasonable level of praise. This will also most likely affect the level of attraction to the target as well as reinforce increasingly specific criteria (in the written material of the target). Thus the individual needs to be assured that they are liked in order to like. For example, Backman and Secord (cited in Berscheid and Walster, 1969) established that by suggesting through a 'personality test' that certain individuals would like a conversational participant, the researchers could manipulate the level of liking to the experimenter's stooge. Individuals who were told that from the basis of the personality assessments they would be liked by the stooge, liked the stooge more than those who were told they would be disliked or to whom they would be perceived as neutral. However, this bogus information lost its impact after several interactions – possibly indicating that the process of social approval must be continual rather than fleeting and superficial.

The susceptibility to liking based on being liked is affected by the person's need or drive level. Thus if an individual is starved of approval, s/he should be unusually receptive to social approval. The effect is even more pronounced when the individual has previously had their self-confidence shattered (Walster and Walster, 1963). Reik (1944) has even suggested that we are unusually susceptible to falling in love when we are dissatisfied with ourselves. Deutsch and Solomon (1959) have also proposed that low self-esteem should affect receptivity to love, affection and praise. However, they make the caveat that low self-esteem individuals are also suspicious of people liking them. Moreover, attitudes expressed towards us should be congruent with our own if we are to like the interactional participant. Thus if an individual feels s/he has completed a task well and is praised, then that form of encouragement will lead to attraction. However, if the individual feels s/he has performed badly then praise will not be taken as genuine and attraction is unlikely to follow. Unsurprisingly, when self-attitude is uncertain we err towards accepting praise rather than criticism.

In the present case the fact that Stagg had been relatively unsuccessful with women up until the point of the enquiry might suggest that social approval by an attractive woman would be highly reinforcing. At the same time it is also quite possible that he would be suspicious of such praise if low self-esteem accompanied this lack of success. Therefore what Britton highlighted as Stagg's 'monitoring, caution and testing' (1997: 227) of Lizzie James may be less a feature of the degree of caution that a murderer would display but rather a normal function of suspicion of the undercover officer's praise. This suspicion may have been fixed in the roots of low self-esteem rather than caution.

Stagg who had at least twice failed to secure a relationship may at that time have been particularly susceptible to the reinforcing properties of encouragement. Consistent praise throughout the enquiry was therefore a necessary device for maintaining contact and for encouraging more and more letters and information regarding Stagg's sexual fantasies. A number of authors have highlighted the importance of the consistency with which praise is given. Inconsistent accounts on similar performances are likely to be unattractive because inconsistency is aversive, it is viewed as inaccurate and therefore may be perceived as unintelligent and insensitive. Further, inconsistency colours subsequent praise, which then comes across as disingenuous and ingratiating.

Mitigating

An inducement to the target to avoid an aversive state (such as, in this case, the threat of withdrawal of an intimate relationship) is the use of 'prompting' to attain commodities that the target does not have. *Mitigating* is defined as a subtle indicator that what the target is producing is not quite what the source wants. The tactic is not so much an order to change the path of the information elicited but rather a tactic to imply as much. Only by performing to a required standard can the target keep this negative emotion at bay.

Mitigating is therefore a 'polite' demand. Ng and Bradac (1993) have noted that mitigators are polite forms of orders such that the comment, 'It's cold in here' is a polite variant of the order 'Shut the window'. Thus James' comments such as, 'I feel you are showing great restraint' are a variant of 'Write me something more extreme'.

The subtleties of levels of speech analysis are particularly pertinent in relation to this device since mitigating covers three domains of speech. The first is the locutionary act – i.e. the actual utterance of the words. The second, the illocutionary act, involves the force or act derived from the meaning of the speech. The third is the effect that the speech has on the listener – the perlocutionary act. These three levels have been discussed by Austin (1962), who focused on what is actually 'done' in speech. The purpose of mitigation is to modify the illocutionary point of affectively negative speech acts, i.e. to 'signal to the addressee that the speaker's intention behind an unwelcome communication has been softened … in terms of speech act theory, mitigation is the attenuation of the strength with which … an unwelcome speech act is communicated' (Ng and Bradac, 1993: 92).

In mitigating the indication is that what is being produced is not entirely acceptable. Thus, there is a subtle but powerful veiled threat of withdrawal, the consequences of which may be uncertain to the target. The target may be left wondering what would occur if something more were not produced. This state of uncertainty can be highly aversive. Indeed as Berger and Calabrese (1987) state, the goal of initial interaction lies in reducing uncertainty in an attempt to determine the future of the relationship. Further, high levels of uncertainty are related to decreasing levels of intimacy. Thus, the promised level of intimate contact may be under threat unless something else is 'delivered'. Exacerbating this may be anxiety over what precisely the source wants. This results in a state of hypervigilance and a rapid search for a variety of alternatives, a condition associated with stress in decision-making (Janis and Mann, 1977). Thus mitigating may follow the initial stages of identifying with the target and from it flow the subtle indicators that a change in attitude is desirable.

Eulogizing

An extension of this tactic is to eulogize qualities of an imagined comparison 'other'. A preferred criterion is held up as the ideal alternative and is compared to the target. Anything less than this desired alternative is considered failure. Eulogizing therefore has very specific criteria as a rhetorical tactic. It is a more extreme demand for the suspect to change the information that he is providing for the satisfaction of the source. It is then a variant of mitigating but includes an added component of clearly illustrating that conforming to the ideal is a worthy endeavour that may bring further 'rewards'. What is implied in using this device is the assumption that unless current behaviours are elevated to the ideal standard, the relationship will break down.

Promising and demanding

Promising

The enquiry team may have believed that they needed to reassure the target of potential 'rewards' (an intimate relationship) by employing the undercover operative to promise them to the suspect. Insko and Cialdini (1971) have examined positive social reinforcers and their influencing effects, suggesting that these are the two central factors that lead to attitudinal reinforcement. A positive stimulus offering information and praise will be attractive and will increase the target's desire to agree with the source due to the tendency to agree with a liked other.

Attraction is based on positive affect accompanying reinforcement. As such, Byrne and Nelson (1965) have suggested that the process of attraction is similar to classical conditioning. Their assumption rests on a number of corollaries: (i) a variety of social communications and other interpersonal events can be classed as reinforcing or punishing; (ii) reinforcing events elicit positive affect, punishing ones negative affect; (iii) stimuli associated with positive or negative affect develop the capacity to evoke that affect; (iv) stimuli that evoke positive affect are liked, those that evoke negative affect are disliked. Thus one likes others who reward one because they are associated with one's own good feelings.

There are a variety of sources of evidence for each of the four hypotheses. It has been demonstrated, for example, that individuals liked a partner more when they received reinforcement in his presence than when they did not. Attitude similarity acts like a traditional reinforcer inasmuch as agreement can lead to liking. Disliking or liking can be successfully manipulated by different affective states incurred through watching unpleasant or pleasant films in the context of the researcher's stooge. It is therefore vital in inculcating attraction that a positive affective state is associated with the attractor.

Promising future success and happiness in the relationship is likely to create positive feelings. When this promise stems from the attractor herself, the link between positive feelings and the object of affection is direct. Therefore, early on in the Stagg enquiry it may have been necessary to create a context in which the undercover officer could convey to the target a sense of a possible future in the relationship. This tactic achieves two things. Firstly, a context for attraction is created since the mention of a possible future of increased intimacy is likely to create positive affect. Because this stems from the source, positive feelings are associated with her. Secondly, the tactic operates directly on promoting the elicitation of specific types of information. For example, the enquiry team were aware that Stagg had written lonely-hearts letters that involved sexual fantasies to another correspondent prior to the operation. They therefore had their first operant ready for reinforcement. Therefore, each time a letter is written it can be reinforced through continued promising. Increasingly specific aspects of the target's response may then be reinforced such that at later stages the tactic may be reserved for increasingly precise criteria.

Demanding (fear/phobos)

Aristotle defines fear as 'a sort of pain or agitation derived from the imagination of a future destructive or painful evil' and further that the state of mind of those who fear is 'accompanied by an expectation of experiencing some destructive misfortune … for fear to continue there must be some hope of being saved from the cause of agony' (Kennedy, 1991: 141). The potential to avoid aversive conditions bears a close relationship to negative reinforcement. Negative reinforcement involves the withdrawing of aversive stimuli in response to the operant. Shaping may therefore occur as a result of increasingly specific criteria on the operant to prevent the aversive stimuli. While this has been well documented in animal studies (see Catania, 1992), it is generally a technique that has been less well documented on human subjects. This may be because of the connotations that negative reinforcement has with 'brainwashing' and cruelty, since noxious rather than pleasant stimuli have to be administered to result in the shaping of the required behaviour. However, there are some 'real-world' examples of reinforcement through negative means that can be seen in cases of torture and brainwashing. An intriguing example of one of these is Farber *et al.*'s (1957) summary of the techniques used by the Communist Chinese in Korea in stimulating co-operative behaviour in a large number of United States prisoners of war. They studied the basis for the success of techniques of false confessions, self-denunciations and participation in propaganda activities. While the intensity of the noxious stimulation – including injury, disease, mal-nutrition, deprivation, sleeplessness, fatigue, isolation and threat, was extreme, the theoretical principles behind shaping compliant behaviour are similar – namely, the avoidance of aversive stimuli through producing the desired behaviour.

Farber *et al.* suggest that the success of these regimes lay in at least three important elements, which they refer to as DDD. 'Debility' refers to the state where semi-starvation, disease and fatigue were induced to create weakness and weariness thus lessening resolve. 'Dependency' was then produced by prolonged deprivation of many factors such as sleep and food needed to maintain sanity. Brief respites from these conditions resulted in reminding the prisoner that it was possible for the captor to relieve the misery if he wished. Finally, 'dread' involved the chronic fear that the Communists attempted to induce in relation to potential death, fear of pain, non-repatriation, deformity and disability, and violence against loved ones. The authors note that DDD does not, in itself, produce the desired behaviours of compliance but rather the occasion for the selective reinforcement of certain modes of response. Even the antici-patory effect of relieving the DDD state was an effective means of gradually shaping the desired behaviour and thus the alleviation of DDD at the time of occurrence of the desired behaviour led to the powerful consequence of the learning of instrumental acts. Very often the desired behaviour was verbal. As Farber *et al.* point out, one learns from infancy to use verbal behaviour as a means of relieving or avoiding noxious stimuli.

While the hypotensive state induced in the POWs is far removed from the present concern, the principles that underlie it are the same. Both rely on the deprived state of the individual, on the dependency that he has formed with the source and on the fear of the withdrawal of the relationship. These are all social aspects of the same underlying principles. It is not suggested that these are necessarily conscious manipulative strategies (Farber *et al.* point out that 'animal trainers and side-show barkers are often extremely competent manipulators of behaviour; this does not mean they are comparative or social psychologists'). They are, nevertheless, powerful inducements to the target to elicit increasingly specific fantasy material.

However, as we have commented, this may be achieved through rhetorical stratagems. That is, feelings of fear might be elicited by making ultimatums upon the target's behaviour. We refer to this tactic as 'demanding'. Demanding involves the direct threat that unless the target conforms to the source's desires then the dissolution of the relationship is imminent. It is, therefore, an explicit threat to the relationship and perhaps, in the target's mind, to a return to loneliness. This tactic is an overt form of control resulting in an asymmetric power relationship in favour of the source.

Lack of mutual control has commonly been shown to be predictive of unstable relationships (Morton *et al.*, 1976; Canary and Stafford, 1992; Falbo and Peplau, 1980). Conversely mutual control is linked to bilateral influence strategies (Falbo and Peplau, 1980) and relational satisfaction and understanding. Therefore the use of demands may be perceived, quite correctly by the target, as the 'beginning of the end' of the relationship. In order to maintain it he will be aware that desired responses are contingent on him adopting a different course to avoid the aversive state of lower control.

Where demanding is concerned there is no doubt in the target's mind as to the course that he should take. There is therefore considerable pressure on the target to expend resources and energies on keeping the relationship together by adopting particular emphases in his attitudes towards the source's specific criteria.

Summary of the tactics and hypotheses

Our suggestion to the defence team was that expected affective reactions of the target can be prompted through a variety of rhetorical tactics. These operate on pairs of contrasting emotional responses – effecting both a positive emotion and its negative associated emotion. Therefore combinations of tactics may be used across the operation to try and promote positive affect. Different combinations can be used to promote or threaten opposite (i.e. negative) feelings. Through this process of 'push and pull', increasingly specific rhetoric may be elicited from the suspect as he also begins the process of interpersonal manipulation.

We were at pains to suggest that there was not necessarily a conscious desire to manipulate the suspect or that any such systematic approach was designed or considered by the enquiry team. However, it is possible that much can be revealed about the enquiry team's narrative by exploring the way in which they set about the operation.

Content analysis

The content analysis of 43 correspondences (12 letters, 27 phone calls and 4 meetings) identified six rhetorical tactics: 'promising', 'mirroring', 'encouraging', 'eulogizing', 'mitigating' and 'demanding' (the content analysis dictionary on page 233).

Each of the 43 transcripts were read through by two independent researchers. Initially a very wide range of tactics was noted though, in many cases, their frequencies were very low. After joint discussion between the two researchers there was clear overlap between the six tactics noted and the content analysis dictionary was then constructed on the basis of these six tactics. A third researcher then went through the transactions using the content analysis dictionary to re-code the information. Inter-rater reliability ranged between .74 and .89 for these variables, indicating acceptable levels of agreement.[3]

Having outlined the tactics and suggested that we will examine their joint action, there are also a number of more specific hypotheses that can be examined as assertions made by Britton regarding the case. These, all taken from Britton's commentary on the case in *The Jigsaw Man* (1997), and are as follows:

- 'It should take two to sixteen weeks for Lizzie to establish a relationship which will lead to some sort of rapport' (p. 181).

- 'She couldn't lead him by revealing new material or lines of discussion; she could only reflect back on subjects already raised by the suspect' (p. 180).

- 'There would be lots of cut outs along the way – decision points where the suspect could choose to go in several directions' (p. 174).

We began with an examination of the frequencies of the various tactics. These are presented in Table 9.1.

The use of encouraging was by far the most frequent tactic throughout the operation, with a mean of 8.6 per correspondence. In some transactions this was used as many as 42 times (meeting 3). Mitigating was the second most frequent tactic and was used a maximum of 39 times in a single transaction (meeting 4). There are stages at which the use of mitigating increases dramatically (phone call 4 – 21 instances and in all three meetings it is used over 15 times). As with encouragement, mitigation keeps alive the central component of the dialogue, i.e. the changing of the genuine features of the target's material to a 'preferred' version.

It is perhaps significant that these two 'softer' versions of the more extreme devices are the most frequent. Perhaps, unsurprisingly, 'polite'

Table 9.1 Table of mean frequencies and standard deviations for the six rhetorical tactics. (Figures in parentheses are percentage frequencies of total sample.)

Rhetorical tactic	Frequency corresp.	Mean per corresp.	SD	Range
Encouraging	370 (38)	8.6	8.3	0–42
Mitigating	225 (23)	5.2	8.8	0–39
Promising	167 (17)	3.9	2.9	0–13
Mirroring	105 (11)	2.5	3.2	0–14
Demanding	84 (8)	2.0	3.9	0–16
Eulogizing	20 (2)	0.5	1.2	0–5

orders are more acceptable throughout an enduring relationship than consistent dictatorial 'bullying' or melodramatic offers of an enduring and passionate relationship. Indeed, studies of gay and heterosexual couples indicate that partners use bargaining and more subtle forms of manipulation more frequently than supplication and bullying (see Kalbfleisch, 1993).

Promising was used a total of 167 times, with a maximum of 13 times in one transaction (phone call 9). This tactic is used early on in the relationship and there are only four transactions where there are no examples (two of which involve discussing terminating the relationship – in the last two transactions). Again, it appears to be relatively important to keep the target's hopes up except in cases where the source has manoeuvred the relationship to a point where their withdrawal may be a more powerful means of influence.

Mirroring is also used early on in the relationship and is fairly consistent throughout although there are stages at which it is used more predominantly (phone call 2 – 14 instances; phone call 19 – 12 instances). As suggested, achieving consensus early on smoothes the path for subsequent forms of manipulation since the target is likely to have become attached to the source.

Both demanding and eulogizing are used far less frequently than any of the other tactics – tending to be used later in the relationship. The first instance of eulogizing is phone call 7; the first use of demanding is letter 8. However, meetings 1, 2 and 4 involve the use of at least 10 instances of demanding. This conforms to the logical development of this tactic – i.e. threatening the withdrawal of what has been achieved necessitates that something actually has been achieved. It is also perhaps significant that these tactics are used more frequently in verbal rather than written interactions (a feature to be discussed).

The relationship of rhetorical tactics to mode of contact

'Mirroring' and 'encouraging' and 'mitigating' and 'eulogizing' may be contrasting sets of tactics since the former pair are softer, more positive forms, while the latter are more negative, harsher forms. Similarly, 'promising' may stand in contrast to 'demanding' since confidence and fear are also opposing emotions. Broadly, these theoretically relate to positive (emulation, confidence) or negative (envy, fear) emotions.

The frequencies of positive or negative tactics within meetings and phone calls are represented in Table 9.2.

Table 9.2 Table of frequencies of positive or negative tactics within meetings and phone calls

Chronological order of phone call/meeting	Phone call Positive	Negative	Meeting Positive	Negative
1	15	0	24	31
2	32	6	35	49
3	5	0	56	32
4	22	28	21	56
5	19	3		
6	3	0		
7	18	6		
8	11	16		
9	31	0		
10	15	3		
11	11	1		
12	5	0		
13	2	1		
14	4	0		
15	8	4		
16	13	0		
17	4	0		
18	12	0		
19	56	25		
20	18	18		
21	33	1		
22	15	1		
23	9	7		
24	15	0		
25	3	0		
26	10	0		
27	0	1		
TOTALS	389	124	136	168

The table shows that 76 per cent of the tactics in phone calls were positive while only 45 per cent were positive in the meetings. What can account for this discrepancy? Firstly, it is possible that, given that the source was not genuinely involved or interested in the target, she did not want to be as positive in face-to-face interactions. This caution may have allowed her to physically and psychologically keep him at a distance. Indeed, since James refused to wear a protective vest and she accepted the possibility that Stagg was the murderer, she may have been particularly reticent in encouraging him. Secondly, it may be in the nature of interpersonal interactions, where one individual is clearly in charge, for more negative and coercive critical aspects to occur since that individual is aware that they can afford to be more captious. This is the aspect of power that French and Raven (1959) refer to as 'coercive' power, where A's capacity for punishing B includes the removal of resources. Ironically enough, this may lead to aggression directed towards the frustrating agent or redirected elsewhere (Dollard *et al.*, 1939; Ulrich and Symannek, 1969). Therefore, despite what appear to be reasonable tactics to avoid aggression they could have incited it.

The relationships between the variables

It is possible that each type of reinforcer is used in tandem – i.e. mirroring with promising and mitigating with demanding and eulogizing. In other words, where one type of tactic increases/decreases, so does its partner. This would lend support to the original hypothesis that mirroring, promising and encouraging are related tactically to promoting positive affect, whereas mitigating, demanding and eulogizing are examples of negative tactics. To explore this hypothesis relationships between the variables are outlined in Table 9.3 as a Pearson's product moment correlation table.

The strongest relationships exist between each group of positive tactics and the group of negative tactics. The fact that all the correlations are

Table 9.3 Pearson's product moment coefficients indicating the relationship between positive and negative tactics

	prom	mirror	encourage	mitigating	demand
prom					
mirr	.70				
enc	.50	.50			
mitig	.30	.45		.63	
demand	.15	.25	.40	.83	
eulog	.12	.30	.55	.65	.87

positive also supports the fact that all of the tactics are related to an underlying theme – in this case the process of persuasive rhetoric. The relationships can be more elegantly represented as a two-dimensional geometric map – the output from which is formed by use of a multi-dimensional scaling procedure known as smallest space analysis (SSA). SSA represents the correlation matrix as points in a geometric space according to the rank order of the relationships between each of the variables and every other variable – such that the more closely related variables will be more closely situated on the plot. In this case the analysis was run to explore the hypothesized relationship between the two groups of variables. The output of this analysis is shown in Figure 9.1.

The SSA confirms the two groupings, with positive tactics to the left and negative ones to the right. Encouragement sits fairly centrally, suggesting that it is a core feature of the rhetoric, and again confirms the notion of persistent prompting as a necessary device for encouraging disclosure. The correlation matrix suggests that the relationship between the variables approximates a simplex – Guttman's unidimensional cumulative scale – in this case of positive to negative shaping ordered as promising, mirroring, encouraging, mitigating, demanding and eulogizing. However, there are two discrepancies in the correlation matrix between the groups demanding and eulogizing and mirroring and encouraging, suggesting

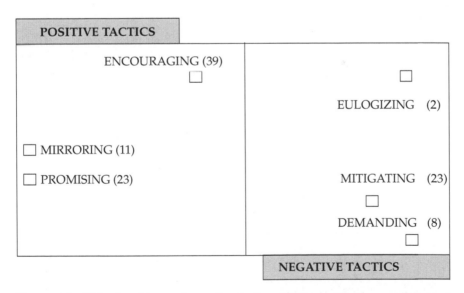

Figure 9.1 SSA of positive and negative tactics – Guttman–Lingoes coefficient of alienation = 0.055. (Figures in parentheses are percentage frequencies of total sample of use of tactic)

that the structure is somewhat more complex. The geometric output approximates a horseshoe structure. This may suggest that a further regional interpretation can be imposed upon the structure – possibly a temporal facet, with promising and demanding both referring to future aspects of the relationship and the others concerned with the present. Both promising and demanding refer to possible future outcomes but one is positive the other negative – i.e. 'The relationship will work if ...' vs 'The relationship will not work unless ...'. This possible interpretation may be represented graphically as below in Figure 9.2.

Although we could not test this hypothesis directly, there was some post-event information from the suspect (Canter and Alison, 1996[4]) that was instructive regarding commentary on the course of his feelings throughout the relationship. Firstly, it appears as though Stagg was pleased to be associated with James – it is known that he spent considerable time talking about her to other individuals on the estate and carried her photograph around. He states in the interview:

Canter: What did you think when you got that [the first letter from James] because you got that out of the blue didn't you?
Stagg: Yeh.
Canter: What did you think of that?
Stagg: Well I just thought my luck was in, more than anything.

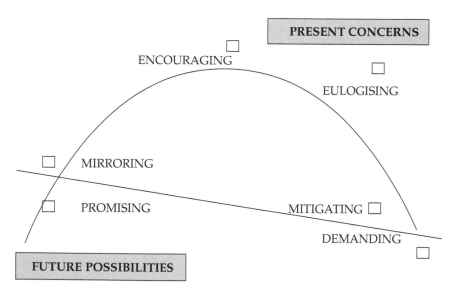

Figure 9.2 SSA of positive and negative tactics showing present and future facet

Moreover, the amount of time Stagg must have spent writing considerable numbers of letters and engaging in lengthy phone calls might be suggestive of a newly found confidence. Additionally, there is some support for the notion that Stagg was attempting both to mirror James and emulate her preferred tastes as well as to conform to a picture that she was creating of an ideal. This is especially evident in the false account of a murder that Stagg admits to 'impress' James:

Stagg: Well that's why I had to make up this story because like at one point I thought I was going to lose her because I kept saying you know I didn't do this murder so you know I'm not like you but yes we can still give it a go you know. But ... erm ... it ... was after one of the meetings when I got back home I thought to myself you know I've got a feeling I'm not going to see her again.

This is a sign of desperation and desire to impress James. Stagg clearly felt he could not match up to the 'ideal' man she had been involved with before or the 'ideal' of the murderer and, significantly, after one of the meetings (which we have identified where instances of more negative tactics were employed) Stagg states he was in fear of losing James:

Stagg: I just thought that she wasn't interested, she was more ... interested in you know if I had actually done the same thing as her ... [she later said] I'm not the right man for her because I didn't do the murder. I keep denying that I was the murderer and that then she just go off er stood up and walked away saying you know we're not going to be good together and that.

Clearly then Stagg was responding with his own range of rhetorical tactics to try to waylay or avoid this loss. In sum, while Stagg's emotions at the time clearly cannot be examined there is some evidence that Britton's first hypothesis of gaining rapport with James was achieved: Stagg spent time trying to impress her, he was clearly more confident during this initial period and he mentions several times, both in the interview with Canter and Alison and more particularly during the interactions with James, that he was afraid of losing her and felt he was not able to come up to her expectations. This fear must have been born of losing what was initially desirable. Further details of the tactics and their potential implications are discussed below.

Relationships between the variables

Disclosure, praise and control

Encouragement is the predominant theme throughout the relationship. It is used 55 times more than its nearest frequency variable (mitigating) and it is used in nearly all of the transactions. Thus in order to maintain the interest of the target, praise is an essential component to subsequent modes of contact and forms of disclosure. Since disclosure is often a device to gain intimacy (known as 'reciprocity' – Cozby, 1973) the target may be particularly susceptible to encouragement if such praise is maintained; i.e. it is a natural step to want to self-disclose if there is uncertainty as to the development of the relationship. When disclosure is encouraged (i.e. when there is consistent praise), the degree of intimate disclosure should theoretically increase. This should also be associated with an increase in inquisitorial behaviour from the target. Berger and Calabrese (1975) state that information-seeking behaviour also increases as a function of the desire to reduce uncertainty and increase intimacy. This should take the form of initially inquiring about low-risk information and then moving to high-risk information (i.e. demographic to biographic). A particular frustration for the target then occurred reasonably early in the sequence where the source reveals that she has a secret but refuses to divulge it. The target spends a considerable amount of effort trying to establish what this might be but to no avail.

In terms of control, partners who disclose the least determine the intimacy level of the relationship (Canary and Stafford, 1992). Thus, both the use of encouragement and the comparably lower level of disclosure on the part of the undercover officer would suggest that it is the source who is in control of the development of the relationship. Moreover, the very fact that the source initiated the relationship gives her the dominant position. Muehlenhard and Scardino (1985) have argued that female initiators are perceived as more sexually active than females who do not initiate dates.

In terms of the asymmetric nature of the relationship, it may have given the source a greater ability to manipulate the target since persuaders who have a favourable power potential are likely to use more influencing strategies (Miller, 1975) and thus the probability of shifting the discourse of the subject would be expected to increase. This is borne out by the fact that there is a fairly high correlation between mitigating and encouragement (0.63), suggesting that both devices were being used in tandem.

Positive and negative tactics and interpersonal proximity

In terms of negative tactics, mitigating, demanding and eulogizing follow a similar pattern – with increases at phone call 2 and all four meetings. Unlike the positive tactics, negative tactics are used particularly in meetings. Interestingly the most sharp incline is in the last meeting (the frequencies across the meetings were as follows for mitigating – 18, 29, 22 and 39), suggesting perhaps that the undercover operation was becoming increasingly more desperate. In fact the relative frequencies of positive tactics are quite low given the amount of interaction. Instead, the source resorted to more forceful demands in threatening the withdrawal of the relationship. High correlations existed between all three tactics (0.83 – mitigating and demanding, 0.65 – eulogizing and mitigating, 0.57 – demanding and eulogizing), showing that all three tactics were being used together.

As stated, the positive tactics tend to occur with higher frequencies in phone calls (promising = phone call 2 – 11 instances, phone call 9 – 13 instances, mirroring = phone call 2 – 14 instances, phone call 9 – 9 instances, phone call 19 – 12 instances). This may be because the source felt that she was more able to use positive tactics when there was physical distance between the pair. Phone calls may have been an opportunity for the source to encourage more fantasy material from the target without fear of intimate contact.

Both mirroring and promising are used with moderate frequency and consistently throughout the enquiry, suggesting that both are important tactics (as with encouraging) to keep the source's interest, even if they appear only once or twice in any one interaction). Bell *et al.* (1987) have asserted that maintenance of a relationship is at least partly contingent upon the communicator being able to increase the partner's affinity. Thus if the source had not used positive tactics it is unlikely that the target would have remained interested for long. In fact, Stagg revealed to Canter and Alison that on several occasions he felt he was 'getting nowhere' with the source and felt at certain times that he was going to lose her (particularly after meeting 2). Mr Stagg also revealed that towards the end of the enquiry he was becoming increasingly frustrated and wanted to finish the relationship. It is possible that this was because of the gradual increase in the joint use of negative tactics over the course of the relationship compared with the general lack of positive ones. Relational features crucial to mature relationships are control mutuality, trust and liking (Millar and Rodgers, 1987). With the lack of openness of the target and relative lack of self-disclosure, the relatively little control that he had over the relationship and the continual pressure on him, it was unlikely that the relationship could have continued for any length of time.

A number of authors have highlighted that unilateral control disrupts relational stability (Falbo and Peplau, 1980). The source is also notably lacking in any strategies, outside the positive tactics, that would help maintain the relationship (Canary and Stafford, 1992), i.e. there are few positive qualities (cheerfulness, lack of personal criticism and spontaneity), openness (direct disclosure about the relationship), assurances (statements of expectations of continuing involvement and caring), social networks (involving friends and family in the relationship) and sharing tasks (taking equal responsibility for a variety of tasks).

A simplex of persuasion?

In terms of the means by which the tactics relate to each other, there is some evidence for a unidimensional scale – from positive to negative tactics – with promising being the most extreme form of a positive tactic and demanding being the most extreme form of a negative tactic. Thus, on the one hand the target is making promises about the future of the relationship as working out well – 'Don't worry you won't be lonely much longer' while on the other threatening its withdrawal – 'If you're not that man you'll never be able to fulfil me' – i.e. giving the target an ultimatum to face the aversive nature of the termination of the relationship. Thus, while both deal with implications about future scenarios, they are set against entirely different outcomes. However, there are some correlations in the matrix that suggest the structure is a little more complex – possibly with the original structural hypothesis of two tactics working as positive tactics and two as negative tactics, with one tactic from each as a 'softer' or 'mitigator' version in each camp. To test this proposal another multi-dimensional scaling technique was employed.

Britton's hypotheses

Having identified and examined the structural relationships between the tactics and the development of the rhetoric over time, we now discuss some related issues that connect with Britton's original hypotheses.

Firstly it is instructive to note that all of the tactics employed bear a resemblance to strategies in more mundane transactions and are therefore not the exclusive domain of undercover operations. Mirroring, promising and encouraging are related to processes of similarity matching in court-ship, while mitigating, eulogizing and demanding are related to issues of control, manipulation and asymmetries in interpersonal relationships. In this regard, assuming that Stagg was at least somewhat attracted to James, then it is possible that she was able to build up rapport in the initial stages of the enquiry. However, this relies on creating a context within which the matching of James' characteristics to those assumed for the suspect were appropriately targeted.

Additionally, the features of James' personality reveal much about the implicit theories of the enquiry team. These accord with those detailed in the previous chapter in relation to the implicit theories drawn from the interviews – including the idea that she should be blonde, 'traditionally glamorous' and interested in deviant sexual activity. It is interesting to note how Stagg perceived James:

Stagg: ... how can I put it, she was sort of mysterious and well what I would term as just weird you know.

In fact on some occasions Stagg's perceptions of James' attempts at seduction were even perceived as embarrassing:

Stagg: ... and er ... every time, when she did er actually mention that she's done this er act or whatever it was she'd done [referring to James' mention of sex orgies and Satanic rituals] she was sort of feigning ... like she was having an org.. orgasm over it and that sort of thing. She'd be sitting there closing her eyes and that sort of panting and that ... and I'd be sitting there trying to eat my chips.

It appears then that there is some evidence that James' bizarre behaviour was simply seen as 'weird' and embarrassing. Thus although an initial rapport may have been built up it is possible that the more extreme forms of persuasion were in fact counterproductive simply because they were too threatening to Stagg. Thus, while elements of the seduction may have been effective in maintaining Stagg's interest, ultimately his level of disclosure and revelations may have been inhibited because of the perceived increasing level of awkwardness he may have felt in her company. In fact it appears that towards the end of the enquiry James became an inappropriate vehicle for eliciting information and eventually Stagg was not even trying to obtain intercourse with her:

Stagg: ... I, I if I was going to get anything this far you know after six or seven months or whatever you know – I'm not going to get it now you know [laughs].

Thus what the enquiry team may have been examining as 'evidence' for the suspect not taking alternative 'eliminating' paths was in fact Stagg's own rhetorical responses designed to gain intimacy and intercourse. Indeed, this is a feature for examination in the next chapter.

Overview

The material in this chapter provides a unique insight into the psychology of interpersonal relationships, processes of persuasion and manipulation. With over a thousand pages of transcripts the Stagg file allows for a fine-grain analysis of everything that was said or written between an (albeit contrived) couple engaged in a relationship. The most striking aspect of this is how rhetoric may be viewed as a powerful means of persuasion through attempts to play upon the emotional needs of the interlocutor. The Stagg file presents a rare opportunity to explore a number of processes between an intense relational dyad. The tactics employed in this case must have been strong inducements to the target to elicit more and more unusual sexual fantasies and possibly to confess to the crime, whether he had committed it or not.

Notes

1   Britton wrote his original profile on a whiteboard. The details of this were erased. It is therefore impossible to ascertain whether the original profile matches the profile that was subsequently written down.
2   The authors visited Stagg and interviewed him about the case.
3   Details of reliability coefficients are: promising (.74), mirroring (.80), encouraging (.89), eulogizing (.89), mitigating (.76), demanding (.78)
4   This was an informal interview carried out with Colin Stagg on 29 May 1996 at Stagg's residence.

References

Alison, L. (1998) *Criminal rhetoric and investigative manipulation*. PhD thesis, University of Liverpool.

Austin, J.L. (1962) *How to Do Things With Words*. Oxford: Clarendon Press.

Azrin, N.H. and Lindsley, O.R. (1956) 'The reinforcement of co-operation between children', *Journal of Abnormal Social Psychology*, 52: 100–02.

Bachman, G. and Zakahi, W.R. (2000) 'Adult attachment and strategic relationship communication: Love schemas and affinity seeking', *URL Journal* http://www.westcomm.org/publications/cr.html (accessed April, 2004).

Berscheid, E. and Walster, E. (1969) *Interpersonal Attraction*. Reading, MA: Addison-Wesley.

Berger, C.R. and Calabrese, R. (1987) 'Communicating under uncertainty', in M.E. Roloff and G.R. Miller (eds), *Interpersonal Processes: New directions in communication research*. Newbury Park, CA: Sage.

Billig, M. (1996) *Arguing and Thinking: A rhetorical approach to social psychology*. Cambridge: Cambridge University Press.

Boninger, D., Krosnick, J.A., Berent, M.K. and Fabrigar, L.R. (1995) 'The causes and consequences of attitude importance', in R.E. Petty and J.A. Krosnick (eds), *Attitude Strength: Antecedents and consequences* (pp. 159–189). Hillsdale, NJ: Lawrence Erlbaum Associates.

Boster, F.J. and Mongeau, P. (1984) 'Fear-arousing persuasive messages', in R.N. Bostrom (ed.), *Communication Year book* (vol. 8, pp. 330–75). Newbury Park, CA: Sage.

Britton, P. (1997) *The Jigsaw Man*. London: Bantam Press.

Burnkrant, R.E. and Unnava, R. (1989) 'Self referencing: A strategy for increasing processing of message content', *Personality and Social Psychology Bulletin*, 15: 628–38.

Burnstein, E. and Vinokur, A. (1975) 'What a person thinks upon learning he has chosen differently from others: Nice evidence for the persuasive-arguments explanation of choice shifts', *Journal of Experimental Social Psychology*, 11: 412–26.

Byrne, D. and Nelson, D. (1965) 'Attraction as a linear function of proportion of positive reinforcers', *Journal of Personality and Social Psychology*, 1: 659–63.

Cacioppo, J.T., Petty, R.E. and Sidera, J. (1982) 'The effects of salient self-schema on the evaluation of proattitudinal editorials: Top-down verses bottom-up message processing', *Journal of Experimental Social Psychology*, 18: 324–38.

Canary, D.J., Weger, H. and Stafford, L. (1991) 'Couples' argument sequences and their relational characteristics', *Western Journal of Speech Communication*, 55 (2): 159–79.

Canter, D. and Alison, L. (1996) Audiotaped interview with Colin Stagg.

Carlsmith, J.M. and Gross, A.E. (1969) 'Some effects of guilt on compliance', *Journal of Personality and Social Psychology*, 11: 232–39.

Catania, A.C. (1992) *Learning* (3rd edn). New Jersey: Prentice-Hall.

Chaiken, S. (1987) 'The heuristic model of persuasion', in M.P. Zanna, J.M. Olson and C.P. Herman (eds), *Social Influence: The Ontario symposium* (vol. 5, pp. 3–39). Hillsdale, NJ: Lawrence Erlbaum.

Chaiken, S. and Eagly, A.H. (1976) 'Communication modality as a determinant of message persuasiveness and message comprehensibility', *Journal of Personality and Social Psychology*, 34: 605–14.

Cockroft, R. and Cockroft, M. (1992) *Persuading People: An introduction to rhetoric*. London: Macmillan.

Cozby, P.C. (1973) 'Self disclosure: A literature review', *Psychological Bulletin*, 79: 73–91.

Cramer, D. (2001) 'Consensus change, conflict and relationship satisfaction in romantic relationships', *Journal of Psychology*, 135 (3): 313–20.

Crutchfield, T.N., Spake, D.F., D'Souza, G. and Morgan, R.M. (2003) 'Birds of a feather flock together: Strategic implications for advertising agencies', *Journal of Advertising Research*, 43 (4): 361–69.

Darlington, R.B. and Macker, D.F. (1966) 'Displacement of guilt-produced altruistic behaviour', *Journal of Personality and Social Psychology*, 4: 442–43.

Deutsch, M. and Solomon, L. (1959) 'Reactions to evaluations of others as influenced by self-evaluations', *Sociometry*, 22: 93–112.

Dion, K., Berscheid, E. and Walster, E. (1972) 'What is beautiful is good', *Journal of Personality and Social Psychology*, 24: 285–90.

Dollard, J., Doob, L.W., Miller, N.E., Mowrer, O.H. and Sears, R.R. (1939) *Frustration and Aggression.* New Haven: Yale University Press.

Eagly, A.H., Wood, W. and Chaiken, S. (1978) 'Casual inferences about communicators and their effect on opinion change', *Journal of Personality and Social Psychology*, 36: 424–35.

Falbo, T. and Peplau, L.A. (1980) 'Power strategies in intimate relationships', *Journal of Personality and Social Psychology*, 38: 618–28.

Farber, I.E., Harlow, H.F. and Jolyon West, L. (1957) 'Brainwashing, conditioning and DDD (debility, dependency and dread)', *Sociometry*, 20: 271–83.

Festinger, L. and Thibaut, J. (1951) 'Interpersonal communication in small groups', *Journal of Abnormal and Social Psychology*, 46: 92–100.

Fine, B.J. (1957) 'Conclusion-drawing, communicator credibility and anxiety as factors in opinion change', *Journal of Abnormal and Social Psychology*, 54: 369–74.

Freedman, J.L., Wallington, S.A. and Bless, E. (1967) 'Compliance without pressure: The effect of guilt', *Journal of Personality and Social Psychology*, 7: 117–24.

French, J.R.P. and Raven, B.H. 'The basis of social power', in D. Cartwright (ed.), *Studies in Social Power.* Ann Arbor, MI: University of Michigan Press.

Hanscombe, A. (1997) *The Last Thursday in July: A Memoir of Rachel Nickell.* London: Arrow Books.

Hass, R.G. (1981) 'Presentational strategies and the social expression of attitudes in impression management within limits', in J.T. Tedeschi (ed.), *Impression Management: Theory and Social Psychology Research.* New York: Academic Press.

Hogg, M. and Vaughan, G. (1998) *Social Psychology.* Essex: Prentice Hall.

Hovland, C.I., Janis, I.L. and Kelley, H.H. (1953) *Communication and Persuasion: Psychological studies of opinion change.* New Haven, CT: Yale University Press.

Hovland, C.I., Lumsdaine, A.A. and Sheffield, F.D. (1949) *Experiments on Mass Communication.* NJ: Princeton University Press.

Insko, C. and Cialdini, R. (1969) 'A test of three interpretations of attitudinal verbal reinforcement', *Journal of Personality and Social Psychology*, 12 (4): 333–41.

Janis, I.L. (1967) 'Effects of fear arousal on attitude change: Recent developments in theory and experimental research', in L. Berkowitz (ed.), *Advances in Experimental Social Psychology* (vol. 3, pp. 166–224). San Diego, CA: Academic Press.

Janis, I.L. and Mann, L. (1977) *Decision Making: A psychological analysis of conflict, choice and commitment.* New York: Free Press.

Johnson, B.T. and Eagly, A.H. (1989) 'Effects of involvement on persuasion: A meta-analysis', *Psychological Bulletin*, 106: 290–314.

Kalbfleisch, P.J. (1993) *Interpersonal Communication: Evolving interpersonal relations.* Hillsdale NJ: Lawrence Erlbaum.

Kennedy, G.A. (1991) *On Rhetoric: A theory of civic discourse* (Aristotle's volume trns. Kennedy). New York: Oxford University Press.

Leventhal, H. (1970) 'Findings and theory in the study of fear communications', in I. Berkowitz (ed.), *Advances in Experimental Social Psychology* (vol. 5, pp. 119–86). San Diego, CA: Academic Press.

Michael, J. and Myerson, L. (1962) 'A behavioral approach to human control', *Harvard Educational Review* 32: 382–402.

McGuire, W.J. (1969) 'The nature of attitudes and attitude change', in G. Lindzey and E. Aronson (eds), *Handbook of Social Psychology* (2nd edn, vol. 3, pp. 136–314). Reading, MA: Addison-Wesley.

Morton, T.C., Alexander, J.F. and Altman, I. (1976) 'Communication and relationship definition', in G.R. Miller (ed.), *Explorations in Interpersonal Communication*. Beverly Hills: Sage.

Muehlenhard, C.L. (1988) 'Misinterpreted dating behaviors and the risk of date rape', *Journal of Social and Clinical Psychology*, 6: 20–37.

Muehlenhard, C.L. and Scardino, T.J. (1985) 'What will he think? Men's impressions of women who initiate dates and achieve academically', *Journal of Counselling Psychology*, 32: 560–69.

Muehlenhard, C.L., Friedman, D.E. and Thomas, C.M. (1985) 'Is date rape justifiable? The effects of dating activity, who initiated, who paid, and men's attitude toward women', *Psychology of Women Quarterly*, 9: 297–310.

Mullis, J.P. and Lippa, R. (1990) 'Behavioural change in earthquake preparedness due to negative threat appeals: A test of protection motivation theory', *Journal of Applied Social Psychology*, 20: 619–38.

Newcomb, T.M. (1961) *The Acquaintance Process*. New York: Holt, Rinehart and Winston.

Ng, S.H. and Bradac, J.J. (1993) *Power in Language: Verbal communication and social influence*. London: Sage.

Pedder, K. (2002) *The Rachel Files*. London: Blake Publishing.

Petty, R.E. and Cacioppo, J.T. (1979) 'Issue-involvement can increase or decrease persuasion by enhancing message-relevant cognitive responses', *Journal of Personality and Social Psychology*, 37: 1915–26.

Petty, R.E. and Cacioppo, J.T. (1981) *Attitudes and Persuasion: Classic and contemporary approaches*. Dubuque, IA: Wm. C. Brown.

Petty, R.E., Cacioppo, J.T. and Goldman, R. (1981) 'Personal involvement as a determinant of argument-based persuasion', *Journal of Personality and Social Psychology*, 41: 847–55.

Petty, R.E. and Wegener, D. (1991) 'Thoughts systems, argument quality, and persuasion', in R.S. Wyer, Jr. and T.K. Srull (eds), *Advances in Social Cognition* (Vol. 4, pp. 147–61). Hillsdale, NJ: Lawrence Erlbaum.

Petty, R.E. and Wegener, D. (1998) 'Attitude change: Multiple roles for persuasion variables', in D.T. Gilbert, S.T. Fiske and G. Lindzey (eds), *The Handbook of Social Psychology* (pp. 323–90). New York: McGraw-Hill.

Priester, J.R. and Petty, R.E. (1995) 'Source attribution and persuasion: Percieved honesty as a determinant of message scrutiny', *Personality and Social Psychology Bulletin*, 21: 637–54.

Raven, B.H. and French, J.R.P. (1958) 'Legitimate power, coercive power and observability in social influence', *Sociometry*, 21: 83–97.

Regan, D.T (1971) 'Effects of a favour and liking on compliance', *Journal of Experimental Social Psychology*, 7: 627–39.

Reik, T. (1944) *Of Love and Lust*. Norwich: Souvenir Press.

Rippetoe, P.A. and Rogers, R.W. (1987) 'Effects of components of protection-motivation theory on adaptive and maladaptive coping with a health threat', *Journal of Personality and Social Psychology*, 52: 594–604.

Rogers, R.W. (1983) 'Cognitive and physiological processes in fear appeals and attitude change: A revised theory of protection motivation', in J.T. Cacioppo and R.E. Petty (eds), *Social Psychophysiology: A sourcebook* (pp. 153–76). New York: Guilford.

Rosenberg, M.J. (1960) 'Cognitive reorganization in response to hypnotic reversal of attitude affect', *Journal of Personality*, 28: 39–63.

Schwerin, H.S. and Newell, H.H. (1981) *Persuasion in Marketing*. New York: Wiley.

Skinner, B.F. (1974) *About Behaviorism*. London: Penguin Books.

Slusher, M.P. and Anderson, C.A. (1996) 'Using casual persuasive arguments to change beliefs and teach new information. The mediating role of explanation availability and evaluation bias in the acceptance of knowledge', *Journal of Educational Psychology*, 88: 110–22.

Stagg, C. and Kessler, D. (1999) *Who Really Killed Rachel?* London: Greenzone Publishing.

Stayman, D.M. and Kardes, F.R. (1992) 'Spontaneous inference processes in advertising: Effects of need for cognition and self-monitoring on inference generation and utilization', *Journal of Consumer Psychology*, 1: 125–42.

Tesser, A. and Conlee, M.C. (1975) 'Some effects of time and thought on attitude polarization', *Journal of Personality and Social Psychology*, 31 (2): 262–70.

Thurstone, L. (1928) 'Attitudes can be measured', *American Journal of Sociology*, 33: 529–54.

Ulrich, R.E. and Symannek, B. (1969) 'Pain as a stimulus for aggression', in S. Grattini and E.B. Sigg (eds), *Aggressive Behaviour*. Amsterdam: Excerpta Medica.

Verplanck, W.S. (1955) 'The control and content of conversation: reinforcement of statements of opinion', *Journal of Abnormal Psychology*, 55: 668–76.

Walster, E. and G.W. (1963) 'Effect of expecting to be liked on choice of associate', *Journal of Abnormal and Social Psychology*, 67: 402–04.

Walster, E. and Festinger, L. (1962) 'The effectiveness of "overhead" persuasive communications', *Journal of Abnormal and Social Psychology*, 65: 395–402.

Wittgenstein, L. (1958) *Philosophical Investigations* (3rd edn). Oxford: Blackwell.

Zanna, M.P. and Rempel, J.K. (1988) 'Attitudes: A new look at an old concept', in D. Bar-Tal and A.W. Kruglanski (eds), *The Social Psychology of Knowledge* (pp. 315–34). Cambridge: Cambridge University Press.

Content analysis dictionary

Rhetorical tactics

Mirroring   Any attempt to feign rapport with the target through stating some presupposed similarity between the source and the target. This may relate either to directly stating that both are 'the same', 'alike', 'similar', etc., or by implication through noting the source's interest in something that is known to be a characteristic of the target.
e.g.

'Even though you've written back once I don't feel as if we're strangers, it's nice to know there's a like mind out there'

'The letter was revealing in more ways than one and I think we have a lot in common'

Encouraging   Any praise forthcoming from the source. This may be in the form of assurance or of encouragement of specific aspects of the target's previous commentary. It may also relate to general characteristics of the target.
e.g.

'Write soon Colin. I can't wait to get your letter in my little handies'

'Your lovely fantasy letter was absorbing'

Mitigating   Any inducement to the target to produce something alternative to that which is currently being produced. This must be achieved through 'hinting' rather than as a direct demand. In other words it is an implicit request or polite order.
e.g.

'You write really well and I bet this is just the tip of the iceberg when it comes to your thoughts'

'You know what I wanna hear don't ya?'

Eulogizing   This involves a discussion of an imagined comparison 'other' or alternative 'scenario' – in particular, highlighting the qualities of another lover that are a preferred version of the current attributes of the target. The quality underlying this tactic is that unless the target has these attributes the current relationship cannot continue.
e.g.

'Oh – I wish you had done it [the murder]. It would just be ... brilliant'

'I can only have a relationship with someone who's been and done something like that [i.e. the murder]'

Promising   Any indication that the relationship, or part of the evolving nature of the relationship, will flourish and that the couple will enjoy a successful partnership. This could involve a general comment about the couple or relate to a specific development – i.e. meeting face to face, staying over the summer, living with each other, and so on.

'I'd like to meet you in the park again and then maybe next summer come over and see you or something'

'Don't worry – you won't be lonely much longer, each time you write I know we get closer and closer'

Demanding   Unlike mitigating, this involves a direct indication of what the source require if the relationship is to continue. The demand is specific and relates to a discrete requirement on the part of the source.
e.g.

'I need you to sort me out. I need to feel ... defenceless and humiliated'

'But it'll all go to rat shit if it isn't there. I want somebody like the man who did this thing [the murder]. I want that man that's the kind of man I want'

Chapter 10

Guidelines for profilers

Laurence Alison, Alasdair Goodwill and Emily Alison

A framework for quality

To date, there has been little systematic research of investigative analytic reports, and precious few suggestions as to how such advice might be deconstructed and evaluated. Neither the British Psychological Society nor the American Psychological Society has focused specifically on the way in which such reports should be provided. Neither organization has devoted special attention to the ethical, legal or professional issues that such involvement from psychologists has to criminal investigations. Although efforts have been made recently in the UK (Rainbow, NCOF, personal communication) and in Germany (Bundeskriminalamt, 2004) to regulate and quality assure profiling, many organizations' regulations are in their infancy. A central concern in the provision of such advice involves the extent to which claims are made without adequate scientific support. Indeed, a major criticism of profiling has been the accusation that such advice is often little more than speculation and intuition (Alison and Canter, 1999). While the worst excesses of profiling are unlikely to re-emerge in the UK because of more stringent quality-assurance processes, there remains no agreed systematic process for training individuals in constructing, utilizing and evaluating profiling. Moreover, there is little in the way of research into the quality of such reports or the extent to which they rely on supporting evidence.

In a small study recently conducted on a sample of European and American offender profiles from the last decade, Alison *et al.* (2003b) established that nearly half of the opinions within these reports contained advice that could not be verified post-conviction (e.g. 'the offender has a rich fantasy life'), while over a fifth were vague or open to interpretation (e.g. 'the offender has poor social skills'). In addition, in over 80 per cent of cases, the profiler did not give any justification for the opinion proposed (i.e. they did not clarify what their opinion was based on). In that research report, we proposed a method to assist in evaluating and preparing such material based on an approach to the evaluation of argument developed by Stephen Toulmin (1958) (see Chapter 1). Toulmin's work provides one basis for assisting profilers in generating reports with strict standards of evidentiary reliability and relevancy afforded to court procedures.[1] Further, by applying this framework to their own reports, profilers may gain insight into the processes that they themselves engage in when preparing material for the police. This may assist them in providing reliable and valid reports as well as increasing confidence in their work. An accumulation of cases may enable profilers to develop more robust models and approaches to the filtering of suspects (see Chapter 4; and Alison *et al.*, 2004). Thus, it is important that, through successive iterations of providing such advice, reports are re-evaluated in the light of resolution of the case. Sadly, this transparency has been missing from the profiling arena and the ability (or willingness) to stand back objectively from such material and utilize it to move the research forward has been sorely lacking. Finally, there is a real need to establish which particular elements (behaviours, temporal sequences, geographic targeting, victimology, etc.) prove most efficient in accurately identifying similarities between offences and in identifying characteristics and assisting in the provision of filtering systems.

Not all behaviours are equal

Although previous research has identified patterns of offender consistency (Douglas and Munn, 1992; Craik and Patrick, 1994; Davies, 1992; see Alison *et al.*, 2002, for a review), few studies exist that have identified *which* features are most or least reliable.

The use of victimological information to link crimes and profile offenders has had some success in recent years (Guay *et al.*, 2001). However, the type of victimological information that is used, how it is used, and what specific information is particularly useful are important questions that remain unanswered. Future work on reliability of information needs to address these questions to produce a valid system.

Based on our observations from the material in the Alison *et al.* study, it appeared that profilers frequently relied on crime scene information and, in particular, the notion of a *modus operandi* or 'M/O'. These aspects have been examined previously as a basis for differentiating crimes and can serve a useful purpose. However, they can prove problematic for the following reasons.

M/O involves an action or set of actions functional to the commission of a crime. M/O differs from 'signature' behaviour in that the latter is proposed as a non-functional aspect of the offence that serves some other psychological purpose for the offender. Signature is thought to be highly idiosyncratic and psychologically significant, whereas M/O enables the offender to commit the crime. An example might be a rapist/burglar who regularly uses a jemmy to open windows (M/O) and then attack victims. During the attack, the offender might force the victim to wear an unusual item of clothing, such as a rubber mask (signature). The signature view of behaviour suggests that the latter action is *psychologically* significant but *functionally* irrelevant, whereas the M/O is functionally significant but psychologically irrelevant (i.e. if a window were left open, there would be no need to use the jemmy). M/O is, therefore, dependent on context and signature is not.

What is rarely clear in both situations, however, is what really constitutes M/O or signature behaviour, and in both cases we have to infer the psychological significance of the behaviour. For example, it is difficult to ascertain whether the use of the jemmy is purely functional or whether it has some psychological significance. Similarly, just how important is the use of the clothing to the offender? Could he be aroused without it? These issues and the debate on the influence of situation over behaviour have been considered in depth in Alison *et al.* (2002), where the authors argue that the examination of very specific behaviours as a reliable basis for inferring characteristics of offenders is fraught with difficulty. The major hurdle involves a very lengthy history of research that suggests that behaviour develops over time and is strongly influenced by context (Cervone and Shoda, 1999). Further, there is a question mark over how frequently signature behaviour occurs and it seems rather unlikely that such behaviours occur in most offences. On a more practical note, if the behaviour is extremely unusual (e.g. offender forces victim to wear a particular mask) it would be obvious to the enquiry team that another offence including this behaviour should be considered as a part of a series.

Using discrete offender behaviours (demeaning the victim, complementing the victim) can also present problems because the observation of such behaviours is often based on witness or victim statements. Statements can be made hours, sometimes days, and even years after an offence has taken place and therefore can be compromized by all the attendant issues associated with the reconstructive nature of memory. Research also indicates that, for two principal reasons, sexual elements are not necessarily useful indicators. Firstly, many sexual behaviours have very high base rates and are, therefore, too common to serve as a basis for discrimination. Secondly, such behaviours appear to reflect different psychosexual meanings dependent upon context (Mokros and Alison, 2002). For example, Alison and Stein (2001) identified that actions such as enforced fellatio can serve as either a hostile or a compliance-gaining behaviour depending upon the other actions involved.

A specific focus on geographic information (in terms of the proximity of various offences) appears to seldom be used as a key indicator despite the emerging research that indicates the utility and primacy of geographic information. Canter (2004) has been especially vocal in articulating the primacy of geographic information and there are now many studies conducted by Canter and other researchers with an interest in this field. In particular, this has been noted in linking offences (Goodwill and Alison, in press). We would strongly urge profilers and analysts to focus on such information as the initial filter in the provision of such reports.

Assessment of the validity of input variables for linking

An important aspect of linking offences relates to consistent use of reliable variables for assigning two or more crimes to one offender. Although it is important to link cases based on the consistency of behaviours, actions and crime-scene elements, profilers must also be aware of two critical dimensions associated with those judgements: internal consistency and differentiation. Tversky and Kahneman (2000) state that, 'the internal consistency of a pattern of inputs is a major determinant of one's confidence … [and] people tend to have greater confidence in predictions based on redundant (or correlated) input variables' (p. 41). For example, a profiler may suggest that a rape in which a black male of 23–26 years of age threatened violence with a knife is confidently linked with a rape committed 200 miles away by a black male aged 23–26 who also used a knife to threaten and control the victim. In this example, the internal consistency of input variables of these crimes, without regard to location, is likely to be considered high. However, if on further analysis we find that the majority of black males that commit rape are aged 22–27 and it is very common for these offenders to use knives during rape attacks, then although the internal consistency is high the differentiation is very low. In other words, the input variables used to link these two crimes are poor at differentiating crimes between black offenders of this age group. In fact, the input variables (minus offence location) are redundant; if the vast majority of black males commit rape in the above manner, then it would be sufficient to describe each crime as, simply, rape in said location by a black male.

The decision to link two crimes is a diagnostic question dependent on two factors:

(1) setting a threshold of evidence sufficient to make a decision to determine similarity (the decision 'threshold' question); and

(2) identifying the information that the decision should be based upon in order to make the most accurate decisions (the identification of appropriate elements).

The vast majority of research in offence linking, albeit limited, has focused primarily on the latter aspect of the diagnostic question, namely, 'What types of information are productive in accurately identifying similar cases?' While this question is of course important and, quite deservedly, has recently attracted attention from the scientific community, the former question is also crucial in informing and training analysts.

In any diagnostic situation a decision threshold is set by balancing the impact of the number of hits against the number of misses (false alarms). In such decisions, there is always a trade-off between hits and misses, where an increased number of hits is accompanied by an increase in false alarms. In some situations, one may be willing to accept more false alarms in order to ensure more hits, while in another situation it may be necessary to obtain fewer hits to ensure fewer false alarms. In order to appreciate the issue of decision thresholds one must consider the four possible outcomes to every 'yes' or 'no' decision. As the 2×2 contingency table shown in Figure 10.1 illustrates, the implications of a 'yes or no' diagnosis result in four possible outcomes: hits, false alarms, misses and correct negatives. Hits and false alarms are equally and positively related; as one increases, so too does the other. In other words, to get more hits (accurately identifying links that are in fact linked) from our diagnostic question we have to 'accept' more false alarms (inaccurately identifying links). The extent to which we are ready to accept more false alarms to increase our chances of hits is a question of decision thresholds.

Setting the decision threshold

Swets (2000) states that two kinds of information are needed to calculate the most productive decision threshold: base rates and an analysis of costs and benefits. *Base rates* refer to the probability or frequency of occurrence of an event, e.g. four child abductions occurred within the UK within two months. Reporting base rates for various crime-scene actions within

Actual

	Linked	Not Linked
Linked	√ Hits	X False Alarm
Not Linked	X Miss	√ Correct Negatives

Judgement (row label, left side)

Figure 10.1 A 2×2 contingency table showing the decisions and outcomes of a linking task

reports is an important element of profiling advice. A base rate can identify rare actions, with a low base rate indicating the relative uniqueness of any given action and a high base rate indicating that the behaviour or action is common within that population. The utilization of base rates and cost/benefit analyses helps set acceptable decision thresholds. If abduction is rare (low base rate) and the cost of a miss is considered high (i.e. not identifying that this is a series when it actually is), one must set a low threshold for linking. However, if the base rate is high (e.g. a rapist using demeaning language) and the cost of a false alarm is high (spending considerable time and resources on the assumption of a series when it is not), then one requires a more stringent threshold for justifying a link.

Establishing cost and benefits of making decisions of this nature can be problematic. How does one quantify the cost of missing a correct link leading to the revictimization of a person against the cost of incorrectly linking an offence and thereby potentially wasting police resources? Fortunately, although not as powerful as base rates and cost/benefit analysis, there are other ways to establish the best decision threshold for any given diagnostic question (Swets, 2000). One common way is to set an acceptable false alarm rate. For example, one may set a false alarm rate below a certain level. While this may reduce the number of hits (i.e. correctly linking a crime), it will limit the false alarm rate (i.e. indicating a crime is linked when it is not) to an acceptable level. Using this method to obtain a decision threshold is contingent on what the 'acceptable' rate of false alarms is, and, therefore, relies on the perceived cost of linking crimes to offences that are not in fact linked.

Diagnostic decision-making and the decision to link offences

Contemporary models of diagnostic decision-making (particularly those that have sought to improve diagnoses in the field, e.g. medical, industrial) have great potential significance to the diagnostic question, 'Are these two crimes similar?' Swets (2000) defines a diagnostic decision as, 'one in which repetitive choices must be made between two competing alternatives'(p. 66). A meteorologist looking at low- and high-pressure systems in an area to determine whether a storm is on the way is one example. S/he must ask her or himself, 'What do the current conditions tell me about the probability of a storm within the next few hours?' Another example might include a psychologist considering recently collected psychometric data in order to determine whether a child has a learning disability. In this case the psychologist uses scores on the test to establish the probability that the child may require particular attention in certain areas. The two themes common across all diagnostic questions are that: (i) the decision-maker must identify the presence of a particular condition (storm, dyslexia) and (ii) they must estimate how probable this identification is (Swets, 1996, 1997). For profilers this often comes in the form of the question, 'How likely is it that these two crimes are similar?' or, 'Here is a particular crime (X); what other crimes that we are currently aware of are also possible Xs and how likely is each of them to be linked to one another?'

The decision to link crimes can therefore be considered as a probabilistic and diagnostic decision in which one has to consider how much evidence (how high a probability) is required before two crimes are considered sufficiently similar to draw them to the attention of the investigator. In doing so, one must estimate the threshold criterion for linking offences. Different thresholds for detection exist dependent, in part, upon the context within which a decision is made. For example, very lax thresholds exist where the cost of not linking when one should have done is very high. As an analogy, in our meteorologist example, the cost of not indicating that a hurricane was about to hit would be very high so the threshold for warning the public may be very low. However, less stringent criteria might be applied if the decision involved the possibility of a light shower. Therefore, all relevant parties who might be affected by the decision must agree upon the implications or 'utility values'. *Utility* relates directly to: (1) the threshold of information considered sufficient to make a decision and (2) the types of information that the decision should be based upon in order to make the most accurate decisions. The vast majority of research in offence linking has focused primarily on the latter aspect of the diagnostic question rather than the former, though both are extremely important issues. Indeed, as Chapter 2 indicates, there are many resource and management issues beyond the immediate concern of 'solving the case' that must be considered when deciding whether to use such advice for linking or for prioritising suspects.

Outlined in the Appendix to this chapter is an example of a 'profile' prepared for an investigation in Eastern Europe. We present this case to illustrate the point that comments on cases, while based in part on statistical probabilities, must also rely on a logical approach formed from a cohesive argument as informed by the specifics of the case. Simply 'cranking the handle of the computer' to spew out some figures is not especially helpful unless it is integrated within the context of the case. Subsequent reports flesh out further developments in the process.

Format of reports

Table 10.1 indicates the four broad areas into which we generally provide investigative advice to the police. While the main body of the report is formed by the demographic analyses (what may be seen as 'typical' components of a profile), the other sections are important. In particular, setting out the background details is critical in ensuring that the enquiry team are aware of the limitations of such reports. The behavioural analyses section may not necessarily be of direct use to the enquiry team, beyond setting the case in context and potentially providing them with some insight into the style of offence that they are dealing with. Finally, the investigative recommendations form the bases for investigative decisions and are, therefore, key aspects in how the enquiry team may choose to use the report.

Background: instructions, caveats, competence and sources of the inferences

Of course, a critical aspect of any report involves setting out the parameters of the advice. As well as presenting the material in an accessible and professional-looking format (by including a front page with title, addresses of the provider and the police contact), profilers should ensure that they reflect (in the report) the precise details of what they have been asked to do. We have often found it useful to meet with officers about a case and subsequently agree a list of bullet points on which we feel we might be able to contribute. It is then useful to ask the contact officer to draft a letter including these points. That letter may then be used as the basis for reflecting back to the enquiry team what the parameters are for

Table 10.1 Basic format for 'profiling' reports

Background	Demographic analyses	Behavioural analyses	Investigative recommendations
Title, address, contact	Salient features of the case	Style of offending	Suspect prioritization
Instructions and origin of report	Age		Risk management
Caveats	Relationship to victim		Leaflet drops
Competence	Location		Linking
Sources of inferences	Marital status and employment status		Decision-making
Case summary	Temporal features Criminal Preconvictions		Team/media management

the advice. This 'contract' assists in ensuring that both parties know what the expectations are and that, for the purpose of the courts, the motives for the request for advice can be clearly scrutinized.

Other cases with which we have been involved have often required many other, more specific requests, but in the case described here, the bare bones of what might be considered the 'lay view' of a 'profile' was the central aspect that interested the enquiry team. Because there is little empirical research in Eastern Europe on profiling, the officers involved in this case were, understandably, relatively naïve as to the process of profiling and to the extent of what was possible. It is, of course, important that the work therefore reflects the current knowledge base of the enquiry team and that it is pragmatically oriented to what is usable by the relevant officers.

Another critical issue is that the report clearly outlines the limitations of what is possible. This includes clearly specifying how the report can be used, what is inappropriate and which aspects of the current case may not follow statistical trends. Statistically driven profiles can only consider generalities and, in many aspects, correlations and frequencies are not clear-cut. It is important that the enquiry team do not have too optimistic a view of what is possible. In particular, the caveat needs to consider legal implications of how the report is used and needs to articulate the limitation of the statistical information. An example is included below:

Caveat re contents of the profile

Primarily, the processes reported here are to do with inference and not evidence. That is, they are in no way intended to single out a specific individual or make an incriminatory claim against an individual who may later become a prime suspect for the enquiry team. Profiling methods are in their infancy. Moreover, they can be entirely incorrect. This warning against inaccuracy should be borne in mind if a suspect is perceived as accurately matching the profile. Concern should be given to any suggestion that such a hypothetical suspect therefore must be the offender. Most importantly, none of the information is provided as a basis for any legal action against a potential suspect – i.e. could not be used as similar fact evidence. It is merely designed as an investigative tool to be used at the enquiry team's discretion. This would include particular reference to the warnings regarding the reliability of any information given. This profile is based on research and investigations conducted in the United Kingdom and the United States. The information contained therein must therefore be considered in the context of these cultures and re-evaluated for application in the context of X culture and criminal activity.

Caveat re confidentiality of the profile

No part of this report should be distributed to anyone other than individuals in the enquiry team without the express permission of the authors. This may be achieved through the liaison officer or direct contact with the authors.

Competence

Another factor that must be included is a brief indication of the competence of the authors of the report. If the report ends up in court, it is highly likely that both sides will draw out the background of the individual(s) who provided the material. In our case, this often includes multiple authors, although one individual will ordinarily be asked to defend the report if required. In cases where different authors have different types of expertise, it can be very helpful to indicate what aspect of the advice has been generated by which author (see Chapter 15) because this will help the courts in deciding whether they require more than one of the experts in court. For example, in our work on the case outlined in Chapter 15, the second author had considerable tacit knowledge of working with domestic violence offenders that formed the basis of some of the comments. We felt that it was important to indicate what aspects of the advice were based on this tacit knowledge and which were based on empirical evidence. It is then for the court to decide the validity of any given claim and presents a more honest and transparent process on the part of the expert. Many of the reports evaluated in the Alison *et al.* (2003a) study made no clear distinction between subjective opinion (albeit potentially considerable tacit knowledge) and well-documented research. Making a clear distinction enables the court to evaluate the certainty and strength of any given claim.

Thus, experts should indicate their background, training and as far as possible case-specific training. It is also useful to indicate previous key cases and illustrate the relevance of these to the case at hand.

Sources of inferences

Having outlined the instructions, caveats and competence, authors can more closely consider the case at hand, moving on to the material upon which many of the claims are made. It is useful to note how transferable these data may be to the case at hand. For example, in this case, there was little in the way of detailed empirical evidence on child murder and abduction in Eastern Europe and so we had to rely heavily on the UK and US figures. Particular caution must be exercised in interpreting the relevance of these data sets to the Eastern European case because we did not know how consistent the figures would be across the different cultures. Therefore, as well as specifically noting the sources of the inferences in this section, we made several other references to the source material throughout. For example:

> The sources of the inferences are based on a behavioural approach. That is no reliance is placed upon motive. Assessments have been made purely upon knowledge of the behaviour of the offender. Each of these inferences is backed by the appropriate degree of certainty regarding the work carried out in that field.

The section in the Appendix regarding the abductions is necessarily edited down to include just the most basic facts and known assumptions about the case. We have manipulated many of these aspects to preserve the anonymity of the case. However, it is generally good practice to provide detail here as to the case and to list the materials provided by the relevant police constabulary. There are several reasons for this, though by far the most important is to ensure that the court is made clear about what was available to the expert. This enables the report writer to defend a claim based on the knowledge that was available, thereby circumventing the allegation that the expert might have come to a different conclusion if only they had considered (for example) statements inconsistent with the other evidence. Therefore, it is good practice to be clear on the details of the case as well as the range of material provided.

The Appendix outlines the, by now, rather traditional form of such profiles. As is clear, these basic details are simply based on statistical probabilities, informed by some of the salient details of the case. The statements should be clear and unambiguous. They should also indicate the basis upon which each claim is made. The section that follows provides a little more detail on the way in which the offence was conducted. Commonly, the visual descriptive power of Smallest Space Analysis (or SSA) has been utilized in this regard and there are many examples scattered throughout the work conducted by Canter and his colleagues (see Canter, 2004, for a review), though this method tends to have been used less and less in our work because its direct application is less obvious than the (admittedly) rather more prosaic list of figures. In the current case we simply present the different styles of offending in tabular form. However, the conventional visual display of the plot has proved useful in providing officers with a view on the style in which an offence has been conducted and several officers have stated that such material can assist in developing interview strategies. We have found that where this is the case we have embellished such sections and tied them in more carefully into a formulation for how an offender may respond to different forms of questioning. However, once again, the paucity of work in this area often results in rather more speculative advice than we would ideally like. It does, however, re-emphasize the points made in Chapter 6 in relation to investigative interviewing, namely that the very heavy focus on the cognitive side of interviewing does not really assist in giving officers a 'steer' on the interpersonal aspects of interviewing that may enhance or compromise the success of the interview.

Towards the end of the report, the profiler provides possible recom-mendations. These are, of course, based on what has been highlighted in the report so far and are a logical extension of what has been generated about the possible characteristics of the offender. In many cases, the investigative team will have already been considering these suggestions. Nevertheless, for the sake of completeness and with the potential for reinforcing previously considered strategies (or challenging strategies inconsistent with the report), they provide a useful addendum for the team.

Feedback

Critical to any progression and development of good practice is detailed feedback. In practice this is difficult to obtain from busy, pressured police officers. Our efforts to provide short feedback forms at the tail end of the report have regularly proved unsuccessful in a majority of cases. However, what does appear to work well is a discussion that centres on feedback on the case after provision of the report. Thus, a new standard practice involves a clear indication at the outset (from the profiler) that, after provision of the report, the SIO must set aside some time to be verbally briefed on the report. This gives both parties the opportunity for clarification and, for the profiler, the critical feedback that may enhance subsequent reports.

Note

1 We are also developing this research and considering its application to the thorny issue and recent debates in the handling of sensitive intelligence information. We speculate that such systematic approaches to the evaluation of intelligence may have helped circumvent allegations of a 'too ready to see what they wanted to' approach in the handling of information regarding the question of Weapons of Mass Destruction in Iraq.

References

Alison, L. and Canter, D. (1999) 'Professional, legal and ethical issues in offender profiling', in D. Canter and L. Alison (eds), *Profiling in Policy and Practice* (pp. 21–54). Aldershot: Ashgate.

Alison, L. and Stein, K. (2001) 'Vicious circles: accounts of stranger sexual assault reflect abusive variants of conventional interactions', *The Journal of Forensic Psychiatry*, 12: 515–38.

Alison, L., Bennell, C. Mokros, A. and Ormerod, D. (2002) 'The personality paradox in offender profiling. A theoretical review of the processes involved in deriving background characteristics from crime scene actions', *Psychology, Public Policy and Law*, 8: 115–35.

Alison, L., Smith, M. and Morgan, K. (2003a) 'Interpreting the accuracy of Offender Profiles', *Psychology, Crime and Law*, 9: 175–84.

Alison, L., Smith, M., Eastman, O. and Rainbow, L. (2003b) 'Toulmin's philosophy of argument and its relevance to offender profiling', *Psychology, Crime and Law*, 9: 185–95.

Alison, L., West, A. and Goodwill, A. (2004) 'The academic and the practitioner: Pragmatists' views of offender profiling', *Psychology, Public Policy and Law*, 10 (1–2): 71–101.

Borg, I. and Lingoes, J. (1987) *Multidimensional Similarity Structure Analysis*. New York: Springer-Verlag.

Budeskriminalamt (2004) *The Use of Behavioural Analysis by the German Police*. Federation State Police Forces Project Group. Bundeskriminalamt: Weisbaden.

Canter, D. (2004) *Mapping Murder: The Secrets of Geographical Profiling*. London: Virgin.

Canter, D., Hughes, D. and Kirby, S. (1998) 'Paedophilia: pathology, criminality, or both? The development of a multivariate model of offence behaviour in child sexual abuse', *The Journal of Forensic Psychiatry*, 9: 532–55.

Cervone, D. and Shoda, Y. (1999) *The Coherence of Personality: Social-Cognitive Bases of Consistency, Variability and Organization*. New York: Guilford Press.

Craik, M. and Patrick, A. (1994) 'Linking serial offences', *Policing*, 3: 181–187.

Davies, A. (1992) 'Rapists' behaviour: a three aspect model as a basis for analysis and identification of serial crime', *Forensic Science International*, 55: 173–194.

Douglas, J. and Munn, C. (1992) 'Violent crime scene analysis: Modus operandi, signature and staging', *FBI Law Enforcement Bulletin*, 61: 1–10.

Goodwill, A. and Alison, L. (in press) 'Sequential angulation, spatial dispersion and consistency of distance attack patterns from home in serial murder, rape and burglary', *Psychology, Crime and Law*.

Guay, J., Proulx, J., Cusson, M. and Ouimet, M. (2001) 'Victim-choice polymorphia among serious sex offenders', *Archives of Sexual Behaviour*, 30 (5): 521–33.

Lingoes, J. (1973) *The Guttman-Lingoes Non metric Program series*. Michigan: Mathesis Press.

Mokros, A., and Alison, L. (2002). 'Is profiling possible? Testing the predicted homology of crime scene actions and background characteristics in a sample of rapists', *Legal and Criminological Psychology*, 7: 25–43.

Swets, J. (1996) *Signal Detection Theory and ROC Analysis in Psychology and Diagnostics: Collected Papers*. Mahwah, NJ: Lawrence Erlbaum.

Swets, J. (1997) 'Separating discrimination and decision in detection, recognition, and matters of life and death: Vol. 4. Methods, models, and conceptual issues', in J. Scarborough and S. Sternberg (eds), *An Invitation to Cognitive Science* (pp. 635–702). Cambridge, MA: MIT Press.

Swets, J. (2000) 'Enhancing Diagnostic Decisions', in T. Connolly, H. Arkes and K. Hammond (eds), *Judgement and Decision Making: An interdisciplinary reader*, (2nd edn) (pp. 66–81). New York: Cambridge University Press.

Toulmin, S. (1958) *The Uses of Argument*. Cambridge: Cambridge University Press.

Tversky, A. and Kahneman, D. (2000) 'Judgment under uncertainty: Heuristics and biases' in T. Connolly, H. Arkes, and K. Hammond (eds), *Judgment and Decision Making: An interdisciplinary reader* (pp. 35–52). New York: Cambridge University Press.

APPENDIX:
The Madjenko, Mascav and Eve Case: A Study in Linking and
Suspect Prioritization

REPORT PREPARED FOR X POLICE

By

Prof. Laurence J. Alison
(Director: Centre for the Study of Critical Incident Research, University
of Liverpool, Bedford Street South, L69 7ZA)

Alasdair M. Goodwill, MSc
(PhD Research Psychologist: Centre for the Study of Critical Incident
Decision Making, University of Birmingham)

Emily Alison, MSc
(Treatment Manager, Cheshire Probation, Cheshire)[1]

Regarding the Behavioural Investigative Advice prepared in the case
of the murder of victims 'Eve' and Famke Mascav and the
disappearance of Amelie Madjenko.

Report prepared 16 January 2004

---

1   The views in this document are the authors' and are not the views of the
    service/institutions with whom they are affiliated.

EXECUTIVE SUMMARY

The following summarizes the key points of this document. This does not serve as an alternative to the full document, merely as an aide-mémoire of the core features of our report.

1. There are a number of areas where we cannot be certain of the sequence of events. The enquiry team should proceed with this enquiry with a number of parallel scenarios in mind. Some of these are likely to prove more resource intensive than others but there are some that could be conducted quickly and with minimal resources. In our view, basic and complex searches should be conducted in parallel. The enquiry team may wish to divide up sub-teams to deal with these scenarios. Each scenario may be moderated in light of new evidence.
2. In light of the above, we recommend 'worst-case scenario' planning. Thus, one must consider that the offences are linked and represent a serial murder enquiry in which further victims may be attacked and other bodies may be found that are linked to these offences.
3. In our view, the most productive behavioural lines of enquiry are likely to stem from careful consideration of the geographic information rather than characteristics of the offenders. The fact that the enquiry team have three sites (the bus depot and the disposal sites) can be further exploited.

CAVEATS

Primarily, the processes reported here are to do with inference and not evidence. They are not intended to point towards the innocence or guilt of the individual or make an incriminatory claim against an individual who may become a prime suspect for the enquiry team in relation to other possible offences. Most importantly, none of the information provided should ever be used as a basis for any legal action. This report is merely designed as an investigative tool to be used at the enquiry team's discretion. The recommendations in this report are based upon the information given to Prof. Alison, Mr Goodwill and Mrs Alison. The report is based on research and investigations conducted in the United Kingdom, Canada and the United States. Caution must therefore be exercized in interpreting the extent to which these figures transfer to Eastern European cases. No part of this report should be distributed to anyone other than individuals in the enquiry team. Permission may be granted through direct contact with Prof. Alison.

It should also be made clear that there are a range of plausible scenarios that could account for each victim's death/disappearance and figures reported are NOT derived in order to exclude suspects, merely to generate probabilities. Thus, offenders outside a particular age range or distance from the offence should not be excluded; they are just less probable given the scientific evidence.

COMPETENCE

Laurence Alison
BSc Psychol, MSc Investigative Psychol, PhD, C. Psychol (Forensic).
I hold a Bachelors degree BSc in psychology awarded by University College London, a Masters degree MSc in Investigative Psychology, awarded by the University of Surrey, and a PhD. in Investigative Psychology, awarded by the University of Liverpool. My PhD considered the use of deception and interpersonal manipulation by offenders in (i) controlling their victims and (ii) in explaining their offences. The thesis also considered controversial investigative strategies and police decision making. My subsequent research has focused on many of these issues, with special reference to sex offenders and the psychological processes involved in police decision-making in major investigations. Within this remit I have considered many issues associated with deception and concealment, including police interviewing, the false/recovered memory debate, the use of informants, controversies surrounding 'psychological profiling' and child sex abuse cases. I have provided advice both to investigators and to the courts on many of these issues.

I am a Chartered Forensic Psychologist and a member of the British Psychological Society. My current appointment is as Chair of Forensic Psychology, University of Liverpool. This report has been prepared in my capacity as an independent consultant and not as part of my duties for the University.

Emily Alison
BSc Behavioral Science and Criminal Justice, MSc Investigative Psychol.
I hold a Bachelors degree BSc in Behavioural Science and Criminal Justice awarded by the University of Madison, Wisconsin, and a Masters degree MSc in Investigative Psychology awarded by the University of Liverpool. My Masters degree thesis examined the relationship between crime-scene behaviours and offender characteristics in homicide.

I have subsequently worked as a practitioner in both the American and British correctional services. I was employed as a Correctional Case Manager and outpatient therapist with Attic Correctional Services in Madison, WI, where I worked with a wide range of high-risk offenders, including the treatment of domestic violence perpetrators in a structured group work programme. I now work as a Treatment Manager with the National Probation Service for England and Wales – Cheshire Area and have responsibility for the Domestic Violence Prevention Programme, a 39-week community group work programme for domestic violence perpetrators. I have worked with over 200 perpetrators of domestic violence, interviewing them in great detail about their abusive and violent behaviour toward their partners. I also have regular contact and correspondence with our partnership agency to obtain feedback from the perpetrators' partners and ex-partners about the offenders' behaviour. This report has been prepared in my capacity as an independent consultant and not as part of my duties for the National Probation Service.

Mr Alasdair Goodwill
BSc Psychol; MSc, Investigative Psychol.
Prof. Alison currently supervises Mr Goodwill's PhD thesis on the classification of stranger-related sexual offences for offender profiling. The chief concerns of this work involve an examination of the limits and benefits in the classification of stranger-related sexual offences to provide advice to investigators, the use of offender profiles, problems associated with the interpretation and utilization of expert advice and the development of psychological contributions to understanding sexual offences. He has worked on many sexual assault, murder and child abduction cases with Prof. Alison.

FEEDBACK AND PEER REVIEW

It would be very helpful for the enquiry team to feedback this report to their peers and senior officers **It would also prove extremely useful if the investigating officer could fill in the short feedback form (at the end of this document) in order that we may improve the service for subsequent reports. We have agreed to talk the enquiry team through the details of the report once officers have had the chance for a read through.**

SOURCES OF INFERENCES

It is important to clearly state the assumptions that this report subsumes. These relate directly to the psychological, behavioural and scientific analysis of the key components of the disappearance of Madjenko, the murder and sexual assault of Mascav and the murder of Eve. It is further stressed that the suggestions, inferences and conclusions contained within this report are based upon these assumptions and should not be extrapolated to explain other aspects of the case that do not fall under the framework of these assumptions.

CLARIFICATION

We are happy to clarify any points in the report on the understanding that these are documented carefully and emerge as an addendum to the report.

INSTRUCTIONS
We have been asked to provide a report on the following:

1. A statistical analysis of the murders of Eve and Mascav.
2. A consideration of whether Madjenko's disappearance could be connected to either of the above offences.
3. A consideration of whether all of these offences may be linked.
4. Investigative recommendations and a proposed filtering model for considering suspects.

Further, I confirmed in a telephone conversation with Senior Officer Dravnov that this report would be delivered by 1 March 2004.

CASE SUMMARY AND EVALUATION

The details of this case are now well documented in the reports given to the enquiry team. Briefly, our current understanding in each of the cases is as follows:

Famke Mascav
1. Famke is a 12-year-old girl.
2. The offence occurred in the district of East Y in X.
3. The victim disappeared on 15.01.2003 (Sunday) after purchasing bread from a store near her home at approximately 9:20am.
4. The victim had initially left her home at 8:30am on the day in question with her mother en route to the local shop.
5. The child left this shop unattended by her mother to return home. On the way home, she stopped to look in a toy shop in the X area of Y.
6. At this time, a male stranger approached her and asked her to go to his home. He told her that he was a puppeteer and that he should like to show her how he made the puppets at his house.
7. The victim stated she did not want to and continued on her way. The male stranger followed her to her house. Famke told the stranger that her mother was not at home and would be anxious that she had left without her. At this point, she went into her home. Her mother returned home and Famke relayed this account to her mother at this time.
8. Famke then went out of the house for a second time at approximately 9:10am to get some bread (that her mother had forgotten to buy) from the store. The last sighting of her was at the store at 9:20am.
9. Her body was found on 21.01.2003, six days after her last sighting, at the back of a parking lot approximately 800 metres (as the crow flies) from the shop where she was last seen alive. She was discovered by refuse collectors.
10. She was found naked.
11. She had been sexually assaulted, semen was found in her vagina. Her vaginal area was severely damaged. She had been killed by mechanical ligature that caused asphyxiation, from behind. The ligature was not discovered. The left side of face had been scratched and there was evidence of 'gnawing' marks (possibly due to animal interference with the corpse, though this is not clear from the material that we have been given).
12. Stomach contents revealed that the victim was murdered a short time after her last sighting.
13. Famke's parents have been excluded as possible suspects (due to the timeline involved).

Amelie Madjenko
1. Amelie is a 14-year-old girl.
2. Last sighting of Amelie was Saturday, 3 March 2003.
3. Sighting was at Bus Depot in X.

4. Amelie's uncle (with whom she lives – both parents deceased) has been excluded as a possible suspect (due to the timeline involved).
5. Amelie has been missing for two months. We have been told that she is a happy child and has two sisters and a younger brother. Neither siblings, nor her aunt nor uncle, have any explanation for her disappearance.

We are working on the assumption that she was abducted and murdered.

'Eve'
Remains of a young girl were discovered on 23.07.2003 in a field on the outskirts of X, some 4 miles from the bus depot from which Amelie Madjenko disappeared. However, because of conditions and interference from animals with the bones, it is impossible to ascertain either mode of death, or whether there has been any sexual interference. Identification has also proved difficult beyond the fact that this is a young girl, estimated to be between 10 and 12 years old. Forensics suggest that the remains have been left outside for approximately 2–5 months.

CURRENT RESEARCH ON ABDUCTION MURDER

The following section describes the figures on prevalence of this sort of offence, the circumstances surrounding the offences (and the extent to which they are in line with other abductions); possible characteristics of the offender(s) and the probable sequence of events. We are assuming that this is a non-family abduction murder. However, we would remind the enquiry team that individuals familiar (where familiarity can mean a casual acquaintance or friend) to the child are more often responsible for child murders than strangers (Boudreaux, Lord and Jarvis, 2001).

Characteristics of the Offence
(unless stated, figures are from Hanfland, Keppel and Weis, 1997; US study)

- Abduction of juveniles (under 16 years of age) is **rare** (2% of violent crime against juveniles).
- Most victims are **girls** (76%), average age **11 years** old (supported by Boudreaux, Lord and Dutra, 1999).
- 58% reported as 'missing child' with, typically, **a two-hour delay in making the initial report** from the time of abduction.
- Children were '... **not particularly vulnerable or high risk victims**' (p. 21).

Thus, there is nothing especially unusual about any of the victims in these regards, though Amelie is a little older than the average age. However, we have been informed that she looks physically younger.

Victim Selection, Procurement and Disposal

- 80% of cases **initial contact** between the killer and the victim is within ¼ **mile of the victim's residence**.
- 57% of victim selection is opportunistic.
- 15% selected on the basis of a prior relationship with victim.
- Two-thirds use a 'blitz' attack – the majority are **not** subtle, clever predators using deceptive means to abduct.
- Non-family abduction is often associated with other offences such as robbery or sexual assault, as a means of **isolating** the child (Finkelhor and Ormrod, 2000).
- **Family involvement is less likely than stranger offenders** for victims in this age group (Boudreaux, Lord and Dutra, 1999).
- The vast majority (74%) of the abducted children who are murdered are **dead within three hours of the abduction**.
- 52% conceal the body.

Thus, on the balance of probabilities this is an opportunistic offence and Amelie, Famke and Eve would have been murdered within three hours. It is unlikely that they were selected on the basis of prior relationships with the offender. The victims were most likely taken in order for the offender to isolate them for the purpose of sexually assaulting them.

Characteristics of Offenders
- *Offender's relationship to victim*
  - Prentky, Knight, Burgess, Ressler, Campbell and Lanning (1991) examined the differences between 97 abducting and 60 non-abducting child molesters who were committed to the Massachusetts Treatment Centre for sexually dangerous persons in the US. The offenders were examined on selected typological and antisocial/ criminal variables, and the results identified a number of general characteristics of abductors, such as low contact with children, low social competence, and stranger relationships with victims.
  - **It is highly unlikely that the offender in this case is a family member. There is a much greater chance that the offender is a stranger or an acquaintance of the victim.** Sexual assault is highly unlikely to precede the murder of a child by a parent. The Bureau of Justice in the US reports that when a person under 12 is murdered a

family member is the most likely suspect. However, when family members killed their children the rate of sexual assault occurring prior to death was 1%.

- In the CATCHEM[2] database of sexual murders of children in the United Kingdom, when the victim was a female child, age 6 to 21, there was a 44% chance that the offender was an acquaintance, and 21% chance that the offender was a stranger. However, in cases where the victim's body was **transported** by the offender:
  - **53%** are committed by a killer who is a **stranger** to the victim.
  - **39%** are committed by a **friend or acquaintance** of the victim.
  - **Family** involvement in this type of case is relatively **infrequent** (9%).

- *Offender's age*
  - The offender is likely to be within an **age range of 28 to 35 (CATCHEM)**. However, age has proven an extremely difficult variable to 'profile'. **No suspect should be eliminated solely on the basis that he does not fall within the profiled age range.**
  - Although the average age of child sexual murderers in Boudreaux, Lord and Dutra's (1999) study was 27 years old with the great majority under 30, the CATCHEM data indicates that when the victim's body is transported from the scene of the murder the offender's most likely age group is around **30 to 35 years old**. Offenders who do not transport their victims tend to be younger, around age 18 to 25 years old.

- *Offender's probable location*
  - **The offender may have attempted to lure victims to a secure place, likely indoors (i.e. his home) in order to carry out the assault.**
  - The National Institute of Justice Census reports that for US child molesters, **75% of the assaults occurred in the offender's or victim's home.**
  - Canter, Heritage and Kovacik (1989) conducted a study of cases of adult sexual assault and found that offenders who commit offences outdoors are unlikely to also offend against victims indoors.
  - Due to the lack of forensic evidence found at the site where the body was disposed of in both Mascav and Eve, it is likely that the offender

---

2   The CATCHEM database was developed by DCI Chuck Burton and was generated partly in response to a series of child abductions by Robert Black – an offender who travelled considerable distances to procure victims.

assaulted and strangled victims in another location from where the body was discovered. After the attack he transported victims to the disposal site. **This attack location is therefore likely to be indoors and nearby the abduction site.**

- The vast majority of offenders in the CATCHEM study lived within **five miles** of the point of contact with the victim; 95% had their residence there; 3% had work, previous residence, or relatives within five mile radius of the point of encounter. All offenders were within a 20-mile radius of point of contact with victim.
- 37% of offenders in the CATCHEM database who transported their victim went less than 9 miles from the point of contact to dispose of the body of the victim.
- Previous research has demonstrated that an offender's initial crimes tend to be closer to his/her home than later ones, and that in fact, the **first offence is usually nearest to home** (Barker, 1989).
- Research on serial murder has revealed that abduction patterns reflect this trend of moving out from the offender's home as the series progresses. However, as a series progresses through seven or eight abduction-murders, the 'points of fatal encounter' commonly revert back, drawing once again closer to the killer's home (Godwin and Canter, 1997).

- *Offender's marital and employment status*
  - A review of the CATCHEM database of sexually motivated murders of children in the United Kingdom shows that: 44% of offenders who murder female victims under the age of 18 and transport the victim's body are married at the time of the offence. Thus, **married men should not be ruled out as significantly less likely than single males or males with partners.**
  - The fact that in the Mascav case and Madjenko the offence occurs on a weekend during mid-morning hours means that there is a possibility that the offender has **regular working hours during the week** and may live with someone.
  - Prentky *et al.* (1991) found that 25% of the 97 abducting child molesters they examined were employed in skilled/lower management occupations, 17% had some form of third-level education, and 28% had been married at some time in their life. These findings effectively highlight the existence of a subset of sexually motivated child abductors who can be considered socially skilled, interacting with other people on a daily basis.

- *The offender's previous criminal history*
  - **The offender is likely to have a previous criminal history,**

including sexual offences and more general criminality such as convictions for theft and dishonesty. **The investigation of sexually motivated homicides of abducted children, especially pubescent children, should NOT be limited to or even automatically focus on individuals with a history of sex offences against children.**

- Individuals with a history of social (e.g. multiple jobs, failed relationships) and sexual (e.g. nuisance sex offences, failed assaults of adults) inadequacies would be better suspects in most cases (Lanning, 1994) of child abduction/homicide (though see the point above regarding married men).
- Canter and Kirby (1995) examined the prior convictions of 416 detected child sex offenders and report that contrary to popular belief, child molesters do not have an exclusive offence history relating to assaults on children.
  - **44% had previous criminal convictions**
  - **86% of those had a conviction for dishonesty**
  - **11% had more than 8 prior convictions** for offences ranging from theft and burglary to violence and indecent assault.
- Goetting (1990) examined the case details of 93 incidents of child homicide in Detroit USA, and found that the majority of offenders had an **established criminal history**.
- Prentky et al. (1991) also found that child abductors motivated by a drive for sexual gratification had committed an **average of four previous sexual offences**. Greenfield (1997) further identified this recidivist feature of sexually motivated child abduction, finding that offenders serving time for the forcible rape or sexual assault of a child were more than twice as likely to have other victims than sexual offenders of adults.

- *Offender does not take any forensic precautions (disguise, condom)*
  - The offender displays no overt regard for concealing his identity (if one assumes that the man approaching Mascav earlier is the offender). This may indicate several things:
    1. He is **not widely known in the community** in which he is offending. This may be due to his lack of social skill or that he is not living in the community (i.e. stranger, traveller, etc.) AND/OR
    2. He has **never been caught for any criminal activity before** and is therefore unfamiliar with law enforcement processes (33% of child molesters in the NIJ Census report (US) had never been arrested prior to the charge of assault of a child, 1996) AND/OR

3. He does not understand or has very limited understanding of the process of DNA evidence.

- *Offender's timing of offences*
  - With regard to the most common time-of-day that sexually motivated child abductions occur, Wooden (1996) reports how Operation Police Lure found that abducting child molesters often target child victims in the morning.
  - The fact that the offender chose to commit the offence against Mascav in broad daylight on Sunday and that Madjenko disappeared on a Saturday morning may be an indication that this is a time when:
    1. The offender's movements would not be monitored by anyone else (i.e. wife, roommate, people who share his building, employer).
    2. He would have access to children that are unsupervised.
    3. The child would be less likely to be missed than if she was on the way to school or home.
    4. Shopping districts/motorways/bus depots serving this community are quieter, allowing less risk of an abduction being witnessed.

- *Miscellaneous statistics of child abduction murderers (Hanfland, Keppel and Weis, 1997)*
  - **50% unemployed**.
  - **62% were Caucasian** (Boudreaux, Lord and Dutra, 1999).
  - **70%** of **offenders lived within 5 miles of** the abduction site (Boudreaux, Lord and Dutra, 1999).
  - Those that do have jobs are in **'unskilled' or 'semi-skilled'** labour occupations.
  - 28% (5 times greater than the next common occupation) are employed as construction workers.
  - Of those killers who were 27 years old and over, 34% still lived with their parents, 32% were alcohol abusers and 27% were drug abusers.
  - 60% have **prior arrests for violent crimes** (53% of these were assaults and/or sexual assaults perpetrated against children).
  - 28% of prior arrests are for murders (or attempted murders) of children and 19% of these have histories of kidnapping children.
  - 64% have previous convictions for **crimes against children**.
  - Most are not in any official custody status at the time of the offence, however, 27% are either on parole or probation (of these previous offences against children).
  - 67% of cases the **MO were similar** to that in the abduction murder.

- 70% were **consistent in the way they committed the crime.**
- 28% consistently chose similar victims.
- 21% similar in approach to victim.
- 17% consistent in the specific acts committed against the child.
- 69% of cases involve a **sexual component**.
- Most common precipitating stressors are 'conflict with a female' (45%) or a 'criminal legal problem' (36%).

Thus, this offender is most likely a stranger who is unskilled and with previous convictions. He is more likely to not be married (56% are not married), but married men should *not* be excluded. Preconvictions are most likely to involve violent crimes and crimes against children. Of all possible forms of employment, the most likely is a construction worker. There are a variety of ways in which this offender is likely to have tried to commit a similar offence – either through MO, a similar victim, a similar approach and/or in the acts committed. We should emphasize that not all these qualities are likely to be consistent from crime to crime (thus, one might have similar MO but a different victim type), although in this case (if the offences are linked) the offender appears relatively consistent in terms of selecting girls between the age of 12–14 at weekends between 10am– 12pm. In general, some aspect of this offence is likely to be present in previous offences (i.e. attempted abductions).

Probable Sequence of Events
The following figures focus more closely on the probable sequence of events. This material is taken from two data sets. The first is Giannakaki's (2000) study of a sub-sample (N = 50) of the HITS (US Homicide Investigation Tracking System) database. Although this is a smaller subset it contains more details about behaviours during and after the offence. The second is from Whitehead (2003) and is based on the National Archives of Criminal Justice database, ICPSR 9682 (Finkelhor, Hotaling and Sedlak, 1990), originally collected for the National Incidence Studies of Missing, Abducted, Runaway and Thrownaway Children (NISMART) (US study). The original data set consisted of 313 records. The sample for the Whitehead study was 73 records. The eligibility requirements for inclusion were as follows: (1) the case was a sexual offence that involved physical contact; (2) there was only one perpetrator, who was not a family member, was male, over the age of 18 and more than five years older than the victim; and (3) the victim was under 16, with no disability and was not killed as a result of the offence.

We should note that both sub-samples reflect all of the statistics referred to in Hanfland, Keppel and Weis (1997). They are therefore representative of the larger sample. However, it also enables us to extract some other details about the likely characteristics of the offender. In particular, the Gianakkaki sample illustrates that:

- 70% live in the same type of geographical area as their victims.
- 72% live in the same type of neighbourhood as their victims.
- 59% kill between 1pm and 8pm.
- 52% murder the victim within one hour and 33% within two hours.
- 52% occur in an open area (33.3% in the woods and 18.8% in 'another outside area').
- 43% used a car in the commission of the offence.

Thus, there is a high probability that the offender lives in the same type of neighbourhood as Madjenko and Mascav and that Eve is probably from the same geographical location. These figures reinforce the hypothesis that all three victims were killed within 3 hours of being abducted. Table 1 below outlines the most and least likely components of the offence itself:

Table 1 Frequency of specific behaviours across 50 child homicide offences (Gianakkaki, 2003)

Behaviours	Frequency
Wounds on head or neck	41 (82%)
Hide body	30 (60%)
Vaginal penetration	27 (54%)
Anal penetration	22 (44%)
Cause of death strangulation	19 (38%)
Victim's clothing was missing from the body discovery site	19 (38%)
Offender moves victim's body from death site	18 (36%)
Cause of death blunt instrument wounds	15 (30%)
Offender returns to death site	14 (28%)
Cause of death stab wounds	12 (24%)
Cause of death asphyxia	12 (24%)
Victim was bound	11 (22%)
Offender kept the victim's body after death	9 (18%)
Victim performs oral sex on offender	6 (12%)
Covered victim's face	5 (10%)
Offender redressed victim (redress)	5 (10%)
Offender performs oral sex on victim	4 (8%)
Foreign object inserted in victim's cavities	3 (6%)
Offender bit victim	3 (6%)
Offender staged the body	3 (6%)
Victim's belongings were missing	2 (4%)
Covered victim's eyes	2 (4%)

Stranger vs. Acquaintance Sexual Assault

As stated earlier, it may be useful for the investigative team to look at the 'worst case scenario', that is, a stranger serial offender abducted and murdered the victims. Bownes, O'Gorman and Sayers' (1991) comparison of 500 stranger and acquaintance sexual assaults from Ireland reveals some strong similarities with **stranger** offenders and assumptions surrounding these cases:

- Offender displays weapon in assault/abduction.
- Assault site is away from victim's home.
- Assault site is in a car or at offender's home.
- Victim assaulted/abducted outdoors (60% of time).
- Victim walking home from school (34% of time).

Behavioural Analyses

The offences were analysed using the behavioural model of paedophilic assault developed at the Centre for Investigative Psychology (Canter, Hughes and Kirby, 1998; Bennell, Alison, Stein, Alison and Canter, 2001). This model identifies three themes based on the offender's interaction with the victim:

1. Intimate: this mode of interaction describes an offence in which there exists a range of grooming techniques, often occurring over time, in order to manipulate the victim into engaging in sexual behaviour; this involves 'courting' the victim prior to the assault and attempting to develop a pseudo-relationship with the victim.

2. Hostile: this interaction involves violence and physical force, with the offender targeting victims on the basis of their vulnerability. Sexual violation of the child may stem from anger, hostility, and rage directed at the child through degradation, violence, and in extreme cases, torture.

3. Controlled: this type of interaction involves the sexual abuse of children based not as a function of a stable sexual predilection, but rather as a function of a more controlled interaction, potentially revealing a certain level of planning and targeting behaviour. In the case of Mascav, Table 2 (below) indicates that the principal interaction style of the offender is 'Controlled', engaging in 5 of the behaviours. Of course, it may be that the offender engaged in further intimate behaviours but these are unknown. However, it certainly appears to be the case that, other than the obviously violent act of murdering the victim, this offence is not particularly characterized by hostile behaviours.

Table 2 Frequency analysis of paedophilic behaviours with behaviours engaged in the Mascav case highlighted in dark tone

Intimate	Hostile	Controlled
1. Promise of gifts/treat	*1. Offender undeterred*	*1. Stranger victim targeted*
2. Reassurance	*2. Threats of violence to victim*	*2. Child alone at time of offence*
3. Affection	*3. Initial force by offender*	*3. Offender ejaculates*
4. Desensitization	*4. Anal penetration*	*4. Vaginal penetration*
5. Oral sex (offender on victim)	*5. Sexual/abusive language*	*5. Offence committed outdoors*
6. Kissing	*6. Violence beyond necessary*	

As described earlier, **'controlled'** offenders do not necessarily have a sexual preference for children but use them as sexual objects for gratification due to their opportunity and vulnerability. This type of offender has been identified in other research on paedophile attackers (Lanning, 1992; Burgess, Groth, Holmstrom and Sgroi, 1978) as individuals who offend primarily against **strangers** in a **one-off attack.** When the offender selects a child as a victim, the primary goal appears to be immediate sexual gratification and he is unlikely to have the patience or desire to engage in sophisticated grooming behaviours to gain compliant victims. The principal intent is not to hurt the victim, simply to gain compliance with his demands for sex. The subsequent murder of the victim is most likely motivated by a desire to avoid detection rather than any sadistic impulses.

This hypothesis is supported by the fact that the **damage to the victim Mascav is functional rather than sadistic.**

- In Mascav's case there was no defence bruising or excessive damage to the body to indicate sadism or physical aggression.
- Rather the violence appears instrumental, being sufficient to assist in fulfilling the needs of the offender (i.e. sexual gratification and concealment of the offence). This, coupled with the fact that the offender might be assumed to be the same individual who was involved in a non-violent means of approach, may indicate that he will abandon an attack if he does not gain initial compliance. If he secures a

victim, however, it is probable that **he will again kill the victim to conceal the sexual assault.**

- Somander and Rammer (1991) report that in cases of 'fatal extrafamilial sexual abuse' the killing of a child may not be a necessary component of the offender's gratification but may occur either in an effort to prevent disclosure of the sex offence, or inadvertently as a result of the physical force used to facilitate the sexual assault. Wyre and Tate (1995) report interviewing child sex offenders who had killed a child for the very reason that he or she tried to run and tell.

Congruent with this view is research by Lanning (1991) in which he describes the 'morally indiscriminate child molester' as having a sexual preference for children and at the same time acting without conscience. Such an offender is likely to abduct or murder children as a means to sexually assault them. The offender's use of instrumental violence against the victim indicates that he may previously have selected children as sexual targets based on familiarity and the knowledge that a child provides an easily controlled source of sexual gratification. The offender's sexual preference for children may therefore be a function of his **inability to establish age-appropriate relationships** rather than an actual paedophilic interest (Lanning, 1992; Prentky, Knight and Lee, 1997).

Lang and Frenzel (1988) examined the various strategies used to sexually seduce children among a group of 50 sex offenders who targeted stranger victims, and found that offenders frequented locations such as school-yards, playgrounds, parks, arcades and shopping malls where 'a wide variety of ploys, wheedling, cajolery, trickery or bribery' were used to lure victims (pp. 313–314). The use of lures in sexually motivated child abduction was further highlighted in a study by Asdigian, Finkelhor and Hotaling (1995) that found in a sample of 364 legal-definition child abductions, those with a sexual assault component were almost three times more likely to involve the luring of a victim than those with no sexual component.

Therefore, in relation to the unidentified stranger who approached Mascav, his reported attempts to lure the child by promises to 'see how I make my puppets' is consistent with research into methods used by child abductors. Therefore, this incident must be looked at more closely. He is unsuccessful with his initial use of this technique. However, he does not respond with violence or force when the child resists or when she informs him that she is unattended by her mother. Child molesters with a demonstrated ability to non-violently seduce and control children may kill their victims after the sexual assault to avoid detection (Lanning, 1994). The offender's failure to adapt his approach from a non-violent one may indicate reluctance on his part to change his scripted plan for securing his victim. Thus, a similar strategy may have been used with Madjenko. He may be unable/unwilling to use violence against the child *initially* due to:

- risk of attracting attention;
- inability/unwillingness to adapt beyond his planned approach;
- only using violence as a functional behaviour (i.e. to accomplish sexual assault, to avoid detection).

To summarize, in terms of abduction approach strategy and victim targeting, the type of offender in question is hypothesized to **employ lures to gain access to female victims who will be sought in locations such as parks and playgrounds.** It is **also likely that abductions of this nature will take place during daytime** when target children are available. In such situations it is further probable that there will be potential witnesses to the incident. The homicide in this case is most likely an effort to avoid detection through preventing disclosure of the sex offence. There is likely to have been considerable post-offence activity aimed at concealing the crime (i.e. removing victim's clothing, transporting the victim, etc.). The victim's body was moved to a location that is, on the surface, unconnected to the offender - a deserted public area such as a park or woodland, but **his residence will be very close to the abduction point, likely within five miles (CATCHEM).**

Probable Mode of Death, Sexual Behaviours, MO and Post-offence Behaviour

It is understood that the forensic material can tell us little of the probable cause of death or any sexual behaviours in the case of Eve or Mascav. It may, therefore, be of some use to assess these factors against the behavioural/statistical information. The following is based on Table 1, on the fact that we know the variable 'clothes missing from crime scene' is a feature of all three offences and on the following information about abductors:

Mohr (1981), Marshal and Christie (1981) and Quinsey (1977):
- The age of the child can influence the initial approach that the offender takes with the victim
  - **Older victims tend to recognize the inappropriateness of grooming behaviours quickly and therefore, offenders use emotional appeals, arguments, threats and blaming more often than bribes or rewards against these victims.**
  - Marshall and Christie (1981) – intercourse occurred more often with older children than with younger children.

Whitehead (2003):
Victims moved by the perpetrator are more likely (during the attack phase) to be:
– detained
– strong-armed, forced and/or verbally threatened into sexual assault
– displayed a weapon as a means of threat
– carried or dragged
– sexually penetrated.

Victims who are moved more than once during the offence are more likely to be:
– detained, tied, gagged or locked up, and sexually penetrated.

Victims moved for concealment purposes are significantly more likely to be:
– detained and moved multiple times
– strong-armed, forced and/or verbally threatened with a knife/blade
– sexually penetrated.

Victims detained by the perpetrator were more likely to be:
– strong-armed, forced and/or verbally threatened
– slapped, pushed or kicked and carried or dragged
– sexually penetrated but less likely to be genitally molested.

Older victims were more likely to suffer verbal threats and penetration.

Younger perpetrators were more likely to:
– move the child, move them for concealment and detain the victim
– force or threaten the victim with strong-arm tactics and penetrate the victim.

The smaller the age difference between the victim and perpetrator, the more likely the child would be:
– moved
– moved for concealment purposes
– detained
– strong-armed, forced and/or verbally threatened
– displayed a weapon as a means of threat
– sexually penetrated.

General Summary
The findings around the abduction behaviours of the perpetrator are consistent with Prentky *et al.* (1991) and Lanning and Burgess's (1995)

267

conclusions that abduction is used by the offender as a method of victim procurement and control. Abduction alone appears to be the ultimate form of victim procurement and control, and the subsequent offence behaviours such as force/threat or physical abuse appear to be used to reinforce the control. This offender appears to rely on a fairly unsophisticated and opportunistic attack pattern. Subsequent detainment of the victim was likely to result in even more primitive, threatening and strong-arm behaviour to gain compliance to sexual demands. Indeed, it is quite possible that the children were killed in response to the inability to encourage them through more pseudo-intimate efforts at sexual assault. On balance, we feel that this offender has not had much previous contact with children in a non-offending capacity.

All of the behaviours relating to abduction appear to be interrelated. In other words, as one abduction behaviour occurs it increases the likelihood of other behaviours occurring. Thus, the results show that offenders will not simply move or detain a victim but rather will move and detain a victim. Although Prentky et al. (1991) and Lanning and Burgess (1995) did not find an increase in violence for child molesters who abduct, the current research has found that abduction behaviours increase force/threat behaviours and physically abusive behaviours. What is interesting about this finding is that the increase in the previously mentioned behaviours do not appear to be a function of gratuitous violence but rather, they appear to reinforce the control over the victim. Increases in force/threat behaviours tend to be behaviours relating to gaining control over the victim such as verbal threats, strong-arm and weapons being displayed. The increase in physically abusive behaviours also tend to be in behaviours relating to control over the victim such as being carried or dragged or being tied, gagged or locked up. By physically moving or detaining a victim the offender is able to gain control over the victim.

As the offence progresses the likelihood of more force/threats or physical abuse increases. The movement of the child increases the likelihood of force/threat and physically abusive behaviours, the movement of the child for concealment increases likelihood of such behaviours a little more, and the detainment increases their likelihood the most.

Probable Mode of Death re: Eve

The most likely cause of death associated with the behaviour 'missing clothes' is head injury (35%), followed by strangulation (27%), blunt instrument (17%) and stabbing (15%). Thus, **strangulation and some form of head injury are the most likely physical indicators** and stabbing is the least likely. This is consistent with what is known about Mascav's death (ligature strangulation from behind).

Sexual Behaviours
The highest associations with 'missing clothes' are:
- **Vaginal penetration (35%)**
- **Anal penetration (44%)**
- **Victim masturbates offender (25%).**

MO
The highest associations with 'missing clothes' are:
- Offender **moves body** (36% of cases)
- Offender **returns to the crime scene** (18%)
- Offender keeps **trophies** of victim (11%).

Post-offence Behaviour and Offender Identification
- **The name of the killer is known to police within the first week in 74% of cases**
- **22% return to the body disposal site**
- 21% of child abduction killers left town following the murder
- **18% confide in someone**
- 17% follow the case in the media
- 11% contact the victim's family
- 10% interjected themselves into the investigation.

Thus, it is highly likely that the offender's name is somewhere in the system. Although the probabilities are under 25%, there is a chance he will have returned to the crime scene, left town following the murder and/or confided in someone.

INVESTIGATIVE RECOMMENDATIONS/SUGGESTED LINES OF ENQUIRY

Are these Offences Linked?
Given the relatively high percentage chance that a similar type of offence has been committed before (or attempted), a strong emphasis must be placed on investigating other abduction attempts and other missing person enquiries. We recommend that, if the enquiry team have not already done so, they seriously consider *any* other off-road abduction offence as a serious potential link to this case (particularly given the very rare nature of such offences; see Hanfland *et al.* (1997) for US figures, CATCHEM for UK figures. Further, Boudreaux, Lord and Dutra (1999) found that the transportation of the victim over long distances (>10 miles) was not uncommon when victims were between 12 and 14 years of age.

In light of the research discussed above and details of this specific case, we suggest that the search should be guided by the following parameters:

- Abductions, attempted abductions, abduction rapes and abduction murders
- 9–19 year old female victim
- Vehicle used in abduction
- Victim found naked
- No clothing found.

However, although the search should be on a national scale we agree that any offence with these parameters within a 30-mile radius of all three of the sites (Mascav's body, Eve's body, abduction site of Madjenko) be prioritized over national offences and investigated first. All prioritized points of interest should be plotted onto a map and subjected to geographical profiling analysis.

Search Parameters – Time and Distance

In 74% of such cases the offender is already 'in the system'. Therefore, the enquiry team may wish to consult their records with regard to the basic profiles as outlined. Searches should also be conducted on the basis of chronological timing either side of the offence and with regard to geographic proximity. For example, records should be checked in relation to any driving offences in the area and suspects living closest to the offence should be checked first. Depending upon resources, the enquiry team may wish to check any driving offences 5 days either side of the disappearance of Madjenko and Mascav. Similarly, offenders within 2 miles of the offence should be prioritized. This is because there is a corpus of research that indicates temporal and locational facets of offending provide the most reliable links to any given offence (Snook, Wright, Alison and House, 2003; Bennell, 2002). The recommended search priorities are summarized in Figure 1.

Thus, the enquiry team should work out concentrically in terms of both locations (abduction site and deposition site) and both forward and backward in time regarding offence timing.

Proximal searches: First priority should be given to the closest offender with preconvictions for violence (esp. sexual violence). The next priorities are property offences and then, finally, driving offences. A further filter is then imposed at the 'characteristic priority' stage. This works as follows: first priority should be given to individuals with all of the characteristics in the relevant priority order boxes – i.e. search for an offender with 'a/b/c

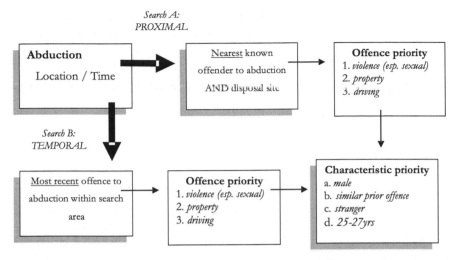

Figure 1 Prioritization filter based on timing of other offences and location of known offenders

and d' attributes. If this generates no suspects, characteristic 'd' (age) is dropped, then 'c', 'b' and so on, and the next search begins.

Search B (temporal) operates in a similar fashion, i.e. select the offence that occurred closest in time to the disappearance of Mascav and Madjenko (two parallel searches). The most likely relevant offence is violence (especially sexual violence). Thus any violent offence that occurred nearest in time (before or after the disappearance) is ranked 1 in priority. Upon selecting the offence closest in time, the 'characteristic priority' filter is imposed again. Searches should be conducted in parallel (i.e. neither search takes precedence). Both searches should be guided, informed and refined in light of the other, more detailed information available within this report.

Geographic Considerations
We have found 'MAP24' (an Internet-based mapping program) extremely useful in working interactively with the local geography involved and the maps provided have come from this website:
http://www.map24.co.uk
By using the routing facility (from Mascav's abduction site to the disposal site) and clicking on 'maximize' on the top right then 'zoom' at the bottom right, one can drag the cursor around the map and zoom in across choice points along possible routes [reference to actual map grid references removed for confidentiality]. This facility also demarcates petrol stations and services, etc. We have found this extremely useful in

guiding our decisions on possible routes, areas of significance, etc. If the enquiry team have not already worked with interactive maps then we would recommend this site as a useful cross-reference. On the basis of the mapping information we view that the following strategies be considered:

- If the offender has used a vehicle to abduct the victims then this is a significant variable that can have an effect on other aspects of the investigative suggestions.
- All other similar abductions, or attempts, should be considered irrespective of their distance from this abduction site due to the offender's mobility.
- It is possible that the offender is a **regular commuter** on this bus route and has a car regularly parked at or near the depot. Thus the victim may have been targeted during the course of the journey and/or on previous journeys. If there is any way of checking individuals whose place of work regularly takes them on this route they should be considered possible witnesses and/or suspects.
- We note that there is a **half way house** not far from the victim's route home. Have individuals within this establishment been checked?
- We have indicated [the geographic co-ordinates were removed for confidentiality] the broad search areas for initial screening of possible suspects. This area represents the preferred search area.

Vehicle

If each case was a forced abduction then there is of course a significant chance that a vehicle was used. Informed decisions might therefore relate to a number of lines of enquiry relating to the use of a vehicle in the offences.

- *Petrol receipts.* We have outlined the various **petrol stations** between the abduction site (s) and the deposition site(s) [the geographic co-ordinates were removed for confidentiality]. If possible, receipts should be checked at these establishments during the relevant time period. Special attention should be given to any individuals with any pre-convictions. If this presents an overwhelmingly large number, the initial filter should be devoted to individuals with more serious convictions (especially assault and sexual assault).
- *Driving offences.* Individuals stopped for **driving convictions** (including parking tickets) anywhere near this route within a day either side of the offence (or as far back or far forward as is reasonably possible given resources) along this route and in the near vicinity should be checked carefully.

- *Car wash/cleaning receipts.* The offender may have washed or cleaned (i.e. vacuumed) the vehicle post-offence to remove forensic evidence. **Local car wash** receipts could be cross-referenced against suspect pool.
- *Vehicle modification enquiries.* The offender may have re-upholstered his vehicle and/or changed the tyres, again to remove forensic evidence. Enquiries at **local garages** for customers modifying their cars days after the abduction date (especially those that didn't seem necessary) may prove useful.
- *Stolen cars.* It is possible that the offender may have stolen a car in an attempt to conceal his identity in commission of this highly visible street abduction. **Local vehicles stolen and recovered** in the days surrounding the abduction could be investigated with attention to the forensic analysis of recovered vehicles.

Of course, all of these suggestions could generate vast numbers of possible suspects but these could potentially be prioritized on the basis of cross-referring them to lists of preconvictions (esp. assault and sexual), the suspect pool and/or sex offender registers.

Internet
The Internet is a very accessible and effective tool for many sex offenders (Quayle, Holland, Linehan and Taylor, 2000). There are a number of possible lines of enquiry surrounding its use by individuals involved in this investigation.

- *Victim forums.* Research has shown that a significant minority of offenders interject themselves into the investigation or contact the family of the victim in some way. On a brief trawl of Internet websites we found several fora for those wishing to help in the investigation, post comments and offer condolences. Of course, these Internet users may be well-meaning, but a background check (through IP addresses and server details) of these individuals could prove invaluable not only for this investigation but for other child sexual offences.

[Example excerpt from an internet site removed for confidentiality]

Legal and Parole Enquiries
As mentioned previously, an enquiry into recent paroles, especially those with legal problems, local to the areas around the time of the abduction could identify further potential suspects.

Prioritizing

Overall, the task should be to prioritize suspects and policy on the basis of proximal and temporal searches FIRST and then examine characteristics of the offender. For example, it would be preferential to base search parameters on the nearest person with a driving offence than a sex offender of the 'right age' who lives 50 miles away.

- *Targeted leaflets.* It is likely the offender has been in the area prior to coming into contact with this victim, may have assaulted other children in this area prior to progressing to murder, and may have returned to the area to scout for future victims. Therefore, an appeal for information should be given to school officials, parents of young children, and park personnel. However, the leaflets must caution parents, teachers, etc., not to interview children zealously because it can lead to innocent fabrication and confabulation on the child's part. The emphasis should be to come forward to police with suspicions and allow police interviewers to conduct a suitable interview.
- *Target homeless persons, addicts and prostitutes in the area for information.* It is likely that the offender had locations pre-selected for commission of assault. Vagrants, addicts and prostitutes using the same area may provide useful witness information, unlikely to be known through regular police enquiries (i.e. house to house, media spots, etc.).
- *Media.* The media can help highlight the potential value of eliciting such witnesses and making the general public more aware of the investigation.
- *Offender volunteering information.* The offender may provide information of seeing the victim with an unknown person in order to deflect attention. It is important to record all interviews where this type of information is obtained and regard the witness as a possible suspect.
- *Witnesses.* It should be noted that hesitation on the part of a witness to produce an alibi or provide their whereabouts may not be an indication of guilt, concealment or obstruction. Many factors can explain the unwillingness to cooperate in police investigations:
  a) Married person in company of person other than spouse
  b) School children playing truant
  c) Person working in area while claiming benefits
  d) Person in employment but conducting personal affairs/business at index time
  e) Distrust of police
- *Entomological investigation.* If body was concealed prior to being disposed of an entomological investigation may link the body to the concealment site and therefore to the offender. An evaluation of the fly larvae present in Mascav's body may uncover larvae that are not

present at the disposal site and could be linked to the assault site, victim residence, etc., when the offender is apprehended.

References

Asdigian, N., Finkelhor, D. and Hotaling, G. (1995) 'Varieties of non-family abduction of children and adolescents', *Criminal Justice and Behavior*, 22 (3): 215–232.

Barker, M. (1989). *Criminal Activity and Home Range: A Study of the Spatial Offence Patterns of Burglars*. Unpublished Master's dissertation, University of Surrey.

Bennell, C. (2002) *Setting Thresholds for Linking*. Unpublished PhD thesis, University of Liverpool.

Bennell, C., Alison, L., Stein, K., Alison, E. and Canter, D. (2001) 'Sexual offences against children as the abusive exploitation of conventional adult-child relationships', *Journal of Social and Personal Relationships*, 18: 155–71.

Boudreaux, M., Lord, W., and Dutra, R. (1999) 'Child abduction: Aged-based analyses of offender, victim, and offense characteristics in 550 cases of alleged child disappearance', *Journal of Forensic Sciences*, 44 (3): 539–53.

Boudreaux, M., Lord, W., and Jarvis, J. (2001) 'Behavioral perspectives on child homicide. The role of access, vulnerability, and routine activities theory', *Trauma, Violence and Abuse*, 2 (1): 56–78.

Bownes, I., O'Gorman, E. and Sayers, A. (1991) 'A comparison of stranger and acquaintance assaults', *Medical Science and Law*, 31: 1–8.

Burgess, A., Groth, A., Holmstrom, L. and Sgroi, S. (1978) *Sexual Assault of Children and Adolescents*. Lexington: Lexington Books.

Canter, D. and Kirby, S. (1995) 'Prior convictions of child molesters', *Science and Justice*, 35: 73–8.

Canter, D., Heritage, R., and Kovacik, M. (1989) *Offender Profiling*. Interim report to the Home Office.

Canter, D. Hughes, D, and Kirby, S. (1998) 'Paedophilia: pathology, criminality, or both? The development of a multivariate model of offence behaviour in child sexual abuse', *The Journal of Forensic Psychiatry*, 9 (3): 532–55.

Finkelhor, D., Hotaling, G., and Sedlak, A. (1990) *Missing, Abducted, Runaway, and Thrownaway Children in America – First Report: Numbers and Characteristics, National Incidence Studies*. Washington, DC: US Department of Justice, Office of Justice Programs, Office of Juvenile Justice and Delinquency Prevention.

Finkelhor, D. and Ormrod, R. (2000) *Kidnapping of Juveniles: Patterns from NIBRS Bulletin*. Washington, DC: US Department of Justice, Office of Justice Programs, Office of Juvenile Justice and Delinquency Prevention.

Giannakaki, T. (2000) *An Examination of Child Abduction Murder*. Unpublished MSc thesis, University of Liverpool. MSc in Investigative Psychology.

Godwin, M. and Canter, D. (1997) 'Encounter and death: the spatial behaviour of U.S. serial killers', *Policing: International Journal of Police Strategy and Management*, 20: 24–38.

Goetting, A. (1990) 'Child victims of homicide: A portrait of their killers and their circumstances of their deaths', *Violence and Victims*, 5: 287–96.

Goodwill, A. and Alison, L. (in press) 'Sequential angulation, spatial dispersion and consistency of distance attack patterns from home in serial murder, rape and burglary', *Psychology, Crime and Law*.

Greenfield, L. (1997) *Sex Offenses and Offenders: An analysis of data on rape and sexual assault*. US Department of Justice, Office of Justice Programs, Bureau of Justice Statistics. Available online at http://ojp.usdoj.gov

Hanfland, K.A., Keppel, R.D. and Weis, J.G. (1997) *Case Management for Missing Children Homicide Investigation*. Seattle: Attorney General of Washington.

Lang, R. and Frenzel, R. (1988) 'How sex offenders lure children', *Annals of Sex Research*, 1: 303–17.

Lanning, K. (1991). 'Ritual abuse: A law enforcement view or perspective', *Child Abuse and Neglect*, 15: 171–73.

Lanning, K. (1992) *Investigator's guide to allegations of 'ritual' child abuse*. Quantico, VA: Federal Bureau of Investigation, National Center for the Analysis of Violent Crime.

Lanning, K. (1994) 'Child molesters: a behavioural analysis', *School Safety*, Spring: 12–17.

Lanning, K. and Burgess, A. (eds) (1995) *Child Molesters Who Abduct: Summary of the Case in Point Series*. Alexandria, VA: National Center for Missing and Exploited Children.

Marshall, W. and Christie, M. (1981) 'Paedophilia and aggression', *Criminal Justice and Behaviour*, 8 (2): 145–58.

Mohr, J. (1981) 'Age structures in paedophilia', in M. Cook and K. Howells (eds), *Adult Sexual Interest in Children* (pp. 41–53) London: Academic Press.

National Institute for Justice Annual Report. http//:www.ncjrs.org/pdffiles1/171679.pdf (accessed 14 March 2004).

Prentky, R., Knight, R., Burgess, A., Ressler, R. Campbell, J. and Lanning, K. (1991) 'Child molesters who abduct', *Violence and Victims*, 6: 213–24.

Prentky, R.., Knight, R. and Lee, A. (1997) 'Risk factors associated with recidivism among extrafamilial child molesters', *Journal of Consulting and Clinical Psychology*, 65: 141–49.

Quayle, E., Holland, G., Linehan, C. and Taylor, M. (2000) 'The internet and offending behaviour: A case study', *The Journal of Sexual Aggression*, 6: 78–84.

Quinsey, V. (1977) 'The assessment and treatment of child molesters: a review', *Canadian Psychological Review*, 18(3): 204–20.

Snook, B., Wright, M., Alison, L. and House, J. (2003). 'Searching for a needle in a needle stack: Combining criminal careers and journey-to-crime research for criminal suspect prioritisation'. 'Internal document', Investigative Psychology Library, University of Liverpool: VOL H41.

Somander, L. and Rammer, L. (1991) 'Intra- and extra- familial child homicide in Sweden 1971–80', *Child Abuse and Neglect*, 15: 45–55.

Wooden, K. (1995) *Child Lures Family Guide for Prevention of Sexual Abuse and Abduction*. Vermont: The Wooden Publishing House.

Whitehead, T. (2000) *Victim and Offender Demographics in Child Abduction*. Unpublished MSc thesis. University of Liverpool. Forensic Behavioural Science course.

Wyre, R. and Tate, T. (1995) *Murder of Childhood*. Harmondsworth: Penguin.

FEEDBACK FORM: OPERATION 'SWAN'

Several officers have now provided us with feedback on previous cases. We hope to increase this feedback with each successive case in order to improve the service. We respect the time it takes to fill in yet more forms but the form below should take no more than 5–10 minutes and all comments are greatly appreciated.

Please briefly indicate how this report was used (if it was used):

_____

_____

_____

Please score the following criteria by ticking the appropriate category:

CLARITY

1. Very unclear, 2. Unclear, 3. Fairly clear, 4. Very clear

Please indicate how clarity could have been improved:

_____

_____

USEFULNESS

1. Not at all useful, 2. Not very useful, 3. Quite useful, 4. Very useful

Please indicate how usefulness could have been improved:

_____

_____

Please write down any other comments/criticisms:

_____

_____

MANY THANKS FOR YOUR COMMENTS

Chapter 11

Assessing the reliability of interviews with vulnerable witnesses

Katarina Fritzon

Interviewing people with learning difficulties

Within the Criminal Justice System there is a general perception that people with learning difficulties do not make reliable witnesses (Milne *et al.*, 1996). In recent years there has been some attempt to examine particular problems associated with interviewing people with learning difficulties for investigative purposes. This research has uncovered a number of areas where problems may arise. In general, the majority of these problems relate to weaknesses in memory coupled with poor comprehension and communication that can lend themselves to an increase in levels of suggestibility. Research has found that people with learning difficulties have particular problems with certain forms of questioning.

Questioning styles can have an impact on the recall of an event by all types of witness, but particularly individuals with learning difficulties (Clare and Gudjonsson, 1993). Broadly, more open questioning styles (e.g. 'tell me what happened') elicit more accurate responses than focused recall, fixed choice or closed questions (e.g. 'was his hair brown or black?') (Kebbell and Hatton, 1999).

In one of the only studies to directly examine police interviewing of people with learning difficulties, Tully and Cahill (1984) identified a number of specific categories of error production as follows:

1 *Acquiescing to leading questions*. These are questions that contain a suggestion as to the answer being sought.

2 *Confabulation*. Pressure by the interviewer, whether moderate or severe, may lead the witness to fill in parts of the account that they are not sure about.

3 *Compounding an original error*. The interviewer assumes an initial (wrong) answer to be correct and elicits further incorrect testimony by accepting this premise. This can occur either through inaccurate interpretation by the interviewer of the statement, or through confabulation by the interviewee.

4 *Overriding clarifications and upgrading of responses*. An inarticulate or ambiguous statement is incorrectly 'clarified' by the interviewer.

5 *Relevant but inconvenient fragment ignored*. Information which does not fit with an already constructed story is ignored by the interviewer.

6 *Alternative choice*. Two restricted options are offered and the interviewee incorrectly chooses one in the absence of the correct option.

7 *Cycles of 'don't know' to line of questioning*. Failures in memory can cause embarrassment and the wish to provide a response. It is important, therefore, to be aware if an interviewee suddenly elicits an answer to a question that follows a series of unanswered questions.

8 *Tendency to say 'yes' rather than 'no'*. In response to a forced choice question, people with learning difficulties tend to say 'yes', or agree with the interviewer.

These errors may be caused by a variety of factors, such as a poor understanding of the importance of telling the truth, a desire to please the interviewer or others present, or to appear competent. In summary, it has been proposed that the tendency to produce errors in testimony in people with learning difficulties is due to both cognitive limitations and the effects of social desirability (Shaw and Budd, 1982). However, it is important to note that research also shows that, with appropriate questioning, individuals with learning difficulties can give accurate accounts (Milne and Bull, 1995).

Research by Gudjonsson has shown that suggestibility is a major factor in explaining why some people make false admissions to crimes for which they are not responsible (Gudjonsson and MacKeith, 1988). A person with learning difficulties may not understand the consequences of making an incorrect admission, but may be more concerned with immediate aspects of the environment such as bringing the interview to an end, or being able to answer questions to the satisfaction of the interviewer.

Assessing the reliability of accounts

The credibility of witnesses depends on both their *ability* to tell the truth as well as their *motivation* to do so (Undeutsch, 1982). Even when people are motivated to tell the truth, accuracy and reliability of statements are influenced by psychological vulnerabilities and questioning styles (Kebbell and Hatton, 1999).

The assumption of unreliability in certain categories of witness, e.g. children and adults with learning difficulties, was challenged in the 1950s when a German psychologist developed a set of criteria that could determine the truthfulness of statements. These criteria were based on what is known as the 'Undeutsch hypothesis' (1982), which posits that statements based on memories of real (self-experienced) events are different in quality from statements that are not based on experience but are products of fantasy, invention, distortion or coaching. Undeutsch's original 'contents of reality' later became refined by Steller and Kohnken (1989) into a set of 19 criteria, listed in the Appendix at the end of this chapter. They named the process 'criteria-based content analysis' to reflect the application of specific criteria to the content of the statement, as a separate issue from the process by which the statement had been generated.

Several studies have found support for using the technique to discriminate truthful from fabricated accounts. For example, Esplin *et al.* (1988) found that every criterion except one was more frequently present in a group of children who had had sexual abuse confirmed than those whose cases had been dismissed. A more recent study by Parker and Brown (2000) evaluated the technique in cases of false allegations of rape by adult females. They found that 10 of the 18 criteria reached statistical significance in differentiating between unfounded allegations of rape versus cases where a perpetrator had been convicted. The unfounded allegations were categorized on the basis that either the 'victim' herself admitted that the account was false, or there were other substantial grounds to believe the allegation had no basis in fact, e.g. contradictory medical or witness statements, or evidence that the 'victim' was suffering a delusional or substance-induced state.

Statement validity analysis has primarily been used in cases involving allegations of sexual abuse of children. However, children and adults with learning difficulties share the impairments in intelligence and social functioning that may contribute to the production of unreliable accounts.

Therefore it is considered appropriate to use statement validity analysis (SVA) to assess the credibility of the account given by Ms X in the case to be described here. However, it is worth noting that this procedure has been the subject of some controversy in recent years (see e.g. exchanges between Horowitz (1998), Lamb (1998) and Tully (1998); and a review by Ruby and Brigham, 1997). First, the application of SVA is dependent on the quality of narrative accounts, with the optimum being a statement in the witness's own words, generated with minimal prompting (Tully, 1998). In the present case, this objective was not met, with the quality of open-ended narrative being very poor both in relation to both the suspect and witness interviews. A second point of relevance to the current application of SVA is the number of criteria that are required to be present in order to support a judgement of veracity. In the review by Ruby and Brigham (1997) different authors offer suggestions ranging from two to 19, but there is no overall consensus of opinion. For these reasons, the application of SVA to the present statement is used only in combination with other analytical techniques to provide an overall assessment of the credibility and reliability of the witness's account.

Writing the report: process and professional issues

Whilst it is incumbent upon forensic psychologists undertaking con-sultancy work with criminal justice professionals to have an awareness of the legal system including some understanding of the professional codes of conduct involved, e.g. PACE (1984) and rules of evidence, the same is not necessarily the case in reverse. Thus, while police officers and solicitors may have a rudimentary understanding of what psychologists do, especially if they have instructed them in previous cases, some of the subtleties of, for example, the professional divisions within psychology are not always well understood. This may be important due to misconceptions about the roles of various specialisms within psychology, in particular about the distinction between forensic and clinical psychologists. While forensic psychologists specialize in the area of offending behaviour, they are not necessarily qualified to undertake psychometric testing in order to provide assessments of general intellectual or psychological functioning. In relation to the present case, for example, a general commentary on the police interviews, with reference to research on the special considerations of people with learning difficulties, could be provided, but an actual assessment of the extent or specificity of the learning difficulty would fall within the remit of a clinical psychologist.

There is also an area of difficulty in relation to the epistemological dif-ferences between the social sciences and the criminal justice professions.

Psychology is an inexact science where, for example, in presenting findings from research in a particular area several studies reach incompatible conclusions with only subtle methodological differences to distinguish between them. This is not tolerated by an adversarial criminal justice system that requires standards of proof in order to reach decisions about guilt or innocence. Therefore a fairly common occurrence, commented on by Gudjonsson and Haward (1998, p. 53–57) in particular, is that psychologists are asked to modify their reports in order to appear to be more confident about their conclusions. Obviously this is not appropriate. It is also important to make the point that in preparing reports, regardless of whether the psychologist is instructed by the defence or the prosecution, the presentation of results should be more or less the same. In other words, if the conclusions reached are not supportive of the particular client, then the report should say so. The client may choose not to use the report in evidence. This point is also important in the area of providing behavioural investigative advice in police investigations, in which the curious paradox exists that while a 'profile' that accurately resembles the defendant is unlikely for evidential reasons to be used by the prosecution to support their case (for discussion see Ormerod, 1996), an inaccurate or partly accurate profile could be referred to by the defence in order to promote its case. It is therefore crucial that the process by which conclusions are reached is clearly elucidated.

In relation to process issues in the present case, for example, there are a number of recognized approaches to analysing interview material, including SVA. For example, a former polygraph examiner (Sapir, 1987) has developed a technique, which is similar in many ways to SVA, called scientific content analysis (SCAN). Fielding (1999) also outlines an approach based on a form of discourse analysis (Fielding and Conroy, 1992) in which detailed interpretations of verbal and non-verbal speech patterns and behaviour are analysed at what Fielding refers to as a 'micro-sociological' level. Alternatively, a more experiential approach could have been adopted, for example a trained police interviewer could have provided a critique based on his professional expertise. Whichever of these methods are adopted must depend on a clearly denoted ethical principle outlined in the British Psychological Society's codes of conduct, that is to operate within one's particular area of competence. The need to be explicit about the process by which conclusions have been arrived at, and the specific area of professional competence, has been adopted by the National Crime Faculty in their Codes of Conduct for Behavioural Investigative Advisers (2001).

A final point in relation to process issues is that made by Canter and Alison (1999). They suggest that the information needed in order to write the report should pertain only to those material facts of the case, as any speculation or opinions held by the client could, if transferred to the expert, potentially bias their report. In the present case, the full set of case papers was provided, and this included video and audio tapes of the police interviews, as well as the typed transcripts. It also included previous social work reports on both the witness and defendant for background information. This was helpful in terms of understanding the extent and specificity of the learning difficulties.

Caveat

Bearing in mind the above issues, it is often useful to include in reports a statement that outlines the terms of reference for the report; in other words, that indicates both what the report does and does not purport to achieve. It is important to delineate these boundaries of the remit of the report so that if questioned in court, for example, over why a particular test was not carried out, the psychologist can refer to these terms of reference.

In the present case, a caveat was issued to the effect that the report considers the interviews in light of research that has been conducted on people with learning difficulties. The research drawn on is contained in the Bibliography. However, it is important to note that this research merely highlights areas where such individuals have a tendency to have problems and does not provide any basis for testing whether a particular individual does have a particular problem. The identification of certain questioning styles that have a tendency to produce errors in people with learning difficulties should not be taken as definitive proof that, in this particular case, they did produce errors in the witness' account.

Assessment of interview with Ms X

Drawing on the literature summarized in the introduction to this chapter, it was possible to highlight a number of potentially significant problems in the interview with Ms X that may have led to her statement being unreliable. In particular, the following areas of concern were highlighted.

Rapport stage

It has been suggested (Tully and Fritzon, 1996) that when interviewing people with learning difficulties, the rapport stage should contain *at least* the following components:

a) assessment of intellectual competence and communication style of witness

b) dealing with the emotional state and demeanour of the witness

c) assessment of the attitude of the witness.

While a) and c) might be done in a straightforward way by having an initial, non-investigative conversation with the witness, including some background information on previous sexual relationships, b) might require the interview to be postponed, a change of venue or even of interviewers.

The only one of these criteria that was present in the police interview was a very rudimentary assessment of Ms X's communication style that resulted in the interviewer asking her to speak slowly.

While Ms X did not seem overly anxious or agitated, it is felt that a failure to properly assess her attitude to the alleged offence, to Mr Y, and to giving an accurate account, could represent a serious oversight. For example, she continually refers to 'hating' Mr Y. This may be an understandable consequence of the offence, but if this negative opinion was present before the alleged offence, then this could represent a motive for a false allegation.

Equally, she refers to various sexual acts, including kissing, as 'disgusting', or 'rude'. Again, this attitude could have important implications for her allegations. For example, given her failure to correctly describe sexual intercourse (see section on Understanding of sexual matters), it may be possible that a less serious sexual assault took place, and that she views this as 'disgusting'. Alternatively, it may be that Ms X consented to sexual intercourse with either Mr Y, *or another person*, and that she is subsequently ashamed of this. Without a proper assessment, coupled with an emphasis on the importance of telling the truth, the issue of what sexual act occurred, if any, between Ms X and Mr Y, is clouded.

Truth-telling

It is particularly important to establish whether a child or vulnerable adult knows the difference between truth and lies, especially if they are to be a competent witness in court. In order to be reliable, the minimum appraisal should include at least the following:

- the person's ability to recognize a truthful statement from a lie
- their ability to say if someone else has told them what to tell the interviewer
- their knowledge of consequences of lying
- their realization that the interviewer needs to know everything that can

be remembered, without guessing or making parts up, or deliberately leaving something out.

Obviously, this assessment should be done carefully, and without conveying to the witness the idea that the interviewer does not believe them. In this case, the interviewer did not address the question of truth-telling with Ms X; therefore we do not know what her understanding of the concepts are.

Questioning style

The majority of questions that were asked of Ms X are closed or fixed choice questions, where she is given two alternatives and asked to select one. Research (Tully and Cahill, 1984) has shown that people with learning difficulties have a tendency to acquiesce with whichever choice is given by the interviewer in response to such questions, as can be seen clearly in the following exchange:

Interviewer:	Did he put his penis inside?
Ms X:	He put his penis inside.
Interviewer:	Or on the outside?
Ms X:	Outside he did do sex with her.

The use of such questions has been shown in a number of research studies (for example, Ceci and Bruck, 1995) to lead to greater inaccuracies in testimony than a more open questioning style. When fixed choice alternatives are given, there is always the possibility that the correct alternative is not in fact presented and the individual with learning difficulties simply picks one of the incorrect options. The individual may make such choices based simply on their knowledge of language, for example:

Interviewer:	When you were on the bed were you facing the ceiling or pillow?
Ms X:	Pillow.

This error could be due to not understanding the word 'facing' (instead of 'was your face towards', or 'pointing at') or because Ms X uses another word ('up' or 'roof') for ceiling.

Timing

There were one or two occasions where the interviewer interrupted Ms X in order to clarify a question or a response. Free narrative accounts are generally the least prone to error, and so it is unwise to interrupt a witness who is trying to give a free narrative account, even if it is initially difficult to understand the content of that narrative. Similarly, it is good practice to allow fairly long pauses after a witness has given an answer to a question, so that there is enough time for her to fully access her memory of the event. In general, the interviewer did not allow enough time between questions or enough pauses for Ms X to gather her thoughts and answer more fully. Apart from the request for her to speak more slowly, the importance of taking her time to think about answers to questions was not emphasized at all during the interview.

Ms X's understanding of sexual matters

There are a number of aspects of Ms X's account in relation to sexual anatomy and acts that are of some concern.

1 When looking at the pictures, she referred to the male genitals as 'vagina' and the female genitals as 'penis'. This doesn't necessarily mean that she doesn't know which is which, but it does make her account slightly more difficult to interpret as we do not know if inaccuracies result from lack of knowledge of nomenclature or lack of knowledge of sexual acts or anatomies themselves. Obviously, the latter interpretation would raise concerns about her accusation in relation to Mr Y.

2 When asked what Mr Y's penis looked like, she said it was blue. A fuller description was not asked for, therefore we do not know whether she was referring to the whole penis, or just parts of it, e.g. the veins.

3 At one point, Ms X says she had her pyjamas on during the incident. Subsequently, when asked how far her pyjamas were taken down to, she indicates only to the top of her thighs. She then says they were taken completely off.

4 She does not answer the question 'could you feel his penis inside you?', although earlier in the interview she does say he 'put his dick in the hole'.

Overall, this tends to suggest that Ms X does not have a detailed understanding of sexual matters, and in relation to the present accusation she is able to provide only a very rudimentary account of sexual intercourse having taken place. Throughout the interview her tendency is to answer a number of questions with 'he did something to me', but she is not able to provide a fuller account of what that 'something' was. This in itself does not invalidate her account, as a short accusation may be just as valid as a longer one. It does mean, however, that it is extremely difficult to assess the reliability of her statement, especially given the prescriptions pertaining to the use of statement validity analysis outlined previously.

Analysis of veracity of Miss X's account

The application of the criteria based content analysis (CBCA) procedure within statement validity analysis to the account given by Ms X identified the presence of only five or six of the criteria listed in Appendix 1. However, as previously stated, since the application of SVA is dependent on the quality of narrative accounts (Tully, 1998), it is important to emphasize that more might have been present in an account generated by a skilled interviewer and that the relative paucity of criteria therefore should not necessarily be taken to indicate a lack of reliability.

The validity criteria that are present include 'reproduction of conversation' (e.g. 'that's what he said, come on do sex'); 'superfluous detail' (e.g. '[A]'s my boyfriend I don't want [Y]'); 'subjective mental state' (e.g. 'it hurt', and 'I don't like that'); 'logical structure'; 'unexpected complication' (e.g. 'he pushed me I banged my head the wall' and 'description of interaction' (e.g. 'he go near me grabbed me banged my head keep pinching me – I said get off me'). None of the criteria is given extra weighting as such, but some are more unusual than others and therefore tend to be taken as more reliable indicators of veracity (Parker and Brown, 2000). Ms X's account contains two of those: reproduction of speech and unexpected complications. These are aspects of an account that someone who was fabricating would be unlikely to incorporate.

Motivation

In any accusation of rape, it is important to examine the accuser's motivation for reporting. This is particularly so if the alleged victim is a child or person with learning difficulties, where there may be external circumstances that influence the child or vulnerable adult. The context of the original disclosure or report is important, as well as any possible pressures to report falsely. As mentioned previously, one possibility is that Mr Y and Ms X had consensual intercourse and that subsequent events have led to the accusation of rape. For example, Ms X mentions that she has a boyfriend and at one point during the interview asks the social worker if she thinks he will be pleased with her now. She also mentions that staff told Mr Y off for his behaviour. These are both avenues that merit further exploration as they could indicate that Ms X has been influenced by external disapproval.

Conclusion

While there may have been aspects of Ms X's account that were unreliable, the overall quality of information was insufficient to reach a firm conclusion on this. Specifically, there was a question over whether Ms X did indeed appreciate the difference between truth and lies, or the consequences of not telling the truth. Throughout the interview, there were a number of examples of the use of question types that have been found by research to elicit errors in testimony from people with learning difficulties. There were a number of inconsistencies within Ms X's account, in relation to the nature of the act(s) that occurred, and other material facts such as the naming of body parts.

In general, the quality of information extracted from Ms X was poor, and lacking in specific detail. A more rigorous analysis of the veracity of her account could only be performed if she was re-interviewed following the procedures outlined in, for example, the Youth Justice and Criminal Evidence Act 1999 (which post-dates the case reported here) or the Memorandum of Good Practice (Home Office and Department of Health, 1992).

Assessment of interview with Mr Y

In relation to the interview of Mr Y, the defendant, there were two main foci of the assessment as instructed by the solicitors. One concerned his understanding of the questions that were asked of him, including the police caution; the second was again to assess the reliability of his account, specifically the apparent admission.

Understanding the police caution

A study by Clare and Gudjonsson (1992) on the former police caution revealed that the majority of people with learning difficulties do not fully understand the right to silence. However, significantly, such individuals tend to claim to have understood the caution when in fact they did not. The new police caution is arguably worded in a more complex way than the old version; therefore it is probably safe to say that an even higher number of people with learning difficulties would not understand than was observed in the Clare and Gudjonsson study.

It is difficult to determine definitively whether Mr Y understood the caution, but interesting to note that when asked to explain what he thought it meant, he attempted to recite what the police officer had said using the same words. A standard test of comprehension is to ask an individual to suggest a different word for one that is given to them. Mr Y did poorly on this aspect of the WAIS-R intelligence test and his inability to rephrase the caution in his own words does tend to suggest a lack of understanding.

Assessment of the interviews

On the whole, the police interview of Mr Y was conducted with appropriate attention to the particular needs of an individual with learning difficulties and appeared to follow the guidelines outlined in the Memorandum of Good Practice (Home Office and Department of Health, 1992).

Interviewing protocol dictates that individuals with special needs must be accompanied by an appropriate adult. Clearly this was adhered to in Mr Y's case since his mother accompanied him. From an assessment of the interview, on the whole the interviewer was sensitive to Mr Y's needs, established rapport, explained his questions in simple terms and elicited information in a professional manner. The interviewer also highlighted the necessity to be precise about sequences of events and allowed an open-ended interviewing format wherever possible. However, there were some specific features that fell into the categories suggested by Tully and Cahill (1984), which therefore suggested that parts of Mr Y's statement may have been unreliable.

General issues

Firstly it was noted that Mr Y was clearly quite uncomfortable during questioning. Although the interviewer spent a minute or two asking him about himself and his family, he was still noticeably nervous upon commencement of formal questioning and might therefore have benefited from a longer rapport stage. In addition to this, the importance of telling the truth was not adequately reinforced, and this may lead to problems in determining the veracity of his account. Clearly, the issue of truth-telling is fundamental to any investigative interview and it is especially important to emphasize this when interviewing children or adults with learning difficulties.

The interviewer made several comments that conveyed disbelief at the responses being given, or indicated that he was not satisfied with the level of information generated. Examples of this include comments like 'get our thinking caps on here' (p. 29), 'I wasn't there but you were' (p.33) and several instances of the interviewer saying 'no, no' before repeating a question. It is a well-known phenomenon that if children or vulnerable adults are continually asked the same type of question they assume that their first answer was insufficient and will elaborate or fabricate different answers in the hope that that will satisfy the interviewer (Underwager and

Wakefield, 1990). This is because they consider that the adult who is interviewing them has superior knowledge about the subject and the reason that questions are repeated is because they (the interviewee) got the answer wrong the first time. In fact, at one point Mr Y said 'I'm not lying' (p. 38) in response to the repeated question 'how did you get into bed with Ms X'.

Specific examples of problematic questioning
Acquiescing to leading questions
In general, the interviewer avoids using leading questions. There are two potentially significant exceptions to this. The first is when he asks about the issue of consent, or permission to have sex. He has already indicated that the answer to this question is important: 'what's the most important thing when you are talking about sex, what's the most important thing, okay, what would you say the most important thing is?' (p. 20), and he himself later gives the answer: 'That's right, permission again and that's one of the main ingredients of all this isn't it, permission.' (p. 20)

The second example of what could be considered to be a leading question is during the section of the interview immediately before Mr Y's admission that he forced Ms X to have sex with him. The interviewer summarizes what Mr Y has just said as follows (p. 47): 'You see what I'm worried about is what you're saying is that you're dreaming of touching her private parts and *then you go into her room and that's what ends up happening.*' (emphasis added). The italicized part has not actually been disclosed by Mr Y at this point, but shortly afterwards he admits 'cos I touched Ms X's [inaudible] again.' The use of the word 'again' raises the possibility that sexual activity *may* have occurred previously. In fact earlier in his statement Mr Y states that 'Ms X was the first' in response to the question 'who touched who first?' (p. 40).

Confabulation
It is suggested that this is more likely to occur when an interviewee is placed under pressure to remember an event. However, the experience of 'pressure' is a subjective one and for some individuals the situation of being interviewed about an alleged offence may be sufficiently stressful to create the potential for confabulation. There are a number of instances during the interview with Mr Y where he changes his answers to questions. A relatively trivial example is in relation to what time he went to bed on the night of the alleged offence (pp. 22–23):

Interviewer:	What time do they put you to bed, do you know that?
Mr Y:	Eleven o' clock.

Interviewer:	I think you said eleven o'clock before.
Mr Y:	No, nine o'clock.

Compounding an original error
It is difficult to assess whether this has actually occurred during the interview because we do not know which parts of the interview are correct and which parts are not. There are many examples of statements which are made and then contradicted later. This may or may not be a product of the interviewer compounding an original error to create a more coherent, but incorrect, narrative.

Overriding clarifications and upgrading of responses
On a number of occasions the interviewer summarizes a sequence of events reported by Mr Y. On some occasions several prompts and repeated questions were required in order to extract this narrative. Therefore, it may be possible that the summary is an inaccurate clarification of what actually happened. For example, on page 28 the interviewer summarizes: 'Remind you where we are, gone to bed, you said you got up to get a coffee, you went to the toilet'. This account differs from the one given by Mr Y later, in which he reports that he was having a dream about Ms X and that was what prompted him to get up and go to her room. We do not know which account is the correct version of events, although it is important to note that the latter was proffered with much less prompting than the former.

Relevant but inconvenient fragment ignored
This is particularly evident in relation to other people who Mr Y states were present during the time of the offence, but whose possible involvement is never explored. For example, on the night in question Mr Y states that 'James wake me up and middle of the night' (p. 30) but the interviewer ignores this and continues 'when you go to the living room' without questioning who James is or why he woke Mr Y up. Other aspects of the testimony that are again ignored include: when asked what Ms X said to Mr Y, he replies 'you don't need that no age common sense authority' (p. 48), but the interviewer only picks up on the next statement 'I am sorry to Ms X'.

Cycles of 'don't know' to line of questioning
Rather than saying 'I don't know', Mr Y tends to convey an inability or unwillingness to answer a question by saying nothing. For example, on pp. 34–35.

Interviewer:	Why did you go to her room though?
Mr Y:	*Pause*

Interviewer:	Can we go back, had you spoken to Ms X that night before?
Mr Y:	*Pause*
Interviewer:	What we're going to talk about now is what happened in that bedroom, right.
Mr Y:	Yeah.
Interviewer:	What we want to know is what happened in that bedroom, right.
Mr Y:	Yeah.
Interviewer:	Cause that's the important bit isn't it?
Mr Y:	Yeah it is.
Interviewer:	But why did you go there?
Mr Y:	Cause there was no staff in.

This is an interesting illustration of the fact that people with learning disabilities have problems answering questions that deal with abstract concepts, such as intention. The interviewer is asking about Mr Y's motive for going into Ms X's room. But the answer that is given is about what *allowed* Mr Y to go into her room, which is the fact that no staff were on duty to stop him.

Tendency to say 'yes' rather than 'no'
Again, there are several examples of this throughout the interview. Notably, during the discussion on permission, there is the following exchange (p. 21):

Interviewer:	Is that word permission very important?
Mr Y:	It is.
Interviewer:	Would you say so, would you say it's important?
Mr Y:	Yes.

This is potentially significant in that it may suggest that Mr Y does not in fact fully understand the issue of consent and does not realize its importance in relation to the alleged offence.

Summary of opinion

Having conducted the analysis of the interviews with Mr Y, it seemed that there were a number of potential problems with his account in general, and with his admission in particular. Firstly, Mr Y showed no evidence of having understood the police caution on the basis that he was unable to demonstrate even basic comprehension of the main constituent parts of the caution, and simply repeated words verbatim. Throughout the interview, there were a number of examples of the use of question types that have been found by research to elicit errors in testimony from people with learning difficulties. There were a number of inconsistencies within Mr Y's account – both in relation to whether consent was given by Ms X for sexual activity to occur, and as to who initiated the contact. There were also several significant aspects of his account that were ignored by the police officer, leading to the possibility that alternative hypotheses about the nature of any sexual activity that may have occurred were not fully elaborated.

Conclusions

This chapter has demonstrated an approach to conducting psychological analysis of interviews that is informed by research. The literature on interviewing in general, and on the issues pertaining to interviewing of people with learning difficulties in particular, was applied to the material in order to reach conclusions about the veracity of the testimony. In this case the accounts of both the defendant and the complainant were found to contain significant indicators of unreliability; the questioning styles of the interviewers were implicated in both cases. This highlights the need for proper training specifically in relation to the interviewing of people with learning difficulties. At the time that this case occurred, the only guidelines that were available were in the form of the Memorandum of Good Practice relating to the interviewing of children (Home Office and Department of Health, 1992). However, this did not adequately cater for people with learning difficulties, and subsequently a new memorandum (Home Office and Department of Health, 2002) has been developed.

People with learning difficulties are at proportionately greater risk of abuse (Nield et al., 2003), perhaps because of a belief in lesser accessibility to the recourse of justice (Westcott and Jones, 1997). The Youth and Criminal Evidence Act 1999 was brought in to attempt to redress this imbalance in perceived inaccessibility to those most vulnerable members of society.

Clarke and Milne (2001) found that police officers' skills were worse when interviewing witnesses and victims than when interviewing suspects, and in part this report reached the same conclusion. This may have been a reflection of the corresponding levels of learning disability by the defendant and complainant (precise IQ measures were not available); however, one particularly worrying incident occurred during the interviewing of Ms X where the police officer left the room saying that she needed to check with someone what further questions she should ask of the complainant. This suggests deficiencies in the training of this interviewer that may in part have contributed to the inability to prosecute this case. The outcome of this particular case was that the court held that the prosecution had provided no evidence.

References

Canter, D. and Alison, L. (1999) *Criminal Detection and the Psychology of Crime*. Ashgate: Dartmouth.

Ceci, S.J. and Bruck, M. (1995) *Jeopardy in the Courtroom: A scientific analysis of children's testimony*. Washington, DC: American Psychological Association.

Clare, I. and Gudjonsson, G.H. (1992) 'Devising and piloting a new "Notice to Detained Persons"'. *Royal Commision on Criminal Justice*. London: HMSO.

Clare, I. and Gudjonsson, G.H. (1993)' Interrogative suggestibility, confabulation, and acquiescence in people with mild learning disabilities (mental handicap): Implications for reliability during police interrogations', *British Journal of Clinical Psychology*, 32: 295–301.

Clarke, C. and Milne, R. (2001) *National evaluation of the PEACE investigative interviewing course*. Police Research Award Scheme. London: Home Office.

Esplin, P.W., Boychuk, T. and Raskin, D.C. (1988) *A field validity study of criteria based content analysis of children's statements in sexual abuse cases*. Paper presented at the NATO Advanced Study Institute on Credibility Assessment, Maratea, Italy.

Fielding, N. (1999) 'Social science perspectives on the analysis of investigative interviews', in D. Canter and L.J. Alison (eds), *Profiling in Policy and Practice*. Ashgate: Dartmouth.

Fielding, N. and Conroy, S. (1992) 'Interviewing child victims: police and social work investigations of child sexual abuse', *Sociology*, 26 (1): 103–24.

Gudjonsson, G.H. and Haward, L.R.C. (1998) *Forensic Psychology: A guide to practice*. London: Routledge.

Gudjonsson, G.H. and MacKeith, J.A.C. (1988) 'Retracted confessions: Legal, psychological and psychiatric aspects', *Medicine, Science and the Law*, 30: 329–35.

Home Office and Department of Health (1992) *Memorandum of good practice on video recorded interviews with child witnesses for criminal proceedings*. London: HMSO.

Home Office and Department of Health (2002) *Achieving Best Evidence: Guidance for vulnerable or intimidated witnesses, including children*. London: HMSO.

Horowitz, S. (1998) 'Reliability of criteria-based content analysis of child witness statements: A response to Tully', *Legal and Criminological Psychology*, 3: 189–92.

Kebbell, M.R. and Hatton, C. (1999) 'People with mental retardation as witnesses in court', *Mental Retardation*, 3: 179–87.

Lamb, M.E. (1998) 'Mea culpa but caveat emptor: Response to Tully', *Legal and Criminological Psychology*, 3: 193–94.

Milne, R. and Bull, R. (1995) *Children with mild learning disability: the cognitive interview and suggestibility*. Paper presented to the Fifth European Conference on Psychology and Law, Budapest, Hungary.

Milne, R., Clare, I. and Bull, R. (1996) *How effective is the cognitive interview as an investigative tool for use with adults with mild intellectual disabilities (mental retardation)*. Paper presented to the Sixth European Conference on Psychology and Law, Siena, Italy.

Nield, R., Milne, R., Bull, R. and Marlow, K. (2003) 'The Youth Justice and Criminal Evidence Act 1999 and the interviewing of vulnerable groups: practitioner's perspective', *Legal and Criminological Psychology*, 8: 223–28.

Ormerod, D.C. (1996) 'The evidential implications of psychological profiling', *Criminal Law Review*, 92: 863–77.

Parker, A.D. and Brown, J. (2000) 'Detection of deception: Statement Validity Analysis as a means of determining truthfulness or falsity of rape allegations', *Legal and Criminological Psychology*, 5: 237–59.

Ruby, C.L. and Brigham, J.C. (1997) 'The usefulness of criteria-based content analysis technique in distinguishing between truthfulness and fabricated allegations: A critical review', *Psychology, Public Policy and Law*, 3: 705–37.

Sapir, A. (1987) *Scientific Content Analysis (SCAN)*. Phoenix Arizona: Laboratory of Scientific Interrogation.

Shaw, J.A. and Budd, E. (1982) 'Determinants of acquiescence and naysaying of mentally retarded persons', *American Journal of Mental Deficiency*, 87: 108–10.

Steller, M. and Kohnken, G. (1989) 'Criteria-based statement analysis', in D. Raskin (ed.), *Psychological Methods in Criminal Investigation and Evidence* (pp. 217–45). New York: Springer.

Tully, B. (1985) Special Care Questioning. *FBI Law Enforcement Bulletin*, November, pp. 9–15.

Tully, B. (1998) 'Reliability criteria based content analysis of child witness statements: Cohen's kappa doesn't matter', *Legal and Criminological Psychology*, 3: 183–88.

Tully, B. and Cahill, D. (1984) *Police interviewing of the mentally handicapped: An experimental study*. The Police Foundation:London.

Tully, B. and Fritzon, K. (1996). *Resource Manual of Specialised Investigative Interviewing*. Psychologists at Law Group, London.

Tully, B. and Tam Kam-Oi (1988). 'Helping the police with their inquiries: the development of special care questioning techniques', *Children and Society*, 1(3): 187–97.

Underwager, R. and Wakefield, H. (1990) *The Real World of Child Interrogations*. Springfield Il: Charles C. Thomas.

Undeutsch, U. (1982) 'Statement reality analysis', in A. Trankell (ed.), *Reconstructing the Past: the role of psychologists in criminal trials* (pp. 27–56). Deventer: Kluwer.

Westcott, H. and Jones, J. (1997) *Perspectives on the memorandum: Police, practice and research in investigative interviewing*. Aldershot: Arena.

Appendix: Statement Validity Checklist

(from Steller and Kohnken, 1989)

General characteristics
1.   Logical structure
2.   Unstructured production
3.   Quantity of details

Specific contents
4.   Contextual embedding
5.   Descriptions of interactions
6.   Reproduction of conversations
7.   Unexpected complications during the incident

Peculiarities of content
8.   Unusual details
9.   Superfluous details
10. Accurately reported details misunderstood
11. Related external associations
12. Accounts of subjective mental state
13. Attribution of perpetrator's mental state

Motivation-related contents
14. Spontaneous correction
15. Admitting lack of memory
16. Raising doubts about one's own testimony
17. Self-deprecation
18. Pardoning the perpetrator

Offence-specific elements
19. Details characteristic of the offence

Chapter 12

Malingering or memory loss in a major collision investigation: reconstructing accounts of suspects, victims and witnesses

Laurence Alison

Introduction

This chapter outlines many of the problems alluded to in Chapter 11. These include the difficulty in unequivocally stating whether statements are true or false, developing clear justifications for claims made about the nature of statements and the need to examine multiple aspects of a narrative account. The present case involves the defendant's controversial assertion that, subsequent to stealing and crashing a car (resulting in the death of a passenger) he retained no memory for the event. The report details the case study notes, the background literature on memory for accidents and the literature on malingering. Throughout, the author pays special attention to the need for further research in malingering and statement validation and highlights how current research is rather limited in helping form expert opinion.

Instructions

The following report has been prepared under the direction of Sergeant McLaughlin, X, Collision Investigation Unit, X Police. I have been asked to assess whether or not the claim of memory loss in a major accident of this type is probable or not. In preparing the report I have been provided with the following details:

- Copy of the transcript of the interview from 4 March 1997.
- Copy of the transcripts from the interview 11 June 1997.
- Copy of the relevant audiotapes.
- Copy of the scale plan/map of location completed by accident investigator.
- Copy of report prepared by Dr Rahanish.

I have not interviewed Mr Stanley or anyone else involved as witnesses or victims involved in this case and my report has been prepared after inspecting the written and photographic evidence alone.

COMMENT BOX:

Sometimes it is possible to interview relevant parties (though there are often legal restrictions – see Chapter 6) but one has to question the utility of such a decision. In this case it was important to concentrate on the evidence at hand and the range of accounts given both by the defendant and the other relevant witnesses. What one is trying to do is gain as comprehensive a picture as possible from the different perspectives of the relevant parties. If the information is consistent across all parties, except the defendant's, one then moves on to explore whether there should be anything unique about this account. One then moves on to consider organic damage and then, if this can be ruled out, a range of possible psychological explanations. This report highlights how evaluation of these claims often becomes a process of elimination of competing hypotheses. It is therefore important to consider all the plausible, legitimate reasons why one might forget such an event.

Background to the Report

The background to this case is well documented in the interviews listed above. Briefly, however, the case involves the following key figures:

- David Matthew Stanley (hereafter DMS)
- Travis Bingley (hereafter TB)
- Ray Bingley (hereafter RB)
- Allan Bingley (hereafter AB)
- Narinder (DMS's cousin)

I understand that the incident involved a collision at approximately 24.10 on X Road in Y. The collision involved three cars: a Ford Focus (driven by the defendant, with RB and AB as passengers), a Citroen hatchback and a

Ford Ka. I understand from a discussion with Sergeant McLaughlin that AB is now dead and RB has very serious head injuries. I also understand that the occupants of the Ford Ka have suffered serious injuries. In the interview, reference is made to the statements of PC Donald and PC Hughes, in which discussion focuses upon both officers seeing a vehicle travelling at speed at approximately 60mph. They follow this car and catch up with it after its collision on the bridge over the River Floch. PC Hughes describes seeing someone trying to slide himself or herself out of the wreckage of the car … sliding from the direction of the driver's seat. He goes on to explain how he assisted a man, who he recognized as DMS from the wreckage. PC Hughes reports assisting DMS to the pavement at which point PC Hughes heard the sound of a baby. PC Hughes goes on to report that, 'I instinctively let go of Stanley and ran over to the child'. DMS then exits the scene. DMS reports several periods of extensive memory loss for many features of this incident. He claims almost complete amnesia from the period at which he left TB's until waking up in the car, though he can't remember whether he was driving or not. One of the few points on which he is adamant and claims very confident memory is that he was not assisted out of the car by PC Hughes.

The following report considers these claims for amnesia. Broadly, DMS appears to be claiming retrograde amnesia. It is unclear what the basis is for the claim on DMS's part, though certain aspects of the account appear to suggest that he thinks it may have arisen as a function of being knocked out by the impact of the crash.

In order to assist me in evaluating these claims I have drawn upon the following literature: definitions of the various forms of amnesia and their respective origin; explanations for forgetting; research on the extent to which accidents are forgotten; and simulated amnesia and malingering.

COMMENT BOX

In constructing an argument and evaluation, one must first introduce the range of possibilities that exist. It is important to let the reader understand as early as possible in the report the range of literature that one is intending to draw upon. It illustrates the fact that the author has considered the most plausible reasons for impaired memory and squarely places the onus on other, potential expert witnesses to validate these competing hypotheses if they are being proposed by the defence/prosecution. Because it is crucial that one does not take sides, it is often very helpful to develop a protagorean framework in which one gives initial emphasis to the counsel that one is *not* providing expertise for. Occasionally, this results in reports that serve the side one is employed by rather poorly but one must

---

remember that such reports are impartial and objective and are not intended to promote one side or the other. It also demonstrates that the author is impartial and is merely pointing out a range of plausible explanations. I have to confess that I have seen several reports (particularly in the area of controversial claims of memory recovery) where it seems apparent that the expert has a particular, preconceived view of the validity of the claim and does very little to consider the competing hypothesis.

I The claim of forgetting[1]

In the claim itself, DMS states that he cannot remember *any* central features of the accident other than the fact that he was not assisted out of the driving seat by a police officer. Other central, forgotten features include being unable to remember where he, RB and AB were going, what they hit, at what speed, who was driving, or, indeed, that there was even an accident. He simply remembers leaving TB's and then waking up in the car after the accident. At this point he is confident and adamant that he was *not* assisted out of the driving seat by a police officer, even though he is uncertain as to the details of how he exited the vehicle. Subsequent to leaving the car, he remembers walking off and being at the chip shop (although there is even some uncertainty at this latter point). He says that he cannot remember which way he went, how he got to the bin shed in the morning or how his shoes got wet. There are, therefore, a number of competing hypotheses to explain this apparent lack of memory:

(i)   Organic amnesia – either through head injury or drug use.
(ii) Functional amnesia – 'psychogenic amnesia' caused by the psychological trauma, normal features of forgetting of accidents and so on.
(iii) Simulated amnesia – i.e. DMS is 'faking' not remembering.
(iv) A mixture of the above – i.e. some features genuinely cannot be well remembered, while those that can are being faked as being forgotten.

COMMENT BOX
On reflection, I feel that this section would have been rather better served either embedding quotes from interviews with the defendant in the text or cross-referring the reader to verbatim quotes in an Appendix. Otherwise, one has to assume either that the reader takes these comments about what the defendant said on trust, or one must go back to the original documents. Additionally, if one were called to give evidence, the author might be expected (quite correctly) to

provide evidence for claims such as 'DMS states that he cannot remember *any* central features ...' One is always striving for clarity and clear justification for claims, and this section would have been far better served by cross-referring to the original statements.

In order to inform the relevant parties and to enable them to make a decision as to which of these is the most plausible hypothesis, I have provided an overview of these related issues within the context of the current case. Thus, this report should be viewed as a device to provide information on issues such as amnesia, memory (especially for accidents) and simulated amnesia and deception. It may, therefore be useful to delineate the various definitions of these issues.

2 Classifications of amnesia: organic and functional

2.1 Organic amnesia

The first broad classification of amnesia is based on whether it is of organic or functional origin. Organic amnesia is a form of pathological forgetting produced by damage to the brain. It is the most intensively studied form and is commonly referred to as the 'amnesic syndrome', a chronic debilitating loss of memory that exists alongside normal intellectual functioning. Examples of this condition are Korsakoff's, closed head injury, encephalitis, damage to the medial temporal region, ruptured aneurysms of the anterior communicating artery and tumours of the third ventricle. Within these conditions there are two discernable classes: *anterograde* (forgetting of facts *after* the onset of the disease or neurological trauma) and *retrograde* amnesia (forgetting of facts that occurred *before* the critical incident).

One possibility then is that DMS has developed some form of organic induced amnesia, either as product of the crash or of alcohol or other drug-related abuse. From the evidence I have been given, which includes a report from Dr Rahanish, there appears to be no accident-induced brain injury, though this must be formally ruled out as an explanation. The second possibility is alcohol-induced amnesia and there is some evidence to suggest that DMS had been drinking quite heavily. Additionally, it is important to establish whether he is a very heavy drinker generally (or if he uses other drugs) since chronic abuse can result in blackouts. Based on Dr Rahanish's report and from DMS's own statements, he does not appear to be a chronic drug abuser. Additionally, DMS denies being drunk on the night in question and he claims to only have had one pint. However, even moderate levels of alcohol can produce memory deficits but not generally of the kind that would produce extensive amnesia of the central features of something as consequential as a major accident (i.e. DMS claims that he doesn't know who was driving, or even that the accident itself occurred). It may be useful to get additional advice on the probability of a moderate level of alcohol as causing such extensive amnesia since I do not have specialized knowledge of the psychopharmacological effects of precise levels of alcohol consumption on memory. In a brief discussion with my colleague Dr Jon Cole[2] (who is an expert on the psychopharmacological effects of drug abuse) regarding the broad details of the claim (i.e. consider an individual has consumed between one and three pints, no other drug abuse at the time and in consideration of an individual that drinks approximately 20 pints on average per week) Dr Cole stated that extensive *en bloc* amnesia in which very central features of an event were entirely forgotten would be highly improbable. However, if the enquiry team seek further clarification on this point I can recommend Prof. Peter Booth, a consultant in clinical psychology at the Windsor Clinic, University Hospital Aintree, Longmoor Lane, Liverpool, L9 7AL, who has very extensive experience of working with individuals who have abused alcohol.

COMMENT BOX

It is inevitable in such complex cases that one will not have the necessary knowledge to consider all relevant aspects of a case. I have often been in the position where the 'opposing' counsel will be keen, in cross-examination, to refer to such claims of ignorance and use these to try and unsettle the expert in the stand and to try and convey to a jury that the expert does not know what s/he is talking about. However, in my experience, it is preferable to be honest and readily identify those areas with which one is not familiar in the very first contact with counsel. In contrast, if the expert finds him/herself trying to defend an area about which they know very little, the cross-examination can far more readily throw the rest of the report into question. I find it extremely useful to draw upon the resources of my colleagues (and to do the same for them) as in this example. It then falls upon the courts to consider whether additional psychological services are required. In such instances it is important to give the relevant parties the addresses and contact numbers of the relevant individuals.

2.2 Functional amnesia

2.2.1 The controversy surrounding functional amnesia

Functional amnesia occurs in the absence of detectable brain injury. In such cases, instances of anterograde amnesia are very rare. In almost all cases of functional amnesia, the forgetting is associated with retrograde amnesia. Some researchers claim that this can entail a loss of personal identity and autobiographical memories, and can include a fugue state in which the patient is unaware of the memory loss. One suggestion is that traumas can induce a limited functional retrograde amnesia – i.e. forgetting of a specific episode. However, there is great controversy surrounding these issues, with some researchers strongly resisting the notion that the central features of traumatic events are forgotten, while other researchers suggest that forgetting of such episodes can happen and is, in fact, quite common (Brewin and Andrews, 1998).

In support of the sceptical viewpoint, many neurobiological findings suggest that emotionally arousing learning tasks generate durable memories and these may explain the clinical observation that patients with post-traumatic stress disorder (PTSD) suffer from persistent and highly vivid memories (Bernsten, 2001). Brown and Kulik (1977) propose that a special neurobiological encoding mechanism is triggered by highly surprising and consequential events. This mechanism establishes vivid memories of the context in which the news was received. The crucial factor is not necessarily the negative or positive features of an event (i.e. whether it was highly aversive or highly pleasurable) but rather, the consequentiality of the event, its distinctiveness and the personal involvement of the individual involved. In this view, an event such as a car crash, entailing loss of life and in which the individual asked to remember the event suffered no organic damage and was interviewed shortly afterwards, DMS should be able to remember whether he was driving or not since the event would be seen as highly consequential, distinctive and personal.

However, according to van der Kolk and Fisler (1995) impairment of memories is more marked shortly after a traumatic experience. They argue that memories improve over time. This is because, shortly after the traumatic event, the individual engages in a process of 'effortful forgetting'. Effortful forgetting can include techniques such as distraction (thinking about other things) and thought-blocking processes (refusing to process recollections) in order to help forget the incident. Thus, forgetting is related to the amount of effort employed to suppress the aversive event. Over time, such defence mechanisms are loosened and the memory impairment diminishes. This is contrary to the way forgetting has been found to occur in ordinary autobiographical memory, because recently remembered events are generally remembered rather better than more distant ones.

Paradoxically, then, extreme stress is cited as an explanation both for forgetting and remembering. Van der Kolk and Fisler (1995) have sought to propose a rationale to resolve this paradox. They suggest that trauma victims often remember the *affect* surrounding an event plus sensory information (e.g. sights, sounds, etc.) in great detail but may be unable to fully articulate what occurred during the event. The individual may later re-experience sensory-laden features (i.e. implicit memories) but declarative memory (essentially, what happened) is often impoverished, fragmented and disorganized. In summary, there remains extensive debate surrounding certain issues in forgetting trauma, with some authors suggesting it is improbable, others suggesting that it can be understood within conventional models of memory, and others asserting that trauma-induced forgetting entails a particular cognitive process, distinct from normal processes of forgetting. Much of this controversy has centred on claims of child sexual abuse (Brewin and Andrews, 1998, Lindsay and Read, 1995), while other research has focused on traumas caused by combat, disasters and accidents.

COMMENT BOX

There are few areas quite so controversial as the 'recovered memory/ false memory, post memory after trauma debate'. I think it is important to reveal to the police, courts and the jury that one is dealing with an area that generates intense disagreement and, not infrequently, emotionally driven arguments and affiliations. One is then alerting the relevant parties to the potential biases that may exist within one's own report (and others), thereby leaving the judgement as to whether the experts or other parties' interests and claims are driven by purely objective reasons or not.

---

3 Remembering accidents

Evidence from a range of studies on potentially traumatic events such as child sexual abuse, disasters, victims of concentration camps and major accidents strongly suggests that individuals do not easily forget accidents. In their review of a number of studies in these areas Pope *et al.* (1998) indicated that none of the individuals forgot that such events occurred. However, according to some researchers, in some cases where injuries were serious, it is possible that some forms of traumatic amnesia were involved in the forgetting (Blanchard and Hickling, 1997). Surveys of self-reported accidents suggest that when respondents are asked to recall accidents at a pre-specified period some time later, they forget about one-third of their road accidents per year. The difference in these findings may well relate to seriousness and the delay between the accident and the request to recall it. It may be quite easy to forget a 'prang' a year later, but rather more difficult to forget a head-on collision that occurred the day before. Loftus (1993) reports how 14% of those involved in injurious accidents did not remember the event one year later. However, in general, the more serious an accident, the more likely it is to be remembered; and the more recently the individual involved is questioned about the event, the less likely they are to have forgotten it. For example, Maycock researched self-reported accidents (Maycock and Lester, 1995; Maycock et al., 1991) and established that when accidents are recalled over a three-year period, more accidents are reported in recent parts of those periods than those longer ago. They established that up to 30% of accidents are forgotten each year. This forgetting rate declines to 18% for accidents involving injuries (a figure comparable to the 14% in the study by Loftus) and they do not report any examples of an individual forgetting an accident one day later.

In a more recent study Chapman and Underwood (2000) used self-report measures for accidents. They asked 80 qualified drivers (50 newly qualified and 30 experienced) to record journey details on a micro-cassette recorder and established that drivers displayed very high levels of forgetting for near accidents, with 80% of near accidents being forgotten in just two weeks. In contrast, there was no evidence that participants forgot actual accidents. The authors state, 'Observing forgetting of actual accidents over two weeks would have seemed highly unlikely' (p. 40). This perhaps demonstrates how, through habitual processes and repetitive near-misses, such information is, relative to the more consequential experience of an actual accident, easily forgotten and how poor driving and dangerousness on the roads are severely underestimated by most people. Moreover, even in near-misses, the authors point out that their research does not imply that the memory was completely inaccessible. With the provision of cues it is possible that participants would be able to recall such incidents.

Thus, according to this research and if organic damage can be ruled out, it would be highly unusual for an individual to forget an actual collision, that, presumably, would hold great significance and in which the individual was questioned about the event a day later. Further, if one were to assume that DMS has forgotten aspects of the event because of arousal or stress, which could have impaired memory, generally memory is impaired in terms of exact details, not in terms of whether the event itself happened at all. For example, Chapman and Underwood state, 'Where impairments for detail information are found, such impairments may only be present for aspects of the event that were not central to the plot or gist of the event' (p. 40). Thus, if precise recall cues were used (i.e. prompts), these may enhance memory. Despite being in an actual accident, involving a high-speed chase that ultimately proved fatal for a child and that caused very significant injuries to a number of individuals (and so, presumably, would be highly consequential) and despite being prompted throughout and being given very many possible recall cues by the interviewers, DMS maintains that he cannot remember the key features of this event. For example:

Q: *Did you know you'd been in an accident?*
A: *I don't think I did.*
Q: *Did you know where you were?*
A: *No, I didn't even know where I was.*

Q: *You say you came to in the Ford Focus is that right?*
A: *Yeah.*
Q: *Where were you in the car at that time?*
A: *I am not too sure where I was in there. I just remember getting out of it. I don't know where I was in the car.*

Further cues include showing DMS CCTV footage (i.e. the car going through a red light), reminding him of the positioning of the cars post-accident, of the scene, of other witness accounts, etc. All fail to remind him of any of the central events.

COMMENT BOX

Once one has outlined the central, concluding arguments about the case in the introduction, one travels from the broad to the particular. In this case, from brain damage, remembering (in general) and forgetting, controversial claims of memory recovery and then memory for accidents. This allows the 'lay' reader to quickly develop some basic knowledge of the area and to place specific events in context.

---

4 PTSD and remembering accidents

Another possibility is that DMS is suffering from post-traumatic stress disorder (PTSD) and that memory impairment may be due, in part, to certain dissociative features associated with PTSD. Murray *et al.* (2002) have recently published a study on these issues. They were able to interview 27 participants (21 men, 6 women) (in-patient sample) and use a questionnaire on 176 out-patients involved in serious accidents in which organic damage could be ruled out as an explanation for any memory impairment. Participants completed the Posttraumatic Diagnostic Scale (PDS; Foa et al., 1997) and the State Dissociation Questionnaire (SDQ) measuring dissociative experiences such as de-realization, depersonalization, detachment, altered time sense and reduction of awareness in surroundings (Murray, 1997). The study indicated that persistent dissociation was a stronger predictor of chronic PTSD than dissociation during the accident. Thus, dissociative experiences held persistently after the accident lead to an increased risk of PTSD. By way of an explanation of this poor prognosis, Murray et al. refer to Harvey and Bryant's (1998) finding that survivors of road accidents with acute stress disorder gave more disorganized trauma narratives than those without, and explain that worse outcomes may come as a result of the individual being unable to integrate the events as part of the recovery process. Thus, in DMS's case, with such widespread amnesia for the event, one might expect strong indicators of PTSD. Of course, in order to fully explore this possibility DMS would have to be clinically diagnosed. DMS states that he has not seen his doctor and has never before suffered blackouts. He admits he has a bad memory usually and that the accident would have made his memory worse. He also says that he has had no medical problems before or since the crash.

5 Simulated amnesia

Several studies have established that simulating amnesia for a crime is a fairly popular method for denying culpability for an offence. For example, Guttmacher (1955) and Leitch (1948) found that just over 30% of convicted murderers claimed that they could not remember their crimes and O'Connell (1960) reported a 40% incidence of limited amnesia in a homicide sample. Bradford and Smith (1979) reported an incidence rate of 65% of individuals claiming amnesia in homicide cases. In almost all of their cases of claimed amnesia by accused murderers submitted to polygraph tests or sodium amytal tests, the claims were not supported. In 60% of these cases amnesia was limited to the crime itself; in other instances it ranged from 30 minutes to 24 hours preceding the crime. Almost all subjects claimed either patchy or hazy amnesia and only one described a complete memory blackout. In comparison with those who did not claim memory loss, the amnesia group was characterized by a higher frequency of alcohol use and emotional arousal at the time of the offence. Similar findings emerge in Parwatikar et al.'s (1985) study. Individuals who claimed amnesia (compared with those who confessed) were more frequently intoxicated or on other drugs at the time of the offence and showed higher levels of depression, hysteria and hypochondriasis on pre-trial Minnesota Multiphasic Personality Inventory (MMPI) evaluations. Moreover, malingered amnesics tended to have higher IQ scores than individuals classified as genuine amnesics. Additionally, the number of earlier arrests for malingerers was higher compared with those who had confessed or who were classified as genuinely amnesic. According to Parwatikar *et al.* this demonstrates that simulated amnesia may increase with increased experience of the criminal justice system. They also suggest that in cases where the individual has no neurotic features, was intoxicated at the time of the offence and claimed amnesia, this may lend additional weight to the suggestion that the claim might be fake.

It should be noted that claims of amnesia are relatively less frequent in offences other than homicide. For example, Taylor and Kopelman (1984) observed amnesia in only 8% of 120 individuals convicted for violent crimes other than homicide and no evidence of amnesia in individuals convicted for non-violent crimes. However, Kennedy and Neville (1957) established that patients who eventually admitted malingering had committed various petty offences and Berrington *et al.* (1956) found that 14 of their 37 patients who presented with functional retrograde amnesia were 'escaping from justice'.

5.1 Distinguishing between simulated and genuine amnesia

Unfortunately, there remains no clear way of distinguishing between genuine and fake claims of amnesia. However, several researchers have suggested that repeated questioning of the accused may yield useful information about the consistency of amnesia and when many inconsistencies emerge, there might be reason to be sceptical of the claim. Further, the belief is that limited amnesia with sudden onset and termination should be viewed with more caution than amnesia that is gradual and patchy and that while genuine amnesia will be defined by its internal consistency, fake amnesia may be marked by inconsistencies and contradictions on repeated interviewing (Power, 1977; Bradford and Smith, 1979; Price and Terhune, 1919; Sadoff 1974). However, Sisler and Penner (1975) found that assessed length of retrograde amnesia fluctuates considerably across test sessions and, thus, caution must be observed in being too definitive about whether a claim is true or false based on inconsistencies.

Schacter (1986) has suggested that one possible means of discrimination might involve 'feeling-of-knowing' ratings. Feeling of knowing refers to the subjective conviction that one *could* retrieve a to-be-recalled item if one were given sufficient useful hints or cues. For example, individuals frequently report that they could recognize previously unrecalled events if they were given enough cues (e.g. Schacter, 1983; Schacter and Worling, 1985). In these experiments, Schacter tested feeling-of-knowing ratings between genuine and simulated amnesic claims. Participants were asked to rate the likelihood that they could recall the forgotten event if they were given more time to remember it and that they might remember the event in the presence of various hints or cues. On the latter question, simulators consistently provided lower feeling-of-knowing ratings than did genuinely forgetful participants. Thus, while genuine amnesic cases were marked by the claim that hints would be useful, simulators consistently claimed that such hints would be less likely to provide assistance. Schacter suggests that one reason for this effect may lie in individuals' beliefs about memory. When simulating, participants may draw upon subjective notions of forgetting and erroneously assume that a genuine participant would state that such cues would be most unlikely to assist recall. This phenomenon has not been restricted to amnesia for criminal events, and other studies have demonstrated its effectiveness in relation to faking scores on the MMPI (Anthony, 1976; Kroger and Turnbull, 1975) neuropsychological assessment (Lezak, 1983) and faking mental illness (Resnick, 1984).

A further complexity is that simulating amnesia may lead to genuine subsequent forgetfulness (Christianson and Bylin, 1999). In their experiment, Christianson and Bylin were able to demonstrate that participants who were asked to simulate subsequently had genuine problems recalling details of the original memory representation.

COMMENT BOX

One has to be extremely careful that one does not convey the idea that one is commenting on the particular defendant's credibility, although one may be asked by counsel quite directly to do so. As outlined in the introductory chapter, the courts work on the basis of the particular, psychologists on the basis of the general. This fundamental difference can sometimes be forgotten and I have often been in situations where counsel (or the police) will try to extract black-and-white arguments and definitive answers about the case at hand. I was pleased to not have this pressure imposed on me in this case and was able to talk in terms of generalities without being pushed into definitive statements about the defendant (which is, of course, a judgement reserved for the jury).

---

6 Select features remembered and forgotten

Outlined in the timeline provided[3] and summarized in the tables below are the features of this incident that DMS states he claims to have

Table 12.1 Forgotten events prior to, during and post-accident, compared with other available evidence

Stages	Forgotten events	Other evidence
PRE-ACCIDENT	Where he was in the morning.	DMS in court.
	How DMS got to TB's.	In car.
	Where he intended to go.	?
DURING	Taking car.	Car was stolen.
	Whether or not he was driving the car.	He was driving the car.
	Being the only one left in the car.	He was only one left in car.
AFTER	Fleeing the scene.	Fled scene.
	Why he has wet clothes.	Ran through river.

Table 12.2 Remembered events prior to, during and post-accident, compared with other available evidence.

Stages	Remembered events	Other evidence
PRE-ACCIDENT	Did not drink at Narinder's	Drank at Narinder's.
	Not violent/argumentative at Narinder's.	Argued and was aggressive at Narinder's
	Had 1 pint in the pub.	Had 3 pints in the pub.
	Did not argue with landlord.	Did argue with landlord.
	Did not argue at TB's.	Argued with TB.
	Leaving TB's via the lift.	?
DURING	Nothing remembered after leaving TB's.	Taking car, driving at speed, crashing car.
AFTER	Waking up in car (though can't remember which seat he was in).	In driving seat.
	Not assisted by PC Hughes.	PC Hughes assists him from driver's seat.

remembered and those that he has claimed to forget. These are employed to illustrate how many of the features that are forgotten relate to potentially incriminating aspects of this particular incident and how many remembered events point to reducing the culpability of DMS.

The significant events[4] that reveal greater intent and culpability are forgotten (in court that morning, what the intention was in leaving the house, stealing a car, driving at speed, who was driving, fleeing the scene) and the events remembered reduce intent and culpability (wasn't drinking, arguing or aggressive prior to incident, not assisted from driving seat by PC Hughes). There does appear to be an extent to which the memory recall is somewhat selective.

COMMENT BOX

This may appear to be a very primitive way of evaluating the claim. However, in generating such reports one is often limited by the available research and the lack of clear, commonly agreed and empirically validated procedures (see introduction to this section). While frustrating for the reader, this proves more so for the psychologist. However, working on real cases does at least alert the psychologist to necessary areas of research while also throwing into sharp relief the current limitations of extant research. Neither CBCA nor any other form of coding procedure would have made as much sense as the simple resumé as tabulated above of what was and what was not remembered (see introductory session for further details of statement validation and CBCA). Further, in striving for clarity one often ends up generating devices that relate very directly to common sense and plausible arguments (albeit supported by the relevant attendant literature).

Summary and conclusions

Given that it is not possible to reliably discriminate genuine from simulated amnesia, it is inappropriate to give any unequivocal statement as to whether the claims for amnesia in this case are reliable or credible. However, there are many features of this case (if the amnesia is genuine and organic damage can unequivocally be ruled out) that would, based on the available evidence and the literature, make this an unusual amnesic claim if genuine. These are as follows:

(i)   Consequential events are generally very well remembered, especially if they are distinctive and personally involving. DMS claims he cannot remember an event that led to his friend and a number of other individuals being seriously injured and in which a child has died, and in which he was in the car driving at speed and which hit a bridge.

(ii)   Traumatic events are generally well remembered (at least in terms of central features).

(iii)   Car accidents are generally well remembered if an actual collision took place.

(iv) Cued recall normally facilitates memory (CCTV footage, cuing DMS into events surrounding the collision). These appear to have had no effect on DMS's recall.

(v) Recall is generally better shortly after an event (in this case one day after).

(vi) Genuine amnesiacs often report 'feeling-of-knowing' experiences. DMS does not indicate that any additional information would help him recall such events.

(vii) Central features of events are generally well remembered. All central features of this event are forgotten.

(viii) Many issues central to establishing culpability have been forgotten. In terms of the events remembered by DMS (many of which reduce DMS's culpability), there is much evidence to contradict his testimony. One must therefore consider the possibility that what has been forgotten *and* remembered is potentially selective and self-serving.

Notes

1   It is important first to highlight the independence of amnesia and automaticity, since it is often assumed that if one has suffered an amnesic episode the sufferer was acting automatically and without intent. Amnesia does not imply automaticity in functioning *at the time* of the event. As Hopwood and Snell (1933) pointed out many years ago, even if one were to assume that an individual was genuinely amnesic for an alleged crime and forget his/her entire past, it does not mean that they did not behave consciously and with intent *at the time of the offence.*

2   Dr Cole also works at the Psychology Dept at the University of Liverpool.

3   This has not been incorporated here because of the restrictions of confidentiality. However, readers should note that the preparation of such timelines in investigating controversial claims is often very useful for the author and the reader of the report.

4   These issues are obviously based only on other evidence, not objectively known facts.

References

Anthony, N. (1976) 'Malingering as role taking', *Journal of Clinical Psychology*, 32: 32–41.

Berrington, W.P., Liddell, D.W. and Foulds, G.A. (1956) 'A re-evaluation of the fugue', *Journal of Mental Science*, 102: 280–86.

Blanchard, E.B. and Hickling, E.J. (1997) *After the Crash: Assessment and Treatment of Motor Vehicle Accident Survivors*. Washington DC: American Psychological Association.

Bradford, J.W. and Smith, S.M. (1979) 'Amnesia and homicide: The Padola case and a study of thirty cases', *Bulletin of the American Academy of Psychiatry and Law*, 7: 219–31.

Brewin, C.R. and Andrews, B. (1998) 'Recovered memories of trauma: Phenomenology and cognitive mechanisms', *Clinical Psychology Review*, 18: 949–70.

Bernsten, D. (2001) 'Involuntary memories of emotional events: Do memories of traumas and extremely happy events differ?', *Applied Cognitive Psychology*, 15: 135–58.

Brown, R. and Kulik, J. (1977) 'Flashbulb memories', *Cognition*, 5: 73–99.

Chapman, P. and Underwood, G. (2000) 'Forgetting near-accidents: The roles of severity, culpability and experience in the poor recall of dangerous driving situations', *Applied Cognitive Psychology*, 14: 31–44

Christianson, S-A. and Bylin, S. (1999) 'Does simulating amnesia mediate genuine forgetting for a crime event?', *Applied Cognitive Psychology*, 13: 495–511.

Foa, E.B. *et al.* (1997) 'The validation of a self-report measure of post-traumatic stress disorder: The post-traumatic diagnostic scale', *Psychological Assessment*, 9: 445–51.

Guttmacher, M.S. (1955) *Psychiatry and the Law*. New York: Grune and Stratton.

Harvey, A.G. and Bryant, R.A. (1998) 'The relationship between acute stress disorder and post-traumatic stress disorder: A prospective evaluation of motor vehicle accident survivors', *Journal of Consulting and Clinical Psychology*, 66: 507–12.

Kennedy, A. and Neville, J. (1957) 'Sudden loss of memory', *British Medical Journal*, 2: 428–33.

Kroger, R.O. and Turnbull, W. (1975) 'Invalidity of validity scales: The case of the MMPI', *Journal of Consulting and Clinical Psychology*, 43: 48–55.

Leitch, A. (1948) 'Notes on amnesia in crime for the general practitioner', *Medical Press*, 219: 459–63.

Lindsay, D.S. and Read, J.D. (1995) ' "Memory work" and recovered memories of childhood sexual abuse: Scientific evidence and public, professional and personal issues', *Psychology, Public Policy and the Law*, 1: 846–908.

Loftus, E.F. (1993) 'The reality of repressed memories', *American Psychologist*, 48: 518–37.

Maycock, G. and Lester, J, (1995) 'Accident liability of car drivers: Follow up study', in G.B. Grayson (ed.), *Behavioural Research In Road Safety V*. Crowthorne, UK: Transport Research Laboratory.

Maycock, G., Lockwood, C.R. and Lester, J. (1991) *The Accident Liability of Car Drivers*. TRRL Research Report 315, Crowthorne, UK: Transport and Road Research Laboratory.

Murray, J., Ehlers, A. and Mayou, R.A. (2002) 'Dissociation and post traumatic stress disorder: Two prospective studies of road traffic accident survivors', *British Journal of Psychiatry*, 180: 363–68.

Murray, J. (1997) *The Role of Dissociation in Posttraumatic Stress Disorder.* D.Phil thesis, University of Oxford, Oxford, UK.

O'Connell, B.A. (1960) 'Amnesia and homicide', *British Journal of Delinquency*, 10: 262–76.

Parwatikar, S.D., Holcomb, W.R. and Menninger, K.A., II. (1985) 'The detection of malingered amnesia in accused murders', *Bulletin of the American Academy of Psychiatry and the Law*, 13: 97–103.

Pope, H.G. *et al.* (1998) 'Questionable validity of "dissociative amnesia" in trauma victims: Evidence from prospective studies', *British Journal of Psychiatry*, 172: 210–15.

Price, G.E. and Terhune, W.B. (1919) 'Feigned amnesia as a defense reaction', *Journal of the American Medical Association*, 72: 565–67.

Resnick, P.J. (1984) 'The detection of malingered mental illness', *Behavioral Sciences and the Law*, 2: 21–37.

Sadoff, R.L. (1974) 'Evaluation of amnesia in criminal legal situations', *Journal of Forensic Sciences*, 19: 98–101.

Schacter, D.L. (1983) 'Feeling of knowing in episodic memory', *Journal of Experimental Psychology: Learning, Memory and Cognition*, 9: 39–54.

Schacter, D.L. and Worling, J.R. (1985) 'Attribute information and the feeling of knowing', *Canadian Journal of Psychology*, 39: 467–75.

Schacter, D.L. (1986) 'Feeling-of knowing ratings distinguish between genuine and simulated forgetting', *Journal of Experimental Psychology, Learning, Memory and Cognition*, 12: 30–41.

Chapter 13

Suicide or murder? Implicit narratives in the Eddie Gilfoyle case

David Canter

Raising questions

Often unusual court cases raise important challenges for psychology and, indirectly, for the ways in which psychologists may help police investigations. This overlap – between the evidence a psychological expert may offer in court and the guidance that may be given to a police investigation – is brought into particularly sharp focus in those rare cases when behavioural and psychological issues are at the heart of determining guilt or innocence. Usually court cases revolve around matters of fact, material evidence, or even circumstantial evidence such as who could have been where when. But sometimes the facts of the case are so indeterminate that it is the character of both the victim and the defendant that are the central issue. If psychology has anything to offer the legal process, surely it must at least be able to comment on such matters?

Cases when the jury's decision revolves around judgements about the psychology of the parties involved create special challenges for the legal system. The courts may act as if they are dealing with something that can be tackled as directly as whether a person was present or not at the crime scene, or if the blood on the suspect was from the victim. The barristers will follow similar strategies when the issues are far less clear-cut, debating the character of the defendant, or in some cases, notably murder or rape, the character of the victim, in a way that suggests that personality is a fact that can be established as readily as a fingerprint. But a psychological perspective raises considerable doubt as to how fixed a person's personality is and how feasible it is for a jury to come to a firm conclusion about the victim's and perpetrator's characters and the meanings of their actions.

The view that personality can be determined, like any other significant fact in a case, from common sense and general knowledge, leads to the assumption that a barrister can help a jury form a view about the personality of a defendant or victim without the help of an expert. The central legal idea is that the expert is someone who knows things not available to a jury of lay-people. Therefore the trial of cases in which the character of key players is at issue may suffer from the simple-minded view commonly expressed in casual conversations in the pub: 'we're all psychologists, aren't we?' The same naiveté is thus also likely to be present among police officers when carrying out their investigations.

A plausible narrative

In these cases where the meaning of people's actions and their inner thoughts are under discussion, the jury is being required to develop or accept a plausible narrative of what went on in an unfolding situation. They are being asked to determine how convincing that story is by considering the people who are the main protagonists of the story. The jury's understanding of the victim and the defendant, the sorts of people they are, has to be built on to give sense to what they are reported to have done.

These problems in court are the same problems that police investigators face when trying to make sense of a crime. Just like the jury, the police try to create a plausible story, a narrative that will help them to see some meaning and sense in a pattern of activity that is often ambiguous. These narratives are based on assumptions of how people typically act under various circumstances and thus are implicit psychological models of what processes influence people's actions. Usually it is believed that police officers and juries have available to them valid psychological models that do not require any input from psychological science. In many cases such beliefs may be appropriate, but in those cases where they are not fundamental questions are raised about the basis of police investigations and the consequent processes that the law follows in putting ideas before a jury. The question can be seen as whether a psychologist can offer alternative, or more plausible, storylines.

These problems are especially significant in cases of murder in which there is only circumstantial evidence to support the prosecution case. In such cases inferences about the motive for the murder become crucial. Such inferences are in their turn based on assumptions about the character of the accused.

If the defence is that the deceased committed suicide or detectives are faced with a crime scene which could be interpreted as either suicide or murder, then there is a need to understand what happened. They have to create a convincing account that describes the sorts of people involved, most importantly the prime suspect and the victim. This account has to be integrated into a convincing narrative which accords with popular understanding of how and why people act as they do. The particularities of the main characters in the story being created by investigators, then before the jury, are an integral part of this story. These particularities are difficult enough to establish for the accused who is present for interview and cross-examination. They are even more problematic when the personality in question is that of the dead victim.

Murder or suicide?

On 4 June 1992 at around 6 pm, Police Sergeant Paul Caddick opened his brother-in-law Eddie Gilfoyle's locked garage door and found Eddie's eight and a half months pregnant wife, Paula, hanging from a ceiling beam, with her feet on the lower rungs of a ladder below the rope. Eddie had a little earlier found a note from Paula that he interpreted as indicating she was leaving him, so he was frantically searching his house and telephoning Paula's friends, after having called in his brother-in-law and his parents to help him.

Having found her dead, they read more closely the note Paula had left. They then formed the view it that it was a suicide note. The coroner's officer who arrived at the house agreed it was obviously a suicide and the body was cut down and put on the floor. No photographs or measurements were taken or forensic examination made of the garage. The rope was removed from the beam without taking details of how it had been tied. The mortician's assistant removed a portion of rope from around Paula's neck and the rope was destroyed. He later reported that he was certain that it was not a slipping knot but had two knots, one tied on top of the other.

The post mortem did not indicate anything suspicious: no violence, no alcohol or drugs. The indications were that Paula died about 2 pm.

From the actions of those in the house on the harrowing evening of 4 June it is clear that everyone – Eddie, his parents, Sergeant Caddick and the coroner's assistant – was convinced Paula had hanged herself. The post-mortem did not raise any doubts about this conclusion.

Everyone was understandably horrified that a woman so close to giving birth should have taken her own life and in the process killed her baby. In the close-knit group of Eddie's and Paula's families and their circle of friends and co-workers, discussion started as to how Paula could have done such a thing. People who worked with her recounted how happy she was about having the baby. They spoke of her buying clothes and equipment for the baby and of arranging to have it christened. A witness emerged who claimed to have talked to Paula at the local post office at 12.40, when she seemed happy. A parcel agent said Eddie signed for a parcel in Paula's name at 5.30. A neighbour also confirms seeing Eddie outside of his house at 5.30. Eddie denied this, saying he had come home from work at 4.30 to take Paula shopping but had not found her. He had found the note and then went to his parents' house, only returning home at around 6 pm.

Against this background of no obvious prior indicators of Paula being depressed, or having mentioned to anyone that she might take her own life, the police began to grow suspicious and to start listening to emerging sceptical accounts of various people who had known Paula. On 23 June a police officer found a 'practice noose' in a cabinet drawer of the garage; although another police officer who searched the garage and every drawer on 8 June had not found such an item.

During this process people came forward to recount to the police a quite remarkable story. They reported that Paula had told them that Eddie had said he was doing some training in his job at the hospital where he worked. This apparently required him to bring to the class an example of a suicide note. They claimed Paula had indicated that she had written a note at his dictation for him to take to the class.

Scenting a subtle plot to kill his wife, the police started exploring further and discovered that Eddie had had a dalliance with a co-worker which Paula had discovered and put a stop to. Here, then, they saw a classic storyline: 'husband kills wife to allow him to run off with lover'. They began to elaborate this story by examining Eddie's character. They decided that he tended to exaggerate his skills and achievements. Among themselves the police described him with reference to an iconic story of a liar and fantasist, saying he was a 'Walter Mitty character'.

To develop the circumstantial evidence for their case they reconstructed the scene in the garage as best they could from the memories of those who had seen Paula hanging. A woman police officer of the same height and build and stage of pregnancy as Paula attempted to climb the ladder and fasten the rope to the beam in the garage. After a few minutes they stopped the re-enactment for fear that the pregnant woman would hurt herself with the struggle to reach the beam. All present at this 're-enactment' were convinced that it would have been impossible for Paula to tie the rope.

It was therefore proposed that Eddie had somehow tricked his wife into putting her head in the tied rope. Then he had stood behind her and lifted her feet, so causing her to die, thereafter placing her feet on the bottom rung of the ladder. They believed they had uncovered a classic murder story in which the devious Eddie Gilfoyle had created a situation in which it appeared that his wife had killed herself, but in fact he had cajoled or conned her into putting herself at his mercy. Eddie was consequently charged with his wife's murder.

'Stylistics' and authorship

In preparing their evidence for court, the prosecution thought it would be of value to determine if the suicide note could have been dictated by Eddie. They therefore approached me to provide a psycholinguistic examination of that note. There was no doubt that the note was in Paula's handwriting, but could it reveal mental processes that were closer to Eddie's than Paula's? Eddie and Paula had been on different shifts at work and were also redecorating their house, which entailed them staying with their parents from time to time. This had led them to leave notes for each other, often on matters of emotional significance. There therefore was a mixture of texts available for consideration.

What drew the police to consider such a possibility is the emergence of a branch of linguistic analysis that attempts to provide mathematical calculations of the components of text that will demonstrate the authorship of that text (e.g. Ellegard, 1962). This activity is sometimes graced with the term 'stylistics' (cf. McMenamin, 1993). It goes back over more than a century and comes into popular awareness with attempts to determine if all the plays attributed to Shakespeare were actually written by him. Such studies typically look at the vocabulary used in plays by various authors and seek to establish whether there is a similar or different mix of words that could be taken to indicate who wrote what.

There is however, a fundamental problem with virtually all of these studies. They never establish that the aspect of style or word use that they are measuring is incontrovertibly, consistently typical of the author in question and clearly distinct from other authors. In other words, there is no *a priori* proof that any aspect of a person's style of verbal expression is unique to that person. Psychologists recognize this as the classic experimental, or 'analysis of variance', problem. Is the variation within an individual's utterances greater than the variation between the utterances of different people? If any given person uses a broader mix of words, varying from one piece of writing to another more than the differences he has from another person, then it will not be possible to use his mix of words to distinguish the writing of the two people.

The approach of identifying unique aspects of the writings of a famous author is rather different from approaches that claim there is some aspect of all utterances that are unique to people, like fingerprints. From time to time, there have been claims that there are general features of what people say or write that will be unique to each person. For example, there have been claims that the proportion of short words to long words is a distinct figure unique to each person. But systematic study has always shown these claims to have established general distinguishing features to be unfounded (Canter, 1992).

Sadly, linguistics is a fundamentally descriptive discipline, not an experimental science. So the people carrying out studies of authorship are usually happy to propose that they have found some distinction that allows them to claim they have identified the actual author of a piece of text, even though they have no proof that they are correct, other than the distinction they claim provides the proof. This form of circular argument does not seem to raise too many questions within linguistic circles.

Challenges to these procedures and demonstration of their lack of scientific validity do not stop the search for such general features because of the popular belief that we have unique ways of expressing ourselves. Indeed, many of us are confident that we can identify the writing of particular students or colleagues. However, such a personal conviction is rarely tested. It also does not have the precision that would have the clarity and proven validity to enable it to be used in court.

I was somewhat ignorant of these complications when the police first asked me, 12 years ago, to examine the suicide note that Paula had written. It seemed to me at least worthwhile to explore a number of Paula's letters and a number that Eddie had written, in order to determine if there was anything about their different writing styles that could be drawn upon to form a view about the authorship of the significant suicide note. Could it be claimed at all that the suicide note was not the words or thoughts of Paula even though it was in her handwriting?

Psychological autopsy

In order to understand how I tackled this task of comparison it is necessary to be aware of how the material was presented to me. I was approached by the senior investigating officer and presented with the intriguing story outlined above. Eddie, the 'Walter Mitty character', had invented a story to convince his wife to write a suicide note, then tricked her into putting her head in a noose. I was not allowed to talk to anyone about this, neither Eddie nor Paula's family, but was asked to examine some notes that Eddie and Paula had written to each other and prepare a report on the likelihood that Paula had written the suicide note with the intention of killing herself.

Although with hindsight I was probably naïve in accepting with too little question the account that the police had given to me, and was far too optimistic about the possibilities for linguistic analysis, I was at least experienced and professional enough to insist that I reviewed the case in general, not looking only at the written material I had been given. For my report I considered the facts of Paula's circumstances as they were presented to me. This included reviewing what the commonly held view was in the published literature on the precursors to suicide.

This report drew on procedures that sit under the title of 'psychological autopsy'. In essence this is an attempt to identify the characteristics of a deceased person from all the information available. It is not a strict process in any very formal sense. There is just a set of ideas and recommendations that provide guidelines on what may be considered. However, as I have discussed in more detail in other places (e.g. Canter, 1999), the published literature rather underplays the considerable difficulties there are in preparing an account of the deceased in a case such as that of the death of Paula Gilfoyle. Not only was I not allowed to talk to anyone, but by the time I was called in the dominant narratives of the various parties – the police investigators, the families of the accused and deceased – had taken hold and were having an influence over all the information being presented.

The report I eventually submitted to the police investigation reflected the fact that there were no strong, overt indicators that Paula had been depressed or not wanting to have her baby. The linguistic analysis concentrated on the vocabulary and themes in the notes between Paula and Eddie. The report came to the conclusion that the suicide note used themes and vocabulary more or less typical of both Paula and Eddie. It raised the possibility that any suicidal thoughts Paula might have had may have been hidden from others, but drew the overall conclusion that Paula had probably not written the note with the intention of killing herself. In total this was taken as lending support to the prosecution case.

My report, though, was not presented to the court. That I am sure was a sensible decision given how little systematic background research there was for me to make use of. However, the report itself bolstered the determination of the prosecution. More importantly, probably, in the curious ways in which the courts work, it encouraged the defence not to bring any parallel linguistic or psychological evidence for fear of opening a way for my evidence. Thus, although it was clearly not directly a consequence of my report, I must carry at least some little responsibility for Eddie Gilfoyle being convicted of his wife's murder and being given the inevitable consequence – a life sentence.

Developments

In the real world, as opposed to the scientific laboratory, coincidences of time and place can have considerable significance. At the time I was approached to contribute to the investigation into Paula's death I was living in Surrey, about 200 miles south of the Wirral peninsula where she had lived with Eddie. A couple of years after Eddie was sentenced I took a job at Liverpool University, a short ferry ride 'across the water' from the Wirral.

Still curious about how a husband could convince his wife into putting her neck in a noose in a garage, especially when there had been a recent contretemps over an extramarital friendship, I was therefore more than ready to talk with members of Paula's and Eddie's extended family when I was contacted by them on arriving in Liverpool. This provided me with new insights into the whole saga and eventually a meeting with Eddie, as well as a written account from him of the circumstances, as he saw them, which gave rise to Paula's death. Let me emphasize the significance of this information. For what might be called 'legal reasons', none of this was available to me when I wrote my original report.

What emerged from all this was a situation that threw into high relief the profound difficulties of carrying out an objective psychological autopsy in a situation where there is a debate over whether a death is caused by murder or suicide. The people who knew Paula best, Eddie and his family on the one hand and Paula's family on the other, each had a psychological investment in totally opposing stories. Her immediate family were reluctant to talk to me, believing that I 'just wanted to show that Paula was mad' and 'get Eddie off the hook'. Most people associated with suicide feel some guilt, thinking that they should have done some-thing to prevent it and therefore would prefer to take the view that there was some other cause for death. Coroners are often sensitive to these feelings by giving an open verdict even when there is a suicide note present.

Eddie and his family clearly had a vested interest in demonstrating that Paula was mentally disturbed in some way, or at the very least deeply unhappy about having a baby. Any view they offered would therefore be extremely difficult to rely on in any court of law. A report based solely on information gleaned from them would be open to strong challenge in cross-examination.

To complicate matters further, by the time that I was involved in these discussions with the various people who had information about Paula, there had been an official enquiry into the initial investigation and even an enquiry into that enquiry. Any details of the actual situation, such as Paula and Eddie's house and the fateful garage, would have been changed beyond recognition. All that could be done was to review the shelf loads of case files that carried details of the interviews collected during the original investigation and later enquiries.

All of these matters brought to the surface a range of psychological questions to which answers were desperately needed: questions that the court should have had answers to in the original case; issues of which the police officers who carried out the original investigation should have been aware.

'Experience of life'

Eddie claimed in his discussions with me that Paula never showed what she was feeling to other people. He described how she frequently presented one face in private and a quite different face in public. He said there had been some indicators that she had been upset the day or two before she died and that this was in accord with other mood swings she had had in the past. His sister and her husband also insisted that Paula was not always the bubbly, carefree person that had been presented to the court. Through these discussions my attention was drawn to considering many aspects of the case. All of these connect with aspects of psychology that are open to scientific study and professional opinion. Yet the courts in the original case and two later appeals have steadfastly refused to acknowledge that these matters are beyond the experience or expertise of a jury. The judge in his summing up of the original murder trial made it clear that he thought the jury could make a decision about Eddie's guilt, and whether Paula was likely to have committed suicide, based on the jury's 'own experience of life'.

Assessing personality

The fact that personality can be a substantive issue in a murder case is shown by the fact that in his summing up the judge at the trial draws attention to discussions of what he calls Paula's 'personality and behaviour', equating personality with behaviour. This does indicate a lack of the learned judge's understanding of professional psychological perspectives. Those who carry out systematic, scientific study of human actions and experiences make a very considerable distinction between 'personality' and 'behaviour'. Personality is the enduring characteristics a person has, behaviour is her actions at particular points in time. To accept that what Paula had done and said to others was a clear reflection of her personality and thus her inner mental state is, at the very least, an assumption open to test. In the trial, as far as I can tell, no detailed accounts of Paula's personality, as a psychologist might talk about it, were presented in evidence.

The discussions about Paula were all at what might be termed surface level, how she was seen by those around her. For example in reviewing the case the Criminal Case Review Commission drew attention to the following from the trial record:

> Mrs Gilfoyle left work three weeks before the baby was due. Family and friends described her as happy and, despite misgivings about the birth itself, looking forward to the arrival of the baby. Mrs Gilfoyle had bought two sets of baby equipment so that one set could be left with her mother who was going to look after the baby when Mrs Gilfoyle returned to work … 2 days before her death, she went to the library and borrowed 6 books on childcare and names.

However, in my original report, before I had met Eddie and heard his account, I did note that:

> She very much wanted the approval of others and would distort accounts of herself and her activities in order to present herself in a good light. She dealt with difficulties and challenges either by presenting a less than accurate account of herself or by hiding away from the stressful situation. This probably did not make her especially vulnerable to suicide but did mean that any suicidal ideation she might have had would have been difficult for others to recognise.

There had also been hints in an earlier witness statement, from a work colleague, that Paula's delight at having the baby was not unconditional: 'she used to say at work that she was worried about having the baby, mainly because she was an older mother and she wouldn't know what to do'.

The judge at the original murder trial did acknowledge that there were contrary indications to the generally positive picture of Paula's delight in having the baby, but brushed them aside:

In October 1991 she wrote to her husband and referred to the baby coming, 'when I am at the lowest ever in my life', and to being undecided whether to bring the baby up herself or to give it up for adoption. The notes, according to numerous witnesses, did not reflect her demeanour and behaviour; she appeared happy and looking forward to the birth of her child.

The judge is thus claiming that what Paula wrote to her husband should be discounted in favour of what she portrayed to less close acquaintances.

Closer consideration of the personality literature could put these ambiguities in another light. Hewitt and Flett (1991) argued that 'perfectionist' people are less likely to look forward to positive events because each event offers an opportunity for failure. They suggest that this trait has three dimensions: self-oriented perfectionism (when the person places unrealistic demands on herself); socially prescribed perfectionism (where the person thinks that significant other people demand perfection); and other-oriented perfectionism (where it is believed that other people make unrealistic and exaggerated demands). This view of 'perfectionism' provides a framework within which a pathway can exist from socially prescribed perfectionism to depression and subsequent suicidal ideation.

These ideas have been developed more recently to show a direct association between the cognitive attribute of the 'perfectionist' trait and suicide (Hunter and O'Connor, 2003; O'Connor and O'Connor, 2003; O'Connor et al., 2004). Could Paula be thought of as having this 'perfectionist' trait, which could have contributed to her thinking about suicide? Certainly in my conversations with Eddie and his sister, they mentioned a number of aspects of Paula's behaviour, such as her approach to housekeeping, even putting tins in alphabetical order on the kitchen shelves, which take on a different significance in the light of these recently published studies.

It is, of course, extremely difficult at this remove to determine the extent to which Paula did hide her feelings from other people and also had traits that could have made her especially vulnerable to fears of failure. Can the fact, for example, that Paula took as many six books out of the library on childcare three weeks before the expected date of delivery, and had baby equipment already stored both at her own and her mother's house, be seen as an indication of anxiety, or form of tension, rather than enthusiasm for having the baby? It may be typical of many mothers expecting their first baby. Were there other aspects of her life that might have indicated the plausibility of a different narrative to the one that Paula was reported to have revealed to the world? Most fundamentally, where there ways in which the police investigation, and subsequently the courts, could have looked at these matters that go beyond a jury's 'experience of life'? Could it have been possible to establish Paula's enduring characteristics, which could have been tested through cross-examination before the jury, and their implications for possible hidden suicidal tendencies explored?

Suicide without precursors

In his summing up at the original trial the judge drew attention to the fact that 17 different people gave no indication that Paula would kill herself. In doing this he is making a fundamental assumption, and one that my original report fostered, that suicide never occurs without some prior indication that would be available to people who had day to day contact with Paula.

A large number of precursors to suicide are identified in the literature. These are the main pointers that are the basis for consideration in conducting a psychological autopsy (Canter, 1999). They include depression, mental illness, previous attempts at suicide, alcoholism and drug addiction, isolation and changes in mood and behaviour, leading up to the time of death.

Yet all these indicators assume that the person who takes their own life gives some sort of indication that their thoughts are moving in that direction. This literature is also based on the premise that others notice whatever cues may be available to the mental state of the intending suicide. Impulsive suicide is not catered for in this framework, as a sudden unplanned event. Nor is a state of secret despair allowed for, in which the person goes to trouble to hide their thoughts and feelings.

Eddie's claims, fervently denied by Paula's family, was that there were indicators, the significance of which he was only aware of with hindsight, that Paula had been nursing a private disquiet with her relationship with him and with the coming baby. This claim and counter-claim therefore raises in stark significance whether such secret despair is possible or at all likely. Establishing that it is possible would not prove that it was the case here, but at least it is an issue that might have influenced the initial police investigation and then the jury if they had been aware of it.

To explore these possibilities I therefore set about trying to see what the likelihood was of suicide without precursors. This study gave rise to a recent paper (Canter *et al.*, 2004). The paper supports the growing evidence that suicide can occur without overt, explicit precursors. Our study looked for the presence or absence of 14 known suicide indicators in 128 case histories (as presented at inquest) of completed suicides. From the co-occurrence of these 14 indicators a model was developed of three suicide pathways: distinct routes to suicide relating to: a) life circumstances (including stressful life events, e.g. financial hardship, relationship crises), b) psychiatric/physical history, and c) suicidal history.

The 128 cases we examined showed considerable variation in the number of overt precursors prior to death. Individuals exhibited between two and ten precursors. Sixteen per cent exhibited fewer than four. This would suggest that not only are there a limited number of psychological processes that lead to people taking their own lives, but that there are also variations in how intentions are expressed, either directly or indirectly. Most importantly, there is a small but significant proportion of cases for which the coroner comes to a conclusion of suicide yet for which there are only minimal prior indicators. It is possible that these individuals are suffering from a state of 'secret despair' in which they feel trapped by negative experiences, and lose hope for the future, but keep such feelings hidden from those around them. This would seem to support the possibility in my original report, that Paula might have exhibited a pathway to suicide related to her life circumstances that were not so clearly expressed to those around her.

Determining authenticity in suicide notes

The idea that a hospital porter, like Eddie, with minimal first-aid training and no counselling or therapeutic experience could dictate a convincing suicide note was never tested in court, or even explored. This therefore raises questions about what the contents of a suicide note are likely to be and the psychological processes that are most probably expressed in such a note. The identification of distinct pathways to suicide would also add a focus to these considerations, because the existence of a limited number of pathways would indicate that a genuine suicide note should reflect one dominant pathway rather than a mixture of processes.

Hopelessness

One dominant factor that has been found consistently in suicide is hopelessness – the degree to which an individual is pessimistic about the future. This is cited as the main component of the depression that is most often associated with suicidal thoughts (Nekanda-Trepka et al., 1983) and completed suicide (Beck et al., 1989). MacLeod et al. (1993, 1997) found that parasuicidal individuals are impaired in their ability to generate positive future thoughts compared with controls. The different pathways we have identified thus are all, in their different ways, routes to the abyss of despair that sees no acceptable future.

327

Certainly the note to Eddie written by Paula expresses hopelessness very clearly:

'this is just too much I can't face up to my problems anymore'

The note implies that Paula cannot face the thought of having the baby, although the full reasons are not expressed in detail in this note. Nonetheless, the pain of a future life is strongly expressed.

The forms of thought of people contemplating suicide have also been elaborated further in studies of depression by Beck (1976). He draws attention to negative patterns of thinking regarding the person's sense of self, their future, and their environment. They are more likely to blame themselves for negative events. They think that the causes will always be present, and will interfere with all aspects of their lives in the future. According to O'Connor and Sheehy (2001), this pattern of thinking is more potent when it is applied to explaining negative interpersonal events (e.g. relationship crises). This thinking pattern sustains the individual's negative state of mind and impairs their ability to problem-solve and deal with an interpersonal crisis. A suicidal person, cognitively rigid with tunnel vision, is less likely to consider alternative solutions to problems, and is more likely to view suicide as an option.

In Paula's note the view that she has never done anything right in her life is strongly expressed in the almost ironic comment:

'maybe it will be the one thing I will do right in life'

The pregnancy is recorded as the epitome of all that she has done wrong:

'I don't want to have this baby that I'm carrying. I wish now that I had got rid of it.'

The feeling of total inability to influence future prospects is also stated. No other alternatives are open for exploration.

'I can't change or alter what I've done.'

A narrative of despair

For these strong declarations of a lack of any acceptable future to carry conviction, they have to be embedded in a plausible narrative. This is where the inventiveness of a fictional letter-writer would be tested. The feelings of utter doom must be expressed strongly if they are to accord with the psychological literature, as they clearly are in Paula's note, but there would have to be some context that makes such a view feasible.

In the case of the Gilfoyles this is hinted at through the earlier documents that I eventually started to consider. In brief, a marital conflict is discussed in which Paula claims that her baby is not Eddie's. The postmortem showed this to be untrue, but of course does not indicate whether Paula thought it was false. This is therefore portrayed as a suicide emerging out of a view that a relationship was being destroyed by the unborn child. The notes build up a rich narrative around this of a lover named as 'Nigel' who in one letter is described as having decided to leave the country and not take Paula with him. This would add further to the proposal of a 'failed relationship' pathway. It certainly requires considerable inventive detail from Eddie if he were the primary author of it as fiction.

Justification

Studies of suicide notes also draw attention to the purpose of writing a note at all. This takes a perspective that owes more to consideration of suicide notes as a form of 'discourse', in the sense that Potter and Wetherell (1987) use the term, examining how people construct themselves and other people through what they say and write. Much of this construction is seen as creating and defending particular views of the self, typically offering, implicitly or explicitly, justifications for actions that might be expected to be outside of what is socially acceptable. Within this paradigm, according to McClelland et al. (2000), the function of suicide notes is to negotiate the potential blame attributable to the deceased and the note recipient. Because suicide violates powerful social norms to keep oneself alive, and further implies that others may have failed in their own social obligations towards the person contemplating suicide, the function of suicide notes is to legitimate a normally illegitimate act.

Thus, individuals will typically be expected to provide some form of explanation for their actions in suicide notes. Whether this is widely known, or would have been known to Eddie, is a moot point. Our studies of suicide notes indicate that explanations or justifications are often not very overt or detailed. Most people seem unable to elaborate on their reasons, but rather indicate that there are reasons and justifications. In one sample of 98 suicide notes we studied, 47% gave only general or constricted comments, e.g. not wanting to continue. The most frequently occurring elements that addressed the social norms against suicide were apologies to note recipients and expressions of love for those left behind.

Again Paula's note is a 'textbook' example of this type of justification. It also relates to comments I made in my original report that genuine suicide notes are more likely to express positive emotions than are simulated ones. An inexperienced writer might assume that the primary purpose of a suicide note is to blame or seek revenge.

Paula wrote:

'no-one is to blame except myself'

and later

'I apologise for all the pain and suffering I have caused by taking my own life. I don't mean to cause any problems for anyone.'

Paradoxically, this natural and common inclusion in suicide notes of apology and self-blame may have been part of the reason the police and jury had convinced themselves that Eddie had written the note. If he was as devious as the police believed then it would be expected that he would make sure the note exonerated himself. The possibility that Paula, intelligently, understood some of the trauma that her death would cause, is a quite different explanation for the purpose of the letter she wrote to Eddie.

Surprise suicides

At the heart of the narrative that the police and jury explored was the idea that people do not commit suicide suddenly, by surprise. Again this is an issue that was not explored in any detail or with any sophistication in either the original court case or in the subsequent appeals. Yet there is a growing literature, not just on the secret despair mentioned above, but also on the awareness in the population at large of the possibility of 'surprise suicides'.

Two studies have examined directly the extent to which individuals believe that 'A suicide attempt occurs with little warning', and 'Usually, relatives of a suicide victim had no idea of what was about to happen' (Domino, 1990; Cruikshank and Slavick, 1994). In a sample of 643 US residents, aged between 21 and 83 years, Domino (1990) found that 76% agreed that relatives might be unaware of a victim's intentions. Conversely, only 23% agreed that suicide happens without warning. A greater proportion of older respondents and those from minority groups endorsed both items. This discrepancy of endorsement is an interesting one, since it may reflect the idea that individuals present themselves differently to different people, and that it may be the ones closest to them who know the least.

In a replication of Domino's study, Cruikshank and Slavick (1994) found 57% and 19% endorsement of these respective items. In addition, they found no differences between individuals who had known someone to commit suicide and those who had not. By contrast, in Alston and Robinson's (1992) study of nurses' attitudes towards suicide, they found that 88% endorsed the view that suicide happens without warning. Nurses have unique access to medical investigation of and a family's reactions to suicide. So it is interesting that their views so contrast with the public at large, for whom only around 20% hold this view. Clearly this is an area in which guidance to a jury could be productive.

An alternative narrative

The story that convicted Eddie Gilfoyle and still keeps him in prison is that he schemed to kill his wife by tricking her into putting her head in a noose, having already prepared the ground by dictating a suicide note for her to write. In addition, his deception had been so thought through that over weeks and months beforehand he had got his wife to concoct an account of an illicit affair and an unwanted pregnancy. There are subtle variations possible on this central theme; for example, that Eddie had built upon some genuine disquiet his wife had about giving birth to create a much more fatalistic scenario. From a psychological point of view, the great invention necessary in this is the note Paula left – a note that all who read it initially saw as a genuine cry of pain. The note has to be regarded as a plausible invention that contrasted with the way Paula was seen by many of those around her; 17 people that the judge counted as disagreeing with the version of events reflected in that note.

I have tried to indicate some of the fascinating assumptions about human behaviour and personality that are enshrined in the gripping narrative that the jury must have accepted when they found Eddie guilty. By unpacking these assumptions it is possible to see how a psychological perspective could have generated a different storyline that may have influenced the original investigation. In this different account the suicide note is genuine and Paula is seen as a person who had secretly harboured despair. The reasons for this related to her perception of her child's father and the consequences of giving birth to it. Within this narrative it has to be assumed that the account Paula is quoted as giving of writing suicide notes dictated by Eddie has either been misunderstood or was part of a convoluted deceit on the part of Paula.

In legal terms, without the alternative narrative being considered by a court of appeal its validity cannot be tested. In psychological terms this case has generated a number of lines of research, including the exploration of what genuine suicide notes consist of, the possibility for determining authorship objectively for written material, the evidence for a 'secret despair syndrome', the knowledge which juries may be assumed to have of the conditions under which suicide happens, and the ways in which plausible narratives shape investigations and jury decisions. The sad fact is that research takes many years to reach conclusions and until such conclusions are clearly available Eddie Gilfoyle may remain wrongfully incarcerated.

Acknowledgements

I am extremely grateful, first and foremost to Eddie Gilfoyle, his family and solicitor Campbell Malone, for allowing me to quote the material in this chapter and for providing me with considerable background information. I am also very pleased to record the considerable contribution made to the preparation of this chapter by Susan Giles. Her PhD work has illuminated much of what I have written.

References

Alston, M. H. and Robinson, B.H. (1992) 'Nurses' attitudes toward suicide', *The Journal of Death and Dying*, 25 (3).

Beck, A.T. (1976) *Cognitive Theory and the Emotional Disorders*. New York: International Universities Press.

Beck, A.T., Brown, G. and Steer, R.A. (1989) 'Predictions of eventual suicide in psychiatric inpatients by clinical ratings of hopelessness', *Journal of Consulting and Clinical Psychology*, 57: 309–10.

Canter, D.V. (1992) 'An evaluation of the "Cusum" stylistic examination of confession', *Expert Evidence*, 1: 93–9.

Canter, D. (1999) 'Equivocal Death', in D. Canter and L. Alison (eds), *Profiling in Policy and Practice* (pp. 123–56). Aldershot: Ashgate.

Canter, D.V., Giles, S.P. and Nicol, C. (2004) 'Suicide without explicit precursors: A state of secret despair?', *Journal of Investigative Psychology and Offender Profiling*, 1: 227–48.

Cruikshanks, D.R. and Slavick, S.P. (1994) 'Further investigation of popular misconceptions about suicide', *Omega: Journal of Death and Dying*, 28(3).

Domino, G. (1990) 'Popular misconceptions about suicide: How popular are they?', *The Journal of Death and Dying*, 21 (3).

Ellegard, A. (1992) *Who was Junius?* Stockholm: Almquist & Wiksell.

Hewitt, P.L. and Flett, G.L. (1991) 'Perfectionism in the self and social contexts: Conceptualization, assessment, and association with psychopathology', *Journal of Personality and Social Psychology*, 60: 456–70.

Hunter, E.C. and O'Connor, R.C. (2003) 'Hopelessness and future thinking in parasuicide: the role of perfectionism', *British Journal of Clinical Psychology*, 42: 355–65.

Kelly, D. and France, R. (1987) *A Practical Handbook for the Treatment of Depression*. Carnforth: Parthenon.

MacLeod, A.K., Rose, G.S. and Williams, J.M.G. (1993) 'Components of hopelessness and the future of parasuicide', *Cognitive Therapy and Research*, 17: 441–45.

MacLeod, A.K., Pankania, B., Lee, M. and Mitchell, D. (1997) 'Parasuicide, depression and anticipation of positive and negative future expectations', *Psychological Medicine*, 27: 973–77.

McClelland, L., Reicher. S. and Booth, N. (2000) 'A last defence: The negotiation of blame within suicide notes', *Journal of Community and Applied Social Psychology*, 10: 225–40.

McMenamin, G.R. (1993) *Forensic Stylistics*. Amsterdam: Elsevier.

Nekanda-Trepka, C.J., Bishop, S. and Blackburn, I.M. (1983) 'Hopelessness and depression', *British Journal of Clinical Psychology*, 22: 49–60.

O'Connor, R.C. and O'Connor, D.B. (2003) 'Predicting hopelessness and psychological distress: the role of perfectionism and coping', *Journal of Counseling Psychology*, 50: 362–72.

O'Connor, R.C., O'Connor, D.B, O'Connor, S.M., Smallwood, J. and Miles, J. (2004) 'Hopelessness, stress and perfectionism: the moderating effects of future thinking', *Cognition and Emotion*, 2, 18: 1099–120.

O'Connor, R.C. and Sheehy, N.P. (2001) 'Suicidal behaviour', *The Psychologist*, 14(1): 20–4.

Polvi, N. (1997) 'Assessing risk of suicide in correctional settings', in C.D. Webster and M.A. Jackson (eds), *Impulsivity: Theory, Assessment and Treatment* (pp. 278–301). New York: Guilford Press.

Potter, J. and Wetherell, M. (1987). *Discourse and Social Psychology. Beyond Attitudes and Behaviour*. London: Sage.

Tanney, B.L. (1992). 'Mental disorders, psychiatric patients, and suicide', in R.W. Maris, A.L. Berman, J.T. Maltsberger and R.I. Yufit (eds), *Assessment and Prediction of Suicide* (pp. 277–320). New York: Guilford Press.

Details of the Gilfoyle case are available on the following websites:
www.mojuk.org.uk/eddie/ed.html
www.portia.org/chapter02/gilfoyl5.html

Chapter 14

A stalking management programme: preparing advisory material for non-psychologists

Emily Alison and Laurence Alison

Historical background

Stalking was recognized by the British legal system with the introduction of the Protection from Harassment Act in 1997. The first anti-stalking law was implemented in California in 1990, prompted by the high-profile murder of television actress Rebecca Schaeffer, who was shot and killed outside her home by an obsessed fan. However, the constellation of behaviours involved in stalking are much more common between acquaintances and domestic partners than between celebrities and their fans (Mullen *et al.*, 1999b; Palarea *et al.*, 1999). A previous relationship does not lessen the impact that stalking behaviour has, nor the severity of the threat. Indeed, in cases where the stalker and victim have a previous relationship there is some evidence to suggest that there is an *increased* probability of physical attacks (Zona *et al.*, 1993; Meloy and Gothard, 1995).

Victims are subjected to systematic and repeated psychological abuse and often feel isolated as they are forced to cut off various forms of social support. Often, the victim can feel abandoned by agencies normally available to support victims of crime. Therefore, any programme to assist victims of stalking must address not only the actions of the stalker and the risk posed to the victim, but the victim's mental health and ability to cope both during and after the stalking incidents.

Stalking management programme aims

The following programme provides a comprehensive package for addressing stalking issues. The current approach to stalking in the UK requires the victim to seek out support from several diverse and separate agencies, such as health professionals, counsellors, security firms and law enforcement. These agencies often have little overlap or co-operation over the course of the case, and it is left to the victim to initiate and maintain working relationships with all of them.

The current programme allows the service provider to comprehensively assess the client's needs and either provide or liaise with outside agencies concerning those needs. This removes the management burden from the client and provides an overall support system for the duration of the case. The current programme also has the potential to be adapted as an education and skill-building workshop for individuals who are fearful of, or at high-risk for, being stalked. Such a workshop would provide information regarding: (1) types of stalking behaviour, (2) factors that increase risk, (3) how to minimize stalking behaviour, (4) how to handle a stalker appropriately should the need arise in the future or be ongoing.

Stalking management programme: outline

The following report provides a four-phase programme for assessing and educating potential or current victims of stalking. The four phases are summarized briefly below.

Phase I: Background and initial assessment

General information on stalking, including the most common behaviours and the different types of stalkers identified in previous research. An information-gathering interview pro-forma is also provided to collect relevant information from victims of stalking. This pro-forma can be modified to assess risk areas for potential victims of stalking.

Caveat: It is important to note that this pro-forma does not allow for a clinical diagnosis of either the victim or the stalker. It simply provides a format for compiling relevant information (as identified extensively in the literature) and drawing on current research to assess possible risk factors and a potential course of action.

Phase II: Determination of risk of harm

A summary of the literature on stalking and associated risk factors. This may be passed on to the client to educate them about elements that increase the risk of physical assault, so they may take appropriate precautions.

Caveat: It should be emphasized that the client should not assume they are at no or very low risk simply because they do not match the identified factors that increase risk. These factors are based on empirical research and probabilities. However, stalking is a varied and complex behaviour and there is still a possibility that the individual case will not follow the trend. No client should ever be advised that they are at no risk of being physically victimized by a stalker.

Phase III: Assessment of symptoms and methods of coping

Examines the psychological distress caused to victims of stalking. Common methods of coping are also discussed. This information is provided to help educate the victim about what they are likely to experience.

Caveat: Such education, however, by no means replaces the need for professional therapeutic intervention. If the client is actively exhibiting major stress symptoms, they should be urged to see a mental health professional or their GP at once.

Phase IV: Determining a plan of action

Provides an intervention plan for the stalking victim. This plan is based on an empirically validated clinical model, but should only be applied after a risk assessment has been completed and with the full co-operation of the client.

'Profile' of a stalker

Because of the wide range of contexts in which stalking occurs, it is extremely difficult to draw one consistent, reliable picture of what type of offender 'stalks'. Therefore, while it is useful to know some basic demographic characteristics that have been identified across research samples of stalkers, an individual should not be ruled out simply because they do not match this profile. Clinical classification systems are also useful for identifying particular 'types' of stalkers and associated characteristics, although, as we have stated, the constellation of behaviours is often complex and cannot be easily classified into distinct categories.

Demographics

Meloy and Gothard (1995) tested whether a forensic cohort of obsessional followers would significantly differ on certain demographic and clinical variables from a randomly selected group of offenders with mental disorders. They used a sample of 20 obsessional followers who had been taken into police custody by the LAPD and a sample of 30 randomly selected offenders in custody who had some form of mental disorder. The demographic criteria from their sample of 20 is compared with Mullen *et al.*'s (1999a) sample of 145 Australian stalkers referred for forensic evaluation in Figure 14.1. While many of the criteria are similar across these two very different samples there are some clear distinctions.

Gender and relationship

Both samples indicate that the majority of stalkers are male. In 14% of the cases, the stalker was the same gender as the victim. In most cases the stalker had a prior relationship of some type with the victim. At the onset of stalking, 36% of victims were employed in professions such as medicine, teaching and the law. The discrepancy in frequencies for victim relationship may be a product of the small sample size in Meloy and Gothard's (1995) study or a discrepancy in the operational definitions

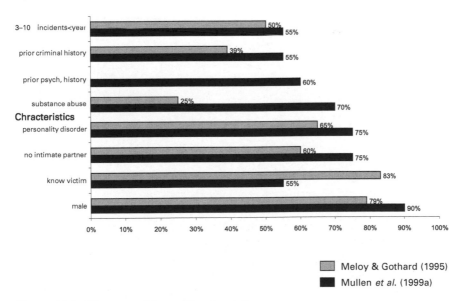

Figure 14.1   Demographic profile of a stalker

used, i.e. 'know' = acquaintance vs. sexual intimate. However, many other studies have found a rate more consistent with Mullen *et al.*'s (1999) of 83%. For example, Harmon *et al.* (1995) found that 71% of their stalking cases involved a prior relationship between victim and stalker. Rates of stalkers targeting complete strangers are generally low, falling consistently around 10–13%.

Marital status

The majority of stalkers had no intimate partner at the time of arrest. Around a third of offenders with no intimate partner in both samples (n = 20–35%, n = 145–30%) were separated or divorced at the time of the offence. This trait has been supported by many other studies. Segal (1989) noted the isolated and lonesome existence of the erotomanic individual,[1] while Zona *et al.* (1993) found that only one of seven of their subjects were married at the time of pursuit, and most (72%) of the erotomanic subgroup never married. Stalkers have a history of impaired or conflicted social relationships. Many of the stalkers whose victims were strangers never had a significant intimate relationship and consistently failed in their courtship attempts. They appeared to lack the social intelligence to form friendships or build an intimate relationship over time. For this type of individual, stalking provides the ultimate passive-aggressive relationship – total consuming involvement with the targeted person requiring little or no direct interpersonal contact.

Psychiatric status

A large percentage of the offenders were diagnosed with various personality disorders (n = 20–75%, n = 145–65%), ranging from histrionic, defined by the American Psychiatric Association (1994) as 'an individual who exhibits a pervasive pattern of excessive emotional reactions and attention seeking behaviour', to borderline personality disorders in which the person often displays a pervasive pattern of instability in personal relationships. Such individuals have also been known to harm themselves by utilizing self-mutilating or self-destructive behaviours. A large percentage of offenders in the Meloy and Gothard (1995) sample were also diagnosed as having suffered from substance abuse or dependence. The frequency reported by Mullen *et al.* (1999a) is significantly lower; however, data were only available for those offenders having co-morbid substance abuse (in conjunction with another diagnosis), which may have impacted the numbers.

Psychiatric/criminal history

A number of offenders also had a record of previous contact with in-patient or out-patient psychiatric treatment and a previous criminal record. Data on psychiatric history were not available from the Mullen *et al.* sample, and a slightly lower rate of criminal convictions was found in their sample, although the majority of these were for interpersonal violence (28%) or sexual offences (7%), perhaps as a by-product of sampling methods. Criminal convictions across both samples ranged from violations of restraining orders, priors for stalking, assault or battery, child molestation, violation of probation, false imprisonment and vandalism.

Duration of contact

The duration of contact for at least half of the stalkers was between three and ten incidents recorded in less than a year. Only 10% of Meloy and Gothard's (1995) sample committed more than ten incidents and continued offending over a year. The median in Mullen *et al.*'s sample was also 12 months, but ranged from 4 months to 20 years. In the National Institute of Justice Survey conducted in 1998 ($n = 16,000$), two-thirds of all stalking cases lasted a year or less, a quarter between two and five years, and around a tenth went on for more than five years. The average stalking case lasts for 1.8 years. Cases of stalking involving former intimates lasts twice as long (2.2 years) compared with non-intimate stalking, which lasts 1.1 years.

Thumbnail

From these results we can draw a thumbnail picture of the 'prototypic' stalker. He is likely to be an unemployed man in his mid-30s. He is likely to have a prior psychiatric, criminal and substance abuse history, and will not be involved in a relationship at the time of the offence. His stalking behaviour may continue for up to a year, ranging from between three and ten incidents in that time. The individual is likely to have already come into contact with either the criminal justice or mental health communities. Informing local health authorities, the probation service and local police may assist in eliminating the stalker's pattern of behaviour. The exchange of information will facilitate their intervention with the stalker, and should therefore not be ignored as a source of assistance.

Theoretical basis for management recommendations

Reinforcement

In order to eliminate unwanted behaviour, the victim must avoid reinforcing the stalker's behaviour. There are two types of reinforcement, positive and negative. *Positive reinforcement* is the most common type of reinforcement for managing others. Examples include promising bonuses to staff for meeting deadlines or using the promise of presents from Father

Christmas to manipulate children's behaviour. In stalking, reinforcement occurs when the victim's behaviour is perceived as a desirable response for the stalker. This may include the perception that the victim is distressed (e.g. the victim crying or swearing at the stalker in response to repeated harassment). Such 'distress cues' will encourage the stalker to repeat the harassing behaviours that elicited those cues.

Negative reinforcement occurs when the stalker can remove an aversive set of cues. For example, if the stalker recognizes that, by touching the victim, this prevents the victim from ignoring the stalker by keeping her eyes on the floor (aversive for the stalker), the stalker will repeatedly touch the victim to inhibit the 'looking down on the floor' aversive stimulus.

Punishment

Another method of extinguishing unwanted behaviour is through punishment. However, as the stalker's main goal is often simply to achieve a response from or impact on the victim, the victim must not only refrain from sending out positive or placatory messages, but also negative or emotional ones. Shouting or swearing at the stalker may not be perceived as punishment but rather as reinforcement. Any expression of emotion may encourage the stalker to continue. Therefore, the victim must attempt to ignore all behaviour by the stalker if possible. When not possible, they must convey an objective, firm message that they are not interested in/do not want contact from the stalker. A lack of response from the victim will assist in eliminating the behaviour of the stalker.

Patterns of reinforcement: the importance of consistent non-responding

The second essential principle of operant conditioning is the impact of timing on reinforcement. The amount of time it takes to eliminate the stalker's behaviour is dependent on the schedule of reinforcement. For example, if the victim has responded to each action by the stalker (*continuous reinforcement*), and the victim suddenly stops responding entirely, the stalker will quickly recognize that their efforts are no longer having the effect that they once were. However, if the victim responds to phone calls after midnight (*partial reinforcement*), the stalker will reinforce their efforts after midnight and it will also be harder to extinguish this particular behaviour because the stalker has found it effective. The most difficult schedule to extinguish is *intermittent* or *occasional reinforcement*, where, for example, the victim answers the phone every once in a while and speaks to the stalker. This type of reinforcement is the most difficult to eliminate because the stalker cannot identify a pattern and, therefore, will keep pursuing the behaviour until the next 'payoff'. A 'classic' example of variable rate reinforcement is gambling, where there are intermittent payoffs. On each gamble, the individual knows that there is a chance of winning. Likewise, the stalker will think they have a chance of contact on each attempt if they recognize that every now and then the victim will react. Therefore, it is essential that the victim resists the temptation to occasionally give in, because the consequences of weakening will make it more difficult to eliminate the behaviour.

Phase I: Background and initial assessment

Stalking need not stem from malice. While obviously hurtful, it is often part of a spectrum of activities that evolve from more conventional patterns of relating. The legal determination of stalking generally requires three elements: (1) a pattern of harassment over time; (2) implied or explicit threats; (3) and intent to harm, intimidate or create great emotional stress (Hickey, 1997). Thus, it is not just the intentions and behaviour of the perpetrator that create a stalking event but how the actions are experienced and articulated by the victim. Stalking is also an unusual offence in so far as it is not determined by one specific act or event but rather by a constellation of intrusive and harassing behaviours committed over time. The most common of these behaviours, as identified in a sample of 145 stalkers (Mullen *et al.*, 1999a) and by self-report of 100 victims (Pathe and Mullen, 1997) are summarized in Figure 14.2.

The percentages in dark tone are taken from the case files of a sample of 145 stalkers referred to an Australian forensic clinic (Mullen *et al.*, 1999a) for evaluation by the court prior to sentencing. Percentages in the lighter tone are from self-reports of victims in 100 cases referred for clinical

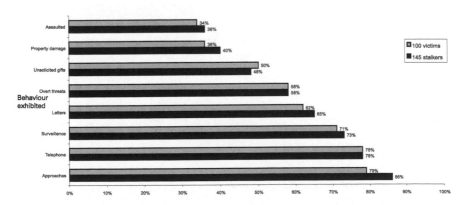

Figure 14.2   Common stalking behaviours

treatment (Pathe and Mullen, 1997) after seeing their GP or by self-referral. Further details of these actions are described below:

Direct approach

A direct approach occurred most often at the target's home, school or workplace. Several assailants refused to leave once they approached the victim, and many had broken into the victim's home. When stalkers approached their victim it was to express their love, plead for a relationship or reconciliation, or to be threatening and abusive (most often only verbally).

Prescribed response: avoid isolation

The victim should try to ensure that they do not become isolated with the stalker. If they are not in a public area, they should attempt to move to one as quickly as possible. They should also not engage the stalker in conversation. Engaging with the stalker in any way will reinforce the behaviour and increase the possibility of future approaches. If the victim's home has been invaded, this is obviously much more difficult. If possible, they should ring the police. They should not wait to call the police because the stalker is known to them or is being calm or reasonable. If unable to ring the police, they should attempt to negotiate a call to a friend or neighbour under the pretence that they were on their way to meet them and they will worry if they are late. Ideally, they should arrange a contact person who can be reached at all times, along with a code word to signify they are in trouble. The crucial element is to inform someone that the stalker is there and they are in danger.

Telephone calls

Repeated and unwanted communication by telephone was also frequently reported (n = 145–78%, n = 100–78%). In many instances the caller immediately hung up, remained silent or attempted to engage the victim in conversations including declarations of love, obscenities and/or threats. Calls were often received in the early hours of the morning or at the victim's place of work. In several instances, answerphones were crammed with stalkers' messages. Stalkers would also go to great lengths to obtain the victim's new number. Employed victims, including professionals, were more likely than other occupational groups to receive harassing telephone calls ($p = 0.016$).

Prescribed response: evidence collection/terminating behaviour

The victim has two choices. They can either use the calls as evidence against the stalker or they can attempt to eliminate the stalker's use of their phone to harass them. If they choose to use the phone to collect evidence, they will have to maintain their existing number. They should invest in a phone where the ringer can be turned off and an answering machine with a volume control and a stock of tapes. They should also inform the telephone company of the situation and that the phone records may be needed as evidence. They will then have to tolerate that their phone may be rendered unusable and they will have to manage recording and cataloguing the tapes to submit to the police. This is obviously a time-consuming and intrusive process but often will provide a wealth of incontrovertible evidence should they wish to bring the stalker to court. Such action can also be rewarding to the victim as they feel they are taking action. If the goal is not to prosecute the stalker but to simply get them to stop the harassment, they should document all calls received so far and then have their number changed. Again, they should explain to the phone company as well as any mobile phone provider that they do not want their number given out to anyone. They should also ensure that friends, family and colleagues know this, as the stalker may try all of these avenues to obtain their new number.

Surveillance

Victims also reported having been kept under surveillance by their stalker (n = 145–73%, n = 100–71%), most often by the individual loitering or waiting in a car outside the victim's home or driving past the victim's home or work repeatedly. In some cases the stalker used surveillance equipment, such as cameras and audio transmitters, to record information on the victim. In a small number of cases the stalker employed a detective agency or persuaded acquaintances to assist in pursuit of the victim. Overtly or covertly, stalkers conveyed their continued knowledge of their victim's movements. Victims in professional employment were less likely to be subject to this form of harassment relative to victims in other occupational categories.

Prescribed response: don't react – record

If the victim suspects they are being kept under surveillance by the stalker, they should again adopt an attitude of non-responsiveness. If they react or interact with the stalker at all, even if the stalker is camped outside their home, they will reinforce this behaviour. They should record all sightings by time, date, location and observed behaviour. They should also report the stalker to the police. The police can then caution, move on or arrest the stalker depending on the circumstances. The victim should not involve unofficial third parties such as neighbours, partners or friends, as the stalker may then target them.

343

Threats

Threats were made to the victim in over half of the cases in both samples ($n = 145–58\%$, $n = 100–58\%$). Threatening behaviour ranged from spreading malicious gossip to discredit the victim, continued harassment until the victim succumbed to demands, threats to kill or rape the victim and threats made to the victim's children or family. Over a third of those who made threats threatened both the victim and a third party ($n = 145–37\%$, $n = 100–33\%$). In the sample of victims, less than half of those stalkers who issued threats went on to assault the victim. Those who did assault their victims had all issued some sort of threat prior to attack.

Prescribed response: dealing with fear

Although in many cases threats are not followed through, the emotional and psychological impact they have on the victim can be profound. Therefore, the victim's concerns should not be dismissed or belittled. Likewise, the victim should not be dismissive of the stalker's threats. Threatening behaviour is an offence and the victim should report all threats to the police immediately. Again, victims should not retaliate or respond to the threats.

Unsolicited gifts/letters

There was also a wide range of behaviours covered in the unsolicited gifts heading ($n = 145–48\%$, $n = 100–50\%$), from quite benign items to very disturbing and upsetting objects. Some stalkers appeared to have sent gifts in misguided efforts to win the victim's affections (e.g. audiotapes, perfume, confectionery, soft toys, jewellery, food parcels and gift vouchers). Other items were sent to annoy the victim (e.g. ordering pizzas, ambulances, magazine subscriptions or airline tickets on the victim's behalf). In a small number of cases the stalker initiated spurious legal action against the victim, often in an attempt to pre-empt the victim's legitimate pursuit of legal redress. Occasionally, stalkers would send items intended to shock, frighten or disgust the victim such as mutilated or intrusive photographs of the victim, and in two unfortunate cases a pig's head and the victim's own cat that had been mutilated.

Prescribed response: refusal

Under no circumstance should the victim accept any item from the stalker. If possible, they should simply return the item, unopened, to the merchant, refuse delivery (flowers, etc.) or, in the case of letters or packages, such items should be turned over to the police. Accepting any item from the stalker could be perceived by the stalker as expressing some interest in pursuing the relationship and can assist in opening up a window of communication with the victim. If the stalker uses particular businesses or services, the victim should speak to the merchant and request that they refuse orders made on his or her behalf.

Property damage and assault

Serious damage to property or assault occurred in a third of all cases (n = 145–40%/36%, n = 100–36%/34%). This included damage to cars (graffiti, scratches, slashed tyres and severed fuel lines) and homes (smashed windows, letter-boxes and fences). In cases where the victim was actually assaulted, most ranged from minor to serious physical attack, but in a minority of cases the victim was sexually assaulted (n = 145–7, n = 100–13). In two cases in the sample of stalkers (n=145), the stalker had attempted to murder the victim, one by strangulation and the other by poisoning.

Prescribed response: report and repair

If the victim's property is damaged, they should again file a report with the police. This can obviously become a continuing drain on the victim and they may be tempted to simply ignore or repair the problem themselves. However, they should be strongly encouraged to continue to actively provide the police with evidence against the stalker. The victim should attempt to have damaged property repaired as quickly as possible as it will only serve as a reminder to them (and the stalker) that the stalker is victimizing them. They should attempt to make their property as secure as possible, but where this is difficult they should be especially vigilant. For example, if their car is parked in an exposed area, they should check for fluid spills underneath or any signs of tampering.

The victim may wish to enrol in a self-defence course. The chief function of such a decision will be to increase confidence and self-awareness. They should also perform behavioural rehearsal, planning for the possibility that they may be attacked. They should run through several scenarios, including worst case (i.e. they are attacked and harmed) and determine how they will deal with it should it occur. Mental preparation and, to a lesser extent, physical preparation may lessen the impact of a physical attack by the stalker. Above all, they should be cautious and aware of their surroundings and should strive not to place themselves in a vulnerable position (i.e. alone in an isolated area).

Phase II: Determination of risk of harm

Risk factors that have been identified by previous research as important to predicting likelihood of harm include: the relationship between the victim and the stalker, the stalker's criminal and psychiatric history, and the use of threats.

Prior relationship

Victims with a prior relationship, and in particular an intimate relationship, are at a higher risk of being physically or sexually assaulted by the stalker.

One is most likely to be stalked by an ex-partner, but also at particular risk are individuals such as psychiatrists, social workers and physicians, whose professions bring them into contact with isolated and disordered individuals, in whom sympathy and attention are easily re-interpreted as romantic interest. The importance of accounting for the presence of an intimate relationship when assessing the dangerousness level of stalking perpetrators is highlighted by studies that have shown that women are at the highest risk of violence from an abusive partner immediately after they terminate a relationship (Schaum and Parrish, 1995; Cordes, 1993). A 1991 study by the FBI reported that 90% of women who were killed by their husbands were stalked prior to their murders. Harmon *et al.* (1995) found that 71% of clinical cases consisted of stalkers who had prior relationships with their victims. Stalkers were categorized into two groups: an affectionate/amorous group that consisted of offenders with a previous relationship or who were pursuing an intimate relationship with the victim, and a persecutory/angry group who did not know their victim and were interested in causing distress and harassment to the victim. Counter-intuitively, the study found that the affectionate/amorous group were more likely to assault their victims than the persecutory/angry group. In a study by Palarea *et al.* (1999), intimate stalkers were significantly more likely to commit violence against persons and property than non-intimate stalkers. Cases in which a threat was made toward a person or property and followed by actual violence were three times as likely to occur in intimate than non-intimate cases. Intimate stalkers also used significantly more physical approach behaviours in contacting their victims.

Suspect's criminal and psychiatric history

Stalkers with previous criminal convictions are at a higher risk of assaulting their victims. Substance abuse and suicidiality by the stalker also increase the risk of assault or property damage to the victim.

Mullen *et al.* (1999a) found that both threats to the victim and assault of the victim were positively correlated with the stalker having previous criminal convictions. Damage to property was strongly positively correlated with substance abuse, though the relationship is less strong in relation to physical assault. Palarea *et al.* (1999) and Zona *et al.* (1998) also found that the presence of substance abuse is a risk factor due to its ability to impede impulse control, lead to paranoid or delusional thoughts in those with other mental health issues, or heighten emotionality. Suicidiality of the stalker has been shown to be a risk factor for attackers and near-lethal approachers who have stalked public figures (Fein and Vossekuil, 1998) as well as for domestic violence situations in which the batterer kills himself and his partner in response to her attempt to leave the relationship (Walker and Meloy, 1998).

Threats

Threats are not reliable predictors of assault. While most stalkers who threaten their victims do not proceed to assault, those that do assault their victims have, in most cases, issued threats.

The use of threats has not been a consistently reliable method of predicting assault. Research has revealed conflicting results, such as the study by Dietz *et al.* (1991a, b) in which threatening letters had no association with approach behaviour toward Hollywood celebrities and had a negative association with approach behaviour toward members of the US Congress. However, many studies have demonstrated that when a stalker does progress to assault, they have previously issued threats to the victim. Meloy and Gothard (1995) found that, while prior intimacy was a powerful predictor for stalkers threatening the victim, threats may be completely unrelated to the risk of physical assault. Most obsessional followers in their sample, even after a year or more of pursuit, did not physically assault their victim.

In the larger study by Mullen *et al.* (1999a), less than half of those who threatened their victims proceeded to assault them, but those that did all had previously issued threats. Therefore, while threats are not reliable predictors of assault, they do indicate an increase in the possibility of assault, as most stalkers who progress to physical attack have previously issued threats to the victim.

The psychological trauma that threats generate can be very significant and should not be overlooked as a factor in managing the case. In a survey by the National Institute of Justice of 16,000 cases, less than half of all male and female victims were overtly threatened by their stalker. In spite of this, stalking victims reported that they were very frightened by the stalker's behaviour or very fearful that the perpetrator would seriously harm or kill them. Fear was generated by the threatening climate created by the stalker's course of conduct, whether or not accompanied by a direct threat.

Phase III: Assessment of symptoms and methods of coping

Victims of stalking are subjected to systematic and repeated psychological abuse. As a consequence they may display any number of stress symptoms. In Pathe and Mullens' study (1997), where victims were clinical referrals or had actively sought the assistance of the authors, there were three common precipitating events that resulted in the victim seeking treatment: (1) escalation in the incidence or severity of the episodes; (2) injury being inflicted whether purposeful or accidental; and (3) relationship and/or employment disturbance. The psychological symptoms displayed and the methods of coping used by the victim should be considered in assisting in the management of stalking incidents. The most common psychological symptoms displayed by victims of stalking are outlined in Figure 14.3.

Arousal symptoms

A very high percentage of stalking victims reported increased anxiety levels, manifest in a variety of ways such as jumpiness, shaking, panic attacks, hypervigilance, exaggerated startle response (often to doorbell or phone) and bruxism (teeth-grinding). The victim may find these symptoms emerge even when they seem to feel relaxed and calm. Victims also experienced chronic sleep disturbance, either due to hyperarousal or repetitive nightmares; appetite disturbances, such as persistent nausea, chronic indigestion, or change in bowel habit; and an increase in frequency and severity of headaches.

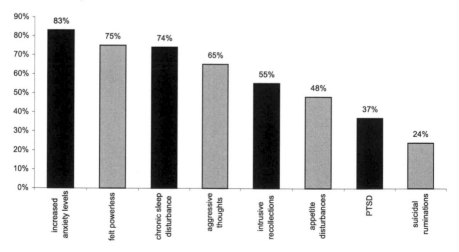

Figure 14.3 Psychological effects of stalking (Pathe and Mullen, 1997)

Suggested response

It is important to explain that these anxiety responses are common stress symptoms. Victims can address these symptoms in the short-term with medication and counselling and clients should be encouraged to seek assistance through professionally recognized counsellors.

Powerlessness

Three-quarters of the victims reported feeling overwhelming feelings of powerlessness. This sense of powerlessness is one of the diagnostic criteria for the more serious (albeit controversial) disorder, post-traumatic stress disorder. Therefore, it is important to combat this by making the victim feel involved in eliminating the stalker's unwanted behaviour.

Suggested response

While the most crucial response by the victim is that they ignore all behaviour by the stalker, this does not mean they should not do anything about it. They should actively compile evidence and diligently pursue the police to take action. They can also participate in support groups for victims of stalking, helping others who are being similarly victimized. These activities lead to more positive coping strategies and also lower stress levels.

Aggressive thoughts/suicidal ruminations

Aggressive thoughts are a common response to stalking. Such thoughts can allow the victim to vent some of the anger and frustration they feel toward the stalker. However, dwelling on these negative/aggressive thoughts for long periods of time can significantly increase anger levels, producing both physical and psychological side-effects, such as increased risk of hypertension and cancer (Speilberger, 1996) and social isolation. Suicidal ruminations, while less frequent, have a similar deleterious impact on the victim.

Suggested response

The victim should be encouraged to move past these thoughts and focus on taking control of their life. If an individual is contemplating suicide, they should be strongly urged to seek professional counselling. Again, focusing on regaining control of their life and feeling as if they can take some type of action toward curing the problem will help combat the feelings of depression and helplessness that lead to suicidal thoughts.

PTSD

Over a third of the sample displayed all of the criteria for a diagnosis of post-traumatic stress disorder (i.e. they had experienced a threat to their life, exposure to injury, helplessness and the manifestation of severe stress symptoms a month post-trauma). Another 18% met all of the criteria except exposure to injury. The rate in this sample is particularly high due to the high rate of physical or sexual assault experienced by the victims (34 were physically or sexually assaulted). PTSD was also more common in those who had been followed by the stalker, as opposed to other forms of harassment. These results emphasize the potential for stalking victims to develop a severely disabling psychological disorder due to the actions of the stalker. Over a third of the victims also reported avoidance or numbing responses, particularly detachment or estrangement from others.

Suggested response

Clinical intervention and a strong social support network are crucial for combating the escalation of severe stress symptoms into such a disorder. Therefore, clients exhibiting detachment (i.e. lack of emotion, eliminating outside contacts, etc.) should be seen as particularly at risk and should be strongly urged to seek professional intervention.

Behavioural responses

All but six victims made major changes in their social and work lives in response to the stalking. The most common responses are displayed in Figure 14.4.

Security measures

Stalking prompted additional security measures in 73% of cases. These measures included: obtaining unlisted telephone numbers and post box

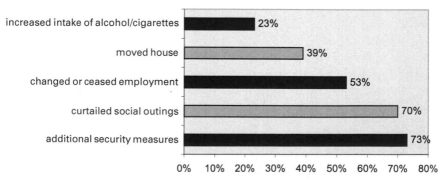

Figure 14.4   Methods of coping (Pathe and Mullen, 1997)

addresses, with a few changing their car and even their surname. Some installed elaborate security systems such as security lights and central monitoring. Three resorted to security guard escorts at work, and others bought guard dogs. These measures often increase the isolation of the victim and the feeling that they are being made a prisoner in their own home. They are constantly reminded that they are under threat and their life is no longer 'normal'.

While victims should be encouraged to take personal security seriously, they should use the least intrusive measures possible. Overt signs of security such as a security guard or an intrusive security system will serve both as a constant reminder of the stalker for them, as well as a sign of reinforcement for the stalker.

Modifying patterns of movement

As a direct consequence of the stalker's actions, 82% of victims had modified their usual activities, avoiding any locations that they thought they might encounter the stalker, such as the supermarket, car parks and train stations. Seventy per cent of victims had curtailed social outings through fear of encountering their pursuer and 53% reported a decrease or cessation of work or school attendance. Often such actions limit the actions of the stalker. However, they also socially isolate the victim and eliminate support networks. Therefore, the victim should be encouraged to modify their patterns of activity but not by excluding or eliminating activities. In other words, they should arrange, if possible, to work unsociable hours. They should vary when they go to the gym, park, grocery store, etc., as much as possible. They should arrange to travel with or meet a work colleague when going to and from work. While the victim may have to exert a great deal of effort and ingenuity to thwart the efforts of the stalker, such action is much more beneficial than eliminating satisfying and rewarding activities or relationships.

Major life changes

In 37% of cases, victims felt that they needed a change in workplace, school or career and 39% relocated their residence, in some cases up to five times. Such drastic upheaval causes distress, with the victim abandoning established community or work relationships. The victim may have to upset the lives of partners and/or children in an effort to evade the stalker. Such efforts were effective (in ceasing the stalking) in 19% of cases (National Institute of Justice, 1998). Therefore, these options should only be considered if the victim has other motivations to move or change employment, or all other options have been exhausted. Many stalkers are very determined and will go to great lengths to track down the victim.

Because this method of coping simply avoids the problem rather than actively addressing it, if the stalker relocates the victim they will simply restart the stalking behaviour.

Summary

All victims felt that their stalking experience had had a deleterious impact on their psychological, interpersonal and/or occupation functioning. Victims drew attention to perceived shortcomings in the responses of both the legal and medical systems. Victims also reported receiving conflicting advice from traditional sources of help, and were often at a loss to know where to turn next for information or positive intervention. Victims often reported that they had considered their ordeal was unique, with some indicating that merely completing the questionnaire in the Pathe and Mullen (1997) study was therapeutic in that it conveyed an awareness of their problems and suffering. Upon entering group counselling, participants reported a sense of commonality, validation and diminished isolation.

The information provided here allows the assessment team to educate a client about the common psychological responses and methods of coping used by victims of stalking. As indicated in the Pathe and Mullen study, simply informing victims that what they are feeling and how they are reacting is normal, allows them to feel less isolated and victimized by the stalker. They should be encouraged however, to seek professional counselling by a qualified therapist to work through their stress symptoms on an individual or group basis.

Phase IV: Determining a plan of action

Based on the goals and outcome desired by the victim, the assessment team and the presenting victim must jointly develop a plan of action in response to the stalking. The client's goals may range from ceasing the stalking behaviour, prosecuting the stalker, or continuing some type of relationship with the stalker.

Plan A: Prosecute

If the client wishes to prosecute the stalker, the focus should be on collecting evidence while limiting the risk to the client and the amount of interference possible by the stalker. The case should also be carefully monitored for any escalation in the stalker's behaviour and both law enforcement and the client's legal assistance should be kept informed.

Plan B: Continuation

If the client wishes to eliminate the stalker's behaviour but would like to continue to have a relationship with the suspect, the best course of action is to educate the individual about the patterns of stalking and the principles of reinforcement. Informing them of the risk of harm from intimate stalkers may encourage them to relinquish the idea of returning to a pre-stalking relationship with the suspect.

Plan C: Cessation

If the client wishes to get the stalker to cease all stalking behaviour, they will have to arrange a carefully planned and rehearsed intervention meeting with the stalker. This meeting will provide a final and objective message to the stalker that the victim is not interested in any future contact. Once the meeting has occurred, the victim must comply with a detailed safety plan for the immediate period following the intervention. The victim must also be educated about how to handle any reoccurrence of the stalking.

The following outline is based on a clinical model, developed by Dziegielewski and Roberts (1995) for assessing and intervening in cases of stalking.

Intervention model

(1) *Collect background* on the stalking case and the client.
- see interview pro-forma in the Appendix to this chapter.

(2) *Complete risk assessment*
- The assessor should also evaluate the risk to the victim by completing not only the background assessment but paying particular attention to the following questions:
    (1) How obsessive is the stalker's behaviour? (i.e. repetitive, intrusive, multiple types of harassment)
    (2) Is the stalker known to be homicidal or suicidal? (i.e. previous history of violence or suicide attempts, threats to kill victim or themselves in the past)
    (3) Does the stalker have access to a weapon? (i.e. location, type of weapon, history of use of firearms or knives)
    (4) Does the stalker have access to the victim? (i.e. how many locations are known to the stalker – work, friends, family, frequent hang-outs/pubs/parks/gym, frequently used shops/garages)
    (5) What is the presence of depression, rage, drug and alcohol dependence of the stalker? (i.e. history of treatment, history of violence, AODA habits/treatment)

- The more of these factors that are present, the higher the risk of possible harm to the victim. If these factors are present, it is ill advised to have a face-to-face meeting between the stalker and the client. The intervention must take place via phone or letter.

(3) **Establish clear objectives** with the client about what they hope to achieve from the assessment.
  - Increase personal security
  - Assess risk of being stalked or being harmed by a stalker
  - Terminate ongoing stalking behaviour

(4) **Intervention plan: notification to stalker that victim is not interested**
  - **Establish ground rules and prepare statement**

  (1) Victim must agree to the importance of establishing very clearly and explicitly that they are not interested to the stalker. They should be made aware that any reinforcement, and in particular a pattern of random reinforcement (i.e. occasionally answering the phone and conversing/shouting at stalker) will encourage and maintain the harassment from the stalker.

  (2) Help victim to deal with the fear of this communication. Often they are fearful of retaliation and will want to mitigate or soften the message. They may also feel extremely angry and may want to shout or use florid language. The message must be communicated calmly and without emotion, which could otherwise be misconstrued as interest by the stalker. Therefore, basic relaxation techniques such as deep breathing or memorizing a repetitive phrase can be helpful.

  (3) The victim should be encouraged to be as direct, concrete and to the point as possible when the stalker is confronted. Behavioural rehearsal of what and how the confrontation will take place is essential. This rehearsal builds the client's security and confidence. The stalker should be told in as few words and with as little emotion as possible. Brevity and shallowness of affect minimize the risk of misinterpretation by the stalker. It is important for the victim to avoid giving reasons for his/her decision, because reasons give hope and leave room for negotiation and argument:

('I am not interested in a relationship with you' vs 'You just aren't my type').

- **Planning the meeting**
  (1) It is essential to advise the victim not to meet the stalker in a private place. No matter how careful the victim is in trying to control confrontation, she/he should always choose a safe place in case the stalker decides to retaliate in anger. This means selecting a place where help is immediately available. Ideally, this can be done over the telephone, where the victim can say their planned speech and hang up.
  (2) The victim should only conduct the intervention when they feel they are ready. They must be clear about their message and confident that they can control their emotions in order to put the message across in the most effective fashion.

(5) *Immediate aftercare for the client*
  - **Safety plan**
    (1) A safety plan should be prepared for the two-week period surrounding this confrontation. Preferably, the confrontation should take place at a location unknown to the stalker previously or not regularly frequented by the victim (i.e. phone from a friend or relative's house and stay with them for a few days). The victim should disrupt their normal patterns as much as possible during the following two weeks (i.e. taking a short holiday, changing work hours, staying with friends/relatives).
    (2) The stalker will attempt to follow up the contact and may seek contact more fervently at this period than any before.

(6) *Follow-up support*
  - Agreement must be established that the victim of stalking behaviour is to cease all contact with the stalker. This is absolutely crucial. Any contact with the stalker, whether positive or negative, may be seen as rewarding and will spark the harassment again.
  - It is important to recognize that the removal of such a continuous pattern/presence in the victim's life will also be difficult for the victim to deal with. As with victims of violence, stalking victims may experience low self-esteem, denial of seriousness of the stalking behaviour, and/or an inability to trust (Bolton and Bolton, 1987). There may be an unhealthy dependency on the

stalker, particularly the longer and more extensive the pattern of stalking.

- Lastly, both the victim and stalker should be evaluated for suicide risk. Depending on the amount of disruption to the victim's life they may feel they have nothing to go back to (i.e. lost employment, relationships destroyed, etc.).
- Stalkers who suffer from borderline traits may try to harm themselves. The victim must be made aware of such a possibility and that they hold no responsibility for such action on the stalker's part. If they attempt to intervene or provide sympathy in any way in response to threats of such behaviour, or actual behaviour, they will only reinforce such tactics and encourage the stalker to start the pattern of harassment again.

(7) *Final assessment*

- The client should be re-evaluated for possible stress symptoms. They should be warned of the possibility that some symptoms do not emerge until after the trauma has been resolved. They should also be advised to consult their GP or counsellor if they are still displaying stress symptoms one month post trauma.
- The goals determined by the client and the assessment team should be reviewed to determine whether or not they have been fulfilled. Such an assessment provides overall closure for the client and the opportunity for the assessment team to review the success and integrity of the programme.

Note

1   Erotomania is described as a type of delusional disorder. Generally, the individual exhibits non-bizarre delusions that involve situations that could occur in real life (e.g. loved at a distance by someone). Specifically in erotomania, there is the delusion that another person, usually considered of a higher status, is in love with the individual. Here the stalker believes that the victim does indeed love him/her but for some reason is denying this emotion.

Appendix

Assessment interview pro-forma – Stalking

Information Collection Interview – Stalking

This pro-forma is designed to collect as much detailed information as possible from the client regarding the behaviour and background of the suspected stalker. The information can be used to advise the client on the best course of action to prevent further stalking behaviour. It will also provide information on how the client should adapt his/her lifestyle to make stalking as difficult as possible. Lastly, it will provide the assessment team with the necessary information to make a determination of risk of harm to the client. Please fill in the following questions with as much detail as possible. Your responses are essential to advise you effectively regarding your case. This information will be held in the strictest confidence and will never be disclosed to a third party without first obtaining your written consent. If you have any questions about any of the items, please ask the interviewer.

Section I: Demographic Information

Name: _____

DOB: [/ /]

Education Level: (please tick the most appropriate choice)

1) some secondary school ___   3) some college____   5) graduate/ professional degree_____

2) secondary school degree____   4) college degree____

Home Address: _____

Postcode: _____

Home Phone number: (____) _____

Mobile: _____

E-mail address: _____

Place of Employment: _____

Work Phone number (if desired): (_____) _____

Suspect: *(please record as much information as you know)*

Name:

_____

Age (approximate):   _____   DOB (if known):   /   /

Gender: M / F / Unknown

Education Level:
1) some secondary school___   3) some college___   5) graduate/
professional degree___

2) secondary school degree ___   4) college degree ___

Home Address: _____
                 _____
                 _____

Postcode: _____

Home Phone Number: (_____) _____

Other numbers: _____ _____
E-mail: _____

Place of Employment: _____
                        _____

Significant contacts (parole officer, siblings, parents, GP, etc.) if known:

Name:_____ Relationship:_____
Phone #: _____
      Address: _____

Name:_____ Relationship:_____
Phone #: _____
      Address:_____

Name:_____ Relationship:_____
Phone #: _____
      Address:_____

Section II: Victim/Suspect Relationship

---

1. Level of intimacy: (please circle the most appropriate category)

(1) spouse/long-term partner   (3) casual acquaintance/ colleague   (5) stranger

(2) close friend/ family   (4) professional/job related contact

2. How long have you known the suspect?
3. Have you had an intimate relationship with the suspect? If yes, for what duration?
4. Have you ever shared a residence with the suspect?

Section III: Contact Behaviours

---

1. When was the first incident of unwanted contact? Please give time of day, approximate date, and type of contact. Include as much detail about the suspect's behaviour and your own reaction.

Approximate Date	Time of Day	Type of Contact	Reaction
			etc.

Phone Calls

---

2. Has the suspect ever contacted you by phone? *(If no, please proceed to question 10)*
3. Is there a pattern to the suspect's calls or is it random? (i.e. certain time of day, time between calls, days of the week)
4. Does the suspect speak into the phone? If not, what do they do? If yes, what is the nature of what is said? (i.e. sexual, romantic, abusive, threatening)
5. What has your response been to these phone calls?
6. Have you kept a record of these calls? If yes, how?
7. Has the suspect spoken to other members of your household? If yes, who and what was said?
8. Does the person leave messages on the answerphone? If yes, have you kept the tapes?
9. Have you been in contact with the phone company? What action have they taken?

Letters/E-mail

10. Have you received any letters/ e-mail from the suspect? How many approximately?

(If no, proceed to question 15)

11. How did correspondence begin between you and the suspect?
12. What was the nature of the content of the letters/e-mail?
13. Do you still have the letters/e-mail in your possession?
14. Did you respond to any of the letters/e-mail? Do you have copies of your responses?

Surveillance/Following

15. Have you suspected or observed the suspect watching you? Please indicate all locations where this has occurred. *(If no, please proceed to question 20)*

Approximate Date	Time of Day	Location	Stalker's behaviour
			etc.
Approximate Date	Time of Day	Location	Stalker's behaviour
			etc.
Approximate Date	Time of Day	Type of Contact	Stalker's behaviour

16. How did you react when you spotted the suspect?
17. Have you suspected you were being followed or have been followed by the suspect? What were the circumstances? (i.e. where was the origin and destination of your journey, was it on foot or by vehicle, how close was the suspect to you?)

Origin/ destination	Time of day	Mode of transport	Proximity of suspect	Duration of event
				etc.

18. How did you react once you realized the suspect was following you?
19. How did the situation resolve? (i.e. suspect waited for you, moved on, attempted contact, etc.)

Attempted or Actual Contact

20. Has the suspect attempted to make face-to-face contact with you (i.e. approached you on the street, come to your place of work or home)? Please provide all locations where this has occurred. *(if no, please proceed to question 27.)*

Location	Time of day	Mode of transport	Proximity of suspect	Duration of event

21. Did the suspect say anything to you or a third party when attempting contact? Please provide as much detail as you can about what was said.
22. How was the situation resolved? What resulted in the suspect leaving the area?
23. What was your response to the attempted contact?
24. Has the suspect made any actual contact with you (i.e. a direct conversation with you, physically touching you, etc.)? Please list all locations where this has occurred.

Location	Type of Contact

25. What did the suspect say or do to you? Please provide as much detail as possible.
26. How did you respond to the suspect? Please provide as much detail as possible. Were you angry or afraid? Did you try to placate the suspect in order to get away?

Threatening or Violent Behaviours

Verbal or Written Threats

27) Has the suspect ever threatened you? Please provide an approximate date. What was the nature of the threat (e.g. to spread rumours, continue to harass you, harm you or your family)? This includes veiled threats, e.g. 'I feel like killing someone, you make me so angry'.
28. How was this threat issued (i.e. in written communication, phone, face to face, third party)?
29. Has the suspect ever issued a threat to a third party directly (written or spoken to someone close to you and directly threatened them)?
30. How did you or the third party respond to the threat?
31. Was there a weapon either mentioned or used as a threat? (saying 'I'll shoot you', holding a threatening object, etc.)

Property

32. Have you ever suspected or known the suspect has damaged your property?
33. What was damaged and how? When and how was it repaired or replaced (i.e. by yourself or by a third party)?
34. Has the offender ever broken into your property (i.e. home or car)? What was taken or done to your property?
35. Have you reported such incidents to the police? Please provide station and name of officer if possible.

Physical

36. Has the suspect ever attempted or actually harmed you or someone close to you?
37. How did the suspect approach you (i.e. attempted conversation, argument, surprise, blitz)?
38. Did the suspect use any type of weapon?
39. Have you reported such incidents to the police? Please provide station and name of officer if possible.
40. To the best of your knowledge, does the suspect have access to or interest in weapons? Please state in as much detail as possible what type and where they are located. (i.e. belongs to a gun club, owns a knife collection, etc.)

Section IV: Personal Security Issues

Patterns of Movement

Please check those statements that apply to you:
I travel to and from work at relatively the same time each day.   ____

I park my vehicle in the same location at work each day.   ____

I travel to other locations according to a predictable routine
(i.e. the gym, grocery shopping, collecting children).   ____

I go to bed at the same time each night.   ____

I go to particular restaurants or pubs on a consistent basis.   ____

I go jogging or walk the dog along the same route, frequently.   ____

Security of Home/Vehicle

1. Do you have a security system on either your home or car? If yes, do you consistently use them?
2. Does anyone have copies of your keys other than yourself? (i.e. roommates, old boyfriends, neighbours, etc.)
3. Do you close your blinds after dark?
4. Do you have an intercom or peephole on your front door? Do you have security lights around the doors and garden?
5. Do you park your vehicle in a garage/on the street/in your driveway when at home?
6. Do you park your car in an isolated area when at work (i.e. large parking garage, unsupervised lot, isolated residential area)?

Personal Security Awareness

7. Have you ever had any self-defence training?
8. Do you carry a personal alarm? What type?
9. Do you take any other personal security measures?

Support Networks

10. Do you have a close network of friends or family with whom you have shared your experiences of being stalked?
11. Have you sought any type of professional support since the stalking started?
12. Have you informed your employer that you are being stalked? What was their response?

13. Have you informed your neighbours that you are being stalked?
14. Who would you say is your closest confidante and support person regarding the stalking?

Law Enforcement Interventions

1. Have you informed the police you are being stalked?
2. Have you ever previously filed a report against someone for stalking or harassment?
3. If you had a prior relationship with the stalker, were the police ever contacted in relation to a domestic incident? If yes, could you please indicate how this situation was resolved?
4. Have you or the police taken any legal action against the suspect in this case? (e.g. restraining order, caution, arrest, etc.)

Note: The next two sections require detailed knowledge about the suspect. If you have no previous relationship with the suspect, you may be unable to answer most of the questions. Please read through them in full and answer those questions you can.

Suspect Psychiatric History

1. Has the suspect ever been hospitalized or received treatment for a psychiatric or psychological problem?
2. Has the suspect ever been prescribed psychotropic medication or undergone psychological counselling?
3. Does the suspect have a history of neurological damage, i.e. severe head injuries, traumatic accident?
4. Does the suspect have a history of or currently have an alcohol or drug problem? Have they ever received treatment for an alcohol or drug problem?
5. Has the suspect ever expressed delusional thoughts, incongruent with reality? This includes things like unsubstantiated jealousy, paranoia or persecution by others.
6. Has the suspect ever threatened to or attempted to kill himself/herself? Has the suspect ever indicated how or where he/she would attempt suicide?

Suspect Criminal/Violence History

1. Has the suspect ever been in contact with the police for suspicion of criminal activity?
2. Has the suspect been arrested or incarcerated at any time? If yes, what was the nature of the offence(s)?
3. Does the suspect have a reputation for or a history of violence? Who is commonly the victim of the suspect's violence?

4. Does the suspect have a history of domestic violence?
5. If the suspect has ever been violent with you, please disclose how and when you were assaulted. Did the violence occur as a situation escalated (argument) or was it without any provocation?

Some basic precautions are outlined in the chart below:
(modified from Houseman, 1993)

How to Protect Yourself ...

At home:	Out walking:	On public transport:	When driving:
Do not leave easily accessible windows open at night.	Don't take shortcuts through lonely areas, day or night.	Avoid lonely bus stops.	Plan your route and check over your vehicle.
Draw your curtains after dark.	Walk facing the traffic so no one can pull up behind you.	On an empty bus, sit downstairs in view of the driver or conductor.	Make sure you have a charged mobile or money for the phone.
Don't put your first name in the phone book or by your doorbell (single woman).	If you go jogging or walk regularly, try to vary the time and the route you take.	On a train, sit near the guard's compartment. Avoid carriages without central walkways.	Let people know where you are going and your expected route and time of arrival.
If you see signs of a break-in, do not enter. Call the police.	Be cautious when unlocking your car or house. Keep an eye out for anyone approaching.	Black cabs are inherently safer than mini-cabs – use only reputable firms.	If you are alone in the vehicle, keep your doors locked while driving. Do not stop to offer directions, etc.

Continued overleaf

Continued from page 365

At home:	Out walking:	On public transport:	When driving:
Do not answer the door to anyone unknown before proof of identification. If you are selling your home, don't show people around on your own.	If you think you are being followed, do not talk yourself out of it. Go to the nearest occupied area and call the police.	Do not answer personal questions (at least not truthfully) such as what neighbourhood you live in, where you work, marital status.	If you break down, do not accept help from anyone but registered emergency services. If you need to speak to someone from the car, keep the door locked and only open the window a couple of inches.

References

American Psychiatric Association (1994) *Diagnostic and Statistical Manual of Mental Disorders* (4th ed). Washington, DC: APA.

Cordes, R. (1993) 'Watching over the watched: Greater protection sought for stalking victims', *Trial*, 29: 12–13.

Dietz, P.E., Mathews, D., Martell, D., Stewart, T., Hrouda, D., and Warren, J. (1991a) 'Threatening and otherwise inappropriate letters to members of the United States Congress', *Journal of Forensic Sciences*, 36: 1445–68.

Dietz, P.E., Mathews, D., VanDuyne, C., Martell, D., Parry, C., Stewart, T., Warren, J. and Crowder, J. (1991b) 'Threatening and otherwise inappropriate letters to Hollywood celebrities', *Journal of Forensic Sciences*, 36: 185–209.

Dziegielweski, S.F. and Roberts, A.R. (1995) 'Stalking victims and survivors: Identification, legal remedies, and crisis treatment', in A.R. Roberts (ed.), *Crisis Intervention and Time-limited Cognitive Treatment* (pp. 175–91). San Diego: Academic.

Fein, R.A. and Vossekuil, B. (1998) 'Preventing attacks on public officials and public figures: A Secret Service Perspective', in J.R. Meloy (ed.), *The Psychology of Stalking: Clinical and forensic perspectives* (pp. 175–91). San Diego: Academic.

Harmon, R., Rosner, R. and Owens, H. (1995) 'Obsessional harassment and erotomania in a criminal court population', *Journal of Forensic Sciences*, 40: 188–96.

Hickey, E. (1997) *Serial Murderers and Their Victims* (2nd edn). Belmont, CA: Wadsworth.

Houseman, R. (1993) *Unleash the Lioness: A women's guide to fighting off violent attack.* London: Hodder and Stoughton.

Meloy, J.R. and Gothard, S. (1995) 'Demographic and clinical comparison of obsessional followers and offenders with mental disorders', *American Journal of Psychiatry*, 152: 258–63.

Mullen, P.E., Pathe, M., Purcell, R. and Stuart, G.W. (1999) 'Study of stalkers', *American Journal of Psychiatry*, 156 (8): 1244–49.

Mullen, P.E., Pathe, M. and Purcell, R. (1999) 'Stalking: False claims of victimisation', *British Journal of Psychiatry*, 174: 170–72.

National Institute of Justice Centers for Disease Control and Prevention (1998) *Stalking in America: Findings from the National Violence against Women Survey.* US Census Report.

Palarea, R.E., Zona, M.A., Lane, J.C. and Langhinrichsen-Rohling, J. (1999) 'The dangerous nature of intimate relationship stalking: Threats, violence, and associated risk factors', *Behavioural Sciences and Law*, 17: 269–83.

Pathe, M. and Mullen, P.E. (1997) 'The impact of stalkers on their victims', *British Journal of Psychiatry*, 170: 12–17.

Schaum, M. and Parrish, K. (1995) *Stalked: Breaking the silence on stalking in America.* New York: Pocket.

Segal, J. (1989) 'Erotomania revisited: From Kraepelin to DSM-III-R', *American Journal of Psychiatry*, 146: 1261–66.

Speilberger, C.D. (1996) *State-trait Anger Expression Inventory Manual.* Lutz, FL: Psychological Assessment Resources Inc.

Walker, L.E. and Meloy, J.R. (1998) 'Stalking and domestic violence', in J.R. Meloy (ed.), *The Psychology of Stalking: Clinical and forensic perspectives* (139–61). San Diego: Academic.

Zona, M., Palarea, R.E. and Lane, J. (1998) 'Psychiatric diagnosis and the offender-victim typology of stalking', in J.R. Meloy (ed.), *The Psychology of Stalking: Clinical and forensic perspectives* (pp. 69–84). San Diego: Academic.

Zona, M., Sharma, K. and Lane, J. (1993) 'A comparative study of erotomanic and obsessional subjects in a forensic sample', *Journal of Forensic Sciences*, 38: 894–903.

Chapter 15

Consent, inference and patterns of abuse in a case of domestic violence

Emily Alison and Laurence Alison

Instructions

The following report has been prepared under the direction of Detective Sergeant Neil Carling, X Police Station, Y Police. We have been asked to assess a set of documentary evidence. In preparing the report we have been provided with the following details:

- A case summary
- And the following witness statements:
- Dr Craig Ealery
- DS Michael Craig, 4 Dec 2004
- PC Michelle Craine, 6 Dec 2004
- PC S John, 17 Nov 2004, 17 Nov 2004
- PC Patrick Michaels, 17 Nov 2004
- PC Theo Gray, 17 Nov 2004
- PC K Perrinel, 17 Nov 2004
- PC Michael Downes, 4–5 Nov 2004
- PC Mary Leess, 5 Nov 2004
- PC David O'Leary, 5 Nov 2004
- PC Warner Southgate, 6 Nov 2004
- PC Jon March, 6 Nov 2004
- PC Patrick Swaine, 17 Nov 2004
- DS Neil Carling, 12 Nov 2004 and 17 Nov 2004

- DC Shelease Davies, 13 Nov 2004
- DC Tony Barret, 12 Nov 2004
- DC Shelley Orton, 15 Nov 2004
- PC Max, 13 Nov 2004
- PC Lawrence Benet, 15 Nov 2004
- PC Julie Citrelle, 17 Nov 2004
- Andy Strauss (neighbour), 17 Nov 2004
- Tracy Parker (neighbour) 17 Nov 2004
- Rosie Casselle (work colleague of A. Winter) (17 Nov 2004)
- A schedule of letters from David Warner to Shelease Winter
- Print of a PNC Record 69/130790M
- Series of police interviews between David Warner (defendant) and the police (3–17 Nov 2004)

Neither of us has interviewed Mr Warner or anyone else involved as witnesses or victims involved in this case and our report has been prepared after inspecting the written evidence alone.

Background to the report

The background to this case is well documented in the interviews highlighted above. Briefly, however, the case involves the following key figures:

- David Warner
- Shelease Winter

Case summary

Our understanding of the current case is as follows: Mr David Warner has been charged with serious assault, rape and false imprisonment as a result of events that took place between 15 November and 3 December 2004, involving Shelease Winter. Warner is a 54-year-old taxi cab driver, with two previous marriages and three children (Sally, 13, Shelly, 8 and Darius, 5). He is a Polish immigrant and served three years as a chef in the Royal Miltary Police in the late 1970s. Since a breakdown involving a previous divorce and his subsequent problems with alcohol, Warner has intermittently attend Trinity House's counselling services for individuals with alcohol-related problems. This establishment has a good track record for working with men who also have had violent relationships with their partners (indeed, Warner makes this point in his statement). He has also worked part-time for 'DriveOne' taxi services in Northton. He has been married to Shelease (34 years) for two years but they have no children.

Warner claims he has been living with Shelease since 1 August (although police found no evidence to suggest a man was sharing Shelease's flat – no clothes, toiletries) and that they had been trying for a baby. (Shelease's boss, Miss Eddies, claims that Shelease kept making comments about how much Warner kept phoning her.) On the weekend of 15 December Shelease went to Northtown for her mother's birthday. While she was there, her phone was switched off for a time and Warner found that strange and thought something wasn't right. Shelease arrived back home on Sunday evening. Warner states that he believed 'something had happened in Northtown' and that he asked some questions that started 'a few minor arguments'.

Tuesday evening Warner picked Shelease up from work and they went to a pub for a drink. Warner became drunk and upset and asked more questions about Northtown. Warner says he found out 'that there had been some form of previous relationship between Shelease and her friend's ex-boyfriend, Oliver'. Warner claims that Shelease 'said that she'd been raped'. (Oliver claims nothing sexual happened between he and Shelease.) They argued and while Warner was in the toilet, Shelease left the pub and went home. It seems Warner's daughter came to pick him up from the pub but an incident with police (possibly involving verbal abuse due to his drunkenness) outside resulted in Warner being taken to a police station although no charges were pressed. Warner then took a cab from the hospital to a friend's house (there is some discrepancy here; in one interview Warner says 'I went to a friend's in Brampton for a little while, then they gave me a lift home' and later says 'when I went to the place the person wasn't there and then I got a lift from someone coming home'). Warner claims the person who drove him home could see he was upset but he didn't talk about it.

Warner claims he was still drunk when he arrived home. He had lost his keys to get in the flat (possibly during the altercation outside the pub) so he banged on the door. (Andy Bach, who lives in the flat above, heard his doorbell at 12.30 pm and reports a man matching Warner's description was trying to get into Shelease's.) The man entered Shelease's flat and Bach heard a lot of door slamming. Shelease opened the door and Warner says he 'lost it and attacked her', 'because she pushed me when I spoke to her about Ollie and that's when I hit back and lost it, I just went crazy'; 'she was pulling at my hair telling me to stop it'; 'I slapped and kicked her'. Warner says he used both his hands and feet but no weapons to hurt Shelease. Warner admits that at one point she was on the floor. (Tracy Parker, Shelease's neighbour, heard a man shouting 'you bitch' among other things at about 1 am and lots of loud bangs and a slap. This went on for over one hour.) Warner claims that after it 'all calmed down' Shelease went to bed.

Warner stayed with her for the following day since she could not go to work. He washed her since she was bedridden and gave her painkillers. Warner claims he asked her if she was all right and wanted to call an ambulance on a few occasions but Shelease said no. He also says he phoned his sister and told her what he had done. The sister advised him to take Shelease to the hospital but Warner says Shelease did not want to go. The day after, Warner left for work (at 'DriveOne' taxi firm). He claims Shelease didn't want the police involved or to go to the hospital. On the Friday evening, Warner admits 'she and I had sex but as on every other occassion … at no point did I ever force her' [in fact] 'she asked me to have sex'. The following day Warner went out to get electricity and gas. He also tried to get Shelease to eat but she said she just wanted to sleep. Warner says he called Shelease's sister, Davina, in Northtown to ask for Oliver's phone number and put the accusation to her. Warner told Shelease to tell Davina what she told him but Shelease wouldn't come to the phone and Davina hung up on him. The following day, Warner bathed Shelease and again tried to encourage her to eat. At this point he said he tried to call an ambulance but there were problems with the phone line and he thought that Shelease may have been cut off by BT. He also stated he phoned Shelease's brother-in-law (Trevor Hairsine, whom he has been friends with for several years) but Trevor denies this. That morning one of Shelease's sisters phoned and then the police got involved. When the police arrived at the flat Warner was returning from a visit to the newsagent. Shelease was found in bed, hardly able to speak, very thin, on a soaking mattress. In hospital, Shelease has been asked who gave her the injuries she had and she was able to reply 'David did it because of Ollie' and that 'he raped me'. She also stated that Warner does not live with her.

Summary of key issues identified in current case

There are two key issues of relevance to the current case that will be addressed by this report, drawing on current research and practitioner experience (EA).[1]

(1) An examination of the role of intent common to domestic violence cases in establishing a pattern of abusive, controlling and violent behaviour.

(2) The frequency and circumstances surrounding the use of sexual violence and rape in domestic violence cases.

This report does not seek to ascertain whether Warner intended to harm the victim on the night of the assault, failed to obtain consent when he had sexual intercourse with her on the night subsequent to the assault, or falsely imprisoned the victim from the time of the assault until the police discovered her. These are clearly issues relevant for the jury. What this report will provide is commentary on research evidence and relevant experience of similar cases to assist in interpreting and examining the particular circumstances in the case at hand.

Domestic violence: background information

Violence in the context of intimate relationships encapsulates many types of abuse: emotional/psychological, physical, sexual and economic. Such abuse can occur within married, separated and divorced relationships or among single people living together or simply dating one another (Paisner, 1991). Many enduring and dysfunctional aspects contribute to the violence that occurs, so it is important to examine how abusive episodes emerge within the context of the ongoing relationship (Dobash and Dobash, 1979). Of all crimes reported to the British Crime Survey in 2000, more than 1 in 20 were classified as domestic violence. Domestic violence accounts for almost a quarter (23%) of all violent crime. Survey reports of domestic violence have also established that repeat victimization is very common within relationships. More than half of all victims of domestic violence are involved in more than one incident of physical violence. No other type of crime has a rate of repeat victimization as high (Kershaw *et al.*, 2000). Work with domestic violence perpetrators and corresponding reports from their partners (EA) indicates that it is uncommon for victims to experience a physically violent attack by their partner as an isolated incident. Reports, both from partners in questionnaires and from perpetrators in treatment, indicate that there is a pattern of non-physically abusive behaviour, comprising verbal abuse (i.e. shouting, swearing, insulting), intimidation (i.e. threats, both verbal and non-verbal, damaging property), financial abuse (i.e. controlling finances, demanding money, theft) and isolation (i.e. cutting victim off from family, friends, taking car keys, falsely imprisoning them in the home) that often precedes physical abuse. In many cases there is no agency involvement until the abuse becomes chronic or escalates to cause serious injury. This is often due to a reluctance by victims to report domestic violence to the police. On average, a woman will be assaulted by her partner or ex-partner 35 times before reporting it to police (Yearnshire, 1997). These reports indicate that there are likely to have been previous incidents of violence before there is any documented evidence of them occurring.

This pattern indicates the progressive and escalating nature of violence within the context of a relationship. Physical violence towards a partner does not simply occur 'out of the blue'. It can be traced back to a build-up of abusive, controlling behaviour that ultimately results in physical aggression and all too frequently murder. In 1999, 37% of female homicide victims were killed by present or former partners, compared with 6% of men. This totals 92 women, one every three days, or two women per week (Criminal Statistics England and Wales, 1999).

Current treatment of domestic violence focuses on unpacking the cognitive intent behind the use of violence. In my work with perpetrators (EA), it is often possible to identify the perpetrators' cognitive processes that lead up to the use of violence. In the current case, there is evidence consistent with the sort of obsessive rumination and anger build-up that frequently precedes violence in relationships: Warner's admission that his suspicions about the victim's infidelity began on Saturday night when he was unable to contact her on her mobile, (extract from int. XYZ, p. 9 'Worried that something was going wrong ...), that Shelease's explanation for switching off her mobile was 'not one that I could accept' and that this led to Warner having negative thoughts (extract from int. ABC, p. 9 'all the negative thoughts start to get to you'). These suspicions and 'negative thoughts' led to 'minor' arguments, resulted in an argument in the pub and finally the assault in the early hours of the following morning. Warner reports that he became upset during the argument in the pub when he found out there had been 'something fishy going on between Shelease and her friend's ex-boyfriend Oliver – it is just the same as what happened with Daisy [his previous wife]'. However, he did not 'lose it' and attack her in the public atmosphere of the pub. In fact he states that 'we weren't like fighting or anything in the pub, we were just, I was asking questions, it isn't the right place and the right time to be speaking about that'. Instead, he left the pub. He was later arrested by the police.

These events suggest that Warner was able to control his behaviour in the public environment of the pub and also that there was a 'cooling-off' period before his next conflict with Shelease at the flat. However, when he did next see her at her flat he states that he became angry very quickly and just 'lost it' and attacked Shelease.

Privacy within intimate relationships is one of the contributory factors that allows domestic aggression to occur unchallenged. Laner (1983) established that most pre-marital violence between college students took place in the absence of witnesses. Similarly, Makepeace (1981) discovered that over half of the violent incidents studied took place in a residence, and a far smaller number occurred outdoors or in vehicles. In similar cases identified in treatment (EA), where there is a preceding argument in a public place and a gap between the initial argument and the physical

373

assault, offenders often report aggressive, violent thoughts toward their partner during the intervening time period. This build-up results in a 'primed' state when they again have contact with their partner and often erupts into violence very quickly, with little provocation from the victim. This pattern had been exhibited by Warner in all three previous relationships. The three previous charges all relate to GBH convictions and in one case (with Daisy Warner) an allegation of rape. In each case, argument emerged in public (at the zoo, restaurant, pub) and in each case there was a delay between the point where Warner walked off and then returned to the victim. In each case, some several hours later, Warner would reignite the argument in the privacy of the home. Interestingly, in the previous conviction against Daisy, he removed his two older children from the house prior to starting the argument but was prepared to beat Daisy in front of their 8-month-old, Darius.

Role of jealousy

Dobash and Dobash (1979) examined how different features of arguments lead to violent episodes. They obtained information on the sources of conflict that led to the first, worst, last and typical violent episodes experienced by victims of abuse. Their study revealed that sexual jealousy and expectations about domestic work were the most frequently reported sources of conflict.

The nature of Warner's correspondence with the victim during his incarceration (See Appendix A: extracts B, F, O, P, S) and comments about his subsequent relationship with her appear to indicate very strong feelings of possessiveness towards the victim:

> (Interview extract DD/MM/YY, p. 8, 'when Shelease went to Northtown she called me and let me know that she got there alright, and then after a while I gave her a couple of calls back, but for some reason after a period of time her phone was switched off for some reason and I don't know why and I found that to be very strange seeing as I said to her not to switch off the phone cos she knew how important it was for me to be able to talk to her because of missing her and things like that'.)

Both men and women in violent relationships frequently report the man's need for constant access to his partner, and rapid suspicion of unfaithfulness based on little evidence (reports from men and their partners in treatment; EA).

Psychological themes of attachment, abandonment and loss underpin interpersonal theories of domestic violence (Murphy et al., 1994). Interpersonal dependency reflects a husband's disturbed attachment to his partner. There is a need to associate closely with, interact with and rely heavily upon valued others. A consequence of these features can lead to an excessive fear of rejection or abandonment from a partner (Langhinrichsen-Rohling *et al.*, 1998). This high level of dependency may predispose some men to control their partner through coercion and violence (Murphy *et al.*, 1994). A result of appraising concern over a partner's autonomy as threatening to emotional security and well-being can lead to arguments about perceived unfaithfulness (fear of abandonment and rejection) and concern over the levels of contact with relatives 'outside' of the direct relationship, which may, in turn, lead to abuse.

Research on attachment theory in relation to offenders who physically and sexually assault their partners suggests that perpetrators have difficulty trusting others and often feel rejected, abandoned or slighted by their partners (Dutton *et al.*, 1994; Murphy *et al.*, 1994). As a result and consistent with the reports of victims of marital/intimate rape, they tend to be jealous of their partners' attention to others and are preoccupied with or over-dependent on their partners (e.g. Frieze, 1983). When these men sense actual or perceived abandonment on the part of their partners, they may use non-sexual or sexual violence in an attempt to re-establish their attachment or hold on her. These considerations lead us into the frequency and role of sexual violence in abusive intimate relationships.

Sexual violence

It is very important to note that sexual violence within the context of intimate relationships is not rare. Various research studies have determined that in a random sample of women in the US, between 10% and 34% are assaulted by an intimate adult partner (Browne, 1993). In these random samples, sexual assault in marriage was reported to occur three to four times *more often* than rape by a stranger. In studies of women who have also experienced physical violence, rape and sexual assault are even more prevalent, and have been recorded in 33% to 59% of cases (from samples of battered women living in shelters). Studies have also found that victims who have experienced both sexual and physical violence are more likely to be victims or perpetrators of homicide (Campbell, 1989). Recent research reports here established sexual violence, possessiveness, jealousy and threats of suicide or homicide within an intimate relationship as reliable indicators of greater risk of harm (Paradine, K., National Crime and Operations Faculty, presentation at NW region DV conference 26/11/02; Adams, P. and Andys, L., Serious Crime Group, Met Police, presentation at NW region DV conference 26/11/02) and by validated actuarial risk-assessment tools (SARA: Spousal Assault Risk Assessment, British Columbia Institute for Family Violence).

To establish how sexual violence is used within relationships, several studies have attempted to establish typologies of 'intimate/marital' rapists. Finkelhor and Yllo (1985) put forth a typology of three types of marital rapists: battering rapists, force-only rapists, and obsessive rapists. In a sample of 50 victims of intimate/marital rape, 48% were classified as the battering type, 40% as force-only and 6% as obsessive type rapists. *Battering rapists* are described as subjecting their partners to a great deal of non-sexual and verbal abuse, most of it unrelated to sex. The sexual violence is believed to be primarily another aspect of the general abuse and is used to further abuse and establish control over the victim. In contrast, *force-only rapists* use force in a more functional way to gain sexual access when it is denied rather than as an extension of other violent behaviour. They rape their partners to satisfy their desire for sex, regardless of their partner's consent. *Obsessive rapists* are postulated to be heavily involved in pornography and to be extremely demanding of sex, often several times a day, and the sex becomes more sadistic and unusual over time.

In my work with domestic violence perpetrators (EA), battering or force-only rapists are the most common type of sexual perpetrator I encounter. (I have worked with only two cases that could be classified as obsessive rapists.) In the majority of cases, the sexual contact or intercourse often occurs during or shortly after a physically or verbally violent incident. This includes behaviour such as grabbing the partner's genitals, digital penetration, forced oral, vaginal or anal sex, insertion of foreign objects, etc. There is often no overt physical or verbal resistance from the woman to the sexual contact but she reports either to the police or to partner support services that she did not consent and only complied because she was afraid for her safety if she refused.

It is often the case, in my experience with men who have sexually abused their partners (10–15% of court-referred perpetrators; EA), that they express positive intentions for the sexual contact ('to make it up to her', 'show my love'). They deny any awareness that their partner may have felt afraid to refuse sexual contact given the violence she had just experienced and often state that 'she didn't say no' or 'she didn't stop me' as an indication of consent, with little recognition of the intimidation and threat of violence that may have forced acquiescence in such circumstances.

While these are the explanations and justifications often encountered with perpetrators in treatment, the question remains of whether it is a reasonable assumption that after a man has physically assaulted his partner, she would freely and willingly consent to sexual intercourse. The case at hand also has the additional factors to consider in that the victim was injured so badly she was bedridden and unable to feed or bathe herself at the time of the sexual encounter. The medical evidence of her mental impairment at the time of the sexual encounter should also be considered a key factor in establishing consent.

Consent

The following is a brief summary of the consent issues considered by the authors when writing this report. It is not presented as 'legal' expertise and is simply included to provide a framework for the consideration of consent in cases of intimate/marital rape. At present, the Sexual Offences Act 1956 defines the mental element in rape as:

A) actual knowledge of the absence of consent or
B) recklessness as to the absence of consent.

The Sexual Offences (Amendment) Act 1976 further provides that in considering if the defendant had an honest belief that the victim had consented, the jury must consider the presence or absence of reasonable grounds. The courts have since found that the defendant is reckless if he does not have a belief that the other person was consenting or his attitude is one of indifference as to whether the other person is consenting or not (i.e. he couldn't care less).

The Ministerial Group on Domestic Violence has made the following proposals on reform based on the independent Sex Offences review set up in 1999. That 'consent' should be re-defined as 'free agreement' coupled with a list of examples where, if found to exist, the defendant will have to prove – on the balance of probabilities – that consent was given. Thus, issues such as:

- victim was abducted or *unlawfully detained*

- victim did not understand the purpose of the act through *lack of capacity to understand* or deceit

- victim was *asleep, unconscious,* or too affected by drink or drugs

- *victim submits because of threats or fear of serious harm or serious detriment to themselves* or another

would bring into question whether free agreement was the case. In the present case Warner indicates that he had to 'clean her up' the morning after the assault. He also indicates that she was in pain and was bedridden (p. 18, DD/MM/YY). He states that the victim was unable to eat for two to three days and that he had to change the bed sheets. He indicates that after witnessing all of these indications that the victim was seriously injured, he himself was concerned enough to want to take her to hospital. However, he then had sex with the victim two days after the initial assault. Clearly, an evaluation of the medical evidence will be crucial in determining the capacity of the victim to consent but one must also consider the potential fear that may have been engendered subsequent to such a physical assault and the resultant fear of resisting sexual advances.

Summary and conclusions

As stated at the outset of this report, it is not possible for any 'expert' to establish the intent of a defendant in such a case unequivocally, either through experience of working with offenders or through knowledge of the literature. However, our report may assist the court in providing informed advice as to general trends and patterns of abuse in physically and sexually violent relationships. In particular it draws attention to the following points:

- Physically violent acts are generally preceded by a history of other abusive events. Indeed, victims rarely report abusive episodes until very severe attacks have occurred. Therefore, it is rare for a perpetrator to suddenly 'lose control', having had no other previous behavioural history of controlling, abusive behaviour.

- A physically abusive attack on a victim can be sufficiently intimidating for a victim to feel too afraid to resist sexual advances and attempts at intercourse. Thus, the victim may not actively resist because of fear of subsequent physically abusive repercussions.

Note

1 Comments that are based on the experience of working with offenders in a therapeutic setting, i.e., Emily Alison, are referenced 'EA'. They are not necessarily based on a body of empirical literature and should be seen as distinct professional experienced opinion relevant to the second author and distinct from comments based on well recognized research.

References

Browne, K. (1989) 'The materialistic context of family violence and child abuse', in J. Archer and K. Browne (eds), *Human Aggression: Naturalistic Approaches*. London: Routledge.

Dobash, R.P. and Dobash, R. (1979) *Violence Against Wives: A case against the patriarchy*. New York: Free Press.

Dutton, D.G. (1994) 'The origin and structure of abusive personality', *Journal of Personality Disorder*, 8: 181–191.

Dutton, D.G., Saunders, K., Starkomski, A. and Bartholomew, K. (1994) 'Intimacy-anger and insecure attachment as precursors of abuse in intimate relationships', *Journal of Applied Social Psychology*, 24 (15): 1367–1386.

Dutton, D.G. (1995) *The Domestic Assault of Women*. Vancouver, BC: UBC Press.

Dutton, D.G. and Browning, J.J. (1988) 'Concern for power, fear of intimacy and aversive stimuli for wife abuse', in G.T. Hotaling, D. Finkelhor, J.T. Kirkpatrick and M. Straus (ed.), *New Directions in Family Violence Research* (pp. 113–121). Newbury Park, CA: Sage Publications.

Finkelhur, D. and Yuo, K. (1985) *License to Rape: Sexual abuse of wives*. New York: Holt, Rinehart and Winston.

Kershaw, C. *et al.* (2000) *The 2000 British Crime Survey: England and Wales*. London: Home Office.

Laner, M.R. (1983) 'Courtship abuse and aggression: Contextual aspects', *Sociological Spectrum*, 3: 69–83.

Langhinrichsen-Rohling, J., Schlee, K.A., Monson, C.M., Ehrensaft, M. and Heyman, R. (1998) 'What's love got to do with it?: Perceptions of marital positivity in aggressive, distressed, and happy marriages', *Journal of Family Violence*, 13: 197–212.

Makepeace, J.M. (1981) 'Courtship violence among college students', *Family Relations*, 30: 97–102.

Murphy, C.M., Meyer, S.L. and O'Leary, K.D. (1994) 'Dependency characteristics of partner assaultive men', *Journal of Abnormal Psychology*, 103: 729–35.

Paisner, S.R. (1991) 'Domestic violence: Breaking the cycle', *The Police Chief*, 35–7.

Walker, L.E.A. (1989) 'Psychology and violence against women', *American Psychologist*, 44: 695–702.

Yearnshire, S. (1997) 'Analysis of cohort', in S. Bewley, J. Friend and G. Mezey (eds), *Violence Against Women*. London: RCOG.

Chapter 16

Conclusions: personal reflections on the last decade

Adrian West and Laurence Alison

Since 'exactness', or accuracy of work, is of so much importance in all branches of research, this accuracy must also be applied to the work of the Investigating Officer. But what is to be understood by accurate work? It consists in not trusting to others but attending to the business oneself, and even in mistrusting oneself and going through the case again and again. By so proceeding, one will certainly bring about an accurate piece of work.

That [the] services to the public are great and [the] labours [of the investigator are] full of interest will generally be admitted, but rarely, even among specialists, is full credit given to the difficulties of the position. (Gross, 1950)

Undiscovered territory

This book is written in the hope that familiarity with the logic of scientific enquiry and a willingness to apply the findings of investigative psychology (Canter and Alison, 1997) will enhance the application of a more rational and systematic method to police investigative efforts. One of our purposes has been to demonstrate how investigative support and advice, linked to the theoretical and research base of behavioural science, can be applied effectively to the investigation of serious crime (West,

2001). We believe that serious crime investigation requires the collaboration of highly able personnel from a range of investigative backgrounds, who are both police and non-police specialists. We also believe that the scientific paradigm, developed by a number of key individuals in the last ten years, incorporating principles and methodologies derived from a number of different disciplines, including decision-making, leadership and management studies, forensic psychiatry, forensic psychology and environmental psychology, has a pivotal role in this combined investigative endeavour.

The application that has attracted most attention, frequently called 'offender profiling', involves an attempt to clarify the actions of a perpetrator and then relate those actions to our varied attempts, either to understand the interpersonal function of the crime or to clarify motivation and determine membership of an offender typology. However, as the chapters in this volume demonstrate, the role of 'offender profiler' has extended beyond inferring offender characteristics from behaviour exhibited during a crime. In fact, subsequent contributions to police work and investigations extend well beyond attempts to set suspect parameters or explain the behaviour of the offender in one-off critical incidents. Rather, as had been recognized by 1996, offender profiling had become a generic term encompassing 'a range of methods that are used to provide advice to crime investigators' (Adhami and Browne, 1996). Such advice might include whether a crime appears to be part of a series or developing specific advice on the running of an enquiry. This might include advice on media strategy; interview strategy; DNA intelligence-led screens; risk assessments and strategies for locating the whereabouts of an offender (geographic profiling). 'In these ways, offender profiling, in all its guises, is viewed as a means of improving crime detection practices' (Adhami and Browne, 1996, p. 1). The recognition that such advice is probably requested more, is found more useful and is probably more reliable and valid than advice on unknown offender characteristics (Copson, 1995) was one of the main reasons that influenced in 2001 the introduction of the less contentious title of 'behavioral investigative advisor'.

As well as the high-profile contributions that may range from advice influencing the decisions made at the earliest stages of a child abduction to the selection of appropriate officers for interviewing a serial offender, these varied offerings increasingly include operational advice that supports day-to-day policing. However, whether that advice impacts on the assessment and management of high-risk sex offenders, or the content and structure of press appeals, or hostage negotiation strategies, the imperative to relate 'the advice from the psychologist' to the theoretical and research base of behavioural science remains.

Recovered ground

Today, it is easy to overlook just how much dismissal and rejection of anything or anyone to do with behavioural science prevailed among some detectives ten years ago. Readers should not underestimate how unwelcoming some incident rooms used to be to newly arrived outsiders. Training in either clinical or investigative psychology was not required to deduce that one's preliminary suggestions counted for little when the senior investigating officer (SIO), in one instance, walked out of the incident room as the psychologist walked in. Such intolerance reflected institutional cynicism and a traditional closed police culture that needed little assistance or training but its own. However, impressed by the developing approach of the FBI's Behavioural Science Unit in the 1980s, Sir John Stevens and other senior detectives had already endorsed the assistance of a small number of psychologists in murder investigations and had supported research into the effectiveness of their advice. Some had also realized that, 'In some instances, profiles do appear to have been little more than ill informed, speculative, impressionistic, personal and ambiguous opinions, based on the perceived status of the profiler as Psychologist' (Canter and Alison, 1999). However, there was still a willingness to consider the contribution of behavioural science, especially in apparently motiveless crimes or protracted murder investigations, where the police still struggle to make sense of an offender's actions and motivation. Nevertheless, at the time of the Nickell trial collapse, offender profiling found itself in a much-maligned position. Then, the outlook for psychologists with aspirations to assist the police in major crime enquiries was very poor.

But in many ways the depth of police scepticism and opposition was warranted. Some psychologists, failing to recognize the complexity of police investigations and the judicial process, had been too swift to criticize police methods. Furthermore, television personifications of the mythical offender profiler and other media attention reinforced police cynicism about the true motives of psychologists and allowed them to justify their resistance easily. Although an entertained public might have been convinced by dramas and airport books, the police were acutely aware that there are no cases where the profiler replaces or directs the investigation team and no cases where the entire prosecution case has stemmed from the psychological profile alone. While the psychological profiler became a crucial part of the stories culture tells about homicide, detectives anticipated that they would appear in a negative light in the profiler's stories. In television series such as 'Cracker', where the police were presented as antagonistic rivals withholding information, the mythical profiler was more intelligent, righteous and morally courageous.

He also supposedly possessed a greater degree of humanity that enabled empathy with the extremes of human behaviour. Such media portrayals irritated detectives whose dedication to victims and their families and unremitting efforts to solve a case were reduced to the tired and worn ways of 'thick plod.'

More damaging still was the notion that offender profiling itself equated with self-serving publicity seeking. Stuart Kind, the forensic science advisor to the Byford Inquiry, had previously noted well before the advent of the mythical 'profiler' that the public's large appetite for crime reading 'will doubtless continue to confer undeserved reputations or oppositely to withhold deserved ones' (Kind, 1987, p. 4). Furthermore, potential abuses of privileged access to police incident rooms and data made a police service with a well-developed ethic of confidentiality towards victims and their families increasingly wary about allowing other interested professionals, including researchers, anywhere near primary data. The corresponding compromise to research efforts into serious crime is still felt.

Less self-serving publicity, less over-confidence and a commitment to working quietly with the police when providing operational advice have led, gradually, to improved relations. Due acknowledgement for an improved situation should also be accorded to a number of police officers, including Rick Holden, Rupert Heritage, Stuart Kirby, Bradley Jones and Steve Watts,[1] who first carried out empirical research in the UK and then worked as 'profilers' or advisors. Their contributions led to a greater willingness among the service to consider the relevance of offender profiling because such advice was coming from individuals who understood the police world intimately, rather than naïve academics who had a limited appreciation of the landscape of policing.

The psychologist as advisor to the police

Anyone embarking upon a career of advising a senior investigating officer directing a major crime enquiry should appreciate from the start that to advise is strictly that. Moreover, in the line of advisors who can assist an enquiry, forensic science advisors are likely to remain primary, especially in light of the superior advances in DNA technology. However rational or evidence-based their advice, keen but naïve psychologists, used to an ethos of multidisciplinary working and an openness to peer review, should be prepared to be frustrated. At the same time, they should also be capable of demonstrating specialized expertise and sound judgement under pressure, appreciating that the urgency of an incident room is a long way from the relative indolence of a hospital case conference or academic seminar. Nevertheless, the psychologist's responsibility to disclose a lack of expertise when asked to undertake an activity for which she or he is unqualified remains (cf. Dietz and Reese, 1986).

Advisors should also recognize the unique pressures confronting a senior investigating officer. The reality is that, especially after the Stephen Lawrence Inquiry,[2] an SIO faces pressure from every direction during the rapid and relentless demands of those first long days of an investigation (see Macpherson, 1999). Police investigators' work often begins with the experience of the visual trauma of a violent death scene and post mortem. Information overwhelms, and can be influenced by a difficult-to-manage media. The necessary immersion in the detail of an investigation often leads to constant preoccupation, rumination and, unsurprisingly, negative personal, emotional and physical consequences for the individual, however resilient. Perhaps students who are keen to investigate serious violent crime and aspire to become profilers recognize that they could not perform the far more demanding role of senior investigating officer.

As the chapter by Ogan and Alison demonstrates, police work often involves a set of complex management skills that extend well beyond the remit of 'catching the offender'. The need to consider the impact of the enquiry on the community carefully, to manage the media and to generate morale among the team requires interpersonal and cognitive skills that are still poorly understood both at a tacit and academic level. The investigator's task can be further complicated by the conflicting objectives of senior figures, sometimes external to the police, with little investigative experience but with reputations and personal ambitions to defend.

It is, therefore, important to appreciate the layers of complexity in managing critical incidents. Crego and Alison's (2004) work captures some of this complexity in their analyses and debriefs of a number of major enquiries. They identified a generic model of critical incident management in which they recognized how critical incident managers must deal with a very wide spread of issues that range from the relatively focused aspect of managing the incident itself, through to the wider political ramifications, many of which had been previously identified by Smith and Flanagan (2000). These are summarized below, in order from the specific to the general, in the 'management pyramid':

- Managing the incident
  (e.g. the complexity of the enquiry, keeping accurate records)

- Managing the team
  (e.g. delegation, team skills, team atmosphere)

- Managing the community
  (e.g. local community, race and diversity, family liaison)

- Managing the culture of the police environment
  (e.g. race and diversity, culture, ACPO)

- Managing political and local/national government issues
  (e.g. local and national government).

Thus, the effective management of a critical incident requires the employment of decision-making and interpersonal skills across a wide range of circumstances and people. The critical incident manager must be able to review this material constantly and remain objective. The joint functions of having to bear responsibility for success or failure while being unable to account for the decision-making of individual investigative staff place considerable stress on the manager. Ultimately, much of the responsibility for the eventual outcome will rest on the shoulders of one person: the senior investigating officer.

Although Innes (2003) claims that the shift towards a more rationalized and bureaucratic organizational system in murder teams has meant that major crime enquiries are less autocratically centred on the figure of the SIO, the reality is that the lead role of the SIO, and his or her competence, analytical skill, leadership and experience, remain critical determinants in the resolution of a major crime enquiry. Maintaining an objective, dispassionate enquiry unencumbered by the surrounding emotional clamour becomes paramount. An investigative mind that weighs the details of the individual, specific case against identified patterns and relationships from the literature and relevant databases becomes a critical support to an SIO under pressure.

Unsurprisingly, however robust the science, it is the psychologist's skill of developing a relationship with an SIO under pressure and communicating useful and timely advice that is one of their most useful attributes. Consequently, advice should be explicit, accurate and concise. Despite the temptation to embed uncertain advice in detailed caveats and counter-arguments, written reports should also be as clear as possible in detailing the forensic psychologist's findings and advice.

Faced with the prospect of legal scrutiny at trial and review of advice in the following months and years, those psychologists who are prepared to put their heads above the parapet should at least be able to rely on having kept detailed notes and produced reports on which they can rely. They should always be mindful of the dictates of their own relevant professional codes and the advice of their most astute critics. As Ormerod and Sturman's chapter indicates, when it comes to the use of offender profiles, the court will not find it too challenging to deconstruct the material systematically if there is any attempt to adduce it as evidence. When you are facing a judge and the barristers, it is too late for second thoughts.

Clarity

In contributing to casework, there are a number of issues that must be clarified before embarking on such reports. Providing advice to the police or the courts is not simply a matter of giving an opinion. Rather, as this book has been at pains to point out, students and practitioners need some understanding of one another's worlds in order to work together effectively. In terms of the communication of advice, this means:

- Specifying agreed objectives, terms of reference and schedules for production of preliminary and final written advice.

- Assessing the available information and developing working hypotheses about the inferred actions of the offender. This stage of the investigative cycle typically requires accessing relevant research literature, databases and discussions with academics and practitioners, including forensic advisors (see Alison, West and Goodwill, 2004).

- Clearly articulating inferences based on crime-scene assessment and information gathering from the context of the crime including analysis of witness depositions and location visits.

- Suggesting practical and achievable lines of enquiry that assist in the search for further relevant information and evidence.

- Providing briefings to senior investigating officers and their teams, ensuring that information is communicated accurately and the rationale for any suggested lines of enquiry is articulated. This is critical where resource-intensive search strategies or DNA intelligence-led screens are influenced.

- When required, providing information and training material from the behavioural science literature to investigators about the aetiology and motivational characteristics relating to various offence types. This is typically used to support and improve skills in investigative interviewing.

- Including recommendations in accordance with legislation relating to disclosure of records and data protection.

The 'investigative credo' set out below is based on the authors' experience and mistakes in the field and provides a number of useful questions that any psychologist can ask him or herself before presenting their findings. This is admittedly a personal set of reflections that may usefully be considered alongside other chapters in the volume (most importantly the chapter by Alison, Goodwill and Alison). Given the potential complexity of the task, to perform the role effectively, one way of avoiding mistakes is for practitioners not to underestimate the time, the stress and the commitment required addressing the following:

1. Will my report be provided on time?
2. Have I discussed fees and have these been agreed?
3. Have I agreed the objectives of the report?
4. Do I know who the central contact is in this enquiry if I need further details?
5. Do I have a realistic idea of how long this case will take me?
6. What features of the case are influencing current investigative priorities?
7. Has an exhaustive crime-scene assessment been used to maximize the information that can be derived to determine the sequence of events and offender behaviour?
8. Have I visited the crime scene and its environs so that I am aware of the geography of the case?
9. Is photographic evidence sufficient for me to appreciate the crime scene and its geographic significance?
10. Has an exhaustive assessment of the emerging statements been conducted to determine what information is convergent or corroborative; divergent or contradictory?
11. What information has been decided is redundant for the investigation?
12. What features of the offence alone or in combination are influencing my interpretation?
13. What are my provisional hypotheses?
14. What are the investigative team's provisional hypotheses?
15. Am I influenced by 14?
16. Is my current interpretation congruent with any related theories?
17. Have any similar (historical) cases been identified as sources for further understanding?
18. Have any cases or incidents been identified as potential links?
19. Have I allowed myself to be subject to peer review?
20. What further enquiries have now been initiated?
21. Have my findings been influenced by external pressures, group dynamics, heuristics or biases in a way that reduces their accuracy or usefulness?
22. Have I based my findings on a clearly defined evidence base, and used this evidence to support any recommendations made?
23. Which datasets have I accessed and are they relevant to the case under investigation?

24. Am I presenting my findings in a way that is unambiguous and will not lead to misunderstanding or misinterpretation?
25. Have I succeeded in meeting the objectives originally defined?
26. What has been the effectiveness of my advice?
27. Have I written up the facts of the case, the process of my decision-making, my analysis, interpretation and discussions with other experts?

It is imperative that forensic psychologists are constantly aware of the investigator's perspective when preparing to present their findings. Consideration of questions such as these will increase the likelihood of producing findings that the police find unambiguous, practical and reliable, thereby reducing the risk of undermining the progress this field has made in the last decade. In turn, this will ensure that the forensic psychologist continues to be invited to contribute to police investigations with increasing acceptance and understanding. Only then will they be able to maximise the spectrum of the contributions they can offer, as well as increasing their reliability and practicality.

The range of contributions

During the last ten years an increasing number of psychologists have advised on an increasing number of enquiries, confident that their advice links to a consolidating research base. In so doing they have gained extensive experience and considerable practical knowledge of police investigative roles and procedures and so have identified areas for research and development. As a consequence, there have been significant improvements in police investigative practices, in particular relating to the investigation of sexual assault, domestic violence, arson, the interviewing of vulnerable witnesses and the training and deployment of investigative analysts. Many of these issues have been considered in this volume, though the reader is invited to extend his/her knowledge base by reference to the many journals, websites, books and references that support the idea that this is a growth area of research where there is considerable optimism that valid contributions can be made. Barrett's chapter notes many of these reference sources and some others are provided at the end of this chapter.

There have also been many positive professional developments. For example, there now exists a process of accreditation of advisors assisting the police in the behavioural investigative advisor (BIA) role. Professional standards are developed and maintained through scrutiny of reports and advice by an Association of Chief Police Officers Board, which includes two professors of forensic psychology.

The BIA role has forced a more careful and thorough review of suspects' backgrounds and personal histories in order to better understand their motivations and actions. This is especially critical for the preparation of investigative interview advice, where it is no longer sufficient to 'tick off' the cognitive interview 'pro-forma' but where officers recognize the need for a deeper understanding of the suspect who is in front of them.

Further, profiling has forced some clinicians to place less emphasis solely on the accounts of offenders, and to consider crime-scene photographs and witness depositions in order to enhance their understanding of the actions of a perpetrator in the commission of a crime. This development may prove especially critical in improving risk assessment and management. As members of the police service develop their role as key players in multi-agency protection work, they will need to continue to improve their knowledge of the heterogeneity of sex offenders. Investigative psychology and behavioural science have brought about a focus on offender actions and interpersonal functions of violence. This has led to the slow realization that the mindset of *modus operandi* and the expectation that one template of a crime has to be exactly replicated with an individual offender is not only an erroneous assumption but can lead to investigative myopia and a failure to see people who are sometimes literally in front of our eyes. Many individuals are contributing to this area and in Wilson and Alison's chapter there are several key references to the central pieces of research in the classification of sex offending.

Conclusions

Overall, through research and practitioner efforts, in providing behavioural investigative advice, forensic psychologists aim to make sense of the myriad issues pertinent to the crime in question and to inform ongoing investigative work. Happily, many of the previous clashes of personality and politics have subsided, to be replaced by a more collegiate atmosphere. In the UK, the Division of Forensic Psychology (DFP; a subsection of the British Psychological Society) has begun to recognize that the academic and practical contributions that psychologists can make extend well beyond therapeutic interventions with offenders or psychometric evaluations and risk assessments. The DFP has begun to challenge previous assumptions about the role of the forensic psychologist and are opening up other professional pathways through to chartership. The recognition that professional practice may include advice to the courts and the court process, advice to the police service in terms of working practices and the management of critical incidents has been a long time coming. However, the DFP has begun to embrace the idea that the remit of what it is that forensic psychologists do is wider than may have initially been assumed. This recognition may, in turn, 'roll the wicket' for investigative psychologists who wish to develop their specialist role in concert with law-enforcement agencies, thereby enabling them to convince the relevant authorities that forensic psychology can make a real and applied contribution.

As the police service realizes that the days of relying on a detective's instinct are gone, an investigative mind that considers the details of the individual case against identified patterns and relationships from the literature and relevant databases is critical in determining the optimal direction of an enquiry. It is clear, based on the number of police officers studying psychology and related disciplines, that the commitment to evidence-based investigative practice is well underway. Several new forensic courses are appearing in the UK and there have been other developments in the US, Canada and Europe. Many police officers successfully complete such courses each year and many more go on to study for PhDs. Further, based on our own experience and anecdotal evidence, many more officers are eager, during the process of discussing casework, to understand the psychology behind the claims. This demonstrates a commitment to using the scientific method as a cornerstone of policing, as well as a healthy questioning outlook on the advice received.

These optimistic developments should, however, be considered against our observation that an ethos that promotes collaborative multi-disciplinary teamwork may still be some way off. Aspirations to professionalize the role of the investigator and the inclusion of investigative science as a core discipline in police training might yet see a more equal partnership in the investigative endeavour. Part of the requirement rests firmly on the shoulders of forensic psychologists. A greater appreciation of the investigator's world and how the effectiveness of an investigation relies upon the competence, analytical skills, leadership and experience of the SIO helps make it clear to psychologists that the need for objective and empirically based advice is paramount. It is also accepted that even if investigators embrace the contribution from psychologists, they should retain a healthy scepticism. As Canter and Alison (1999) noted, 'One must check and treat with caution all opinions and not simply assume that because it is said with great conviction by someone with experience that it must be true' (p. 39). Readers are encouraged to bear in mind this recommendation when considering any work that suggests psychology and psychologists can make a contribution (including, of course, this volume!)

This book is designed to help illustrate the argument that forensic psychologists can benefit from trying to gain some appreciation of the stress, complexity and ambiguity of the investigators' world. Needless to say, it is one thing to gain an appreciation and quite another actually to experience this world, but the simple-minded view that investigation is just about 'catching the offender' can result in a misguided academic contribution.

Notes

1   All of these officers worked under the direction of Professor Canter.
2   See the MacPherson Report. This case was critical in the UK and involved the murder of a young black youth in the Metropolitan area of London. Subsequent allegations of institutional racism, thought to have contributed to the lack of a conviction, resulted in a detailed and highly critical report with attendant recommendations.

References

Adhami, E. and Browne, D.P. (1996) *Major Crime Enquiries: Improving Expert Support for Detectives*. Police Research Group. Special Interest Series, Paper 9. London: Home Office.

Alison, L., West, A. and Goodwill, A. (2004) 'The academic and the practitioner: Pragmatists' views of offender profiling', *Psychology, Public Policy and Law*, 10(1–2): 71–101.

Canter, D. and Alison, L. (1997) *Criminal Detection and The Psychology of Crime*. Dartmouth: Ashgate.

Canter, D. and Alison, L. (1999) *Profiling in Policy and Practice*. Dartmouth: Ashgate.

Copson, G. (1995) *Coal to Newcastle? Police use of offender profiling*. Police Research Group. Special Interest Series, Paper 7. London: Home Office.

Crego, J. and Alison, L. (2004) 'Control and legacy as functions of perceived criticality in major incidents', *Journal of Investigative Psychology and Offender Profiling*, 1: 207–25.

Dietz, P.E. and Reese, J.T. (1986) 'The perils of police psychology: 10 strategies for minimizing role conflicts when providing mental health services and consultation to law enforcement agencies', *Behavioural Sciences and the Law*, 4: 385–400.

Gross, H. (1950) *Criminal Investigation: A Practical Textbook for Magistrates, Police Officers and Lawyers*. London: Sweet and Maxwell Limited.

Innes, M. (2003) *Investigating Murder: Detective Work and the Police Response to Criminal Homicide*. Clarendon Studies in Criminology. Oxford: Oxford University Press.

Kind, S.S. (1987) *The Scientific Investigation of Crime*. Forensic Science Services.

MacPherson, W. (1999) 'The Stephen Lawrence Inquiry' (www.archive.official-documents.co.uk/document/cm42/4262/sli-00.htm (accessed 9 August, 2004).

Smith, N. and Flanagan, C. (2000) *The Effective Detective: Identifying the Skills of an Effective SIO*. Police Research Series. Paper 122. London: Home Office.

West, A. (2001) 'From offender profiler to behavioural investigative advisor: The effective application of behavioural science to the investigation of major crime', *Police Research and Management*, 1(1): 95–108.

Websites

The Stephen Lawrence Inquiry
www.archive.official-documents.co.uk/document/cm42/4262/sli-00.htm

The Soham Murders
www.bichardinquiry.org.uk/

The Victoria Climbié Inquiry
www.victoria-climbie-inquiry.org.uk/

The Centre for Critical Incident Research
www.incscid.org

The Centre for Investigative Psychology
www.i-psy.com

Index

Abberline, Inspector 28–30
academics, working with practitioners
    xxvi–xxvii
acceptable behaviour, 'blurred lines'
    xxiii
accidents
    remembering 304–6
    and PTSD 306–7
accountability for delivery 99, 101
accounts
    assessing the reliability 280–1
    reconstruction 297–312
    see also statements
accreditation of profilers 176, 388
accused, use of offender profile
    evidence 189–90
ACF (Arson Control Forum) 57
ACPO (Association of Chief Police
    Officers) 97
admissibility of evidence 178
    from investigative psychologists
        183–90
    regulation governing 182–3
    and reliability 180–1
advice, communication of 386

aggressive thoughts, as a response to
    stalking 348f, 349
amnesia
    classifications 301–4
    simulated 307–9
        distinguishing between genuine
            amnesia and 308–9
'amnesic syndrome' 301
analysis of crime see crime analysis
anger-excitation rapists 70
anger-oriented sexual murderers 76
anger-retaliation rapists 70
anterograde amnesia 301, 303
Anti-Corruption Group 146
anti-stalking laws 334
appraisal process in the police 163
apprehension methods for serial
    killers xxi, 10–13
    frequency distribution 12–13, 16–17
apprehension roles 13–16
argument, Toulmin's philosophy 6–7,
    81–2, 236
argument quality 206–7
arousal symptoms of victims of
    stalkers 348–9